The Seventh Earl Beauchamp

For Halina

Contents

List of Illustrations

Alfred Emmott, 1st Baron Emmott
bromide print by Walter Stoneman, 1917
© the National Portrait Gallery, London

Edmond Warre
mixed-method engraving probably by Thomas Lewis Atkinson,
1889, thought to be after Francis Hall
© the National Portrait Gallery, London

William Lygon, 7th Earl Beauchamp
dry-plate glass negative by Walter Stoneman, 1917
© the National Portrait Gallery, London

Lady Mary Hepburn-Stuart-Forbes-Trefusis (née Lygon) as
Marie de Lorraine, a lady at the court of Marguerite de Valois
by Thomas Bennett & Sons; photogravure by Walker & Boutall,
1897, published 1899
© the National Portrait Gallery, London

Hallam Tennyson, 2nd Baron Tennyson
half-plate glass negative by Walter Stoneman, 1917
© the National Portrait Gallery, London

Sir Almeric William FitzRoy
bromide print by Walter Stoneman, 1917
© the National Portrait Gallery, London

Arthur John Bigge, Baron Stamfordham
whole-plate glass negative by Walter Stoneman, 1917
© the National Portrait Gallery, London

Eton College
vintage snapshot print taken by Lady Ottoline Morrell, 1915
© *the National Portrait Gallery, London*

William Lygon, 8th Earl Beauchamp with William Lygon,
the 7th Earl
whole-plate glass negative by Bassano Ltd, 25 April 1924
© *the National Portrait Gallery, London*

'A view taken from Christ Church Meadows, Oxford', showing
James Webber and Cyril Jackson
hand-coloured etching by Robert Dighton, published May 1807
© *the National Portrait Gallery, London*

Joe Chamberlain
*pen and ink drawing by Walter Stoneman, done between
1880 and 1910*
© *the National Portrait Gallery, London*

Rufus Isaacs, 1st Marquis of Reading
bromide print by (Arthur) Walton Adams, 1910s
© *the National Portrait Gallery, London*

Herbert Henry Asquith, 1st Earl of Oxford and Asquith
bromide print by (Arthur) Walton Adams, 1913
© *the National Portrait Gallery, London*

Francis Paget
*water colour by Sir Leslie Ward, published in Vanity Fair,
22 November 1894*
© *the National Portrait Gallery, London*

David Lloyd George, 1st Earl Lloyd George
*oil painting on canvas by Sir William Newenham Montague
Orpen, 1927*
© *the National Portrait Gallery, London*

Preface

My knowledge of the 7th Earl Beauchamp began accidentally. I first became acquainted with his name while writing the history of House of Lords reform. Beauchamp was one of the very few hereditary peers who, in 1910, strongly favoured limitation of the powers of the Lords. In addition, I came across a note by the writer Paula Byrne in her entertaining book *Mad World*: in this note, she stated that, because of the 'scandal' associated with the person of Beauchamp, nobody had undertaken a 'full-scale political biography of this remarkable man'.[1] This provoked my interest and made me consider trying to correct the omission. I was also much inspired and encouraged by David Cannadine's erudite study, *Aspects of Aristocracy*. Introducing his work, this distinguished historian advises 'other historians' to 'delve more deeply and more originally into the modern aristocracy'.[2] Finally the determining factor that impelled me to engage in this book was the entry for the 7th Earl Beauchamp in the *Oxford Dictionary of National Biography* by the renowned biographer Richard Davenport-Hines.[3]

The 'scandal' to which Paula Byrne refers had two motivational sources, each different from the other: one was the jealousy of a member of the aristocracy and the other the infantile outpourings of a coarse novelist. In both cases the smearing of the Earl was unjustified. The 2nd Duke of Westminster, a playboy and dandy but a total nonentity in high politics, could not bear the thought that his brother-in-law, the 7th Earl Beauchamp, had earned the confidence of the King, proved a diligent cabinet minister,

---

1   See Paula Byrne, *Mad World: Evelyn Waugh and the Secrets of Brideshead* (London: Harper Collins, 2010 paperback edition), p. 353.
2   See David Cannadine, *Aspects of Aristocracy: Grandeur and Decline in Modern Britain* (London: Penguin Books, 1995), p. 5.
3   See Richard Davenport-Hines, 'Lygon, William, seventh Earl Beauchamp (1872–1938)', in *The Oxford Dictionary of National Biography*, vol. 34, ed. H. C. G. Mathew and Brian Harrison (Oxford: Oxford University Press, 2004).

was promoted to high state offices and had become a successful and eloquent member of the House of Lords. Apart from pursuing his extravagant life, the Duke's chief interest was to demean Beauchamp. He seized his opportunity when he heard it mentioned in private circles that the Earl enjoyed sexual relations with his male servants. This was true. But nobody was particularly bothered – certainly not the Earl's immediate family. However, in Britain, the notorious Criminal Law Amendment Act, 1885 was still in force. It made all homosexual acts between men illegal, 'in public or private'. Those prosecuted could be sentenced to two years' imprisonment. The fallout from the Oscar Wilde case had been appalling, and it could not be forgotten. In Britain, as A. L. Rowse recalled, it 'led to an accumulation of barbarous inhumanity, and incalculable suffering', which forced people to flee abroad.[4] The Duke was to dish out the same fate to Beauchamp. This distinguished man was ruined: while still in his prime, he lost his wife, his family and his home.

After Beauchamp's death his memory was publicly dragged through the mud by Evelyn Waugh. What had stirred Waugh's animosity against the Earl? When Waugh came up to Oxford and met the Beauchamp sons he began to develop an inferiority complex. The firstborn Beauchamp son was at Magdalen and the second at Christ Church – patrician colleges for aristocratic progeny. Waugh was at Hertford, which no doubt accommodated outstanding students but was not a province the aristocracy frequented. The future novelist thus initially formed 'a withering contempt' for these 'arrogant scions of noble and country families', who drank champagne at breakfast and then took to breaking windows in Peckwater Quad in Christ Church,[5] as the Earl of Birkenhead[6] (one of Waugh's earlier friends) recalled. In time, however, Waugh's 'tastes matured' and he 'began to find pleasure

---

4   See A. L. Rowse, *Homosexuals in History* (New York: Dorset Press, 1983), p. 169. This
     book is highly instructive. It portrays the homosexual life of many eminent historical
     personalities and tells us how natural this life was.
5   Birkenhead, 1st Earl of, b. 1872. A Unionist.
6   See The Earl of Birkenhead, 'Fiery Particles', in David Pryce-Jones (ed.), *Evelyn Waugh
     and His World* (London: Weidenfeld and Nicolson, 1973), p. 138.

in aristocratic society and the houses these people inhabited'.[7] This was not
due to 'latent snobbishness', but rather that there was an 'inherited ease in
their manners and an elegance in their surroundings which made a strong
appeal to one side of his nature'.[8] Waugh found compensation first in the
homosexual company of Hugh Patrick, Beauchamp's second son, at Christ
Church, and, later, in becoming acquainted with Hugh Patrick's sisters at
Madresfield, the Beauchamp family house. The Beauchamp girls, all four of
them, took a fancy to Waugh's wit,[9] so that he was a welcome guest, and he
often spent days or weekends at Madresfield. Here he felt self-assured. He
had failed to find his own identity, but sought solace in his association with
the Beauchamp girls. They accepted him – but not fully. He fell deeply in
love with one of them, Mary Lygon, and wrote affectionate letters to her all
his life. It appears, however, that she refused to have intimate physical relations with him, and preferred to marry an exiled Russian prince, a drunkard
and a parasite, whom Waugh loathed. Are we to presume that Lady Mary,
despite her adoration of Waugh's wit, would not marry him because he did
not belong to her social class? Waugh must have felt the pain deeply. How
did he get revenge? On 6 June 1944 Waugh recorded in his diary that he 'sat
down early to work and wrote a fine passage describing Lord Marchmain's
death agonies. [Lord Beauchamp had died in 1938.] ... I sent for the priest
to give Lord Marchmain the last sacrament.'[10] In this way, Waugh 'finished
the last chapter' of *Brideshead Revisited: The Sacred and Profane Memoirs*

---

7   *Ibid.*

8   *Ibid.*, p. 139.

9   Dorothy Lygon, one of the Beauchamp girls to whom Waugh was closely attached
     and with whom he corresponded regularly, writes: 'In looking back on my friendship
     with Evelyn down a perspective of forty-odd years, the most predominating features
     are his consistent, spontaneous, irreverent wit, and his capacity for turning the most
     unlikely situations into irresistibly funny jokes which continued to be woven into
     our conversations and letters with an increasing richness of texture over the years.'
     See Lady Dorothy Lygon, 'Madresfield and Brideshead', in David Pryce-Jones (ed.),
     Evelyn Waugh and His World, *op. cit.*, p. 50.

10   See *The Diaries of Evelyn Waugh*, ed. Michael Davie (London: Weidenfeld and
     Nicolson, 1976), p. 567.

of Captain Charles Ryder, which was published a year later, in 1945.[11] The narrative portrayed the 'profane' life of Madresfield in full detail. Waugh vehemently denied that this is what he had done. Dorothy Lygon recollects that during Waugh's visits, 'he talked about his next book'. Waugh told her: 'It's all about a family whose father lives abroad, as it might be Boom [Lord Beauchamp][12] – but it's not Boom – and a younger son: people will say he's like Hughie, but you will see he's not really Hughie – and there's a house as it might be Mad [Madresfield], but it isn't really Mad.' He talked on, writes Dorothy Lygon, for:

> some time in this vein, at pains to emphasise that, although he had chosen a situation which might be compared to ours at one time, he was going to treat it in a very different way – he had taken bare bones, the skeleton, and intended converting it with muscles creating tensions, quite different from those which had influenced us – the Roman Catholic element, so powerful for him, and an integral part of the story, never affected us, and the Marchmains' matrimonial problems can in no way be equated with those which beset my parents. ... I think that Evelyn conceived Brideshead in a mood of violent nostalgia for what he thought was a vanished past; he put into it all he most regretted and missed in pre-war life. ... I think that the resemblance between my family and the Marchmains has been exaggerated; when I first read it, it did not seem to me he had used us as characters, nor do I think so now; he had used a situation, not the people involved in it.[13]

This has not been the general view. The gifted writer Paula Byrne has analysed *Brideshead* closely and comes to a different conclusion:

> Despite the prefatory author's disclaimer,' she writes, 'the Lygons [the Beauchamp family] suffuse the book. The portrayal of their ancestral home with its Arts and Crafts chapel, their painful domestic situation, their startling beauty (like faces carved out of Aztec stone), the father as a disgraced Liberal politician who is now a social pariah exiled in Italy, the young people left to run wild in the great house, the pious

11   See Evelyn Waugh, *Brideshead Revisited: The Sacred and Profane Memoirs of Captain Charles Ryder* (London: Chapman & Hall, 1960 edition).
12   Lord Beauchamp was known as 'Boom' to all of his children 'behind his back'. 'Mad' was what they called Madresfield.
13   See Lady Dorothy Lygon, 'Madresfield and Brideshead', in David Pryce-Jones (ed.), *Evelyn Waugh and His World, op. cit.*, pp. 53–4.

mother, the alcoholic second son drifting from failure to failure, the lovely daughter who becomes a society beauty in an unhappy marriage, the cold and pompous heir to Brideshead unable to produce an heir himself, the plain and tender-hearted youngest daughter. The Lygons inspired all of these elements and more.[14]

A few quotations from *Brideshead* support this claim. Waugh's note on the novel, which reads: 'I am not I: thou art not he or she: they are not they',[15] misleads the reader. 'I' certainly is Waugh; Sebastian Flyte is definitely Hugh Patrick: 'Lord Sebastian Flyte ... A most amusing young gentleman. ... The Marquis of Marchmain's second son, the Earl of Brideshead [Viscount Elmley] went down last term'.[16] And Lady Marchmain! 'Very, very beautiful; no artifice, her hair just turning grey in elegant silvery streaks, no rouge, very pale, huge eyes ... pearls and a few great star-like jewels, heirlooms, in ancient settings ....'[17] Readers need only take one look at the Countess Beauchamp's charcoal portrait by John Singer Sargent to see how perfect Waugh's description is.[18] But it is Lord Marchmain that interests us. He is 'a little fleshy perhaps, but very handsome, a magnifico, a voluptary ... He daren't show his great purple face anywhere. He is the last, historic, authentic case of someone being hounded out of society.'[19] Lady Marchmain 'has convinced the world that Lord Marchmain is a monster. And what is the truth? They were married for fifteen years or so and then Lord Marchmain went to the war; he never came back but formed a connection with a highly talented dancer. There are a thousand such cases. She refuses to divorce him because she is so pious. Well, there have been cases of that before. Usually, it arouses sympathy for the adulterer; not for Lord Marchmain

14 Paula Byrne, *op. cit.*, p. 301.
15 Evelyn Waugh, *op. cit.*, p. 6.
16 *Ibid.*, p. 37.
17 *Ibid.*, p. 64. Dorothy Lygon asserts that she did not think that Waugh 'ever met my mother, but he could not have created a character more unlike hers than Lady Marchmain's'. See Lady Dorothy Lygon, *op. cit.*, p. 53.
18 The portrait is printed in Jane Mulvagh, *Madresfield: The Real Brideshead* (London: Doubleday, Black Swan edition, 2009), p. 308.
19 See Evelyn Waugh, *op. cit.*, pp. 64–5.

though.'[20] Why not? Because Waugh believes that Lord Marchmain has committed a great sin – and Waugh is heavily obsessed with this.[21] The 'I' of *Brideshead* even feels embarrassed when he visits Lord Marchmain in Italy: 'Lord Marchmain's mistress arrived next day. I was nineteen years old and completely ignorant of women. I could not with any certainty recognise a prostitute in the streets. I was therefore not indifferent to the fact of living under the roof of an adulterous couple, but I was old enough to hide my interest.'[22] Later, however, Waugh indulged in paranoia:[23]

20   *Ibid.*, pp. 65–6.

21   Waugh never really knew Lord Beauchamp, although he met him casually once. Mary Lygon took Waugh to stay with her father when he rented Gerald Berners' house in Rome (see Lady Dorothy Lygon, *op. cit.*, p. 53), and it is probable that the Earl completely ignored Waugh. On the other hand, Beauchamp was quite fond of Waugh's friend Robert Byron, the celebrated travel writer (*The Byzantine Achievement*, 1929; *The Road to Oxiana*, 1937). In fact Beauchamp went sightseeing with Byron in Italy, and inspired Byron's love for Byzantine art. Byron remembered Beauchamp as 'a man of exquisite and unusual taste' (Paula Byrne, *Mad World*, *op. cit.*, pp. 89–90). Did Waugh assume that Beauchamp and Byron had intimate relations, and thus became jealous, so that he began to hate Beauchamp? The only time that Waugh showed any feeling of sympathy for Beauchamp was when Hugh died in September 1936. 'I know,' he wrote to Mary Lygon, '[what a] loss it will be to all of you and to Boom.' See *The Letters of Evelyn Waugh*, ed. Mark Amory (London: Weidenfeld and Nicolson, 1981), p. 111. Waugh continued to bear malice towards Robert Byron. This he admitted in a letter to Harold Acton. Byron was killed in 1941. 'It is not yet,' Waugh wrote to Acton on 27 April 1948, 'the time to say so, but I greatly disliked Robert in his last years & think he was a dangerous lunatic better dead.' See *The Letters of Evelyn Waugh*, *op. cit.*, p. 277. What caused this dislike, one wonders? Perhaps the same paranoia!

22   See Evelyn Waugh, *op. cit.*, p. 113.

23   The distinguished historian Hugh Trevor-Roper had his own rather bitter experience with Evelyn Waugh. Trevor-Roper once made some critical remarks about Jesuits. Waugh never forgave him and never stopped heaping insulting comments on the historian. These denunciations, Trevor-Roper writes, became 'somewhat paranoid'. though. Waugh's 'wild fantasy and black humour' were 'aspects of his genius as well as of his warped character'. Waugh was, Trevor-Roper believes, 'utterly cold-hearted: all his emotions were concentrated (apart from his writing) upon his social snobbism and his Catholicism ...' See *One Hundred Letters from Hugh Trevor-Roper*, ed. Richard Davenport-Hines and Adam Sisman (Oxford: Oxford University Press, 2014), p. 316.

> Lord Marchmain lay dying, wearing himself down in the struggle to live ...[24] The priest bent over Lord Marchmain and blessed him. ... 'Now,' said the priest, 'I know you are sorry for all the sins of your life, aren't you? Make a sign, if you can. You're sorry, aren't you?' But there was no sign. 'Try and remember your sins; tell God you are sorry. I am going to give you absolution. While I am giving it, tell God you are sorry you have offended him.' ... 'God forgive him his sins' and 'Please God, make him accept your forgiveness.' ... Lord Marchmain made the sign of the cross. Then I knew that the sign I had asked for was not a little thing.[25]

That was how Waugh pursued Lord Marchmain, and literally Lord Beauchamp, with what A. L. Rowse fitly calls 'such barbarous brutality'. That was what *Brideshead* brought about. Was not this super-Catholic (or rather, pseudo-Catholic) himself suffering from a kind of infantilism, from 'a mood of violent nostalgia for what he thought was a vanished past', and was he not diverting his feelings about 'all he most regretted and missed in pre-war life' to the downfall of Lord Beauchamp. Homosexuality was neither a sin nor unnatural. Homosexuality, wrote Sigmund Freud in 1935 is 'nothing to be ashamed of'. It is 'no vice, no degradation, it cannot be classified as an illness; we consider it to be a variation of the sexual function produced by a certain arrest of sexual development. Many highly respectable individuals of ancient and modern times have been homosexuals, several of the greatest men among them (Plato, Michelangelo, Leonardo da Vinci, etc.).[26] It is a great injustice to persecute homosexuality as a crime, and cruelty too.'[27] Yet British social norms were such that Freud's words would go

---

24   *Ibid.*, p. 367.

25   *Ibid.*, pp. 370–1.

26   A. L. Rowse has skilfully analysed this in his study. See Rowse, *op. cit.*

27   Quoted in Graham Robb, *Strangers: Homosexual Love in the Nineteenth Century* (London: Picador, 2004 edition), p. 80. This book enriches our knowledge of homosexuality. Equally instructive and fascinating is the study by Richard Davenport-Hines, *Sex, Death and Punishment: Attitudes to Sex and Sexuality in Britain since the Renaissance* (London: Collins, 1990). Chapter Four, 'Dance as They Desire: The Construction and Criminalization of Homosexuality', is the main part commanding our attention. 'Questions,' we read, 'of maleness and femininity, or of aggression and passivity, whether explicitly erotic or not, were liable to as many different answers as there were individuals. Yet in nineteenth century Britain there was a craving for the

unheeded. With the wide circulation of his novel, Waugh achieved what the 2nd Duke of Westminster had failed to accomplish. The Duke sent Beauchamp into exile, but Waugh did more: he ruined the Earl's reputation.

The 7th Earl Beauchamp did not deserve to be treated as a social outcast. Whatever his sexual proclivities, they were private: they did not interfere with, or in any way influence his public life. His children did not make a fuss about them. The Earl's tendencies did not even worry the Countess, his wife, at first. For 'many years', she wrote to her daughters, she had 'strongly suspected' that 'all was not as it should be' with her husband.[28] And she kept silent. But in the end, bullied by her brother, she changed her mind and filed a divorce case. Only then did she come to think that 'one side of his life and desires went contrary to everything that is Natural'. This again is paranoia.

Earl Beauchamp was indeed a remarkable man. He had rich talents. His knowledge of ancient art and architecture excited envy. He was an affectionate father. He showed capacity in the high state offices that he held: Governor of New South Wales, Captain of the Gentlemen-at-Arms, Lord Steward of the Household, Lord President of the Council and First Commissioner of Works. His eloquence and work in the House of Lords met with high regard and won the approbation of the House.

It is chiefly to the political side of the Earl's life that the attention of the present volume is devoted. This book is almost entirely based on the unpublished archival collections. All along, I have maintained the methodological principle that the subject 'shall be his own biographer'. Accordingly,

----

certitude of universal rules and axioms. ... Surrounded by religious perplexities, by fears of social dissolution, and by the sense of personal isolation which became so characteristic of western Europeans in the nineteenth century, people wanted rules which were strict and certain. Anomalies of gender and desire, individual feelings which went so deep and could be so different, were frightening in their implications for conscientious souls trying to live a straightforward moral life according to eternal precepts – dismaying, too, for those who were feeling the essential isolation of modern life.' See p. 115 (of the Fontana Press edition, 1991). We may be allowed to add that, in our day, the views of certain 'conscientious souls' have not basically changed.

28   For the full text of the letter, see Jane Mulvagh, *op. cit.*, pp. 396–7.

I have cited appropriate documents fully and extensively. These include: state papers, official records, extracts from speeches made in the House of Lords, and also diverse correspondence – with the court, with party leaders and prime ministers and with other institutions and individuals. These all help illuminate the character of the Earl. This study is more a portrait than a complete biography. I hope to give a more accurate picture of a person who has been unjustly treated by history.

Jowett Lodge   *Peter Raina*
Oxford
Michaelmas Term 2015

Acknowledgements

The author gratefully acknowledges his debt to:

Her Majesty Queen Elizabeth II for her gracious permission to use the Royal Archives at Windsor
Professor Laurence Brockliss, Vice President, Magdalen College, Oxford
Professor Sir David Nicolas Cannadine
Professor David Clary, President, Magdalen College, Oxford
Ms Julie Crocker, Archivist, Royal Archives, Windsor Castle
Miss Judith Curthoys, Archivist, Christ Church, Oxford
Dr Richard Davenport-Hines
Mrs Isabel D. Holowaty, Bodleian History Librarian, Oxford
Mr Peter Hughes
Mrs Keeley Mortimer
Mrs Elizabeth L. Taylor, National Portrait Gallery, London
Professor Tom Melham, Praefectus, Holywell Manor, Balliol College, Oxford
Sir Michael Wheeler-Booth, Honorary Fellow, Magdalen College, Oxford
Dr Helen Wicker

also to:
Mr Jon Ashby, copy-editor
Mrs Lucy Melville, publisher

The author records his debt of gratitude to the following archives:

The Royal Archives, Windsor
Bodleian (Weston) Library, Oxford
The British Library, London
Cambridge University Library, Cambridge
Christ Church Library Archives, Oxford

Eton College Library Archives, Windsor
Gloucestershire Archives, Gloucester
Kent History and Library Centre, Maidstone
The Madresfield Archives, The Estate Office, Madresfield, Malvern
The National Archives, Kew, London
National Portrait Gallery, London
Nuffield College Library Archives, Oxford and the Warden and Fellows
of Nuffield College
Oxford Union Library Archives, Oxford
The Parliamentary Archives, London
Senate House Library Archives, University of London, London
State Library of New South Wales, The Mitchell Library, Sydney
State Records of New South Wales Government, Australia
Worcestershire Archives & Archaeology Service, Worcester

While every effort has been made to trace copyright holders, if any have been inadvertently overlooked, the author will be happy to acknowledge them in future editions. However, it is understood that documents and correspondence cited in the present volume concerning the province of the realm are covered by the Crown Copyright.

Early Years

Ancestral lineage

The roots of the Lygon (or Ligon) family go back to the descendants of Norman knights. The family intermarried with a line that was perhaps French: the Beauchamps (pronounced 'Beechams' in English). Between them, the Lygons and the Beauchamps divided up vast acres of agricultural land in Worcestershire over which they claimed ownership. The family records tell us that in 1450, by deed, William Lygon, obtained a manor, called Madresfield in the Malvern Hills. It is described as 'an island of independence in an ecclesiastical see'. On this 'island', over the course of centuries, a huge building was constructed known as Madresfield Court. It was held in demesne by the Lygon family and has been theirs ever since without interruption.

The first Lygon of Madresfield, we are told, was called William. In 1495, a Thomas Lygon appears, whose son, Richard, married Anne Beauchamp of Powke. Her ancestry can be traced back to William Beauchamp, Lord of Elmley Castle and hereditary castellan of Worcester. Anne's grandfather was a younger son of the Warwick family, who was rewarded with the title of Baron Beauchamp of Powyke 'in consideration of his service' to Henry V and Henry VI. He was also Master of the King's Horses, Treasurer of the Isle of Wight and a Knight of the Garter.

This long and complicated, but fascinating, genealogical history of the Lygon-Beauchamp families has been well recounted by Dorothy Williams in *The Lygons of Madresfield Court*,[1] and I have drawn heavily on this book for information.[2] What concerns us, however, is the immediate ancestral lineage of the protagonist in our story, and we will move forward to more modern times.

William Lygon, born in 1747, was an acquaintance of William Pitt the Elder and became a close friend of Pitt the Younger. He entered the House of Commons as the Member for Worcestershire, and in 1780 made an arranged marriage to Catherine Denne, who was of Irish descent. In 1798 William suddenly became rich, when part of the family estate was left to him after the death of William Jennes, an ancestor of William's mother, Susanna Hanner. Up to 1798 William and Catherine had lived 'in the fringe of London society', but now that they were rich, all changed. Catherine, an 'attractive and vivacious' woman, employed her charm to secure a baronetcy for her husband. It seems that Catherine paid £800 for the title Baron Beauchamp of Powyke in 1805, and that, when a reshuffle of Admiralty appointments took place that same year, Pitt seized the occasion to recommend William Lygon's ennoblement. William had to resign from his seat in the Commons, which he did in 1807, and he took his place in the House of Lords.[3] A decade later, in 1815, Catherine paid the Exchequer £10,000 for William's earldom.

The 1st Earl Beauchamp died on 19 October 1816, and his wife Catherine twenty-seven years later on 2 March 1844. They had had twelve children. The 2nd Earl Beauchamp, also called William (1782–1823), was the second child of the 1st Earl (the firstborn was a daughter who died in infancy). The 2nd Earl was educated at Westminster and Christ Church, Oxford. He was Member of the House of Commons for Worcestershire

1   Dorothy Williams, *The Lygons of Madresfield Court* (Almeley, Herefordshire: Logaston Press, 2001).

2   Another equally helpful historical narrative of the Lygon family, is the graceful portrayal by Jane Mulvagh, *Madresfield: The Real Brideshead* (London: Doubleday, 2008).

3   The Lygons bought a house in Belgrave Square in London; Catherine spent time collecting the fine art collection, French and Italian furniture from the continent and the historical portraits with which Madresfield Court was furnished.

from 1810 until 1816, when, at the age of thirty-four, he succeeded to the title of his father. In parliament, he defended Princess Caroline against the charges of adultery that were made against her. Otherwise, he spent time as a landowner, and travelled widely on the continent collecting historical portraits and *objets d'art*. He never married, and died at the age of forty on 13 May 1823.

He was succeeded by his younger brother, John Reginald, who had been born on 21 November 1783. This 3rd Earl was also educated at Westminster and Christ Church, Oxford. On 14 March 1814 he married Lady Charlotte Scott, daughter of the First Earl of Clonmell and Chief Justice of Ireland. Charlotte brought with her a dowry of £60,000. John resided at Madresfield and took a keen interest in his agricultural estate, especially in the living conditions of his farm labourers. He also established an Emigration Fund to enable emigrants from South Australia to work in Worcestershire. He was described as 'the peasants' Earl'. When his first wife died, John remarried. This was in 1850 and the bride was Catherine Braye, a widow. He died in 1853, leaving no children by either wife.

The earldom consequently fell to the third son of William Lygon and Catherine Denne. This son, Henry, was born on 7 January 1785. He went to Westminster and Christ Church, Oxford and, having obtained a commission in the army, served in the 13th and 16th Light Dragoons in the Peninsular War under Wellington. In 1815 he was transferred to the 1st Life Guards, being raised to the rank of Major General in 1837. Henry had already entered the Commons as MP for Worcestershire in 1816 and he held this seat until he succeeded to the title, as the 4th Earl Beauchamp, on the death of his brother in 1853. He rarely spoke in parliament. In 1824 he married Lady Susan Caroline Eliot, daughter of the 2nd Earl of St Germans. They had seven children. Henry was the first estate owner to introduce mechanized farming in Worcestershire. In his will, he also provided for the building of three bridges over part of the back drive in Madresfield Court. Major General Lord Beauchamp died in 1863.

The 5th Earl Beauchamp, born on 13 February 1829, was also called Henry. The eldest son of Major General Henry, he was the first Lygon sent not to Westminster, but to Eton. He commenced his military carreer in May 1848. When his father became Earl Beauchamp, Henry took the title of Viscount Elmley, sold his commission and travelled in Europe and America. In the family tradition, he served as MP for Worcestershire until he succeeded to the earldom in 1863. Henry died on 4 March 1866. He never married.

Frederick, the 6th Earl Beauchamp (1830–91) was the second son of Major General Henry Lygon and Lady Susan Eliot. He was educated at Eton and Christ Church, Oxford, where he showed early signs of having a scholarly temperament. He was President of the Oxford Union in 1851, and became a fellow of All Souls College, Oxford in 1852. At Oxford, he got to know Dr Edward Bouverie Pusey[4] and, through him, John Keble,[5] who often visited Madresfield Court. With these connections, Frederick took much interest in the work of the Tractarians.[6]

Frederick also cultivated the acquaintance of Lord Philip Stanhope, the historian. One Christmas, the historian invited Frederick to stay at his home at Chevening. There, Frederick fell in love with the historian's only daughter, Lady Mary. She was very intelligent and widely read. As a little girl she fascinated Lord Macaulay, a friend of the Stanhope family, who wrote a verse for her:

> There was a little girl,
> Who had a little curl,
> Right in the middle of her forehead,
> And when she was good,
> She was very, very good,
> But when she was bad she was horrid!

4   E. B. Pusey (1800–82), Anglican theologian, a leader of the Oxford Movement, which sought to return to seventeenth-century ideals of the Church of England.

5   John Keble (1792–1866), Anglican priest, helped lead the Oxford Movement; Professor of Poetry at Oxford (1831–41); one of the authors of *90 Tracts for the Times* (1833–41).

6   The nineteenth-century Oxford Movement, begun in 1833 and centred in Oxford University, was established by John Henry Newman (1801–90), later a cardinal in the Roman Catholic Church, Richard Hurrell Froude (1803–36), John Keble and Edward Pusey. The ideas of the movement were published in *90 Tracts for the Times* (1833–41). The authors of the *Tracts*, known as the Tractarians, asserted that the doctrinal authority of the catholic Church was absolute. By 'catholic' they meant that which was faithful to the teaching of 'the early and undivided' Church.

As Frederick's wife, Mary displayed her diverse talents. She was a gifted artist, who drew and painted; she refurnished and redecorated Madresfield Court. Mary's interests went well beyond decoration of the family home. She founded an Industrial School in the village, which took orphaned and abandoned girls between the ages of 6 and 14, helping them towards a future career. Mary also cultivated friendships with members of the royal family.

Frederick himself was elected MP for Tewkesbury in 1857, and then for Worcestershire between 1863 and 1866. He took an active interest in local government and sat on various boards of local schools. However, his chief interest seems to have been in the workings of various religious communities, including Anglo-Catholic organizations. He was a keen enthusiast for Gregorian plainsong and a founder of the Gregorian Society. He was also a member of several commissions, especially ones involved with education and child welfare. He acted as Lord of the Admiralty in 1859, was Lord Steward from 1874 to 1880, and was Paymaster-General from 1885 to 1887. In Oxford, Fredrick helped in the establishment of Keble College and Pusey House.

In June 1876 Frederick lost his very close and affectionate associate of eight years when his wife, Mary, died. She had been his partner, his colleague and his adviser. Mary left him two sons and three daughters. Mary's loss was felt well beyond her immediate family. Queen Victoria's daughter, Helena (wife of Prince Christian of Schleswig-Holstein) very much regretted her death. In a letter to Frederick, she wrote: 'How dearly I loved your dear Mary I think I could not tell you, nor the true friendship I bore her, and her loss is very great grief to me.' Another letter of deep sympathy arrived from Windsor Castle.

> The Queen hardly knows how to write to Lord Beauchamp on the occasion of the dreadful misfortune which has befallen him, or how to find words to express her deep and true sympathy with him in this hour of awful bereavement! All the Queen can say is – that having herself gone through the *same* terrible trial, she is *able* to understand his present sufferings and to feel deeply for him![7]

---

7   Quoted in Dorothy E. Williams, *The Lygons of Madresfield Court, op. cit.*, p. 81.

Frederick remarried in 1878. This was to Lady Emily Pierrepont, daughter of the 3rd Earl of Manvers. By her he had two sons and two daughters. On 19 February 1890 Frederick died. The earldom fell to his eldest son, William, the 7th Earl Beauchamp, the subject of this study.

Childhood and education

William Lygon was born on 20 February 1872, the second child of Frederick and his first wife, Mary. The first child had been a girl, also Mary, born in 1869. The birth of a male heir was the cause of family celebration which spread to the surrounding countryside. Church bells rang not only in Madresfield Church, but also in the churches in Worcestershire, Gloucestershire and Herefordshire where the 6th Earl was patron.

William's mother died when he was three years old. His step-mother, Lady Emily, lavished much care and affection on the young child, and his father applied himself to the his heir's general upbringing. But it was William's elder sister, Mary, who increasingly gave attention to her brother, slowly making him aware of the rich artistic, intellectual and social life at Madresfield Court. The early cultivation of artistic taste which he got from Mary stayed with William all his life. At Madresfield the young heir 'enjoyed all the charm of patrician adolescence'.[8]

William was sent to Eton in 1885, where he lived in the house of Thomas John Proctor Carter and Rev. Sydney Rhodes James. This house, known as Drury's, was demolished in 1899. William was registered as Lord Elmley. There is little of distinction to note from his time at Eton. There are no sports or school office positions mentioned; and no prizes are awarded to him. However, he seems to have been active in the Literary Society. The *Eton College Chronicle* records that a meeting of the Literary Society was

---

8   This is how Vita Sackville-West characterized Sebastian in *The Edwardians* (London: Virago Press, 1983), p. 13.

held on Monday 23 September 1889 'in the School Library, when the following members were elected, exclusive of Sixth Form: Nathan, Ponsonby, Jex-Blake, K. S., Lord Elmley, R. E. R. Brocklebank, Austen-Leigh, K. S., P. C. Sherbrooke. The Society is now full.'[9]

William was fortunate to attend Eton at a time, when important reforms were being initiated by the new headmaster, Dr Edmond Warre, who had been elected by the governing body in July 1884, just before William's arrival.[10] The choice of Warre as headmaster had caused controversy, since, it was said, he had 'made no mark as a scholar, a preacher, or a man of letters' and his name was 'associated with no question of educational reform'.[11] On the other hand, he was 'well known as the best rowing coach in England and as an able field-officer of Volunteers'. He was regarded as 'an *oppidan* of the *oppidans*'.[12] This criticism did not deflect the members of the governing body from their decision: when they met 'nine of the eleven votes went to Warre'.

Warre proved to be a successful reformer. The frightful system of flogging was drastically reduced. The classical curriculum was slightly diluted, with modern languages such as German and French allowed as an alternative to Greek – and these languages were to be taught by native speakers. The study of history was emphasized as well. Warre seems to have been

9   See *Eton College Chronicle*, 26 September 1889, p. 434.
10 My chief source on this topic is 'Doctor Warre', in Tim Card, *Eton Renewed: A History from 1860 to the Present Day* (London: John Murray, 1994), pp. 82–90. See also 'Dr Warre confounds his critics', in L. S. R. Byrne and E. L. Churchill, *Changing Eton: A survey of conditions based on the history of Eton since the Royal Commission of 1862–64* (London: Jonathan Cape, 1937), pp. 53–72.
11 Percy Lubbock, a contemporary of John Maynard Keynes at Eton (1897–1901), remembers that Warre 'absolutely lacked the gift of the kindling spark, nothing that he touched ever sprang to fire in his teaching'. Warre 'brought forth his lore, he quoted the poets, he harangued us upon the grammar of the ancients' and his 'musing wandering speculating humour caught the attention of the boys'. Quoted by Richard Davenport-Hines in his magnificent *Universal Man: The Lives of John Maynard Keynes* (New York: Basic Books, 2015), p. 41.
12 An *oppidan* is any boy at Eton who is not one of the seventy scholars on the Foundation.

'more interested in training character than training the mind'. He did not
inspire the boys with his sermons, but when 'he spoke to the boys briefly
about some particular disciplinary issue, the very distinctions he would
draw between right and wrong were effective. He had the gift of appeal-
ing to boys' better nature.' The number of boys to be accommodated in
each house was changed: the smaller houses were to hold thirty-six, and
the larger houses forty boys. During Warre's time the academic standard
of the school improved, and the boys showed better discipline. The 'great-
ness' of Warre had become clear by the time of his retirement. It is recorded
that Warre was 'no theorist, but a practical man'. He desired Etonians to
'take their places as leaders of the country, upright in the service of God
and their fellow men'. It was his fairness, his friendliness and his generosity that the boys at Eton appreciated. Trained under Warre's new system,
William left Eton in 1890.

Time at Christ Church, Oxford

In 1891, William went up to Christ Church, Oxford. This was not only
because his father had been at this grandest of Oxford colleges, but also
because it had now become a tradition with the English landowner class
to send their sons to Eton and then on to Christ Church, which was seen
as the natural home of young English aristocrats.[13] Of all the titled sons of
the aristocracy who went to Oxford in these years, 35 per cent went up to
Christ Church.[14] Such was the case with William. He entered as a nobleman styled Viscount Elmley, but changes to the college constitution made

---

13   See the scholarly and fascinating study by Judith Curthoys, *The Cardinal's College:
     Christ Church, Chapter and Verse* (London: Profile Books, 2012), p. 250.
14   *Ibid.*, p. 221.

in 1867 had abolished the distinctions once made between undergraduates from different social classes.[15]

Yet a certain distinction was still preserved so far as the residences of the undergraduates was concerned. When Henry Aldrich had been installed as Dean in June 1689 he had ordered the reconstruction of Peckwater Quadrangle, which was built in the Palladian style. The ample sets of rooms there were designed to provide somewhat grandiose accommodation for noblemen and their servants.[16] The adjoining Canterbury Quadrangle was classier still, and Viscount Elmley resided in Canterbury 4:4, up a staircase built specially for the grander and richer students at the end of eighteenth century.

What exactly Elmley read at Christ Church we do not know, but it would be reasonable to speculate that he may have read modern history and jurisprudence. This was a new curriculum created by William Stubbs after his appointment as Regius Professor of History in 1866. Stubbs strongly believed that the study of history and constitutional law would be most proper for Oxford men, preparing them for public service.[17] And it is very

---

15   The undergraduates had previously been formally divided into: noblemen (the sons of dukes, earls, marquesses, etc.); gentlemen commoners (sons of knights and the gentry class); commoners (sons of rich businessmen) and servitors (sons of parish clergy, respectable businessmen and those who could not afford to pay college fees). These distinctions were changed under the Christ Church Oxford Act of 1867, when a governing body was also created to run Christ Church in its collegiate role. A motion passed in December 1868 and ratified by the governing body on 27 January 1869 stated that 'there shall be no distinction in respect of academical dress, designation, college charges, or college payments among undergraduate members of the House, not being Junior students nor Exhibitioners within the House'. See Judith Curthoys, *The Cardinal's College, op. cit.*, p. 265.

16   *Ibid.*, pp. 141–2.

17   *Ibid.*, p. 270. During his term as Dean of the college (1855–91), Henry George Liddell attempted to bring Christ Church into 'an era of higher intellectual and artistic achievement'. A former Student [Fellow] of Christ Church, enlightens us more on the history of his college in J. F. A. Mason, 'Christ Church', in *The History of the University of Oxford*, vol. VII, ed. M. G. Brock and M. C. Curthoys (Oxford: Clarendon Press, 2000), pp. 221–31. On the teaching and scholarship that might have been of interest to Beauchamp during his time at Oxford, see W. H. Walsh, 'The

likely that the young William must have been conscious of the fact that
Christ Church had produced men who attained very high public office.[18]

In late February 1891, while William was at Christ Church, the Dean
told him that he should return immediately to Madresfield Court because
his father had been taken 'seriously ill'. William was not told that his father
had died. At Worcester, when he got off the train, he saw a poster on a
newspaper stand with the announcement: 'Death of Lord Beauchamp'.
This, he later said, was his first intimation of what had happened: the 6th
Earl had passed away on 19 February. Viscount Elmley succeeded him as
the 7th Earl Beauchamp on 20 February 1891. He had just turned nineteen.

Coming of age

A year later, when Elmley turned twenty, he received a large number of
congratulatory letters from friends and relatives. Below are some of these
letters:[19]

1
Padworth House,
Reading[20]

---

zenith of Greats', *Ibid.*, pp. 311–26; Richard Jenkyns, 'Classical Studies, 1872–1914',
Ibid., pp. 327–32; Oswyn Murray, 'Ancient History, 1872–1914', *Ibid.*, pp. 333–60;
Reba N. Soffer, 'Modern History', *Ibid.*, pp. 361–84; Barry Nicholas, 'Jurisprudence',
Ibid., pp. 385–96.

18   Christ Church had produced thirteen prime ministers and eleven viceroys of India.
With the exception of one or two, all of them came from aristocratic families. *Ibid.*,
p. 337. See also *Christ Church University Calendar* and internal admissions.

19   These letters are bundled together and scattered in various Boxes: A 6; B 2–6; C 4–6,
at Madresfield Court, Malvern, Worcestershire [hereafter cited as Beauchamp Papers].
I am grateful to Mr Peter Hughes of the Estate Office, Madresfield, Malvern, for
making these accessible to me.

20   Padworth House was owned by a bachelor called Christopher Darby-Griffiths.

Feb., 20th 1892

My dear Willie,

I must write a short note to wish you very many happy returns of the day. I have thought so much about you all just now. ...

I am yours affect. S.

Alice [full name illegible]

2

13 King Edward Street, Oxford

Feb. 20, 1892

Dear E.,

Had I the [illegible] as I have the will I would say more. But failing the former I can only wish you all my heart many, many happy returns of this day. ...

Yours ever,

Landon [Surely Perceval Landon (1867–1927), dramatist and war correspondent, who was Beauchamp's private secretary when Governor of New South Wales, 1900.]

3

111 Eaton Square

Feb. 19, 1892

Dear Willie,

One word to wish you many very happy returns of your birthday. It cannot, for this year at least, however, fail to bring back some recollections of last year, & ...

[name illegible]

4

Feb. 19

My dear Beauchamp,

I cannot let so momentous a day pass without sending you congratulations and good wishes. To succeed to a position like yours would be a tremendous thing in your case; and I do think it is made easier by the special lustre which your father's life has added to your name. But still, being his son, (and not merely a successor) you have the best chance of knowing how he was prepared for his work, & where he sought his strength; and knowing this, of following his steps.

With the truest and best wishes,

I remain,

Yours ever,

Thomas B. Strong

5

Feb. 20

My dear Beauchamp,

At the risk of adding another to the collection of notes which you already possess, I venture to offer congratulations this morning. One use of birthdays is to make it possible for friends to say what they are always thinking. May I then assure you that I look forward with real love and hope to a long line of anniversaries, increasingly blest to yourself and others?

Yours ever,

Thomas B. Strong

And Beauchamp's coming of age, on 20 February 1893, brought him many more messages of congratulation:

1

Ist Sunday in Lent 1893

My dear Willie,

If I may continue still [word illegible] to address you in youthful terms now that you are of full age, let me wish, and that very heartily, that you may have many years enjoyment of the position which God has given you to fulfil its responsibilities to His glory – the [word illegible] good of others, and to your own personal and future happiness.

Yours always sincerely,

George [full name illegible]

2

Christ Church, Oxford

Feb. 22nd

With best congratulations on coming of age –

from

J. T. Carpenter-Garnier[21]

3

18 Feb. 1893

[Words illegible] Many congratulations on attaining your majority and wishing you a long and very happy life.

Believe me,

faithfully yours,

R. Smith Carington[22]

4

Feb. 20, '93

... May He guide & enlighten as well as bless you in all your ways – in you going out & coming in, and bring you hereafter to His eternal joy.

Reginald Stourton[23]

5

New College, Oxford

Monday [no date]

Dear Beauchamp,

I am sending you a very slight offering in the form of a book for your birthday. I wish I could give you something better but I am really very short indeed; however I hope you will like it & will understand that with it go all my best wishes for the future in every form.

21 John Trefusis Carpenter-Garnier, b. 1874; came up to Christ Church in Trinity Term 1892 from Eton; killed in action as a major in the Scots Guards, September 1914.
22 R. Smith Carington, b. 1852; lived at Southbury House, Malvern, near Madresfield.
23 Reginald Stourton (1877–1943); later settled in Tasmania.

Believe me,

Yrs very sincerely,

Maurice Glyn[24]

6

Magdalen College, Oxford

Monday [no date]

My dearest Elmley,

One formal line to wish you all the good that this world brings and all the happiness of the next. I was so glad to have seen you yesterday. It was very nice of you to have come. At any rate I saw the last of your boyhood!

God bless you always,

B.

7

The College,

Worcester

Feb. 20, 1893

My dear Lord Beauchamp,

Will you permit me to offer you, on behalf of Mr [name illegible] and myself, our heartiest good wishes on the attainment of your majority and to express our most sincere hope that the future may, in the good [word illegible] of God, be abundantly blessed to you and yours.

Every yours sincerely,

[name illegible]

The Malvern Link Local Boards, unanimously adopted a resolution on 20 February 1893 to congratulate the Earl Beauchamp on his coming of age. The resolution was sent to the Earl on 23 February.

Further letters arrived:

24   Maurice Glyn (1872–1920); a member of the Glyn banking family.

8

The Marriage Law Defence Union,

7 King Street, Westminster, S. W.

20th Feb. 1893

Dear Lord Beauchamp,

The remembrance of the most kind friendship shown me by your Father for thirteen years makes me send you my most hearty good wishes on your coming of age, but I hope you will not trouble to reply.

Yours truly,

George [full name illegible]

Sister Gertrude [full name illegible], Abbess, wrote [no date] to 'My Lord', wishing 'my sincere congratulations, on your account, to your sisters whom I have the pleasure of knowing'.

The Oxford Union Debating Society

William was very active in the Oxford Union Debating Society. During the Easter Term of 1892 he is listed as being on the standing committee of the Union as 'Earl Beauchamp, Christ Church, Secretary'. From this time on, he proved to be a frequent debater. Here we list his contribution to the Union debates.[25]

1

Thursday, March 24, 1892
Mr Magee; Merton, President, in the Chair.

25 See *Proceedings of the Oxford Union Society* (Oxford: printed by W. R. Bowden, 1823–1924), v. 3 (M. T. 1890 to E. T. 1904). I am most grateful to Niels Sampath, Senior Library Assistant, Oxford Union Library, for his kind help in my research.

Mr F. R. C. Bruce, Worcester, moved: *That this House condoles with ratepayers of London on the unfortunate result of the County Council elections.*

Speakers:
In the Affirmative
Mr Bruce, Worcester
Hon. W. Gibson, Merton
Mr Lake, Lincoln
Earl Beauchamp, Ch. Ch.

In the Negative
Mr Ridgeway, Lincoln
Mr Morrah, St John's
Mr R. C. Phillimore, Ch. Ch.
Mr Stewart, St John's

Mr Bruce replied.

Division:
Ayes 36
Noes 34
Majority 2

2

Thursday, May 19, 1892
Mr Galbraith, Oriel, President, in the Chair.
Mr P. Landon, Hertford, moved: *That the present is the truest age of Chivalry.*

Speakers:
In the Affirmative
Mr P. Landon, Hertford
Mr R. Bruce, Worcester
Mr Baker Penoyre, Non-Coll.

In the Negative
Lord Beauchamp, Ch. Ch. (Secretary)
Mr Hatton, Hertford
Mr Christian, Lincoln

Mr Landon replied.

Division:
Ayes 46
Noes 28
Majority 18

3

Thursday, December 8, 1892.
Mr R. C. Phillimore, Christ Church, Peresident, in the Chair
Mr J. H. Peachey, B. A., Queen's, Ex-Librarian, moved: *That this House regards the Irish Evicted Tenants Commission as unworthy of its serious consideration.*

Speakers:
In the Affirmative
Mr J. H. Peachey, B. A., Queen's, Ex-Librarian
Earl Beauchamp, Ch. Ch. (Ex-Secretary)

In the Negative
Mr W. F. K. Stride, Exeter
Mr W. Whitaker, Exeter
Mr W. Stewart, St John's

Mr J. H. Peachey replied:

Division:
Ayes 17
Noes 21
Majority against 4

In Michaelmas Term 1892 and Lent Term 1893, 'Earl Beauchamp, Ch. Ch.', is listed as serving on the Standing Committee:[26]

4

Thursday, February 2, 1893
Mr C. H. Eliot, Merton, President, in the Chair.
Earl Beauchamp, Ch. Ch., Ex-Secretary, moved: *That this House has no confidence in Her Majesty's Ministers, and considers their position eminently unstable.*

Speakers:
In the Affirmative
Earl Beauchamp, Ch. Ch., Ex-Secretary
Mr W. G. Howard Gritten, B. N. C.
Mr B. Christian, Lincoln
Mr A. S. Owen, New Coll.

26   The Oxford terms, Michaelmas, Hilary and Trinity, were then known as Michaelmas, Lent, and Easter respectively.

Mr H. B. Parker, Hertford
Mr F. E. Samual, Magdalen
Mr H. W. Liversidge, Hertford, Librarian

In the Negative
Mr C. G. Robertson, B. A., Hertford
Mr W. Whitaker, Exeter
Mr R. C. Phillimore, Ch. Ch., Ex-President
Mr J. H. Harley, Non-Coll.
Mr J. J. Cotton, B. A., Corpus

Earl Beauchamp replied.

Division:
Ayes 117
Noes 49
Majority 68

In the Easter Term of 1893, Earl Beauchamp, Ch. Ch. was elected President of the Union.

5

Thursday, April 27, 1893.
Earl Beauchamp, Christ Church, President, in the Chair.
Mr W. F. K. Stride, Exeter, moved: *That the House of Lords will be justified in rejecting the Home Rule Bill.*

Speakers:

In the Affirmative
Mr W. F. K. Stride, Exeter
Mr H. W. Liversidge, B. A., Hertford, Ex-Librarian
Mr W. G. Howard Gritten, B. N. C.
Lord Balcarres, Magdalen, Junior Treasurer
Earl Beauchamp, Ch. Ch. President

In the Negative
Mr J. S. Phillimore, Ch. Ch.
Mr K. E. Chalmers, Balliol
Mr J. H. Harley, Non-Coll.
Mr J. J. Cotton, B. A., Corpus
Mr R. C. Hawkin, Pembroke

Mr F. E. Smith, Wadham, moved the adjournment of the Debate.

Division on the adjournment.
Ayes 24
Noes 15
Majority 9

A week later the adjourned debate took place.

6

Thursday, May 4, 1893.
Earl Beauchamp, Christ Church, President in the Chair.
The Motion before the House: *That the House of Lords will be justified in rejecting the Home Rule Bill.*

Speakers In the Affirmative: 13
Speakers *In the Negative*: 6

Beauchamp did not speak.

Division:
Ayes 90
Noes 28
Majority 62

7

Friday, May 12, 1893
Earl Beauchamp, Christ Church, President, in the Chair.
Mr P. J. Macdonell, Brasenose, Librarian, moved: *That our present system of political parties is productive of political immorality.*

Speakers *In the Affirmative*: 7
Speakers In the Negative: 6

Beauchamp did not speak.
The Mover waived his right of reply.

Division:
Ayes 35
Noes 27
Majority 8

8

Thursday, May 18, 1893.
Earl Beauchamp, Christ Church, President, in the Chair.
Mr H. Belloc, Balliol, moved: *That this House would approve of any measures which gave Undergraduates a share in the government of this University.*

Speakers *In the Affirmative*: 5
Speakers In the Negative: 7
Speaker *Neutral*: 1

Mr Belloc replied.

Division:
Ayes 114
Noes 70
Majority 44

9

Thursday, May 25, 1893.
Earl Beauchamp, Christ Church, President, in the Chair.
Mr F. R. C. Bruce, Worcester, moved: *That this House would welcome the adjournment of the House of Commons for twenty years.*

Speakers In the Affirmative: 7
Speakers In the Negative: 5
Speaker Neutral: 1

Beauchamp did not speak.

Mr Bruce replied.
Division:
Ayes 25
Noes 58
Majority against 33

10

Thursday, June 1, 1893.
Earl Beauchamp, Christ Church, President, in the Chair.
Mr R. R. Marett, M. A., Ex-Secretary, moved: *That this House approves of the principles of the Local Veto Bill.*

Speakers In the Affirmative: 3
Speakers In the Negative: 9 (including Earl Beauchamp. Ch. Ch., President)

The Mover waived his right of reply.

Division:
Ayes 43
Noes 50
Majority against 7

11

Thursday, June 8, 1893.
Earl Beauchamp, Christ Church, President, in the Chair.
Mr J. R. L. Rankin, Corpus, moved: *That this House would welcome the outbreak of an European war.*

Speakers In the Affirmative: 4
Speakers In the Negative: 7 (including Mr H. Belloc)
Speaker Neutral: Baron von Born (Worcester)

Mr Rankin replied.

Division:
Ayes 29
Noes 70
Majority against 41

12

Thursday, June 15, 1893.
Earl Beauchamp, Christ Church, President, in the Chair.
Mr K. Lake, Lincoln, moved: *That this House approves of the principle of the Imperial Federation League.*

Mr A. M. McMullen, Balliol, moved the adjournment of the House.
Speakers For the Adjournment: 3
Speakers Against the Adjournment: 2

Mr B. Christian, Lincoln, moved the Previous Question, which was carried.
Speakers *In the Affirmative*: 3
Speakers *In the Negative*: 2

Beauchamp did not speak.

Division:
Ayes 32
Noes 14

This was the last time that Beauchamp would chair the Union debate. Some rather unpleasant events caused his expulsion from Christ Church.

Expulsion

Not all aristocratic members of Christ Church conformed to good sense, which Jonathan Swift so aptly formulated as 'the principal foundation of good manners'.[27] And the noblemen who resorted to vandalism in November 1893 lacked both good manners and good breeding. The cause of this insolent behaviour was the restriction administered by the Dean on those who were invited to attend a ball at Blenheim Palace to celebrate the coming of age of the Duke of Marlborough.[28] The noblemen refused to accept what they thought was a restriction of their 'aristocratic privileges'.[29] The offended aristocrats voiced their anger by painting slogans, 'Damn the Dean' (Paget) and 'Damn Sampson' (the senior censor), on the doors and walls of the Great Quadrangle. A piece of satire was circulated comparing the College to an institution which united 'all the advantages of a preparatory school with the affectionate superintendence of home life. Puritan principles! Venial porters!! Indifferent dons!!!'.[30] A second incident, still more offensive, happened in the summer of 1894. After a

27   See Jonathan Swift, 'A Treatise on Good Manners and Good Breeding', in John Gross, ed., *The Oxford Book of Essays* (Oxford: Oxford University Press, 1991), p. 34.
28   Marlborough, 9th Duke of, b. 1871.
29   'Many undergraduates at Christ Church looked forward to [moving naturally into high positions because of their aristocratic backgrounds] irrespective of the outcome of their studies at Oxford, and keeping the well-born in order, or encouraging them to scholarly application, represented a perennial challenge to the college's disciplinary resources. ... Their protest was against the refusal of the authorities to waive the normal regulations about college gate hours to enable them to attend a ball at Blenheim Palace. ...'. See *The History of the University of Oxford, op. cit.*, p. xxiii.
30   See Judith Curthoys, *The Cardinal's College, op. cit.*, pp. 267–8.

Bullingdon Club dinner,[31] a rowdy, drunken group of 'noblemen' broke windows in Peckwater Quad. This was now too much for Francis Paget, who had been appointed to the deanery only recently, in 1892. Discipline had to be restored. It is not entirely clear how deeply Earl Beauchamp was involved in these incidents. But it must have been serious enough to cause the Dean to have him expelled from the College along with those guilty of this scandalous conduct. Perhaps the punishment was too harsh, especially on Beauchamp. It is surmised that the young Earl only put up notices criticizing the Dean for sending down the undergraduates, but that he had not himself participated in the hostile acts.[32] There are no records to prove or disprove this conjecture. However, could it be that Beauchamp's subtle nature and delicate upbringing aroused his compassion on his fellow undergraduates, the objects of the Dean's wrath, and that this compassion proved fatal?

---

31   The Bullingdon Club is said to have been founded some time in 1780, primarily as a horse-racing and cricket club in Oxford. It still exists, and holds annual dinners. It is a club of rich people, notorious for the drunken, noisy behaviour of its members. The club has no official association with the University.

32   Beauchamp is said to have sent 'an insolent letter' to Dean Paget. See *The History of the University of Oxford, op. cit.*, p. xxiii.

A Seat in the House of Lords

As a hereditary peer, Beauchamp was automatically entitled to a seat in the House of Lords after the death of his father. Having come of age on 20 February 1893, he sat in the House for the first time on 14 March 1893 as 7th Earl Beauchamp.[1] However, while he remained at Oxford, he did not have time to participate in the Lords' debates. All this changed after his expulsion from Christ Church in 1894: he became involved in public affairs. First of all, in 1895, he secured for himself the office of Mayor of Worcester. Here he was following the family tradition, since the Beauchamps had been active in Worcestershire local politics for decades. The young Mayor – he was twenty-three – had little difficulty in coping up with his new duties, and he fulfilled them with dedication. But he stayed in this office for only a year. In June 1897 Beauchamp retired from being Mayor of Worcester. He sent a letter of thanks to the 'Citizens and Children of Worcester'. And so did Lady Mary Lygon, his sister:[2]

> I must write a line to say how much touched and delighted I am by your very kind and generous thought in giving me such a delightful token of your goodwill and affection. I shall certainly wear it, and it will remind me every day of the happy time when I was your Mayoress, and of the sympathy and warm welcome which I always met with from you.
>
> Yours gratefully and sincerely,
>
> Mary Lygon
>
> *Madresfield, June 1897.*

---

1   See *Parliamentary Debates*, House of Lords, vol. X, 14 March 1893.
2   Source: Beauchamp Papers, *op. cit.*

Lord Beauchamp wrote:[3]

> I want to join Lady Mary in thanking all the citizens & children of Worcester who
> have made my Mayoralty such a pleasure to me & have given me so handsome a
> memorial of the past year. I am indeed very grateful to all of you for the very many
> kindnesses you have shown me & as I cannot thank you each individually, will you
> accept this the gratitude wh I feel from the bottom of my heart & remember that
> nothing will give me more pleasure than to hear the prosperity & well-being of the
> City of Worcester & all its inhabitants.
>
> Beauchamp
>
> *Madresfield, June 1897.*

Each letter had a photograph of the author attached to it.

Beauchamp's main occupation was in the House of Lords. From early
1896 onwards he devoted his time and energy to the problems debated in
the House. His seriousness of purpose is shown in his deep involvement
and varied interests.

On 1 May 1896, Beauchamp moved that the Sewers and Drains Bill
be read a second time.[4] He said:

> that by the Public Heath Act, 1875, it was provided that a pipe into which the sewage
> of more than one house ran became a sewer repairable by the public authority. That
> position was in no way recognised by local authorities until a decision was given
> in the case of *Travis v. Uttley*, in December 1893, which revealed their obligation
> to the local authorities, who had up to that time thought that owners or occupiers
> were obliged to maintain all drains on private property. An attempt was made in
> the Public Health Act, 1890, to bring the law into accord with practice by enact-
> ing that when one or more houses were connected with a public sewer by as single
> drain, and these houses belonged to different owners, then the public authority
> might compel the occupiers to put the drain into order. But last year, in the case
> of *Hill v. Hair*, the judges held that there were two defects in this Act which made
> it inapplicable to the drains that were sewers under the original Act, and to houses
> which belonged to the same owner. In these circumstances the Bill was introduced

---

3   *Ibid.*

4   See *Parliamentary Debates*, House of Lords, vol. XL, 1 May 1896, cols 321–3. This
      was perhaps Beauchamp's maiden speech in the House of Lords.

to define the expressions 'sewer' and 'drain'. In Worcester there were 47 miles, and in Nottingham 230 miles of drains, which, unless this Bill were passed would remain sewers repairable by the public authority. There were two ways in which landowners would be affected; they would retain drains which would not be compulsorily taken from them as they might be at present; and they would have power to build over or alter any drains which were on their property at present. The other clauses were comparatively unimportant. The second section provided that the procedure adopted in the case of streets should be followed by the local authority in requiring a drain in a dangerous state to be put in order. The third clause gave a local authority power to declare a drain to be a sewer; and it was not likely to be abused, because no local authority would undertake the charge of more sewers than it could avoid, for fear of unduly burdening the local rates. The Bill had received the approval of the Association of Municipal Corporations, who were of the opinion that the definitions of sewer and drain in the Bill were the best that could be devised.

Lord Stanley of Alderley[5] rose to say that, since the bill was being 'strongly opposed' in Liverpool, Manchester and Salford, he thought it justified to move for the adjournment of the debate.

The Prime Minister, the Marquess of Salisbury,[6] said that it 'would be rather a strong measure, without hearing any arguments going to the substance of the Bill, to refuse a Second Reading and the objections to the Bill could be heard on going into Committee'.

Lord Harris[7] suggested that the House 'should have a fortnight to consider it before going into Committee'. And he congratulated Earl Beauchamp on the 'lucidity with which he had introduced the Bill'.

The Earl of Morley,[8] the Chairman of Committees, hoped that the bill would be read a second time. He agreed that a better definition of drains and sewers 'was wanted'. But any amendments could be discussed in Committee.

Amendment, by leave was withdrawn, and the original motion agreed to. The bill was read a second time and committed to a Committee of the Whole House.

---

5   Stanley of Alderley, 3rd Baron, b. 1827. A Liberal.
6   Salisbury, 3rd Marquess of, b. 1830. A Conservative.
7   Harris, 4th Baron, b. 1851. A Conservative.
8   Morley, 3rd Earl of, b. 1843. A Liberal.

The bill was considered in Committee on 12 June, was amended and ordered to be read a third time on 30 June 1896. The amendments were unsatisfactory to the author of the bill. Earl Beauchamp argued that the amendments would, if passed, make 'confusion worse confounded'. He therefore thought it advisable to withdraw the bill, in the hope that 'before the next Session, in consultation with the Local Government Board and the noble Earl (the Earl of Morley) whose Amendments were embodied in it, they would be able to introduce a new Bill which would be entirely satisfactory to all parties'.[9]

Lord Russell of Killowen[10] observed that the 'noble Earl deserved every credit for tackling this difficult and thorny subject'. The bill was by leave withdrawn.

Beauchamp joined in the debate on the Lunacy Bill, which was considered in Committee on 15 July 1897.[11] The debate centred round an amendment which gave the Commissioners of Lunacy power to 'require the visiting committee of any asylum, or the committee of management of any hospital, to make such alterations in, and addition to, the rules and regulations of the asylum or hospital as the Commissioners may consider expedient, and if the committee do not within two months after the notice make such alterations and additions to the satisfaction of the Commissioners, and send to the Commissioners a printed copy of the amended rules and regulations, the Commissioners may make a report to a Secretary of State, and the Secretary of State shall have power to determine whether the alterations or additions required by the Commissioners, or any of them, with or without modification, ought to be made or not, and any alterations or additions which the Secretary of State may approve shall be observed as part of the rules and regulations of the asylum or hospital.'

Earl Russell moved that the amendment be omitted. Lord Monkswell[12] agreed that the amendment gave too much power to the Commissioners.

---

9   See *Parliamentary Debates*, House of Lords, vol. XLII, 30 June 1896, col. 374.
10   Russell of Killowen, Baron, b. 1833. A Liberal.
11   See *Parliamentary Debates*, House of Lords, vol. LI, 15 July 1897, cols 134–43.
12   Monkswell, 2nd Baron, b. 1845. A Liberal.

The Earl of Northbrook[13] expressed objections. Earl Beauchamp referred to the inadequate pension scheme for those officers working in lunatic asylums. He gave notice of his amendment, the object of which was 'to express the opinion which would be largely shared by noble Lords who were acquainted with the condition of affairs, that with the onerous and disagreeable duties they had to discharge these officers would not be fairly and adequately treated under the provisions in the Bill'.[14] But he did not move his amendment. The bill was re-committed to the Standing Committee.

A topic of another nature had come to interest Beauchamp by 8 March 1898.[15] He was troubled by the condition of the Church of St George in Botolph Lane, London. He rose to ask the Lord Bishop of London if he was:

> aware that the Church of St George, Botolph Lane, has been closed for over five years, and the rectory house let for business purposes; and if any, and what, provision has been made for the spiritual oversight of the parish by the rector? I do not propose to detain your Lordships. I would merely say that this appears to me to be a very gross case of neglect of duty on the part of the rector of St George, Botolph Lane. The rector at the present moment receives over £600 a year, including the sum which he receives as income for the rectory house, which is let for business purposes. For that stipend he performs no duties whatever on behalf of his parishioners. Putting on one side the question of doing duty for wages received, I would merely say that what makes the question more deplorable is that almost within a stone's throw of St George's Church admirable work is being done by the Church Army and the London City Mission. There is no doubt that if the rector re-opened the church he would have a large congregation to which he might administer with advantage.

The Bishop of London replied thus:

> The facts of the case are these: The fabric of the Church of St George's, Botolph Lane, was some years ago reported to be insanitary and dangerous. The church was, therefore, closed for services on sanitary grounds. A scheme was then set on foot for the union of the parish of St George with the adjoining parish of St Mary-at-Hill. Such unions involve, as your Lordships are aware, many complicated arrangements, and the question has not yet been entirely settled. But in a very short time the parish of

13   Northbrook, 1st Earl, b. 1826. A Liberal.
14   See *Parliamentary Debates*, House of Lords, vol. LI, 15 July 1897, col. 141.
15   See *Parliamentary Debates*, House of Lords, vol. LIV, 8 March 1898, cols 946–7.

St George, Botolph Lane, will cease to exist, and will be united to St Mary-at-Hill. Meanwhile, the rector is responsible for the spiritual work of the parish, and I have no reason to think that it is neglected.

On 1 July 1898 Beauchamp moved the second reading of the Borough Funds Bill.[16] The provisions of the bill, he said,

do not deal with any matters of principle, but only with matters of detail, which have been found to be inconvenient, insufficient, and also unnecessary. The Bill chiefly proposes to amend both the Borough Funds Act, 1872, and the Borough Funds (Ireland) Act, 1888, with regard to public meetings. We find that those electors who chiefly come to public meetings are not those whose opinions weigh most. A matter in which we propose to make an Amendment is to take away from a single voter the power of putting the town to the enormous expense of having a poll. There was a case at Newcastle-on-Tyne, which was put to the expense of having a poll of 600, because one or two individuals were 'cranky'. We propose in the Bill to limit the right to one-twentieth of the electors. I confess that the exact number would be better dealt with in Committee, but the reason why one-twentieth is put down is because we follow the precedent of the Municipal Corporation Act. A second large and important detail is with regard to the division of the Bills into parts. At the present moment, if a Bill deals with two separate subjects, such as washhouses and parks, and a large number of the electors object to one, although they do not object to the other, it is necessary that they should reject both. However much a large majority may wish for washhouses, those washhouses have to go by the board, because a majority of the electors object to public parks. We wish to give facilities for the division of the poll into parts, in order that each may be rejected in accordance with the opinion of the electors. Another thing is with regard to the vote by ballot. At present the system is entirely different from that in vogue under any other regulations of local government. Initials have to be placed upon the papers, the papers are distributed all round the houses, and they are cleared afterwards. When there is an election for a School Board and for municipal purposes afterwards, it is invariably found that a large number of papers are invalidated because they were marked on papers for municipal elections with their initials instead of their crosses. The last matter to which I wish to call your Lordships' attention has regard to the payment of expenses. It is now found that considerable expense must be gone to in the matter of preparing a Bill. With complete confidence I ask your Lordships to give a Second Reading to this Bill.

16   See *Parliamentary Debates*, House of Lords, vol. LX, 1 July 1898, cols 771–4.

After a brief debate in which the Chairman of Ways and Means, the Earl of Morley, and the Earl Wemyss[17] participated, the bill was read a second time, and committed to a Committee of the Whole House.

Work for the London School Board

In addition to attending the House of Lords sessions, Beauchamp worked on the London School Board from 1895 until 1899, when he was designated to the Governorship of New South Wales. He describes his work in his diary.[18] It gives a rare insight into the local politics at the time in London.

> The members of the London School Board were especially kind & tho' my visits were fairly regular my interest in the work ceased.

> For some reason I was glad to have so dramatic an end placed to my work on the Board. My heart was always at Madresfield & being constitutionally lazy, it was a constant

---

17 Wemyss and March, 9th Earl of, b. 1818. A Liberal-Conservative.
18 The 7th Earl Beauchamp was not a regular diarist. But he made an exception in January 1900, because 'So many friends have told me I shd keep a diary that I have at last resolved to spur my usual indolence into some semblance of the thing. Not only shall I write down Australian events as they occur but also such things as I remember of the past as are likely to be interesting. It will probably be unstudied & ungrammatical, but the New South Wales portion will at least form the basis for a book wh is now in my mind on Australia. Just now we are all agitated by the Transvaal crisis – or war as it is now & by the excitement of speeding our own contingent. There has been a very loyal feeling shown as usual throughout the colony.' Oct. 1899. Jan. 1900: 'Alas! for the frailty of my good resolutions. It is only now Jan. 8 on board the *Pylades* on my way to Norfolk Island that I find time for these execrably written lines. She rolls horribly & I must try to find some quieter place for writing than that part of the captains cabin wh has been very generously made over to my use.' The diary is first dated 'Oct. 1899', then 'Jan. 1900'. The diary is written in long hand, and is at places illegible. A microfilm copy of it is accessible at the Mitchell Library, State Library of New South Wales, Sydney, under Manuscripts, Call No. ML A3295, Frame Nos 259–301: *Beauchamp, Lord – Diary, 1899–c.1900*.

trouble to me to be each week running up to London. It generally happened that I stayed there as little as possible & therefore found myself too busy. The routine was to arrive in London Tuesday nights – visit schools on Wednesday morning, perhaps a 'notice B.' meeting then to a Committee at the Board offices wh wd last till 5.00. It generally meant an early start from my room at 125 Piccadilly by 8.30 a.m. & very hurried luncheon at the Travellers. Thursday the same thing happened again except that the Board itself met at 3.00 & seldom finished before 7.00 p.m. Then very often there were evening meetings & the train left at Paddington again for Madresfield at 9.50 a.m. Then in addition to all these there were divisional members meetings in Finsbury every first monthly Monday wh were a constant trouble to me. Nor did I feel that without a great deal more attention & lengthier stays in London I cd effect much on the general policy of the Board. For that reason I never spoke but thrice, once when nearly a year had passed since election when an opportunity somewhat suddenly arose on the question of attendance. I had rather taken a special interest in it & therefore I spoke for some 10 min. & was rather pleased at the way the members received me. The other time was to second very shortly some amendment moved by some moderate member on the religious question. It was defeated by the Progressive & intolerant majority. The more one saw the inside of the work the more it became clear that the Progressives had used the religious cry as an electioneering cry. The same remark is equally true of moderates. Mr Athceston Riley with his famous Circular had split up the Moderate Party as led by Mr Diggle. Till then the Moderates had used the religious as a cloak for the economical cry. This seemed proved when Mr Diggle refused to give effect to the principles he had hitherto expressed by voting against Mr Riley & was obliged at the 1897 election to go to the Electorate on a programme wh was little better than a promise to 'save the ratepayers pocket'. For myself Mr James Adderley then incumbent at May Fair Chapel asked me in the summer to stand for the combined principles of Church & progress. The situation had been discussed at a meeting of the U.S.U. at Mr Scott Hollands & after some hesitation I agreed to stand. My platform was the maintenance of the 72 religious compromise & progressive education. I had little hesitation because it seemed clear to me that the religious question was not one for the Board to settle. Rightly or wrongly it had been settled by Act of Parliament & tho' we might not think it ideal, it had to be altered by Parl. & not by the Board. Progressive education with increased payments to teachers & general improvement I heartily & thoroughly supported. Mr Corriegrant was the general organiser of victory, Miss Eve a sitting member & Mr Bowden a former teacher from the North were my colleagues. We were chosen at a weird meeting in the Middleton Hall off High St Islington. The constituency was huge. It had six members of whom our party nominated & carried 3. Four candidates turned up at the caucus meeting composed of delegates from all the labour – radical & socialistic organizations in the district. We each spoke & were heckled. I came I think the third in the list & just beat Mr Morgan Browne who got in afterwards for the Strand. The contest began about Oct., the election was at the end of November. London was apathetic – some nonconf. objected to my being Ch. of E., some radicals to my being a Lord. The Radical agent was excellent, shoved me about & we managed some how to get in 4th on the list of six. My two Radical colleagues were on the top, then came a lady Mrs Dildin for whom Finsbury plumped. There were also several Independent & unsuccessful candidates. Lord Reay[19] we chose as chairman from outside the Board & Mr Lyulph Stanley the progressive leader vice-chairman. The Progressives were every where triumphant, but what they did I must write later.

Beauchamp had now to turn his mind to other matters. He was soon destined to be posted to occupy an important high office in the Empire. Many Christ Church men had served the Crown in this capacity: why should not Beauchamp follow suit?

19   Reay, 11th Baron, b. 1839. A Liberal.

Governor of New South Wales

Appointment

Earl Beauchamp was Governor of New South Wales, Australia from 18 May 1899 to 30 August 1901. He was offered the post at the end of December 1898. He was travelling in Europe with his friend, and at the time sightseeing in Greece, when the letter with this offer reached him. The Secretary of State for the Colonies, Joseph Chamberlain,[1] had suggested Beauchamp's appointment, and the Earl later recorded the circumstances in his diary:[2]

> Landon & I left London just before the Christmas of 1898 & had spent it in Paris – mostly in the restaurants. ... we were joined by my uncle Philip Stanhope & aunt Ina for our Xmas dinner. It was much too large & much too rich, but more than excellent. Frederics – as much a statesman to look at as ever had risen from a bed of sickness to cook for us & the result was beyond comparison. High Mass we saw at Notre Dame where I had seen it before with Eddie on one of the Sundays in Oct. 95. This occasion of course was far finer & the Cardinal Abp Richard – most saintly of cardinals celebrated mass with great pomp. I was in the front row on the south side outside the rails & saw completely. The music was not very striking but the procession with its long line of tapers in the dim cath. was fine. The only piece of ritual I cd not understand was the changing of mitres wh was a prominent part the Epiphany mass in S. Mark's Venice earlier in the same year. The afternoon we spent at a most curious church of wh P .L. [Perceval Landon] so like him knew. From my recollection it was called Ruthenian, its construction was that of the Greek Church but it was reconciled to Rome. We waited long for Vespers wh however never took place, altho' several people – largely I thought strangers wandered in & out again.

---

1   Joseph Chamberlain (1836–1914), Liberal M.P., 1876–86; Unionist M.P., 1886–1914; Colonial Secretary, 1895–1903.
2   See *Beauchamp, Lord – Diary, 1899–c.1900*, *op. cit.*

It is in some slum near the Luxembourg & is – to those curious in such things well worth a visit. Then to the Louvre, where the Milo statue attracted me as strong as ever. What does her expression mean? The downward curve of the outward lips is so curious & so [unmissable]. Is there a hint of a sneer in the benignity with wh she regards us? Scarcely too a Venus, to me she seems rather a Mother of Nature never the Venus of Tennyson's (*Oenone*).[3] What a mixture the picture galleries are? The vulgar jewel room first & early Italians – Murillo & Raphael spoilt by their vulgar reproductions & the Ary Scheffer (ugh!). The loping gallery wh always depresses me & the occasional masterpiece in the larger room. On the whole however it is I think to the Lancret that I turn with most pleasure in Paris.

Next day we were off – after a déjeuner at Pruniers with my uncle to eat oysters by the night train by Mont Cenis to Brindisi. It was a horrid journey – a few hours at Turin wh we used walking about the town & on again, this time I think without beds. Turin was not interesting & tho' the next days journey by the side of the Adriatic was charming we felt when we met again at Brindisi some of our fellow travellers from Paris who had arrived via Rome & Naples in a train de luxe that we were ill repaid for the discomfort of the night. Faithless Cook!

The Austrian Lloyd wh stopped at Corfu brought us with little delay to Patras where we arrived very early in the morning & where to our joy the guide from Athens turned up. P. L. was late, we bundled as before & just arrived in time to catch the train. Without his breakfast or a view wh the pouring rain blotted out. P. L. was rather unhappy but the aforesaid Charles – always full of resources speedily produced cold eggs & we ate. The men at the wayside stations were uninteresting & we arrived in time at Olympia. Happily the three damsels from America whom P. L. declared had been persuaded to come to Olympia of wh they then heard for the first time took up their quarters in the more magnificent hotel wh Charles disliked. We spent New Years day at Olympia & had plenty of time to explore. The Hermes of Praxiteles in the Museum is most beautiful – the finest of all male statues as the Venus of Milo represents the women. The head & body are perfect. The restorations are few & unobtrusive. Alas that in Greece we saw no one who for face or figure compared with this. Mahaffy[4] in his *Rambles* declares the statue larger than life size but to us it seems little over 6 ft. The winged Victory with her flying robe & the remains of the temple were of comparatively little interest. It is pleasant however to record that all was well cared for.

3   A poem by Alfred Tennyson written in 1829. Oenone is deeply in love with Paris, who is off to Troy to be with Helen. Oenone expresses her grief.

4   John Pentland Mahaffy (1839–1919), Irish classicist and papyrologist; wrote extensively on Greek art and culture.

The guide books to Olympia are so admirable that it wd be foolish for me to emulate them. Let me only record with how much pleasure both here & at the Parthenon wd I subscribe to have the pillars restored. In both places they lie separated into their component parts, lying in order, scarcely injured. I cannot [believe it is] beyond the skill of modern archaeology or engineering to restore them in such a way as wd give us a more perfect impression of their appearance. Nor need we fear that earthquakes wd hurt them more in the future than they have in the past. The Basilica was very interesting & with little effort we were able to reconstruct Olympia as it was in her [illegible] & most coloured days.

We started at last on ponies & mules – our cook had been telegraphed for by Charles from Athens & had arrived the night before with beds & provisions. Andritsaena was our object but we slept a night at Grecko on our way where our arrival caused the greatest astonishment. The view was beautiful. The valley of the Alpheus ran at right angle to the village in the blue & purple distance. A smaller valley ran from the foot of the mountain on wh Grecko was perched to join the Alpheus. On each side & beyond were mountains stretching a way into the distance or gently running down to join the green meadows below. After dinner the moon came out & we sat a long time on the balcony in silence. The next day on again over the mountain to country less wooded & less [illegible] interesting. The track itself was near the Turkish road wh it some times joined & much as I hated the Turk. The abominable pavement [illegible] land of ragged stones made me hate him more – with reason they were slippery & in places laid on too steep an incline. It is only fair to add that the neglect with wh the Greeks had since treated the track had probably added to its dangers. For the first day & a half indeed the journey was very beautiful. A bright sun, clear air, trees & cheerful villages gladdened both heart & eye. We passed thro' groves of Olive & arbutus & by the way side were growing crocus & anemone, wild iris & cyclamen. Most veracious Theocritus!

Andritsaena treated us badly. It rained when we arrived, it rained as we left. A pause in the bad weather alone persuaded us to start before 6 a. m. to see Bassoe wh was the goal of our journey in the Peloponnese.

A pile of letters was awaiting my arrival in Athens, we had really been for a fortnight without news & we fell upon them eagerly. In the course of them I came upon one from Mr Chamberlain in wh to my enormous surprise he offered me the governorship of New South Wales – I scarcely knew where the colony was & certainly nothing about it – my few wits indeed were rather scattered on reading the letter; as usual P. L. to the rescue. The offer was very forthwith refused, so ridiculous did it appear to me but the prospect brightened under P. L.'s account & after an evening wh we imagined myself having filled every honourable post in the Empire I wired & wrote asking for the fuller particulars wh were mentioned in the letter. The next steamer left Athens in a week for Constantinople & the only thing to do was to curb my impatience, seek at Legation a little information about the colony & see the sights. The journey home cd only be shortened from Turkey. The British Minister & Lady Egerton were most kind. We dined often with them & Spicer one of the attachés gave us a very clear insight into the politics of the legation.

Arrived at last in London. I dined at the Beefsteak & there found Lord Kintore[5] who strongly advised me to accept & after a lot of letters retired to bed certain of what my decision shd be. Lord Kintore I had met in the Spring of '95 on a Sat. to Monday visit to Battle Abbey – with my dear old aunt the Duchess of Cleveland & had liked him immensely. He had just then returned from South Australia & came on to Madresfield at very short notice to meet Princess Mary when she came in April to a function in Malvern. From him first I heard of the *Bulletin* of wh he had no favourable word & he told me of its account of Lady Jersey's[6] departure. 'M. E. J's departure' – 'Not an eye but was dry, but stop, we had forgotten a drunken old Irish woman', etc. Leslie Ward as usual & many enquiries after Dick Somerset. Pandeli Ralli pleasant as ever & full of enquiries about Athens as he intended a yachting trip later in the year.

Next day to the C. O. [Colonial Office], where Oliver was affable & kind. He read me Lord Hampden's[7] letter of resignation complaining of the expense wh he put down at some £12,000 a year. Then he took me to see some officials who looked up N. S. W. in their books & after gathering a lot of very inaccurate information, I wrote from a table in the corner of the P. S.'s room a formal note of acceptance to Mr Chamberlain who was in his own room next door but who was too busy to be disturbed. The information was afterwards tiresome in its inaccuracy. They told me that neither plate, linen or glass was provided, that there was no country house, that some £600 was allowed for an A. D. C. The matter was so far settled, but until the Queen had approved nothing cd be said or done in public.

When Chamberlain approached the Queen to seek her approval, Her Majesty did not appear enthusiastic about it. Was there no other, or rather better, candidate? the Queen enquired. In a lengthy letter dated 17 January 1899 the Secretary for the Colonies had to explain why the choice had fallen on Earl Beauchamp.

5   Kintore, b. 1852, 10th Earl of. A Conservative. Governor of South Australia, 1889–95.
6   Wife of Earl Jersey (1845–1915), Governor of New South Wales, 1890–93.
7   Viscount Henry Hampden (1841–1906), Governor of New South Wales (1895–99).

Colonial Office[8]

Mr Chamberlain presents his humble duty to your Majesty and in reply to your Majesty's letter he begs to say that he approached several other Peers before saying anything to either Lord Beauchamp or Lord Tennyson[9] on the subject of the vacant Australian Governorships. Among them were the Duke of Somerset, Earl of Dudley & the Earl Camperdown, but none of these noblemen were willing to have their names submitted to your Majesty.

Mr Chamberlain has recently found the greatest difficulty in getting candidates for these appointments, owing chiefly to the fact that the expenditures exceed the salary allowed by the Colonies to the extent of £3,000 and sometimes of much more per annum.

It was under these circumstances that Mr Chamberlain at last recommended Lord Beauchamp and Lord Tennyson who both desired an opportunity for public work and were willing to spend what was required.

In the case of self-governing Colonies the constitutional powers of the Governors are very limited and the responsibility is not great, as is the case in a Crown Colony.

Lord Beauchamp served as Mayor of Worcester and, although the office is not in itself an important one, it enabled him to give evidence of great industry & good judgment, and it was universally conceded that he made a most excellent host which is an important qualification in Australia.

As regards Lord Tennyson, Mr Chamberlain has little knowledge of his personal qualifications, but his father's name and the fact that Lord Tennyson is the author of the poet's life will secure for him a good reception in the Colony.
Mr Chamberlain consulted Lord Salisbury about both these appointments before submitting them to your Majesty, and he hopes that they may prove to be worthy of your Majesty's approval.

27 Jan., 1899

Her Majesty's approval was soon conveyed to the Secretary for the Colonies. An official announcement appeared in the *Gazette*. The newspapers indulged in much gossip about Beauchamp's youth. He would soon be 27. However, his family, his friends and his acquaintances were 'all most kind'.

---

8   Source: Royal Archives: VIC/ADD/C/22.
9   Baron Tennyson (1852–1928), eldest son of the poet laureate Alfred Tennyson; Governor of South Australia (1899), Governor-General of Australia, 1902–3.

The Queen now invested Beauchamp with the insignia of his proper rank[10] and invited him to dine with her at Windsor. Here is how Beauchamp remembers the event:[11]

> Lord Tennyson was appointed at the same time & a short time after our appointment we were both made K. C. M. Gs. The old rule had been to make all outgoing governors G. C. M. G. But of late that rule had been suspended in order to make the lower rank of higher esteem in colonial eyes & also in order that the higher rank shd be a sort of reward after good service. As a matter of fact the ribbon had been attractive to me throughout & it was with much pleasure that I heard that the Queen wd herself invest us both. Lord & Lady Tennyson & I received command to Windsor for the same night. They arrived by an earlier train & I left London with Ld Denbigh[12] who was Lord in Waiting about 5.30 in some trepidation. He showed me my room at once & at 7.30 we met in the corridor for the investiture. A picture by the Queens Italian marine painter of the naval '97 review stood on an easel & occupied our attention with several introductions to members of the household for a dreadful half hour. An equerry in uniform carried the orders on a red velvet cushion & various subordinate officials were about. At last a commotion. The Queen was going into the room where it wd take place. Sir Fleetwood Edwards instructed us & at last the first victim was summoned. The Queen seemed to be attended only by Princess Henry & sat in a low chair. The room was tiny, so small indeed, that tho' H. M. was seated in the middle, there scarcely seemed room for the door to shut behind me. I knelt on one knee & Lord Denbigh produced a light Court sword with wh he helped the Queen to touch me on both shoulders. He prompted her also with the words 'Sir William' & the Queen inaudibly murmured something wh I took to be 'Rise Sir William.' I had kissed her hand on kneeling but omitted to do it again then as was strictly correct, but tho' ready to do it, did not find the opportunity. Then the

10   Earlier, on 9 February 1899, the Secretary for the Colonies had sent Beauchamp a letter stating the following: 'It has usually been my privilege in the case of all gentlemen appointed to Australian Governorships to present their names to the Queen for the honour of Knight Commander of St Michael & St George, and I shall be very glad to be permitted by you to make this recommendation in your case. The higher honour of Grand Cross of the Order has usually been subsequently offered either on leaving office, or during its term. Trusting that it will be agreeable to you that it should follow the usual precedent.' See manuscripts in Mitchell Library, State Library of New South Wales, Sydney: *Beauchamp, Lord: Letters received, 1899–1901*. Call No. ML A 3012.

11   See *Beauchamp, Lord – Diary, 1899–c.1900, op. cit.*

12   Denbigh, 9th Earl of, b. 1845. A Conservative.

Queen hung the ribbon round my neck fixed the star into a large pin wh had been inserted in my frock coat – helped again to do both by Lord Denbigh. I kissed her hand again & retired backwards.

Lord Tennyson then went thro' the same ceremony & afterwards took me to his room where I was introduced to Lady T.

Dinner at 9.00 by wh time I had arranged the ribbon to hang higher round my neck & had arrayed myself in breeches & stockings. Lady Ampthill was there & Miss Minna Cochrane Lady-in-waiting to Princess Beatrice. At 9.5 the Queen passed across the corridor leaning heavily on a stick & supported on the right by an Indian. We followed into the dining room wh is called I think the oak dining room. The Queen who never sits next to a stranger had on her right Princess Henry, next to whom I came, then Lady Tennyson – on her left Lady Ampthill, then Lord T. Conversation was subdued. Princess Henry or Lady A. repeated to the Queen any thing they thought wd interest her, but the only time she really brightened was when I spoke of the Duchess of Cleveland as likely to come to Australia. The dinner was good with excellent claret & the Queen seemed to eat heartily, & drank, I think, whisky & water. There was no pause between the courses & each person seemed to be served separately. The waiting was excellent. Indians waited on the Queen. After dinner we all passed into the corridor where H. M. sat in a chair, & after interviewing Lady T. sent for me. It was very difficult as she sat low in her chair – very low to speak without being heard by all. I kept bent accordingly & the Queen asked most kindly after various relations & then several questions on matters of fact wh made conversation very difficult. However I tried my best &, having thought of her anxiety to be called Empress of India expressed some hope that H. M. shd honour the various colonies by assuming some title such as Empress of India, Canada & Australia. This did come round to me afterwards, but vaguely. After I had been dismissed, Lord T. was interviewed. Lady A. & I watched, & wondered what it was when he produced something out his waistcoat pocket. It turned out after to be a Saxon flint found in the Isle of Wight. He told me he found the Queen very easy to talk to!! So the Queen went to bed & we went many miles to a billiard room where we drank or smoked & talked etc. Next morning breakfast with the household in the same room & so – away.

The household always are charming & delightful people. I had written my name as directed by a groom of the Chambers in a birthday book wh H. M. sends regularly round. Lady Ampthill afterwards declared the Queen's verdict was 'Lord B. was easy to get on with but he looked as if he ought to take a tutor out with him' – an opinion wh pleased me. I was much struck by what I had chiefly noticed when the H. of L. was received by H. M. in 1897, that the top part of the head seemed to weigh down the lower – an impression produced by the chin being sunk. Indeed there seemed to be little chin – the cheeks I suppose dwarfed it. The Queen was dressed in nondescript black with a white [illegible] cap ornamented with two jet feather like ornaments in front – her face red & her hair silvery white.

Departure

Now that it was all settled that Beauchamp would take up the governorship of New South Wales he set out to make the necessary arrangements. His chief task was to assemble and recruit a strong staff. And naturally, before the journey, leave-taking from the family and friends became equally necessary. Beauchamp's diary gives us further details.[13]

> My telegrams & mysterious return a week early had thoroughly upset the family who were agog with excitement. My marriage to a slave bought in the Constantinople market was the romantic production of the Pull Court schoolroom. That the Vice-chairmanship of the London School board had been offered me was Mary's idea. However as silence was imposed, London was impossible for me, my plans were upside down & a true answer to almost every question was impossible. So I fled to Madresfield & broke the news to Mr Munu on the Sunday. Then Pull Court had to be told & the anxious fluttering atmosphere of a feminine establishment scenting a wedding was very amusing. Mama was prepared to fall upon my neck & that of the bride whom she wd not have been surprised to see emerge from the brougham & the conversation at luncheon where all knew a mystery overhang our previous talk was embarrassed. That same night I left for Middleton to consult Lord & Lady Jersey who then & always have been most kind. A telegram that aft. told me it wd be next day in the papers so in gt hurry I wrote to many friends & relations to tell them the news. Meanwhile only Lady Mary Villiers & her younger sister were at Middleton & the peals of laughter with wh they received the news was not very gratifying to my vanity! However, Lord Jersey gave me much good advice, Lady Jersey gave me much information & after dinner I saw photos of the house at Sydney. It had always been a pleasure to me to see or to talk to Lady Jersey & this was no exception. Next morning I went back to London & found the papers not unnaturally reproduced my own surprise at my appointment. Not only was it a gt surprise but it was especially gratifying as it had been earned by no payments to political party funds, by no asking on my part. In accepting it indeed the prospect of the order of SSM & G. was

13   See *Beauchamp, Lord – Diary, 1899–c.1900, op. cit.*

a certain inducement & my age the youngest of all colonial governors was the record. All thro' since the first night at Athens P. L. had told me of Federation, it had some influence on my decision. Five years is dreadful. Three years wh seemed in London the probable time was possible. At the Bachelor's where I lunched my entrance was rather sensational. Gillet at once congratulated me & voiced the general surprise. Every body was very kind & many were the letters wh had to be answered during the next two months & a half. The first thing to do was to get together a staff. The first idea was my dear cousin Dick Somerset, Prince Algy of Teck & Perceval Landon as secretary. A cable was sent to Dick in West Africa – he notes it in his diary, Prince Algy refused & P. L. was found impossible. Victor Corkran next was offered the secretaryship & he accepted with joy. A telegram to Russia offered Robin Lindsay second place on the staff & on his return he with joy also promised to come. From Dick came a refusal as he was bound to the Company & tho' the place was kept open in the hope that his fever wd prevent his return to the Niger, his death in March left me a bare month before leaving without a chief of the staff. Most happily after a refusal from Wilfrid Ashley I was lucky enough to get Wilfrid Smith on Eddie's recommendation. As the name conveyed nothing to me, the experiment was a risky one wh has however since turned out a brilliant success.

From that time onward I lived in a whirlpool of distraction & excitement. It was only on *the Himalaya* on our way out that there was a period of rest before we were engulphed [sic] in the vortex of New South Wales. The appointment had been announced on Jan 23 & a few days – 2 or 3 after was held the annual dinner of New South Wales people in London. Lord Jersey had asked me to come & as he was in the chair, it was a pleasure to accept. Many eminent colonists were introduced & by good luck more than by forethought I made a happy speech. It was short & 'modest'(!) & in promising to try to follow Lord Jersey's example a right note was struck.

Beauchamp received a letter from the Governor of New Zealand giving him information about his forthcoming travel.

Earl Ranfurly[14] *to Lord Beauchamp*[15]

Government House,
Wellington,
New Zealand

14   Ranfurly, 5th Earl of, b. 1856. A Conservative.
15   Source: Manuscripts in the Mitchell Library, State Library of New South Wales, Sydney: *Beauchamp, Lord: Letters received, 1899–1901*. Call No. ML A 3012.

4.I.99

My dear Beauchamp,

Hill Trevor has received Capt. Smith's telegram, and Cook & Son have been told to arrange for your transit from Milford Sound to Mossbum the end of the Railway or Lumsden if better, at Milford Sound there is a settler named Sutherland who has rooms in fact he called it an Hotel, but there is no licence. My children had tea there, tho' I have not been to the house myself, they say it was clean & the food was all right, this was 2 years ago, it is however probably a poor place; you should have with you whatever liquor you require from the ship to Mossbum, as none I fancy can be legitimately obtained. The route to Te Anau Lake is only a bridle path so all luggage has to be carried on men's backs, I presume therefore you will send all to the Bluff to be sent on by train to Lumsden to meet you there, only taking what can be carried by two men viz 100 lbs between the two. I have told Hill Trevor to cable Capt. Smith about this, as the men are very difficult to communicate with, there is only a Mail to Milford Sound about once a month, so arrangements have to be made from the other end (Te Anau). I wrote to you a letter on 23 Dec., but accidentally it was never posted, and has just been discovered, in it I gave you my plans, which as they are somewhat altered I will now give you, destroying the former letter. Up till Febry 1st I shall be chiefly travelling (North Island) by train, attending one or two fetes & prize givings that I have fixed. In Febr. I am due on the West Coast South Island at Okarito & several very out of the way places. Leaving there for the East Coast of North Island also for un-get-at-able places where I have to meet Maoris and finally reaching Auckland about the middle of March.

I shall be on the telegraph almost if not quite daily, as in these war times I do not like not getting the news, & also being about in case anything exceptional occurring. My best address will be 'Wellington or Forward'.

I almost fear I shall altogether miss you, but shall know more after this contingent leaves. We do not take up our residence in Auckland anyhow before the middle of March.

I will see that every possible arrangement is made on the Railways for you, & you have only to let me know anything, & I will see what can be managed.

Believe me,

Yours sincerely,

Ranfurly

Before Beauchamp left England, he sent messages to various people. He wished a happy New Year to the Tennysons, who had earlier arrived in Australia. Lady Audrey Tennyson thanked for the good wishes:[16]

> Marble Hill,
> Adelaide
>
> January 7th, 1899
>
> Dear Lord Beauchamp,
>
> I feel as if I had behaved most ungratefully to have let several days lapse without writing to thank you for your kind telegram of warm wishes for the New Year which we reciprocate most cordially. I have had every minute of my time taken up with stitching hospital jackets & belts etc. for our Contingent, & have let all letters go till today, Sunday. I have also to thank you for your photograph & hope you have received mine, which you asked for, from Melbourne. I told the man there to send it to you, as I did not think you would care for a group of me with the boys.
> We came up here to this perfectly lovely, delicious place about three weeks ago and are blissfully happy, grudging every day passing, thus shortening our time here.
>
> You must come and see us here sometime. I wonder if you ever have any stamps you do not want for other collectors. You would let Capt. Wilfrid Smith just put them in an envelope for my boys.
>
> Believe me,
>
> Yrs sincerely,
>
> Audrey Tennyson
>
> P.O. Please forgive my stupid mistakes, I have got one of my horrid headaches so can't write the letter again.

Beauchamp wrote to the Secretary for the Colonies, letting him know the date of his departure. From the Secretary's answer it is clear that Beauchamp must also have enquired about his A. D. C.'s salary and the country house in Sydney.[17]

---

16   *Ibid.*
17   *Ibid.*

9th February 1899

Dear Lord Beauchamp,

I have received your letter of the 5th inst. saying that you propose to start on the 7th April. I am sorry that you should have been misinformed as to the salary of your A. D. C. and the existence of a country house, but I understand that this was due to the fact, with which you were at once acquainted, that the available information in the Colonial Office is unfortunately out of date. I imagined that it was generally known that the acceptance of an Australian Governorship involved considerable personal expenditure, a disadvantage I am endeavouring to remedy, and I can only hope that the information which was unfortunately given to you too late is not such as would have affected your acceptance of the Governorship if you had obtained it earlier.

I am,

Yours very truly,

J. Chamberlain

Beauchamp also informed the retiring Governor of New South Wales, Viscount Hampden, about his arrival. The latter responded with a message, which must have amused his successor:[18]

Government House,
Sydney

March 5, 99

My dear Lord,

I have left an American wagonette which you will find a very useful and, indeed, a necessary carriage in the country. I used it myself a great deal in the city.

I gave £60 for it, & have had two years work out of it. The carriage requires some slight repairs, but I think it should be worth £30.

I am,

Yrs faithfully,

Hampden

18   *Ibid.*

To Beatrice Webb, Beauchamp sent a bouquet of flowers. She dispatched a thank-you letter.[19]

> 41 Grosvenor Road,
> Westminster Embankment.
>
> March 28, 1899
>
> Dear Lord Beauchamp,
>
> The flowers are lovely [illegible] very kind of you to have thought of us, with all your preparation for departure. We should be immensely interested to hear from your [illegible] if you should find time to write to us.
>
> With best regards
>
> Yours sincerely
>
> Beatrice Webb
>
> P. S. Please remember us to W. Reid[20] & W. Wise[21] and especially to W. Ashton[22] for whom we [illegible] a very much liking. BW

Arrival in Australia: A diplomatic *faux pas*

Earl Beauchamp sailed for Australia on 7 April 1899 in the mail steamer, the *Himalaya*.[23] In those days, Albany was first port of call for mail steamers from Europe. Beauchamp's steamer dropped anchor in King George's Sound on 10 May. High State officials bid the new Governor welcome.

---

19   *Ibid.*
20   Sir George Reid (1845–1918), premier of New South Wales, later Prime Minister of the Australian Commonwealth.
21   Percy William Wise (1870–1950); Anglican priest, curator at Christ Church, North Adelaide.
22   Julian Ashton (1877–1964), journalist, critic and artist.
23   The *Himalaya* had been built about 1850 to be commandered for the trooping service at the outbreak of the Crimean War. She was later converted into a P & O liner, and still carried masts and sails to supplement her engines. Her average speed did not

A prying young journalist was also present. His impertinent inquiry into the Governor's purpose occasioned an embarrassing start to Beauchamp's work. This 'cub' reporter was called Ernest R. Power. Power had an assignment with the *Sydney Evening News* and *The Sydney Morning Herald* to interview various notables on their arrival at Albany and report on them. Something extraordinary happened when the mail boat carrying Lord Beauchamp arrived at Albany. The steamer, writes Power,[24]

> lay out in the middle of Albany's magnificent harbour, and as the tug drew alongside, I recognised the good-looking, boyish face peering down from the liner's rail as that of the young nobleman. Immediately I got aboard, I walked up to His Excellency, informed him who I was and requested an interview. He was quite taken aback, and quickly observed, 'You want to see my private secretary.' I replied, 'No; it is your Excellency I want.' By this time he was half-way along the deck, with myself in pursuit.

<hr />

exceed 9 knots. For details see: Alan Clark (ed.), *A Good Innings: The Private Papers of Viscount Lee of Fareham* (London: John Murray, 1974), p. 25.

24   This narrative and a whole mass of information related to this and other incidents are to be found in *The Papers relating to the 7th Earl Beauchamp William Lygon*, 'Birth-stain message'. Source: manuscripts in the Mitchell Library, State Library of New South Wales, Sydney, Call No. ML DOC 2561. Even years later, Beauchamp's *faux pas* was not forgotten. The gossip columns continued to write about it. We quote an instance: 'Earl Beauchamp crops up again. When B. Chump was suffering the consequences of his bitter pill, the unfortunate remark about Australia's *birth-stains*, he lamented to George Reid that for too much had been made of the incident. "Why," said he, "I heard an Australian, giving a speech in London, declare that Australia's advance was marvellous, considering how recently her ankles had been freed of the chain. He also commented on the marked partiality Australian women show for chain bangles, and assumed, he said, that it was the influence of heredity. In fact I got the birth-stains phrase from him." "Who was that Australian?" asked George, and Beauchamp mentioned the name of a cockney journalist who had scampered through this country in about three weeks. "I understood he was an ex-Premier," mournfully said his innocent Excellency, "and was led to believe Australians gloried in the speed they had shown in getting away from the tiger and the ape." "Yes," replied Reid, thoughtfully, "but next time you see a man running from a tiger you won't stop him to discuss its marks, will you?" This is how Reid told it to a small gathering of Australian artists in London.' *Smith's Weekly*, 10 May.1919. Source: Manuscripts in the Mitchell Library, State Library of New South Wales, Sydney, Call No. ML DOC 465b.

He disappeared down the companion way, and in a few moments I was met by the private secretary, Hon. Victor Corkran, who informed me that his Excellency had decided that he would not be interviewed in Australia. I replied that his Excellency would not be able to maintain that attitude for any length of time, unless he wished to become unpopular. The Hon. Victor then said his Excellency would answer questions through him.

It was an inauspicious start, but it led to what I regard as about the best scoop I was ever able to secure. Among other things, I asked for a message to the people of New South Wales. The Hon. Victor conveyed my request to the blue-blooded nobleman, and, on returning, said that Lord Beauchamp was 'looking up a message'. We chatted for some time – there was no snobbery about the genial private secretary – and then he received the message, which was written by Lord Beauchamp in lead pencil, on his 'Madresfield Court, Malvern Link' notepaper – I still have it. The message, as many Australians remember, was an adaptation of a verse from Kipling's *Seven Seas*. The following is a facsimile:

> Greetings! Your birth-stains have you turned to good
> Forcing strong wills perverse to steadfastness
> The first flush of the tropics in your blood
> And at your feet Success
> – *Beauchamp*, 10 V 99

Immediately I read the lines I realised the blunder he had made, but after a mental wrestling match, determined to say nothing, but leave it to my Sydney principals to decide whether he should be 'saved from himself'. Future events justified my decision, as the 'Seidlitz powder's' invitations[25] to Government House, and other like incidents, showed that this amiable but tactless scion of a noble race was apparently born to blunder.

A blunder it certainly was. Beauchamp's 'birth-stain' message was published by the Sydney papers the very next morning. Needless to say, it created a considerable stir among the local population. And when Beauchamp reached Sydney on 18 May he realized what a poor first impression he had made. The 'dashing' Governor acquitted various uncomplimentary nicknames at

---

25   The Governor sent out two classes of invitations to guests at a levee: a blue ticket allowed a guest to meet the Governor, a white ticket allowed a guest to roam only a cordoned-off area.

once: some called him 'Billy Big Chump', others 'Birth-stain Beauchamp'.[26] The harshest criticism was voiced by the *Bulletin*, the most radical of the Australian journals, which was 'an unprecedented and unrivalled forum of all who rebelled against the colonial or imperial Establishment'.[27]

Welcome to Sydney

Earl Beauchamp was scheduled to arrive in Sydney on 18 May. Preparations were being made to welcome the new Governor. The office of the Consul General of France in Sydney addressed a formal note to Sir Frederick Darley, the Lieutenant Governor,[28] on 8 May:[29]

26   See 'Birth-stain message', *op. cit.*, Call No. ML DOC 2561.

27   See O. H. K. Spate, *Australia* (London: Ernest Benn Ltd., 3rd revised impression, 1971), p. 59. Beauchamp's unintentional *faux pas* drew criticism from various other quarters. Earl Carrington [(1843–1928); President of the Board of Agriculture, 1905–11; Lord Privy Seal, 1911–12; created 1st Marquess of Lincolnshire, 1912] wrote: 'That ass Ld Beauchamp has made a real good start! as Governor of New South Wales.' Diary entry from 28 June 1899, London. Bodleian Library: Carrington (Ld Lincolnshire) Papers, MS. Film 1135 (2). Another entry made in London on 5 December 1899 reads: 'From Australia Rupert [Lord Carrington's younger brother, living in New South Wales] writes: I fear Beauchamp is impossible. He seems detested by everybody: & his staff are worse then he is ...'. *Ibid.* Much later Rupert writes again from Australia: 'We are excessively warlike here ... Our Governor Ld Beauchamp is awful. He went to the Melbourne Races instead of seeing our contingent off, & now has gone to New Zealand for a month. He was away on Commemoration day at the University & is generally considered a pig headed prig.' Entry written at Wycombe on 25 February 1900, *Ibid.* As will be shown later, Rupert Carrington's observations were highly exaggerated. There is plenty of evidence to show that Earl Beauchamp conducted his official duties scrupulously, and that he became increasingly popular in the Province.

28   Sir Frederick Darley (1830–1910), Chief Justice and Lieutenant Governor from 1891 on.

29   Source: *Correspondence between Earl Beauchamp and the Consul General of France, G B d'Aunet, 1899–1900.* Manuscripts in the Mitchell Library, State Library of New South Wales, Sydney, Call No: ML A 1829 or CY 3233.

Office of the Consul General of France,
Sydney (Australia)

To His Excellency
Sir Frederick M. Darley, KCMG
Lieutenant Governor

Sydney, 8th May 1899

Sir,

I have the honour to inform Your Excellency that at a meeting of the Consular Body held the day before yesterday, Saturday, and at which the Consuls General, Consuls and Vice Consuls at present in Sydney assisted, – comprising those of Germany, Austria-Hungary, Belgium, Denmark, Spain, United States, France, Greece, Japan, the Low Countries, Peru, Portugal, the Republic of Ecuador, Russia, Norway and Sweden, and Switzerland, – the following resolutions were unanimously adopted:

(1) The Consular Body decide that, on the occasion of the approaching arrival of His Excellency Earl Beauchamp, Governor of the colony of New South Wales, and subject to the approval of the new Governor, there is no reason for changing anything of the precedent established at the time of the arrival of His Excellency Viscount Hampden, in that which concerns the form in which the representatives of foreign nations desire to offer to His Excellency Earl Beauchamp their compliments, good wishes and congratulations.

(2) That, in consequence, the Consular Body will abstain, as in November 1895, from participating in the procession which it has been invited to join by an insertion in the *Government Gazette* of the 2nd inst.

(3) That the Consul General for France in his capacity of elder, is charged to communicate to His Excellency the Lieutenant Governor the designs above-mentioned, and in the second place to take suitable steps in order that His Excellency Earl Beauchamp may fix the day and the hour when he will be pleased to receive the Consular Body in official audience.

In fulfilling the mandate which has been conferred to me by my colleagues, I take this opportunity of renewing to Your Excellency the expression of my very high consideration, with which I have the honour to be,

Your obedient Servant,

Georges Biard d'Aunet

(Translated from the French by G. Whiteford)

The French Consul, Georges Biard d'Aunet, a senior diplomat in Sydney, was a very boastful character. The Frenchman took upon himself to dictate rules with regard to the rank and precedence of consuls at formal ceremonies. Perhaps he thought the new Governor was a young and 'inexperienced' nobleman. This was to lead to constant friction between the two men.

The French Consul sent a further letter to the Lieutenant Governor.[30]

To His Excellency
Sir Frederick M. Darley, Kt, KCMG
Lieutenant Governor
9 May 1899

Sir,

The usual custom of this colony in regard to the rank and precedence of Consuls, occasionally gives rise to difficulty and even to some friction. Almost always, a most natural hesitation on the part of representatives of powerful foreign governments hinders them from demanding an explanation on these delicate questions.

I have, however, become certain that these difficulties do not proceed from the design to diminish the prestige and the moral authority which attach to the position of official agents accredited in this country, but are due rather to the absence of some general rule, and to the fact that the precedents more or less established to-day, date from a remote period. In those days foreign agents were all of subordinate grades, and represented only less important interests, but these interests are now very considerable, and each year are becoming more so.

Having appreciated in many circumstances, the benevolent sentiments and the high courteousness of Your Excellency, I thought I might be permitted to call attention to the utility that would result, in my opinion, from the rank and precedence of the consuls being determined with a little more exactness, – and the approaching arrival of a new Governor in this colony seemed to me a favourable occasion for communicating with Your Excellency on the subject.

[Page missing] ... the position of those, who, by their grades, length of service, and the importance of their nation and the interests they represent, seem to merit more honourable treatment.

I will add, that, in a self-governed colony the positions of the consuls, and particularly the deputy consuls, borrows a special meaning from the rule under which the

30   *Ibid.*

country is governed. They do not gain from it a more representative character than in a European country; but their relative independence, and therefore their responsibilities, are increased in the same measure as the relative independence of the country in which they exercise their functions.

These considerations, I hasten to add, do not appear to me to have been entirely unknown here; but it has been marked, as far as I can judge, only in an intermittent and variable style.

To speak for myself, I have noticed that sometimes I am treated with the most flattering respect, and at other times, without apparent reason, I find myself placed much below my rank. It has happened to me that dining at the table of His Excellency the Governor, in the company of persons before whom, according to the usual course of things, I should take precedence, I have been seated at the lower end; some time after, at a Government House dinner at which two Governors of Australian Colonies (not including Lord Hampden) and several important personages were assisting, I was placed on the right of Lady Hampden. It seems to me that I was not in my proper place on either of these occasions.

I do not wish to weary Your Excellency by citing the numerous occasions on which I have regretted accepting very amiable invitations to dinners, banquets, reunions or ceremonies more or less official, because the place reserved for me was really a little too far below that to which I had a right. I would make your Excellency smile in relating to you how, when at a grand banquet of the Town Hall, my colleague the Consul General for Germany (at that time M. Pelldram) and I, met at the moment when we were retiring, because when we had asked where we ought to sit, we were answered: 'where you will, except at the table of honour'.

Without attaching to these questions of etiquette more importance than they deserve, I must confess that they possess some weight, especially for a foreigner in a public position like mine.

It is only at Government House, by an example emanating from the highest authority, that these questions can be resolved. Then gradually a *modus vivendi* will be established, giving satisfaction to the allowable sensitiveness which, I am certain, nobody intends to hurt.

If it is not possible to have a fixed rule, as I said before, does not Your Excellency think, that to those whom it concerns, at least to the most important agents, there could be a general indication from which it would not be desirable to depart too much? It would be for us, then, whom it most concerns, to submit to the conditions, and not to bring into this matter excessive sensitiveness, which would then be out of place.

Your Excellency can be assured that I would submit to it. What I particularly wish to avoid are these embarrassing surprises, which are repeated too often and have inclined me more and more to abstain from appearing on occasions when it would have been most pleasant to have done so.

If Your Excellency will permit me, I will take the liberty of recalling that which concerns me personally.

I have been titular envoy of the French Consulate General for six years, as well as Consul General and Lieutenant of the Reserve Fleet. I was for thirty-seven years in the Navy and the Foreign Office. (In France Consuls generally rank after the rear-admiral Commander in Chief, and before the other rear-admirals. They give precedence to Governors of the First Class, but take it of governors of all other classes.) I am moreover, the elder of the consular body in this colony, that is to say, I have been longest appointed in the highest grade.

Under these conditions, I presume I should give precedence to His Excellency the Admiral, to His Honour the Chief Justice, to the Prime Minister, to the Presidents of the two Chambers, to His Eminence the Cardinal, to the Governors of the other Colonies of Australia, and to distinguished strangers to whom it is wished to do exceptional honour. There are other persons occupying, or who have occupied official positions in New South Wales, to whom I would not object to give precedence contingently, but I do not think that any of them could take offence in a contrary case.

I would be thankful to you, Sir, if on the arrival in Sydney of His Excellency Earl Beauchamp, you would be so good as to make part of these representations to him, joining them with whatever your large experience may suggest. I have full confidence in the high impartiality and the perfect courtesy of the representative of Her Majesty the Queen. I cannot forget that it is for him to decide, and for me to submit, even as my colleagues do, to his appraising, never doubting that it will be equitable and kind.

I have the honour to be,

Your Excellency's most obedient Servant,

Georges Biard D'Aunet

(Translated from the French by G. Whiteford)

The office of the Lieutenant Governor reacted as follows:[31]

Minute For His Excellency The Lieutenant-Governor

Mr Brunker presents his humble duty to His Excellency the Lieutenant-Governor, and begs to suggest that the accompanying communication, addressed to His Excellency

31   *Ibid.*

by the Consul General for France, should be reserved for the consideration of the Right Honourable Earl Beauchamp, as the matters therein referred to can, apparently, only be decided by the new Governor.

Mr Brunker would be glad, also, if the Consul General for France could be advised to that effect.

The Treasury, New South Wales,

Sydney, 11th May 1899

But happily the arrival of the Governor was well greeted by many public organizations. Below we produce a few of the typical ceremonious greetings. All these communications, written in beautiful calligraphy, were addressed to 'His Excellency, The Right Honourable William, Earl Beauchamp, K. C. M. G., Governor and Commander in Chief of the Colony of New South Wales and its Dependencies'. We offer a few samples below.[32]

1

Congregational Union of New South Wales

Sydney, 18th May 1899

May it please your Excellency,

On behalf of the Ministers, Office Bearers and Members of the Churches of the Congregational Union of New South Wales, we respectfully tender to your Excellency, as the representative of our Most Gracious Sovereign Queen Victoria, a very hearty welcome to our Shores.

---

32   In all, Earl Beauchamp received over 50 such letters from various organizations, some of which were: the New South Wales Literary and Debating Societies' Union, the New South Wales Public School Teachers' Association, the Society of Artists, Tweede River District, the United Licensed Victuallers' Association, the Broken Hill Ministerial Association, the Chinese Community of Sydney, the Consul Generals and Consuls Accredited to New South Wales, Coraki Municipal Council, Goulburn Catholic Schools, the Manchester Unity Independent Order of Odd fellows, Moss Vale. These addresses are catalogued in *Beauchamp, W. Lygon, 7th Earl – Addresses, N. S. W, presented, 1899–1900*. Manuscripts in the Mitchell Library, State Library of New South Wales, Sydney, Call No. ML D 233 or C Y 1164.

We give thanks to God for the safe conduct which has been vouchsafed to you during your voyage, and join with our fellow citizens in earnest wishes that you may be blest with good health during your stay in our Colony. We also trust that your residence amongst us may be one of great happiness to yourself and prosperity to the people, and that, in exercising the duties of your position, you may be richly endowed with Divine wisdom and guidance.

We beg to assure you of the unfeigned loyalty of the Members of our Denomination to Her Majesty's Throne and Person and of the reliance you may place upon their hearty support in the performance of all the duties your high office and in all that contributes to the happiness, prosperity and true well-being of the people of our land.

In name of the Congregational Union of New South Wales,

A.J. Griffith (Chairman)
James Buchan (Secretary)

2

Committee of the Chamber of Commerce of the City of Sydney
Sydney, N. S. W.

May 18th 1899

May it please your Excellency.

We the Committee of the Chamber of Commerce of the City of Sydney on behalf and in the name of the Mercantile Community, approach your Excellency with the assurance of our devoted loyalty to Her Most Gracious Majesty the Queen.

We congratulate your Excellency on your safe arrival, and venture to express the hope that your term of Office may be as agreeable to you as it doubtless will be beneficial to the Colony.

The commercial interests of the Colony are suffering, as you are aware, from the effects of a long and severe drought, resulting in a serious diminution of the flocks and herds, as well as of agricultural products.

The resources of this territory however are so varied that the value of its exports has continued to increase, and we trust that under Divine Providence, during the term of your office, such favourable seasons may be experienced that a larger measure of success may attend the operations of our several industries, whereby the general prosperity of the Colony may be speedily restored.

Tendering your Excellency our heartfelt Welcome to New South Wales we beg to subscribe ourselves,

Your Excellency's obedient servants,

President

V. President

Hon. Treas.

[Signatures illegible]

3

Centre of the St John Ambulance Association
New South Wales Centre

Sydney, May 18th 1899

May it please Your Excellency,

We the Council and Members of the New South Wales Centre of the St John Ambulance Association desire to offer to Your Excellency a very hearty welcome to this Colony, expressing at the same time our loyal devotion to Her Majesty Queen Victoria, and our earnest hope that your Governorship may be agreeable to your-self and conducive to the best interests of this the Mother Colony of Australasia. Her Majesty Queen Victoria being the Sovereign Head and Patron of the Order of St John of Jerusalem (of which Order we are the Ambulance Department) we feel sure that Your Excellency as Her Representative will note with satisfaction our great philanthropic work in Australasia.

We are,

Your Excellency's obedient Servants,

President
Chairman

on behalf of the Council and Executive Committee and Members

[Signatures illegible]

4

The Diocese of Bathurst
Dubbo, May 31, 1899

May it please your Excellency,

We the members of the Church of England in the Diocese of Bathurst in Synod assembled, desire to approach Your Excellency and welcome you to N. S. Wales.

The high reputation Your Excellency has attained at home, and the interest you and your family have ever manifested in the welfare of the Church to which we all belong, encourage us to hope that you will extend the same kindly interest to the Diocese of Bathurst, which forms part of New South Wales, the Government of which you administer on behalf of Her Gracious Majesty, the Queen.

With every best wish for Your Excellency's success and happiness during your residence amongst us.

(Signed on behalf of the Synod)

President

Chairman of Committees

[Signatures illegible]

5

The General Assembly of the Presbyterian Church of New South Wales

Sydney, May 1899

May it please Your Excellency,

We the Ministers and Elders – Members of the General Assembly of the Presbyterian Church of New South Wales, now in Session in this city, respectfully approach Your Excellency with assurances of a cordial welcome to yourself and of loyal devotion to the Person and Throne of our beloved Sovereign Queen Victoria, of whom Your Excellency is the worthy representative.

We congratulate Your Excellency on your safe arrival on these shores, and unite with our fellow citizens in the recognition of those eminent abilities for which you are distinguished, and join with them in wishing you all prosperity.

We pray that the Divine Blessing may rest upon you and guide you in the discharge of the duties of Your Excellency's high and responsible office.

In name and by authority of the General Assembly of the Presbyterian Church of New South Wales.

Moderator
Clerk

[Signatures illegible]

6

Sheep-breeders Association

Your Excellency,

The members of the Sheep-breeders Association desire to welcome you (their Patron) to their Fifth Exhibition. We wish to point out that the Association was formed more particularly as an educational institution; and that it has succeed in its object, every one who has witnessed the successive exhibition must truly acknowledge.

At the first Show under the auspices of the Association many inferior sheep were exhibited – on the second occasion very few of such sheep – while now we have perhaps the grandest assemblage of Merino sheep in this Pavilion that the world could show.

This is a proof that we are progressing, and that many sheep breeders had much to learn. The last few years have been very disastrous to the pastoral industry of Australia, while probably New South Wales has suffered more than any other Colony by the late terrible drought. Yet in spite of this we see congregated here a magnificent sample of Merino sheep, with a lesser number of English breeds, aggregating in value many thousands of pounds.

Your Excellency is no doubt aware that wool growing is our great staple industry; Australasia exporting no less than twenty-one millions in value annually, and that this may be very largely increased by careful breeding, is the great object we have in view; an increase of ½ lb. weight per fleece or one penny per lb. in value, would add to the material wealth of these colonies, no less a sum than two millions sterling per annum.

To extend the usefulness of the Association, the Committee introduced into its schedule, prizes for small land holders, with the hope that we should attract their sympathy and support, and although the response this year is somewhat discouraging, we shall hope in the future to see a healthy rivalry amongst our smaller brethren.

Your Excellency will thus see that our aims are well worthy of the support of all classes in the community, and we rejoice to acknowledge that this is freely recognised by those who are more immediately interested in our great staple industry; donations from whom have been generously given.

Notwithstanding the heavy losses of the past, we look forward with confidence that providential rains will once more make out barren lands to bring forth abundantly.

On behalf of the members of the Sheep Breeders' Association,

I am, my Lord,

Yours faithfully,

Geo. H. Cox

President

[No date]

7

From the Society of Artists

May it please your Excellency,

We, the President and council of the Society of Artists, offer you a Cordial Welcome to New South Wales, and desire to express our Loyalty to the Throne and Person of her Most Gracious Majesty Queen Victoria, and we trust that your residence here as her representative may be a pleasant and happy one.

We are your Excellency's most obedient servants,

Sid Long (President)

[Signatures illegible]

8

Lord Tennyson to Lord Beauchamp.[33]

Government House,
Adelaide

May 12, 1899

My dear Lord Beauchamp,

I am very glad that you and your party are able to come to us. Lunch and a special train will be ready for you. But I fear that it is a tall hat business, as I could not get you off a guard of honour of sailors at the jetty, and of police at the station here. It is quite natural for they want to give you a loyal welcome. My A. D. C., Captain Lascelles, will go off in the launch and bring you up. My wife & I give you all hearty greetings.

Yours sincerely,

Tennyson

Captain W. [illegible] my P. S. will meet you at Adelaide station and make any necessary presentations.

---

33   Source: *Beauchamp, Lord: Letters received, 1899–1901.* Manuscripts in the Mitchell Library, State Library of New South Wales, Sydney, Call No. ML A 3012.

The letters of welcome to the new Governor included messages from the Consuls General and Consuls accredited to New South Wales, the Chinese community in Sydney and the New South Wales Literary and Debating Societies' Union.

The office of Governor

Earl Beauchamp was the tenth Colonial Governor of New South Wales to take office since the Constitution Act of 1856 came into effect.[34] In 1899 New South Wales was an entirely different country from what it had been in 1788, when founded as a penal colony for British convicts. The original convicts had by now wholly ceased to exist as a class. A nation had come into being: a nation of colonial-born citizens and of free British and other European immigrants who had engaged themselves in developing pastoral farming, agriculture, viticulture, digging for gold and in a flourishing sector of small industry. The social elite of New South Wales included wealthy landowners, ex-military officers, professional politicians, artists and writers. But it was formally an Imperial colony, run from London through a Governor appointed by the Crown. The Governor exercised supreme powers which were transmitted to him by the Secretary of State for the Colonies. He could, 'at his discretion, dismiss ministers, refuse the Royal assent to legislation, exercise the prerogative of mercy, dissolve Parliament against the wishes of his ministers or refuse to dissolve it on

---

34 The previous Governors were: Sir William Denison (1855–61); Sir John Young (1861–67); Lord Belmore (1868–72); Sir Hercules Robinson (1872–79); Lord Augustus Loftus (1879–85); Lord Carrington (1885–90); Lord Jersey (1891–93); Sir Robert Duff (1893–95); and Viscount Hampden (1895–99). Source: G. N. Hawker, *The Parliament of New South Wales, 1856–1965* (New South Wales: Victor C. N. Blight, 1971), p. 303.

their recommendation'.[35] As chief executive officer, he was responsible for the government of the colony. The Governor's powers had been absolute until 1823, when the colonial administration was reorganized. In this reorganization, an executive council and a legislative council were established: 'the executive council derived its powers direct from the Crown and its officers were officers of the Crown; the legislative council was established by statute, and its power was statutory'.[36] The Governor was assisted in his administration by the executive council, which included the Governor, the Colonial Secretary (who also acted as premier), the Colonial Treasurer, the head of the military, the head of the Anglican Church, the Surveyor-General and, at times, the Chief Justice.[37]

The Constitution Act 1856 introduced substantial democratic reforms. It gave the colonies the right to elect two Houses: a Legislative Council of twenty-one members nominated by the Governor on the advice of the Executive Council for an initial term of five years; and a Legislative Assembly of fifty-four members wholly elected by the franchise, which required a salary qualification of £100 per annum, and a lodger's qualification. Yet the Governor still had 'important powers over the appointment of the first members of the Legislative Council'.[38]

The governments of the Australian colonies were now designed on the 'principles of well-regulated freedom'.[39] Although Australian society was 'deeply influenced by ideas from Britain and by the presence of immigrants who had grown to maturity in the old world, the characteristic attitudes of the people were a product of the new'. Thus Australian nationalism

---

35   For a detailed survey of the powers of the colonial governors, see G. H. Hawker, *op. cit.*, p. 59.
36   See R. M. Hartwell, 'The Pastoral Ascendancy, 1820–50', in Gordon Greenwood (ed.), *Australia: A Social and Political History* (London: Angus and Robertson, 1955), p. 52.
37   See R. M. Hartwell, *op. cit.*, p. 52, n. 14.
38   See Hawker, *op. cit.*, p. 5.
39   Quoted by I. D. McNaughtan, 'Colonial Liberalism, 1851–92', in Gordon Greenwood, *op. cit.*, p. 99.

became 'an essential component of Australian political and social life'.[40] And if this nationalism had to be assertive, it must be 'protected from the malign influences of the old world'. The celebrated Australian prose writer Henry Lawson[41] warned strongly against the danger of Australians admitting to have 'the good old English gentleman over them; the good old English squire over them; the good old English lord over them; the good old English Aristocracy rolling around them in cushioned carriages, scarcely deigning to rest their eyes on the common people, who toil, starve, and rot for them; and the good old throne over them all'.[42]

New South Wales saw the beginnings of a strong trade union movement. The Australian Labour Federation advocated its policies on the principles of the British Labour movement. The robust columns of the *Bulletin*, founded in 1880, voiced the grievances of the best Australian creative writers, thus becoming 'the most important avenue of publication'.[43]

By 1890 the powers of the Governor were somewhat neutralized. He now came '*not to govern but to reign*',[44] that is, he would not interfere much in the daily working of the political machine, but keep a close eye on the execution of the state constitution. Thus, when Earl Beauchamp arrived in 1899, he found New South Wales very consciously a nation, with a highly developed political and social elite. Two major issues dominated the politics of the colony at the time: fiscal problems (free trade or protection, factory legislation and taxation) and the question of whether the colony should join other colonies in forming the Australian Federation. At the State Premier's conference in 1895 New South Wales had displayed very little enthusiasm for this move. But in a June 1899 referendum, by a tiny majority, the colony voted to form the Federation. Beauchamp, who was now in Sydney, had

40   See R. A. Gollan, 'Nationalism, the Labour Movement and the Commonwealth, 1880–1900', in Gordon Greenwood, *op. cit.*, p. 145.

41   Henry Lawson (1867–1922), short story writer and balladist; major work: *While the billy boils* (1896); critical essay: 'Pursuing literature in Australia', *Bulletin* (Sydney, January 1899).

42   Quoted by R. A. Gollan, *op. cit.*, p. 147.

43   *Ibid.*, p. 148.

44   See Hawker, *op. cit*, p. 59.

little or no role in the politics surrounding this. But the Governor was confronted with a problem created by the 'paunchy and tricksy'[45] George Reid, Premier since 1894. In 1899, Reid was to be censured by the state parliament over his handling of a case to which Beauchamp refers in his diary (as quoted below). Reid requested the Governor to dissolve parliament. Suspecting mischief, Beauchamp refused this. Reid was forced to resign, and was succeeded by W. J. Lyne,[46] the leader of the Protectionist Party. Lyne's term of office was viewed differently. Some called him 'a suitable Premier'; others described him as a 'drab, doleful and monotonous Premier'; while a further group thought he had 'no bold ideas of national policy'.[47] Yet Beauchamp and Lyne got along together well. The lengthy correspondence between the two helps establish this fact.

The French Consul General's wrangling over precedence

However, Beauchamp had, first of all, to face a question that had little to do with high politics, but which required some solution. The French Consul General had raised the subject of 'table precedence' for the diplomats – and persisted with it, presenting his case directly to the Governor. A lengthy

---

45   This is how the historians have judged him. See O. H. K. Spate, *Australia, op. cit.,* p. 65. Reid had 'won a reputation for lazy wit, poor attendance and good living. He was a fat man, not afraid to use his appearance to make an audience laugh, and hardly seemed a serious politician for most of the 1880s'. And yet he made a decent political career: State Premier (1894–99), leader of the Federal opposition (1901–4), High Commissioner for Australia in London (1910–16), and then a member of the House of Commons (1916–18). See G. N. Hawker, *The Parliament of New South Wales, op. cit.,* p. 184.

46   Sir William John Lyne (1844–1913), Premier of New South Wales, 1899–1901.

47   See Hawker, *op. cit.,* p. 183.

exchange of letters was the consequence, which the Governor may perhaps have regarded as trifling but which the Frenchman pursued fussily.[48]

Croissy,
Hunter's Hill

4 July 1899

Your Excellency,

I shall be extremely obliged if you will be good enough to convey to your sister, with my humble respects, my thanks for her gracious invitation to tea on Thursday, which I shall be happy to accept.

The reply of Your Excellency respecting the dinner of our Chamber of Commerce and principal French residents places me in a position of serious embarrassment, because no one understands better than I the advantage that is taken of Your Excellency's graciousness. However, I must take the liberty of insisting upon it, because it would be a great disappointment to my countrymen if they were deprived of the honour that you intended to them. The occasion is an exceptional one. Our commercial community represents here considerable interests. The presence of Your Excellency on this occasion would have an effect as excellent on the one hand as your refusal perhaps would be badly interpreted on the other, and might leave a false impression which, although I have their confidence, my moral authority over these merchants would be hard to remove.

On leaving Government House yesterday I went to invite Mr Reid, who accepted with the cordiality which, I may say, he has always shown towards my countrymen and myself. We shall have also Mr Carruthers, your new Minister of Finance and Commerce. The question of date is at your decision and there is nothing to prevent the date being postponed to next month. Everything will be arranged to suit the convenience of your Excellency, upon which you rely on me. Let your Excellency be convinced of that. If I did not fear to use too strong an expression, I should say that, in acceding to the wish which I have been requested to express, Your Excellency would be doing an act of good policy. May I add that I would be personally obliged? The 'table of precedence' will have my full attention.

Yours etc., etc., etc.,

Georges Biard d'Aunet

---

48 Source: Correspondence between Earl Beauchamp and the Consul General of France, G B d'Aunet, 1899–1900. Manuscripts in the Mitchell Library, State Library of New South Wales, Sydney, Call No. ML A 1829 or CY 3233.

Beauchamp responded on 14 July, but first communicated his views on 12 July to the chief executive.

Minute for the Honourable Prime Minister

In forwarding this document for the consideration of my Ministers, I desire to make a few observations with regard to the Table of Precedence which I found in use at Government House.

It appears to me desirable to allocate places on the List to The Chancellor of the University and to the Public Service Board.

The place in which the Consuls are found seems based on the great authority in use 'at home' – *Burke*. In the edition for 1899, page 1825, occurs the following passage:

> The Comparative Rank of Consular Officers, and of Officers in Her Majesty's Naval and Military Services, is as follows:
> Agents and Consuls-General rank with, but after, Major Generals and Rear Admirals.
> Consuls-General rank with, but after Brigadiers and Commodores.

It would, to my mind, be perfectly impossible to give any Major Generals or Rear Admirals precedence before that of the Major General Commanding the Forces.

It appears, therefore, that the Consuls-General are quite properly placed. It might, however, be well to draw the proposed distinction between Consuls sent here, and Consuls living here. This would give, e.g. to the American Consul an equal rank, in order of seniority with the other Consuls who are sent.

My own inclination, therefore, would be to suggest to the French Consul-General no alteration except to alter No. 22, in the Table of Precedence, into reading 'Consuls sent by their own Governments in order of seniority here'; other Consuls would thus be omitted.

It would be well, however, to ask the Chief Justice for his advice.

Beauchamp
Governor

12th July 1899

Here, in translation, is the French Consul General's reply:

Consul General to Earl Beauchamp

Croissy,
Hunter's Hill

31 July 1899

Your Excellency,

I beg you to excuse my taking the liberty of recalling the explanations which I had the honour to give you in reply to your confidential letter of the 14th. I refrained, in sending to Paris an account of the celebration of our National Fete, to mention the omission of the felicitations that His Excellency the Governor has been accustomed to make to the Consulate General on that occasion. It would however be particularly agreeable to me to learn that Your Excellency does not intend to create a precedent which appears to me not to be in accord with the kindly intentions which you have personally manifested to me.

I take this opportunity to thank Your Excellency for the invitation which I received for the 7th August and to which I sent an official acceptance. But, being desirous of acting with as much frankness as deference in my intercourse with Your Excellency, I must inform you privately that I do not think I can be present on that evening. I think that owing to your decision in respect to the inaugural dinner of the French Chamber of Commerce of Sydney, it would be better for me to remove somewhat the impression produced on my countrymen by your refusal to attend at that dinner – a refusal which I cannot but take into account.

On the other hand, the reception in question having been preceded by other receptions for which I had not the honour of an invitation, I do not hesitate to confess to you I feel under a certain embarrassment. I believe that custom in most, if not in all, the capitals accords to the envoys of foreign governments what we call *l'entrée*, that is to say, that they are invited either individually or collectively to all receptions which have not a special or private character. It has been thus at Sydney up to now, at least so far as I am concerned, and I do not remember any 'at home', garden party or ball given at Government House to which I have not been invited. This fact no doubt it will be easy to verify.

Be it as it may, the abandonment of this custom, combined with certain circumstances about which I have already been led to make respectful comment, would tend to establish a new *classement* [procedure] – or rather want of procedure – which, in my particular position, imposes upon me, at least for a time, a discrete reserve.

Needless to say, this reserve in no way affects the feelings of high esteem and personal sympathy which I have for Your Excellency, or the private intercourse with which Your Excellency and family have been good enough to honour me.

In begging you to offer my humble respects to Lady Mary Lygon, I remain etc.,

Georges Biard d'Aunet

Beauchamp answered the same day.

Government House, Sydney
31 July 1899

My dear Sir,

The celebrations of the 14th July will be a subject upon which I shall desire my Ministers' opinion, and I shall take care that every consideration is given to your letters on the subject.

Allow me to congratulate you on the success of the dinner on Saturday night, which I was unfortunately unable to attend.

I shall very much regret your absence from the Party next week, especially since you have accepted the invitation. It will be so significant that I fear I shall be quite unable to ignore the matter.

I have the honour to be,

Yours faithfully,

Beauchamp

It was not long before there was another letter from the French Consul General (all his letters are reproduced in G. Whiteford's translation):

Consul General to Earl Beauchamp

Croissy,
Hunter's Hill

2 August 1899

Your Excellency,

Misunderstandings create difficulties. I must say that in officially accepting your gracious invitation for 7th I desire to choose the least 'significant' course – its refusal would have been brusque (*Un refus surait en un allure cassante*). I do not wish to hurt the feelings of Your Excellency, and if my absence at the 'evening party' were to have that effect I should be present. I desire nothing so much as good and easy intercourse, with the maintenance of my office – neither more nor less. But my particular and prominent position is a delicate one. It has become more so since recent incidents. If you will be so good as to take it into consideration, and it will be easy for you to give me an indication of having done so, you will find me extremely happy to forget my rank, precedents, and all similar matters, for other occupations leave me but little leisure.

I am, &c.,

Georges Biard d'Aunet

The premier, Mr Reid gave his advice to the governor.

Treasury Minute

The Treasury, New South Wales, Sydney,

21 August 1899

Subject: Minute for His Excellency the Governor – respecting Table Precedence

Mr Reed presents his humble duty to your Excellency and begs to state that it has not been usual for Ministers to advise in matters of this kind.

When questions have arisen in regard to such matters, Mr Reed's impression is that they formed the subject of reference to the Colonial Office.

GHR

Following this advice, Lord Beauchamp wrote to the Colonial Office in London, and there was the following exchange:

1

Government House, Sydney

[no date]

Sir,

I beg leave to forward a correspondence with the French Consul on the question of precedence. I shall be much obliged by any advice from the C. O.

I will only add that he is a gentleman with whom it is found generally difficult to keep on cordial terms & that he is the only member of the consular body who has complained.

I have the honour to be, Sir,

Beauchamp

2

Consul General to Victor Corkran, Private Secretary to Lord Beauchamp

Croissy

8 September 1899

Dear Sir,

I have received your note of the 6th inst., and beg you to thank His Excellency the Governor especially in respect to the form of official correspondence.

In regard to the question dealt with in my letter of the 30th August and the accompanying note, I shall be obliged if you will tell His Excellency that all communications which he will forward to me on that subject will be received, like former ones, with a sincere desire to meet his private views. Nevertheless, I am convinced that we should arrive at the desired result by an exchange of views verbally than by means of written correspondence.

I know that His Excellency is at present very closely occupied with official duties, and perhaps it would be convenient to him to allow this somewhat uneasy period to pass by. In any case I wish to say that I remain entirely at his convenience.

Believe me, &c.,

Georges Biand d'Aunet

3

Lord Beauchamp's Private Secretary to the Consul General

Government House, Sydney

13 September 1899

Dear Sir,

I received your letter of the 8th instant, and in reply I regret to find that I did not express myself sufficiently clearly. On the first page of the letter, which accompanied your 2nd note, you mentioned that the communication was *unofficial* and I concluded that your request also related to unofficial matters. In the case of the correspondence relating to the interference with Seamen by Boarding Masters at Newcastle, His Excellency received your answer through your Secretary, but as he is sure this was unintentional he desires me to say that he will overlook the matter on this occasion.

What his Excellency intended me to convey – and I am sorry that there should have been a misunderstanding – was that in order to save you trouble he would be quite agreeable to unofficial communications from you being made through your Secretary and such communications would, in the ordinary course come through me.

I have &c.

Victor Corkran

Private Secretary

4

Consul General to Lord Beauchamp's Private Secretary

Sydney,

14 September 1899

Dear Sir,

I beg you to inform His Excellency the Governor that I much regret the misunderstanding of which you were good enough to acquaint me. He will excuse me for declining the responsibility of it.

I wrote on the 30th August: 'I beg you to ask His Excellency if he would see any objection to my addressing him in the manner he has employed towards me, and which besides, is usual here, that is to say, through the medium of "my Secretary".' I was then answering an *official* letter dated 24th August, respecting the question of procedure, the form of which letter was 'I am directed by His Excellency, the Governor'.

You were good enough to reply on the 6th September by a private letter, 'His Excellency further desires me to say that he hopes that you will always address your communications to him in the way which best suits your own convenience ...'.

The expressions 'in the manner he has employed towards me' (referring to a letter to which I was replying) as well as 'always address your communications to him' could leave no doubt in my mind, nor leave me to suppose that any doubt existed in the mind of His Excellency, that it referred to *official* correspondence.

That is why on the 8th September I asked you to thank His Excellency the Governor 'concerning the form of official correspondence'.

I was thus authorised to use the form which I employed in my communication respecting the Newcastle matters.

If I rightly understand your letter of yesterday, His Excellency now expresses the desire that I should address myself to him in *official* communication, whilst he reserves to himself the right to address similar correspondence to me through you. His Excellency adds that, in respect to *non* official letters, he sees no objection to my sending them through my Secretary, who will forward them to you for transmission to His Excellency.

I regret that I am not able to share the feelings of His Excellency on these two points, but I hope, as you will see, that it will be easy to reconcile these opinions.

In regard to private correspondence, I would not take the liberty of addressing any communications to His Excellency, even with his sanction, which did not come directly from myself. I should be wanting in the deference which I owe to him did I do so. This view of the case extends to all private communications, as between all gentlemen the same consideration is due. It is then understood that I have no intention, in respect to *non* official correspondence, to use the authority, which His Excellency grants, of signing through my Secretary.

As to *official* correspondence, the custom followed in this Colony up to now is that we correspond with the Prime Minister on all general matters. My records are full of such correspondence, which has always worked regularly, and the form of which has never raised difficulty.

It is my duty, nevertheless, to reply to all communications, whatever their object, which His Excellency favours me with. I am always ready to do so, but now the question of form has been raised.

The general custom is to reply in the form adopted by the person who writes first, with the necessary difference in manner of address according to position, which I have always respectfully observed. That is why I asked His Excellency, when he wrote to me through you, if he had any objection to my replying in the same way. His Excellency, after apparent hesitation, saw an objection. I am only too happy to comply with his wishes, and I will write directly to him henceforth.

It appears to me, however, difficult to establish as a fixed rule and precedent that whilst His Excellency addresses me through a medium, that is to say under the form 'I am desired ...' or 'I am directed ...', I should, nevertheless, reply direct to him, and I consider it is a request more than I should perhaps grant. I beg you then, my dear Sir, to be good enough to inform His Excellency the Governor that I shall be very thankful if he will consent to sign all his official communications to the Consulate General of France, or at least to cause them to be signed 'by order'; or, if he prefers to continue the use of indirect official correspondence, I hope he will see no objection to my sending my replies in an impersonal form, as the following: 'The Consul General has the honour, &c., ...'.

I fear I have not grasped the sense of a phrase of your letter of yesterday, 'As, however, His Excellency is sure this was unintentional, he desires me to say he will overlook the matter'. I understand that His Excellency the Governor, knowing that I had no intention to hurt his feelings by writing through my Secretary, has been kind enough to forgive me.

If I have not been deceived in translating, I beg you to say to His Excellency that I received his sanction on this matter by your letter of the 8th inst., and that I do not intend, by availing myself of it, to fail in the respect that I owe His Excellency, any more than His Excellency desired to cause offence by addressing to me in the same form the official letter to which I was replying.

You will personally oblige me, my dear Sir, by assuring His Excellency that I see with a keen regret, after a long residence in this country, so many difficulties accumulating in so short a time, on the ground where we both meet, but that I sincerely desire to see them disappear, and am ready to make, to this end, all concessions that are not incompatible with the dignity of the position I occupy.

I am &c

Georges Biard d'Aunet

5

Lord Beauchamp's Private Secretary to the Consul General

Government House,
Sydney,

16 September 1899

Sir,

His Excellency desires me to say that he has learnt your views with regret and is sorry to find you are unwilling to fall in with the arrangements he proposed.

He is very serious to settle the matter in as simple and as satisfactory a way as possible. I am desired, therefore, to make another suggestion for your kindly consideration and to ask if you would agree to another arrangement by which correspondence should in future be conducted between your Secretary and myself?

His Excellency is in favour of the idea and would esteem himself happy in being able to settle it in this way – if it is agreeable to yourself.

I have, &c.,

Victor Corkram

Private Secretary

6

Consul General to Lord Beauchamp's Private Secretary

Croissy

Hunters' Hill

18 September 1899

Dear Sir,

If I properly understand the proposition you are good enough to send me, on behalf of His Excellency the Governor, by your letter of the day before yesterday, the exchange of official correspondence between His Excellency and my Consulate General will be such that you will write according to the instructions of His Excellency to my Secretary, who will inform me of these communications, and my Secretary will reply to you in accordance with the instructions I shall give him. And vice versa if the first communication comes from the Consulate General.

I beg you to say to His Excellency that I thank him for the intention which has inspired this suggestion, and I am happy to see that His Excellency has recognised the justice of the remarks which I took the liberty of making. I have, neither personally nor in my official capacity, any objection to this method of correspondence, and I shall adopt it as His Excellency desires.

However, I take the liberty of pointing out the unusual form of this form of procedure. It is a general principle that official correspondence should be addressed to the authorities whom it concerns. It is thus that His Excellency the Minister for Foreign Affairs (although I am his direct subordinate) writes to me without any medium, and signs all letters, excepting those transmitting documents and dealing with simple formalities.

I think then that direct correspondence is to be preferred, save in differences of rank, but the right should be reserved of signing through the medium of an authorised person. I employ the latter means but little myself, and out of courtesy have never used it in respect to constituted authorities.

However, if His Excellency persists in declining direct and reciprocal correspondence, I shall conform, as I have said, to the method indicated in your letter of the 16th.

I shall be obliged if you will let me know whether His Excellency considers my letter of the 8th September (respecting the Newcastle matters) as null and void owing to lack of form, or if he will be good as to accept it in spite of the misunderstanding dispelled today. In the latter case, I would be thankful if you would send me the information asked for in the fourth paragraph of that letter, in view of the inquiry to be held in reference to the matters pointed out in the first paragraph of the letter from Government House, dated the 4th September.

I am, &c.,

Georges Biard d'Aunet

The local press observed that the Consul General for France, M. Biard d'Aunet, had not been:

> present at any of the Government House functions last week. His absence was distinctly conspicuous, and it appears from an explanation in the *Courier* that the French residents of Sydney consider that the Governor has insulted the French nation. Earl Beauchamp attended in person at the American Consulate on the Fourth of July, and made much of Colonel Bell, whose labours in the country have been principally in the direction of the spread of infidelity. But his Excellency neither attended the French Commemoration a few days later, nor sent his card by the aide-de-camp. Until this discourtesy is explained, M. Biard d'Aunet says, he cannot attend Government House.

Life as Governor: Earl Beauchamp's diary

Much worse things were to follow. But let us return to Earl Beauchamp's other activities. His governorship lasted a little more than two years. From his own brief narration we get some knowledge of his sojourn in New South Wales, his encounters with government officials and how he estimated the quality of local politics. We can also retrace his spheres of action on the basis of communication of letters he sent to various people or received from them. Let us then first quote his diary:[49]

> Anyhow behold me at last after a great function sworn in at last as governor of New South Wales & its dependencies. It is not now any more than before my intention to record at length the daily round or common tasks of the Gov. The diary is to be a record of impressions rather than of facts & a history written with a broad pen. The first two months were months of constant functions. At the beginning the Gov. is regarded with too critical – later with too neglectful an eye. No ceremony is complete if he is absent during the months immediately succeeding his arrival – & it is his own fault if he does not – by judicious absences make his presence of some value. We were all strange to the duties & their novelty relieved the tedium. We began by

---

49 Source: *Beauchamp, Lord – Diary, 1899–c.1900*. Manuscripts in the Mitchell Library, State Library of New South Wales, Sydney, Call No. ML A 3295, Frame Nos. 259–301.

asking all with whom we came into personal contact to luncheon. The Darleys, Sir Frederick & Lady Darley dined immediately. He was as delightful as we had heard. Tall & dignified with white hair & blue eyes – ruddy face – rather heavy eyelids he was a most impressive Chief Justice. Lady Darley also tall – grey hair & portly was of the greatest help. They were both anxious to be of service & both then & afterwards were always ready to help in the many difficult questions wh arose. Meanwhile, newspapers, admiral general & officials followed one another in bewildering confusion. Sunday to early Church at St James'. 11.00 Mattins at the Cath. All this was duly reported in the next day's papers somewhat to our embarrassment, since at home early devotions are not generally considered of importance to the world. Apparently however it had a great effect & came back to us from England as a most strange & weird action. For Mattins we separated. Mary going to St James with my aunt & the rest to the Cath. where the Abp preached the sermon – of course referring to the new Gov. What really did make me sit up however was that I suddenly heard a prayer for the Governor wh was inserted after that for the Royal Family. However it was not long before I found out how badly he needed it! It is one of the few modern prayers wh have any approach to the style of those in the Prayer Book. It has often astonished me that people are seldom able to compose a modern prayer. Not even Stevenson wrote one wh in rhythm or beauty approaches the peroration of his essay *Aes Triplex*[50] wh stands out as one of the finest pieces of modern English. Dr Johnson was sonorous, but Abp Benson was the best. It may be the want of association, there is none of the modern prayers wh compares for instance with the Advent Collects. themselves the best of all. Even the unknown ones for special occasions surpass the Jubilee or special prayers. The whole question is rather like that of hymns. Here again the proportion of good modern hymns is very small. *Hymns A & M* are full of absurdities. What can be more ridiculous than an evening congregation of healthy country folks singing 'Art thou weary, art thou languid?' Or another question to wh I have never had a satisfactory answer is why clergymen so often choose a bad hymn. The best rule is to exclude any hymn wh includes the words 'I' or 'me'. There are many very devotional poems admirably suited for private use wh commonsensically considered are ridiculous at 'common prayers'. My pet abomination is one on alms giving wh includes this verse:

---

50   R. L. Stevenson, *Aes Triplex* (1878). Perhaps the following lines might have moved Earl Beauchamp: 'All (writes Stevenson) who have meant good work with their whole hearts, have done good work, although they may die before they have the time to sign it. Every heart that has beat strong and cheerfully has left a hopeful impulse behind it in the world, and bettered the tradition of mankind.' See *The Works of R. L. Stevenson*, Vailima Edition, vol. 2 (London: Heinemann, 1922), p. 130.

Whatever, Lord, we give to Thee,
Repaid a thousand fold shall be,
Then gladly will we give to Thee
Who givest all!

Of course – who would not, at 1000 per cent rate of interest! Or again, 'Oh for wings that I may taste & see'. The fact is that for sentimental association's sake many hymns are passed wh wd be rejected as merely secular poems but for wh favourite tunes earn acceptance – Mrs Heman's lines are always amusing.

Mr Reid prime minister of New South Wales came to Albany just then on a holiday trip with two members of the Leg. Council. He came from there on the *Himalaya* & took gt pains to impress on us all that he had had no idea of meeting me till he reached Albany. He evidently lied because I got a letter from Capt. Fielden saying that Mr Reid had promised to talk to me on one or two things & it had also been a subject of immense gossip. The caricaturists were busy as usual. Of course he was intensely interesting to us all & we compared notes about him every day. The chief thing we concluded was that he was a complete humbug. No sooner did I tell him who Lady Bertha[51] was than he said very civil things to her about Lord Lathom,[52] & having extracted particulars from me brought in very touching references to both her father & mother. To my aunt he spoke tenderly, to me great grand paternally & I hoped he thought he took me in. We had long conversations & after what I had been led, from his photos & what people had told me about him, to expect I found him very different. His aspect was grotesque but his manner was admirable. Short, fat & with an eyeglass, he was almost a figure of fun. He slept about the deck, with mouth wide open & snoring loudly to the delight of the amateur photographers on board. In talking he had a deliberate way wh was impressive & certainly considered himself – perhaps like Wilkes, a ladies man. He gave me at great length an account of the Federation from his point of view & strove hard to show himself the patriotic far-sighted statesman. He began with a long account of Sir Henry Parkes[53] & the Federal Council – how the movement had become more earnest – how the Melbourne Conference – the Hobart meeting & others had taken place. Then of course came the weak point of his account over wh he passed lightly – the part he had himself taken over the First Referendum. He explained that there had been various points in the Bill to wh he had been unable to give his entire adherence: that recognising tho' he did fully the immense importance of this measure he felt himself unable

---

51 Lady Bertha Bootle-Wilbraham was sister of the second Earl of Lathom.
52 Lord Lathom (1864–1910).
53 Sir Henry Parkes (1815–96), Australian politician; sat in the New South Wales Legislative Assembly from 1856 to 1895.

conscientiously to support it with his whole heart, that etc. etc. His anxiety for the successful issue of the movement was so great that, in spite of the declared will of the People he had brought the matter forward again in Parl., had persuaded the Assembly to agree to a further conference at wh a settlement very satisfactory had been arrived at & wh he hoped wd shortly be ratified by the inhabitants of the Colony. Happily from previous knowledge I was able to supply mental comments on the position as he expounded it. His enemies declared that the result of the first Referendum had been a gt surprise to him: that his wish had been to curry favour with big wigs at home by an outward support of the Bill wh he recommended to the electors in a most lukewarm manner. There had been a majority but not the 2/3 majority wh a successful amendment in the N. S. W. Leg. had demanded, contrary to the other colonies whom the simple majority satisfied. But the fact of there being a majority had been a surprise & Mr Reid from that moment determined to alter his plans & to strive for the Federal Premiership. On the Premier's suggestion various resolutions had been carried in Sydney embodying the alterations wh were likely to satisfy the public of N. S. W. Armed with these Mr Reid had been to a Premiers Conf. & after some bargaining had emerged with a Bill wh he was ready to support heartily. As a matter of fact the alterations in the Bill were scarcely important enough to justify so great a change of policy. Unfortunately the standard of political morality was not high enough to interfere with these tactics & when retribution did overtake him, it was rather from personal motives of revenge on the part of the successful intriguers.

A month after my arrival the Bill was carried by a large majority of some 30,000 on a poll of 170,000 & after being passed by the Parliament was agreed to by me & forwarded home. This cleared the way for the intrigue which ended in the overthrow of his ministry & establishment of Mr Lyne.

At the time of the election of the Parl. in the Australian summer of '98 Mr Barton[54] was chosen to lead the Opposition. Barton was a man – disliked by the Labour party who had held unimportant offices in a former government & had also been Speaker. Of his administrative abilities nothing was known, but he was said to be too lazy & over fond of a good glass. As the prime champion of Federation however he was a fit opponent to the head of a govt. who lukewarmly told the electors that were he a Victorian he wd vote for the Bill, but as a member of N.S.W. he contended himself with laying the facts before them. But as I have said before the strength of the Federation vote surprised Mr Reid who forthwith made up his mind to turn & an astonished public saw the leaders of the two sides agree on the chief topic of the day. Mr Barton blessed Mr Reid when he departed to Melbourne to join the Premier's

54   Sir Edmund Barton (1849–1920), federationist, first Prime Minister of the Commonwealth of Australia.

Conference with the resolutions wh had been carried by the Sydney House, & people began to think some change was necessary.

Mr Reid succeeded in getting few of the alterations put into the Bill, but came back from the conference happy in an excuse for recommending it. It was about this time that I reached Sydney – whose claims to the Capital of Federated Australia Reid had somewhat unnecessarily given up. For a month the contest raged & concluded at last with a majority none too large for the Bill. It was forthwith introduced into the Parl. wh I opened amid the usual ceremonies – passed after debate in both Houses & sent home to the Imperial authorities. Once Federation was out of the way, Mr Barton announced that his chief object had been crowned with success & that he shd retire. The Opposition chose Mr Lyne as his successor. Rumour declared that the compact between the two provided that if the governor general were to send for Lyne, he wd recommend that Mr Barton be made the first Federal Premier. Later on while Barton was in England another rumour ran that the agreement had been only to give the Chief Justiceship of the Federal Supreme Court to Barton while Lyne became Premier. In any case Barton's retirement was necessary because the Labour party whose vote turned the scale wd never have voted to put him in, while Mr Lyne was not averse to making himself pleasant to them. Lyne had been minister for works in Sir George Dibbs[55] government & was said to be concerned in certain jobs of the time. He had not paid his landlord rent, but made him firstly government architect, & afterwards raised his salary. Mrs Lyne was a nice plain homely & motherly woman. No sooner elected, than Mr Lyne whose method was chiefly by buttonholing & interviewing individuals & so commending himself to them personally – began to look round for a handy weapon of attack & found one in Col. Neild.[56] Col. Neild was a rather notorious M. L. A. who had raised a regiment of volunteers wh for some time had been in a state of ridiculous insubordination: officers abused officers, the men never attended. Not unnaturally the regiment showed signs of incapacity wh were noticed at the Easter manoeuvres of 1898. Col. Neild retorted on his military critics & superior officers in the public press, alleging as his excuse, parliamentary privilege. He was placed under arrest & became for some time the object of much ridicule. His place in public estimation is shown by his nickname of Jawbone Neild. Some 18 months before this gentleman had been to England & being anxious of some notice at home asked Mr Reid the then Premier for authority to enquire into the question of old age Pensions – assuring him that the work shd be a labour of love. This assurance Mr Reid communicated to the Assembly promising to pay him no public money without the direct assent of Parliament. Unfortunately for himself

55 Sir George Dibbs was thrice Prime Minister of New South Wales, 1834–1904.
56 John Cash Neild (1846–1911), politician, precipitated the downfall of the Reid government in Sydney in September 1899 on a motion of no confidence.

Mr Reid broke this promise under pressure from Col Neild who is supposed to have threatened to vote for the opposition whose minority at that time was only 4. A sum of £350 was paid for personal expenses incurred & no more wd have been heard of the matter if Neild had been a popular man.

Lyne brought in a vote of censure to wh was appended by a supporter – a rider specifically condemning payment to Col. Neild. The Labour party met in caucus & after long debates found itself pledged to vote as a body for the motion. This meant 19 votes. The party are pledged under penalty of dismissal to vote always with the majority. The reason why so many were ready to vote against Reid was that several members had gone further than he had at the first Referendum – so far indeed that they wd not execute the volte face with wh Reid had surprised the colony & therefore desired revenge.

Reid tried every way of escape. He made able speeches & at last came to me one afternoon about 2.45. He expatiated at first on my youth & ignorance – the difficulties of constitutional government – the readiness of the Col. Office to support a premier rather than a governor. He had been much affected at this charge of personal corruption against him – so different to any ordinary vote of censure & had that morning consulted the Chief Justice. It seemed to him that an extraordinary charge required extraordinary measures & he proposed therefore to appoint some commission on the lines of the Parnell commission to try the case. The C. J. had expressed himself as ready & willing to meet his wishes & to appoint some member of the Supreme Court Bench to sit on the commission. He had therefore come down to ask me to sign a prorogation of Parliament to take effect for 10 days or so while the enquiry proceeded after wh the House wd meet again & resume the debate with the advantage of an un-biassed opinion before it. Meanwhile the House met at 4.00. Wd I please sign at once the document in his pocket wh wd prorogue the House?

Briefly I refused & Mr Reid who took it very well went off to tell the Cabinet. It was a clever idea, but obviously a trick only to use the prerogative of the Crown as a party move. The Judge cd only have said there was no evidence of bribery & to have allowed Reid to take from out the hands of Par. a question it had begun to discuss wd have laid me open to much discussion. Besides a majority meant to turn him out & turn him out it did a few days later. Meanwhile I spent an uncomfortable afternoon, but learnt with pleasure a few days after, that so far from approving, as Mr Reid implied, that C. J. had strongly opposed the idea & tried to stop it. However he had been unable to withhold his promise of a Judge if the commission were appointed.

After this the crisis pursued a normal course. The resolution was carried & then communicated to me by Sir Joseph Abbott, the Speaker. The Premier asked for a dissolution in a lengthy memo wh I shortly answered with a refusal, giving as few reasons as possible. I did not ask for his advice as to who I shd send for, fearing lest by naming Mr Barton unnecessary complications shd follow. I sent for Mr Lyne who accepted the task of forming a Ministry, but asked for a few days. Generally indeed universally my action in refusing to grant a dissolution was approved of & tho' the former request never was made public, I am sure that it wd have been still more heartily approved.

This happened just before the Sydney race week, & the political negotiations went on throughout the festivities. These were celebrated as the origin of the blue & white ticket fuss. When I reached Sydney there was only one door wh was used both by the governor, people on business & callers. Accordingly there were constantly awkward meetings in the front hall wh was at any time liable to invasion from anyone who wished to see the private secretary. One of us had a brilliant idea. It was to turn the large room then used by the A. D. C. into a side entrance & hall – to use the then porter's room for the staff & to send every one who came in the day time into the new entrance where those who wished to see the Gov. or P. S. passed to their left – those for the A. D. C. to the right. The new system worked excellently tho' the drawback was that the room for the staff was somewhat small. However we no longer met importunate visitors whom we had to refuse to see in the hall, nor as we came in at the front door found others writing their names in the book. Very innocently we then thought of following the plan they had at Melbourne of giving to the important people tickets by wh they cd use the new side door & find themselves in comfort away from the crush of the cloak room. Further we conceived the idea of recruiting the entrée as being a more friendly & popular act than, only walking in procession. These tickets were strictly limited to judges & ministers etc. There was no exception made as at Melbourne in favour of private friends. Never were our hopes that these arrangements for the comfort of our guests less fulfilled. The colony was shaken to its depths – Australia outraged rose in revolt. From end to end the blue & white tickets became a byword & abuse poured on our unlucky heads. Sydney gossips lied & believed every lie wh those fertile clubs produced. It was the only topic of conversation – became a proverb – was even used as term of reproach in Parliament. Why to this day, I cannot understand. Seidlitz powder story of course was an amusing variety – quite untrue. Else the arrangements, like all those made by Wilfrid were excellent, & Lady Darley assured me, as indeed did others that the balls were among the best & cheeriest she had ever seen in a government house. As a matter of fact, I fancy that the old set wh had ruled previous staffs seized the opportunity to be disagreeable & thought that here was their chance of revenge. The smart set had been treated no better than the rest & resented the treatment. A little later Melbourne wh had experienced the system for many years laughed at the tea cup storm & Sydney in the end was a little ashamed.

Mr Lyne had meanwhile formed his cabinet. My friend Col. Mackay was moved to the Upper House, & made Vice President of the Executive Council – a post of honour but of small emolument. Wise was made Attorney General, & See Chief Secretary, etc. etc.

The previous cabinet had held few men of capacity. Mr Reid had gathered round him a body of men of little ability. Carruthers was the ablest & filled in turn the Land Office & the Treasury. His deafness struck me as being often feigned as several times I noted he cd hear well enough if he wd. John Hughes as V.P. of the Executive Council & also preceded Col Mackay as leader of the Upper House. He was a tall handsome Roman Cath. with red face, white hair & gold rimmed spectacles. Very respectable & presentable. A leading Roman with a pleasant stout wife who squinted. The others were dull – Varney Parkes a son of the famous Sir Henry was postmaster, but seldom appeared at the Council meetings.

In the new Cabinet shd be noted:

Wise – the original of the youthful ministers in Anthony Hope's novel of *Half a Hero* [1893]. He had come out from England where he had been educated tho' Australian born with a gt reputation. He had done well at Oxford & been president of the Union. Sir Henry Parkes had early made him Attorney General since then he had been a rising young man who somehow had never risen. He & Reid were bitterly opposed to one another & carried on a personal feud. Its origin I never made out. People generally said *'chercher la femme'* & declared that he had had relations with Mrs Reid before her marriage. A Judge told me that he never took Wise's quotations of law cases as accurate till he had verified them as he had been known to misquote. Generally indeed that was what was felt of Wise that he cd not be trusted. He had married a sister of the Lady who afterwards became known to fame as 'Trilby'[57] in the Haymarket production. They were both pleasant, & he was a most agreeable companion, full of stories & far better read than were most others in the colony. We however had been careful not to make friends with one so violently opposed to the Premier.

See was a self-made man of good heart but a most pushing & disagreeable manner. As president of the Agricultural Society & a leading merchant he was of much weight in the community. The last I shall mention was Mr Sullivan[58] who became famous for his continual promises to develop to their utmost the various districts of the colony.

Behind all these was one Dr MacLaurin, the Chancellor of the University a most clever Scotchman, whose advice was constantly sought & followed by the Premier. One rather interesting little point rose over one nomination that of Crick to the postmaster-generalship. Lyne recommended it to me with hesitation, prepared apparently, considering Crick's previous history, to withdraw his name. He told me however

---

57   *Trilby* was the play adapted from George du Maurier's novel.
58   E. W. O'Sullivan (1846–1910), Australian politician and journalist.

that the pressure to put him in was strong & it did not seem to me that I had any constitutional right to object. In any case the Colonial Office wd have refused to back me up, tho' Lyne wd scarcely have referred it home. Generally on the whole question of the politics of the Country I must confess to have been disappointed. There was one admirable feature indeed in the absence of any bribery. Through & through politics appeared to me perfectly pure. One premier after another had died or retired from office a poor man. On the other hand there was much to regret. The standard of the average member was distinctly low. Socially & intellectually they were quite uneducated. Cruickshank indeed was in the house but had little influence. Ashton was a clever exception. The best class of lawyer or merchant or squatter held himself aloof & scorned politics & politicians alike. They maintained indeed that the payment of members had introduced a low class of men, but to me it appeared that the abdication of the better men was the cause of the mischief. To begin with, had there been at the time a majority of squatters, the bill for the payment of members wd not have passed. Certainly the bill has allowed poor demagogues to enter the House, but I cannot persuade myself that the people wd have continued to elect the worse man if a good candidate had appeared.

From one cause or another indifference or poverty the squatters had neglected parliament & the occasional good man who now tries to get in finds that the ordinary voter has ideas with wh he cannot easily comply. Nemesis has overtaken the richer class & I cannot easily sympathise with their constant abuses.

That the democracy do recognise a good man is happily shown by the list wh was chosen to represent the colony at the Melbourne conf. It was an admirable list, on wh the best interests of the community were represented, & the most careful autocrat cd scarcely have made a better selection from the names of those who stood. The excellence of that list indeed has made me wonder whether the same thing may not happen again under the Federal Senate elections. If so, the Upper House composed as it wd be of the best men, might not unlikely prove of greater influence in the country than the H. of Representatives. The natural result followed from the election of such men to the colonial parliament. Inefficient Speakers tolerated disorder – opportunism took the place of principles – fear of a dissolution & loss of income prevented the usual play of Parliamentary practice. There was a low tone throughout the Lower House.

Catchwords were allowed to rule – ministers promised & introduced many advanced reforms such as wd be popular & please the easy ear of the people. But of the deeper objects of politics – the reason for their existence – members thought little. Thus it came about that in a colony wh prided itself upon its name for democracy there was practically no self or local government. Centralisation & bureaucracy wh meant an appeal to the minister of the day ruled the local affairs of each district, till to be a good 'roads & bridges' member was one of the first reasons for his re-election wh a candidate wd urge. The political power wh the gov. thus possessed was considerable.

Again, in England, few objects are dearer to the true democrat than education. The education of N. S. W, was 20 years behind the times. Things however in some way muddled along all right & no one seemed to think a change was in any way necessary.

More glimpses of the Governor's life

Our reliable source of information on how Beauchamp passed his time is his extensive correspondence. We expose to view some of it here:[59]

I

Baron Lamington[60] *to Earl Beauchamp*

Government House,
Brisbane

14th June, 99

Dear Lord Beauchamp,

Would there be any chance of you & your party coming to pay us a visit here? It would be a great pleasure to Lady Lamington & myself were you to do so. I write thus early before you have perhaps had time to settle yourself as we propose going

---

59 Source: *Beauchamp, Lord: Letters received, 1899–1901.* Manuscripts in the Mitchell Library, State Library of New South Wales, Sydney, Call No. ML A 3012. Further letters arrived from: Capt. P. H. G. Feilden, 19 May 1899 (thanks for settling Viscount Hampden's affairs); Julian Ashton (Australian journalist), 18 June 1899 (regarding a slight incurred by his wife); Viscount Henry Robert Brand Hampden, 27 June 1899 (congratulations on Beauchamp's performance at Sydney; regarding the Commonwealth Bill and a place of residence for the Governor General); Thomas Brassey, 1st Baron, 29 June 1899 (accepting an invitation to stay); and Sir Edmund Barton, 4 July 1899 (arranging a time for meeting).

60 Baron Lamington (1860–1940), Governor of Queensland, 1896–1901.

home in September for a month's leave. If a visit cannot be arranged now, we shall hope to see you on our return.

I am,

Yours very truly,

Lamington

2

Viscount Hampden to Earl Beauchamp

104 Mount Street

June 27, 99

Confidential

Dear Lord Beauchamp,

I congratulate you sincerely on your pleasant voyage and on your reception at Sydney of which I have had accounts in the Sydney Press. I was sure you would be pleased with the hearty loyalty of the great mass of the people. ...

Hampden

3

Lord Tennyson to Earl Beauchamp

Government House,
Adelaide

July 24/99

My dear Lord Beauchamp,

...

We are delighted to be able to come to Sydney on a visit to you in September. If possible no functions for us, please, and certainly no speeches, for I want a little rest [illegible].

We are told that one day we ought to go [illegible]. Are there not some fine waterfalls near you? I remember a picture of the '[illegible] Falls' somewhere among your mountains. You mention education in Sydney. My impression is that Adelaide State schools are as good as any good Board Schools in England, but that the denominational schools are not up to a high standard. Here the University standard is equal to good public school averages in England. ...

Yours very sincerely,

Tennyson

4

Members of the Legislative Council of New South Wales

May it please Your Excellency,

We, Her Majesty's loyal and dutiful subjects, the Members of the Legislative Council of New South Wales, in Parliament assembled, desire to express our thanks for Your Excellency's speech, and to assure you of our unfeigned attachment to Her Most Gracious Majesty's Throne and Person.

We will give our best consideration to any further measures for the purpose of carrying out the decision of the electors accepting the Federal Constitution.

We join with Your Excellency in the prayer that our deliberations may promote the general welfare.

President

Legislative Council Chamber,

Sydney, 18th July 1899

5

Members of the Legislative Assembly of New South Wales, Sydney, 27th July 1899

May it please Your Excellency,

We, Her Majesty's loyal and dutiful subjects, the Members of the Legislative Assembly of New South Wales, in Parliament assembled, desire to express our thanks for your Excellency's speech, and to assure you of our unfeigned attachment to Her Most Gracious Majesty's Throne and Person.

We join with your Excellency in the hope that the decision recorded by the electors upon the 20th June will be fraught with lasting benefits to the Australian people, and we are prepared to take the necessary steps to give full effect thereto without delay.

We will give due consideration to such of the important measures enumerated in Your Excellency's speech as may be submitted to us.

We trust that our labours may prove of benefit to all classes of the people.

J.P. Abbott

Speaker, Legislative Assembly Chamber

6

Joseph Chamberlain to Lord Beauchamp

Private

31 August 1899

My dear Beauchamp,

Many thanks for your letter of the 25th July with regard to our exchange of telegrams on the subject of New South Wales troops for South Africa. The voluntary offer of their services on the part of so many Officers, N. C. Os and men has demonstrated the patriotic spirit prevailing in the Colony just as well as an offer of troops by the Government would have done, and together with numerous similar and spontaneous offers from other Colonies has afforded a most satisfactory proof of the unity of the Empire.

I had already realized before I received your letter that you had done all that was possible to persuade Mr Reid.

I am,

Yours very truly,

J. Chamberlain

7

George Houston Reid to Lord Beauchamp.

Sept. 12/99

Dear Lord Beauchamp,

Your letter of 15th instant gave me sincere pleasure, for it is regarded as something more valuable and kindly than any 'official utterance' could possibly be.

In the wide sphere beyond party politics it will always be my hope to occasionally meet your Excellency; and I need not say that, on the broader basis referred to, my services will ever be at your Excellency's command.

I feel sanguine that 'Colonial experience' will play no slight part in the broader career in the Imperial councils which await you, and I will always watch that career with feelings of personal interest, and a conviction that you will not 'live in vain'.

Mrs Reid also desires to thank you for your message.

I am glad Lord Rosebery[61] has not forgotten me. If you can remember, will you assure him of my pleasure at his remembrance; and say that in my opinion, whether he will or no, the next hand at the Empire's helm, will be his.

Your very faithful servant,

G. H. Reid

8

Baron Lamington to Earl Beauchamp

Government House,
Brisbane

20th Sept. 99

Dear Lord Beauchamp,

I thank you for your kind letter, & reciprocate your regrets at our not meeting. But you are right to do all the travelling you can.

Your decision in not granting Reid a dissolution was sound – as you suggest he will not be probably long in a back seat.

I am grateful to Lady Mary for a kind letter & am glad their visit was not altogether unpleasant, or without [illegible] for so long a journey.

Believe me,

Yrs sincerely,

Lamington

---

61   Lord Rosebery, 5th Earl (1847–1929), Liberal cabinet minister, 1885; Foreign Secretary 1886, 1892–4; Prime Minister, 1894–5.

9

Telegram from the Governor of New South Wales, Australia, Earl Beauchamp[62]

28 October 1899

Given at Sydney 2.30 pm

Received in Balmoral at 9.50 am

To Sir Arthur Bigge,[63]

Windsor

Please convey the following message to Her Majesty on the occasion of the first portion of New South Wales contingent.[64] I am desired by my ministers and a representative gathering of citizens to express my humble duty to Your Majesty and to assure Your Majesty of the grateful appreciation of the people of this Colony of Your Majesty's gracious expressions of interest in the contingent now leaving our shores. The people of this Colony will always be ready to share the duties and responsibilities of Your Majesty's Empire.

Governor

New South Wales

Beauchamp travelled widely in the colony. He showed interest not only in the fate of white farmers, but learnt to appreciate the life of the Aborigines and the Maoris. He showed concern for the education of the local children. It is said that in December 1899 alone the Governor entertained 4,525 children in Government House.[65] He had not 'tied himself to stale old

---

62 Source: Royal Archives: VIC/MAIN/P/2/223.

63 Sir Arthur Bigge (1849–1931), Private Secretary to Queen Victoria, 1895–1901 and to the Prince of Wales, 1901–10; created Baron Stamfordham, 1911.

64 During the South African War (1899–1902) Australia marshalled over 16,000 volunteers to fight along with the British Imperial troops. See Deryck M. Schreuder, 'Empire: Australia and Greater Britain, 1788–1901', in Alison Bashford and Stuart Macintyre (eds), *The Cambridge History of Australia*, vol. 1 (Cambridge: Cambridge University Press, 2013), p. 521.

65 See Jane Mulvagh, *Madresfield: The Real Brideshead, op. cit.*, p. 304.

customs'.[66] He welcomed artists, poets, musicians and even poor clergy-men to his house.[67] All this helped to increase Earl Beauchamp's popularity among the people in New South Wales.

66   This is what one Australian journalist, Miss Gouli Gull, reported. Quoted in Jane Mulvagh, *op. cit.*, p. 306.

67   Of course, there were other duties the Governor was obliged to attend to. Here, for example, is an emergency conveyed in 'Minutes for His Excellency from the Chief Secretary's Office', dated 11 June 1899: 'In view of the very great anxiety with regard to the missing ship *Perthshire* and the strong public feeling expressed in favour of one of Her Majesty's ships being sent in search of the vessel, I have the honour after consultation with my hon. Colleague, the Premier, to request that Your Excellency will be so good as to communicate with His Excellency the Admiral setting forth the desire expressed and suggesting that in order to satisfy the public anxiety for the safety of those on board the missing vessel he will cause a search to be made.' Source: Beauchamp Papers, *op. cit.*

CHAPTER 4

The Governor and the French Consul General: Further Estrangement

On 27 September 1899 Lord Beauchamp made an official tour of Cobar, where he visited the Cobar Gold Mines and the Great Copper Mines. He even went underground and inspected the huge workings. In the evening a banquet was held in his honour. About 'seventy people, representing the town and district, were present'. After the toast to the Queen had been made, the chairman proposed, 'The Governor'. Earl Beauchamp replied saying that he 'took the flattering reception as a mark of the people's confidence in their Governor'. He said he had the 'highest appreciation' for men who undertook their duties scrupulously. He was, he added, especially pleased to have noticed 'the marked feeling of loyalty, respect and affection' with which the guests had received the toast to the Queen: 'No Queen ever deserved it better.'[1] Then, quite unexpectedly, the Earl shot a bolt from the blue at the audience. He referred to an incident which hardly befitted the occasion. Referring to the Dreyfus trial[2] in France, he described what had happened as 'a hideous travesty of justice'. It was all very well, he declaimed, to speak of Liberty, Equality, and Fraternity, but the Dreyfus case had shown that these were just empty phrases in contemporary France. And the way Dreyfus had been treated made him feel glad, Beauchamp

---

1   See 'The Governor's Tour', *The Sydney Morning Herald*, Sydney, 28 September 1899.
2   Alfred Dreyfus, French army officer, a Jew, was in December 1894 accused of selling military secrets to the Germans. He was convicted and sentenced to life imprisonment by a French court. It turned out later that the document implicating Dreyfus was a forgery and that Dreyfus had been implicated because of his being Jewish. The affair attracted widespread public criticism.

confessed, that he was 'an Englishman, not a Frenchman'.[3] The Governor's words received loud cheers.

Now, whatever opinions people may have had on the Dreyfus case it does seem a breach of etiquette that Her Majesty's Colonial Governor should publicly express such views at an official function. Was it another *faux pas*, or did the Earl intend to take vengeance on the French Consul General for his ever more insolent behaviour towards him? Whatever the case, the consequences put him in an embarrassing situation. His remarks caused the French citizens of New South Wales to fly into a rage. And perhaps no one felt the censure so keenly as the French Consul General himself. The Foreign Ministry in Paris and the Colonial Office in London got involved in the affair. Earl Beauchamp was later obliged to write a letter assuring the Consul General that no offence had been intended and that he now felt sorry that he had made such utterances. The whole story can be traced in the correspondence reproduced below.[4] (The French Consul General's letters are again relayed in translation.)

I

Consul General for France to Lord Beauchamp

Sydney, 30th September 1899

To His Excellency, Lord Beauchamp, Governor of New South Wales

Your Excellency,

In a speech delivered at a banquet at Cobar, Your Excellency, according to accounts published in the Sydney journals, made certain remarks which could not fail to attract my attention.

Your Excellency, replying to a toast proposed by the Mayor of Cobar, expressed your opinion on a case recently tried in France in the following terms: 'it is all very

---

3   See 'Lord Beauchamp Lets Himself Out', T*he Evening News*, Sydney, 27 September 1899.

4   Source: *Correspondence* between Earl Beauchamp and the Consul General for France (Biard d'Aunet) during 1899 and 1900 (including letters, news cuttings and observations made concerning the Dreyfus case). Manuscripts in the Mitchell Library, State Library of New South Wales, Sydney, Call No. ML A 1829.

well to speak of Liberty, Equality and Fraternity in France, but there is certainly neither liberty nor equality where the soldier is not treated as a citizen and the Jew is denied fraternity. The sentence of Dreyfus is a hideous parody of justice', and the speech of Your Excellency concluded with the following phrase: 'I am glad to be an Englishman and not a Frenchman.'

I have no desire to make any comment on this remark, however much it may indicate a spirit offensive to the French nation.

The high position which the representative of the British Government occupies in this colony gives to such bitter expressions a significance to which it is my duty to draw Your Excellency's attention.

The banquet had an official character and Your Excellency was accompanied by two of your ministers. From the commencement of the speech, Your Excellency touched on recent political events in connection with which your constitutional prerogative as Governor had been exercised.

In short, the toast to which Your Excellency replied was 'The Governor'. It was, consequently, in your official capacity that your Excellency thought fit to express yourself in the manner mentioned above.

It is likewise in my official capacity as representing France in this Colony that I beg of Your Excellency to inform me if your statements have not been misrepresented in the published accounts to the extent of giving to the words of your Excellency an offensive signification which was not intended. If it were so, I ask your Excellency to be good enough to let me know what expressions were employed in referring to French Justice and the French nation, in order that I may transmit the correction to the Minister for Foreign Affairs, and close this incident.

Your Excellency will observe, no doubt, that in so delicate a matter it is expedient that the explanation should be precise, so that any misunderstanding may be avoided. I shall, therefore be obliged if your Excellency will have the goodness to forward to me direct that which I have the honour to ask for and to sign the reply with your own hand.

Be good enough to accept, &c.,

Georges Biard d'Aunet

2

Lord Beauchamp to the French Consul General

Johnson's Freemasons' Hotel, Broke Hill

6th October 1899

Sir,

I have to acknowledge this [illegible] of your letter dated September 30th.

Its contents are so important that I beg leave to delay my answer until my return to Sydney, which will follow so immediately after your receipt of this letter as to cause you, I trust, no inconvenience.

I have &c.,

Beauchamp

3

Government House, Sydney, 11th October 1899

Sir,

In reply to your letter of the 3rd September, I beg leave to say that I have now read the reports of my speech at Cobar you enclosed for my perusal. They are about as accurate as could be expected under the circumstances. The few lines in each report (which do not, by the way, coincide with one another) are the summary of some 15 or 20 minutes address.

The extracts which you send me torn from their somewhat lengthy context fairly represent, however, so far as they go, a portion of what I said, and still feel in the matter.

The evidence given at Rennes by Colonel Mercier and Freystaetter show how the trial of 1894 was conducted and the verdict obtained. I should be both sorry and surprised to think that my reference to that verdict which the Supreme Court of Justice in France has itself reversed and sent back to a fresh Court Martial could wound the feelings of your compatriots in New South Wales.

I have &c.,

Beauchamp

4

The French Consul General to Lord Beauchamp

Sydney, 12th October 1899

Your Excellency,

Your Excellency, replying under yesterday's date to my communication of the 30th inst., was good enough to inform me that the account of your speech at Cobar, which I had the honour to send you with my letter, was as nearly correct as circumstances permitted. Your Excellency is of the opinion that these extracts reproduced pretty faithfully a part of that speech.

Your Excellency adds that the witnesses called together at Rennes by the Court Martial (before which Captain Dreyfus appeared) gave evidence by means of which the judgment that was obtained in 1894 condemned that officer.

Your Excellency concludes in declaring that you would be displeased and surprised at the thought that the mention made in respect to a verdict annulled by the Cour de Cassation of France should have wounded the feelings of my countrymen in this colony.

The first part of your Excellency's letter gives satisfaction to the request I made, at least as much as it was possible to do, for I understand that it would have been difficult to reproduce *in extenso* the developments of Your Excellency's speech in connection with the matter under discussion.

Since Your Excellency has acknowledged that the extracts from the press are in substance correct, I cannot ask for more precise statements.

In regard to the decision given in France in the case of Captain Dreyfus, it is not for me to discuss the opinion of your Excellency.

In respect to the feelings of my countrymen in this colony, I beg Your Excellency to observe that I have not introduced the matter. It is as the representative of France and the envoy of the French Government alone that I have taken the liberty of asking Your Excellency for explanations.

I think I can nevertheless assure Your Excellency that if the feelings of my countrymen could be wounded, it would not be because Your Excellency has criticised in an official speech a judgment which has been in effect set aside by the Supreme Jurisdiction, but because that reference was accompanied by general remarks of a character offensive to our country.

It is these general remarks which have imposed upon me the duty of writing to your Excellency to ascertain if they really had been made; and by the reply of your Excellency, which contains neither amendment nor extenuation they acquire the official character which they could not until now have in my eyes.

I am thus in the presence of a fact which I cannot disregard and of an occurrence which I have not the power to explain by reason of its nature and importance.

I consider, however, that I should neglect nothing to bring about an explanation. That is why I beg Your Excellency to be good enough to examine with attention and in a conciliatory spirit the statements I have just laid before you. I do not doubt you will see the possibility of a satisfactory explanation, which I shall be happy to bring under the notice of the Minister for Foreign Affairs at Paris.

Be good enough to accept, &c.,

Georges Biard d'Aunet

5

Lord Beauchamp to the French Consul General

Government House, Sydney, 13th October 1899

Sir,

I beg leave to acknowledge the receipt of your letter of the 12th instant.

It is always dangerous to jump at conclusions and it is a matter for regret that, before publishing hastily the letter which was addressed to you by your fellow countrymen, it was not thought necessary to ascertain more accurately the facts of the case.

To condemn the trial of 1894 and to congratulate my hearers on the fact that they could not be tried before such a tribunal does not seem to me to travel far beyond the limits usually observed.

I join with you in a desire for a 'satisfactory solution' of the difficulty. Such a solution is generally obtained more easily by whoever creates the difficulty, and therefore, I cannot think that any remarks of mine are necessary.

Beauchamp

6

The French Consul General to Lord Beauchamp

Sydney, 16th October 1899
Your Excellency,

I have received the letter, dated 13th inst., with which Your Excellency has honoured me.

In this second communication Your Excellency has been good enough to speak again of the feelings manifested by my countrymen in Sydney and of your opinion on the judgement of the French Court Martial.

I have already (on the 12th inst.) begged Your Excellency to note that I did not apprise you of the emotion produced amongst the French residents by Your Excellency's speech at Cobar. It is true that these gentlemen wrote a letter, sent it to me and published it: but I did not acquaint Your Excellency of that matter.

The attitude taken by my countrymen could not, nor had it a right to, affect the necessity I felt under, in my official capacity, of asking for some explanation on the subject of the speech at Cobar. I did not ask before the principal French residents of Sydney had written that letter. And in terms in which Your Excellency has recognised a conciliatory intention.

I do not, consequently, grasp the motive of your Excellency in referring officially, in your communication of the 11th and 13th inst., to a document which can have no official value to you and which has neither been addressed or transmitted to you.

In my letter of the 12th inst., I made a similar remark concerning Your Excellency's opinion on the Dreyfus case. I begged Your Excellency to observe that my request for explanations had no connection with that matter, but with certain expressions used by Your Excellency, cited between inverted commas in my letter of 30th September, and applying to the moral valour of the French nation. The general remarks of Your Excellency, of which the Dreyfus matter had been the point of departure, were finally summed up thus: 'I am glad to be an Englishman, and not a Frenchman.'

In the letter of the 11th October, Your Excellency has confirmed the exactness of the accounts given in the press. Neither in that letter nor in the one of the 13th October, have I found any correction nor extenuation of the expressions employed by Your Excellency. I am obliged to declare that in attempting to justify them you maintain them.

Under these circumstances, I shall not trouble Your Excellency any longer with a correspondence which appears to me futile and I must express my most sincere regret at the failure of my efforts.

I have the honour to inform Your Excellency that I am transmitting a copy of the documents relating to this affair to His Excellency the Minister for Foreign Affairs at Paris, begging him to deal with the matter as appears to him advisable.

Georges Biard d'Aunet

7

Joseph Chamberlain to Lord Beauchamp

Telegram of Dec. 7th

Government House, Sydney

Personal – French Ambassador has twice urged the Foreign Office to express concern at observations respecting France and Dreyfus case made in your speech at Cobar, and your subsequent correspondence with the French Consul generally. Attitude of the French Government towards us is extremely friendly, and they appear most anxious to dispel impression produced by the language of their press. If any remarks of yours have been misunderstood, it might be well to take some public opportunity of pointing out in general terms that they did not imply any want of consideration for the French Nation or Government.

Yrs

Chamberlain

8

Lord Beauchamp to Joseph Chamberlain

Reply

Telegram of Dec 9th to the Secretary of State

Pray express my regret for any unwarranted impressions caused by my speech at Cobar. Have already informed French Consul here of my regret if feelings of French residents are wounded.

Governor of N. S. W.

9

The French Consul General to Lord Beauchamp

French Consulate, Sydney

31 March [1900]

Monsieur,

H. E. the Minister for Foreign Affairs in Paris has just informed me that in consequence of official communications made by your Ambassador in London Your Ex. has been so good as to express your personal regrets on the subject of the incident which occurred at Cobar, the 26th Sept. last. In making this communication under the heading 'Confidential' – H. E. M. Delcasse requests that I should consider the incident closed & should make every effort to dissipate the unhappy impression which had been produced among my compatriots residing in this Colony. It will be more agreeable to me to carry out these instructions because I saw with regret a situation being prolonged of which the abnormal character was certainly not in harmony with the intimate sentiments of myself or Your Excellency.

I am sure that Your Excellency will appreciate this fresh testimony of the conciliatory intentions of the French Government and of its desire to remove everything that could trouble the good relations which the representatives outside each of the two countries have as their mission to maintain & to consolidate.

I should therefore be happy if Your Excellency would be so good as to inform me that on his side, you consider the incident as closed & that it should leave no trace in the future.

I seize this opportunity to repeat to Your Excellency etc. etc.,

Georges Biard d'Aunet

10

Lord Beauchamp to the French Consul General

Government House, Sydney

3. IV.00

My dear Sir,

I welcome warmly yr suggestion that the Cobar incident should be considered closed. It has always seemed to me to have attracted a quite unnecessary amount of attention.

I am particularly pleased that the explanations made thro' Mr Chamberlain – identical with those I made to you – shd on the Quai d'Orsay have been considered satisfactory. I was very much surprised that the matter was raised at all, & still more at the way in which it was raised. In my desire that this colony shd have friendly relations with your country, it was an especial regret to me, nor can I think that any good purpose was thereby served. I am therefore the better pleased that you shd now desire it to be considered closed & have the greatest pleasure in acceding to your request.

I have the honour to be, Sir,

Yours etc.,

Beauchamp

11

Lord Beauchamp to the French Consul General

Government House, Sydney,

6.v.00

Dear M. d'Aunet,

I am sure you will understand my diffidence in refusing to receive a vice consul before his appointment has been submitted to my ministers.

I shall however be glad to see him as soon as the usual formalities are complied with. If that day is convenient to you, I shall be glad to see you to say good bye on Saturday next.

Pray let your secretary inform Capt. Smith what hour suits you. That is a course of procedure which will save us both trouble.

Yours faithfully,

Beauchamp

12

French Consul's Secretary to Lord Beauchamp's Secretary

7 May 1900

Sir,

M. Le Consul General desires me to acknowledge the receipt of his Excellency's letter of yesterday's date & sends his thanks. The Consul General will be much honoured, in accordance with His Excellency's suggestion, to present him Mr Albert Boudet next Saturday at any hour most convenient to His Excellency. As to the formalities, the Consul General desires that His Excellency may be informed that there can be no difficulty on this account, as the Consul General does not know what formalities are necessary – as the vice consuls have no authority except the name & under the responsibility of their chief – from which it follows that their admittance to office, as long as they are of the lower order does not usually necessitate an official communication. However that may be, to satisfy the wish expressed by His Excellency, the Consul General has the honour [by] this letter to notify to His Excellency the entrance into office of M. Albert Boudet on the 6th of March & his taking up the duties at the Consulate from the 13th of this month pending the arrival of M. Voisson, Consul of France; so the Minister for Foreign Affairs has [illegible] to take the place of the Consul General during his absence.

Yours

P. Marcus

Secretary

13

Lord Beauchamp's Secretary to the French Consul's Secretary

Government House,

Sydney

Sir, I have officially acknowledged your letter with reference to the appointment of Mr Boudet.

I have to add that His Excellency will be pleased to see M. D'Aunet on Saturday morning (the 12th) at 11 a. m. to bid him goodbye.

He will be glad to see M. Boudet when his appointment has been gazetted, of which I will give you the usual official notice. His Excellency regrets that etiquette forbids him from seeing him before.

Secretary

Thus ended the 'feud' between the Governor and the French Consul General.

CHAPTER 5

A Most Charming Hostess: Lady Mary Lygon

Earl Beauchamp's life in Sydney was quite intense. He must have been glad to have at his side his elder sister, Lady Mary, who had agreed to accompany him to Australia as his hostess. She was indeed a remarkable woman.

Lady Mary's background

Lady Mary was the eldest child of the 6th Earl Beauchamp and his first wife Lady Mary Stanhope. From childhood Mary and her younger brother, William were emotionally attached to each other. Mary had grown up with a deep religious faith and acquired a keen passion for music. Still in her teens, she organized a boys' choir at the village church, and helped produce Christmas plays with musical interludes which she herself composed. Later she organized the annual Madresfield Music Competitions. In this capacity she got to know a young Malvern musician who already showed uncommon talent – Edward Elgar. Elgar was also instrumental in founding the Malvern Musical Festival. He was often the guest of the Lygon family at Madresfield, and Lady Mary tried never to miss the first performances of Elgar's works. In November 1897, when a new society, the Worcestershire Philharmonic, was established with Elgar as conductor, the administrative committee, headed by the Earl of Dudley and Lord Hampton, included Lady Mary Lygon.[1] Together with another young

---

[1]   Whenever Lady Mary planned Madresfield musical competitions or concerts she was eager to invite Elgar. Elgar would gladly accept the invitations if time allowed. On

woman, Winifred Norbury, Mary Lygon exerted her efforts to keep the young composer 'in order' and make him 'work as well as amuse him', so as to 'spur on Edward's music'[2] and his career. This in due course led to a strong mutual affection between Mary Lygon and Elgar. When, in January 1899, it became known that Mary would be accompanying her brother to Australia, Elgar composed his *Three Characteristic Pieces*, Op. 10 and, on 24 March, sought her permission to dedicate them to her. It was given. The composition had to be printed before Mary sailed for Australia, and Elgar wrote to his publishers: 'I want to know if you could get the *title* done *very soon* as Lady Mary is going away & I should like her to see it first ... She is a most angelic person & I should like to please her – there are few who deserve pleasing ...'[3] When Lady Mary and Lord Beauchamp started out on their journey at the beginning of April, Elgar headed the Worcester delegation at Foregate Street Station to see them off.

Elgar's affection for Lady Mary appears to have lingered. His *Enigma Variations*, Op. 36 are famously based on 'my friends pictured within'. As its dedication line, Variation XIII (the *Romanza*) has three asterisks, almost universally believed to stand for Lady Mary (and, indeed, Elgar himself at first wrote her name in). The movement quotes Mendelssohn's overture *Calm Sea and a Prosperous Voyage*, and contains in its orchestration the chugging of a ship's engines – the ship taking her away to New South Wales. Elgar's magnificent biographer, Jerrold Northrop Moore, believes that, even after the *Enigma Variations*, the composer's thoughts were preoccupied by 'the pretty lady': they were still drifting 'towards the spring voyage of Lady Mary Lygon'[4] when he was working on a cycle of songs for the Norwich

---

3   April 1898 he wrote to her that the 'whole of my northern expedition is put off & so I am free on the day of your Concert & will come and, if you still wish it, conduct the two trios'. Lady Mary replied, thanking him and saying that she was 'very glad' that he could come and that it was 'most kind of you to say that you will help us at the concert by conducting the trios'. Quoted by Jane Mulvagh, *Madresfield, op. cit.*, p. 248.

2   See Jerrold Northrop Moore, *Edward Elgar: A Creative Life* (Oxford: Oxford University Press, 1987), p. 241.

3   *Ibid.*, p. 267.

4   *Ibid.*, p. 277.

Festival in October 1899. *A Sea Song* – a short poem – was composed to be set to music, though it seems that the lyric[5] 'was made too poignant for the innocent music of Edward's setting'.[6] The lines of the poem ran thus:

> Closely let me hold thy hand,
> Storms are sweeping sea and land,
> Love alone will stand.
>
> Closely cling, for waves beat fast,
> Foam-flakes cloud the hurrying blast;
> Love alone will last.
>
> Kiss my lips, and softly say:
> 'Joy, sea-swept, may fade to-day;
> Love alone will stay.'

The text of this 'poignant' lyric had not yet reached the ears of Lady Mary, who was at the time exceedingly busy hosting her brother's guests at Government House in Sydney.

Lady Mary in New South Wales

Lady Mary took care of the social events at Government House: she would arrange balls, invite high officials to tea or to dinner, and welcome any other personal guests. Government House became a home where many in the colony could receive a friendly reception. Lady Mary also looked after her brother's health and comfort. It seems to have been a convention at the time, that when British civil servants went abroad to occupy senior posts in the Empire they would, if they were not married, invite their sisters to act as hostesses. Thomas Babington Macaulay had set the precedent. Earl Beauchamp became ever more indebted to his sister's presence.

---

5   *Ibid.*, p. 278.
6   *Ibid.*

We get a glimpse of Lady Mary's personality and the energy she showed while in Australia in a letter she wrote to her sister, Lady Ampthill:[7]

Hill View, N.S.W., August 13th, 1900.

After all I cannot expatiate on the glories of the lace dress, as the silly shipping company had not sent it up when I was in Sydney on Wednesday! So it must again wait another week. Meanwhile our glorious weather here continues – and is a real joy. We spend hours talking to Mr Percival Landon; how interesting he is about the war! He has aged a great deal I think. Mr Arthur Somervell arrived on Friday – and will stay up here this week with us – as his work does not again begin till next Monday. On Saturday we had an expedition to the FirzRoy Falls – a very beautiful gorge 14 miles from here. Mr Wilfred (Smith), Mr Harris, Captain Clark and I rode and all the others drove. Coming back we lost our way in the bush – did an extra ten miles and arrived back at 6 after a good 35 miles! Yesterday Lord Richard Nevill arrived from Melbourne for a two days visit – so we are a large party of men. Tonight Willie goes off to a place called Corowa, 200 or 300 miles off – and tomorrow Susie, Bertha, Mary Gilmour, Mr Wilfred, Mr Harris and I, are going to a place called Coolangatta – which is about 44 miles off – and to reach which we have to cross the Kangaroo Valley. We are going to ride half and drive the other half of the way, coming back in the same manner the next day. We shall then have three more quiet days here and return to Sydney on Saturday – to plunge into a giddy whirl of Missions, Bishops, Meetings etc. etc. Lady Ranfurly has thrown us over for the race week – so we are trying to get Lady Lamington – and Mr Zulu (Farquhar) – and possibly Mr Le Hunte, the Governor of New Guinea. Did I tell you about our four Bishops, who are coming to us? First the Bishops of Melanesia and New Guinea – who are both young men and very attractive, albeit the latter rejoices in the name of Stone-Wigg!!! Then the Bishop of Grafton and Armidale (most charming) and his wife – and the Bishop of Adelaide and Mrs Harmer (née Somers Cocks) and a cousin of the Duchess of Bedford's. There are mission meetings nearly every night – and the festivities consist of garden parties, tea-parties and luncheon parties to meet the Bishops and their wives, singly, or *en bloc*. We shall be ecclesiastical at the end of it all!! This is a dull letter but our life here is slightly monotonous – compared to the giddy whirl in Sydney. Bertha and I were much pleased last week, as we had collected £101.12 for the Seamen's Mission before the meeting and electrified them with our success ...

7   Source: Royal Archives: VIC/ADDU/27: Letter 13/8/1900.

The return to England

Lady Mary stayed in Sydney only a few months, because she was expected back in England to attend to her own official duties. In 1895 she had been appointed Lady-in-Waiting to H. R. H. the Duchess of York (by royal order, she was to remain with her as Lady-in-Waiting when she became Princess of Wales, and then Queen Mary). So, in September 1900, Lady Mary returned to England. Beauchamp missed his precious hostess. And many friends regretted her departure too. An Australian poet put his thoughts in these elevated words:[8]

> *To Lady Mary Lygon*
> *On her Departure from Sydney*
> *Sept. 12th 1900*
>
> You leave us, lady, in the Spring
>   When, all the wide land through,
> The perfumed winds go wandering,
>   On days of gold and blue.
>
> The wattle's floating incense thrills
>   Like music of a lyre;
> Its altars on a thousand hills
>   Are plumed with golden fire.
>
> Great white winged clouds on far-off heights
>   Are gathered; and below
> Are little clouds, like acolytes
>   In surplices of snow.
>
> Ah, lady, when in England stands
>   The Spring so young and fair,
> With slender blue-bells in her hands,
>   And roses in her hair –

8   Source: *Beauchamp, Lord: Letters received, 1899–1901*. Manuscripts in the Mitchell Library, State Library of New South Wales, Sydney, Call No. ML A 3012.

Then you will see the primrose dear,
  In many a deep green lane,
  And, in the sky above you, hear
The English lark again.

But, in the time of frost and snow,
  Your thoughts will turn, may be,
Unto a land that lies below
  The grey dividing sea.

O then when winter winds have chilled
  The earth, no longer green –
May our remembered sunshine gild
  The darkness of the scene!

Victor J. Daley[9]
Sept. 12/1900

Lady Mary devoted almost all her adult life to the service of Queen Mary. When she died in 1927, the Queen was greatly distressed. She expressed her sorrow in a letter addressed to the 7th Earl Beauchamp:[10]

> The Queen commands me to try and tell you how deeply she sympathises with you over the loss of our beloved Mary, and how much Her Majesty feels her going. She valued Mary as her best friend as well as her faithful, devoted, clever and wonderful servant, and she is very, very sad ...

Sad indeed was this early death. Lady Mary died much too young – she was only fifty-eight. The death was also most unfortunate for Lord Beauchamp. Not only did it cause him great sorrow at the time, but a few years later the Earl must have realized quite how much her absence meant: for, had Lady Mary still been alive in 1932, she might perhaps have persuaded Lady Lettice, Beauchamp's estranged wife, from laying ignominy upon her husband.

---

9 Victor J. Daley (1858–1905), a Celtic poet and journalist; his first book of verse *At Dawn and Dusk* was published in 1898.
10 Quoted in Dorothy Williams, *The Lygons of Madresfield Court, op. cit.*, p. 98.

CHAPTER 6

The Governor's Profile: The Year 1900

The backdrop to Earl Beauchamp's governorship was the final hammering out of the Constitution Bill and Commonwealth Act which brought the Australian colonies together in a Federation; and the 'South African' (Second Boer) War, which preyed on a lot of people's minds. But, in the day-to-day matters of the Governor of New South Wales, the year 1900 was not marked by any particularly significant events. Earl Beauchamp followed a routine of normal administrative and other obligatory social functions. He found a good Prime Minister in Lyne and the two worked well together. They cultivated a mutual respect and even developed a liking for one another. In the course of the year Beauchamp became increasingly popular with the local public, and he fostered friendships with a large circle of people. The voluminous correspondence from this period is an obvious testimony to this. Some of the letters are very curious: one such letter is by Henry Lawson, the Australian author of *The Union Buries its Dead*, but he was not yet famous and was asking for financial help. Further, we have access to an extensive exchange of letters between Lyne and Beauchamp. The letters rouse our interest: they are at places amusing, but equally informative with regard to official business. A selection of this correspondence is reproduced in the following pages.[1]

---

1 Source: *Beauchamp, Lord: Letters received, 1899–1901*. Manuscripts in the Mitchell Library, State Library of New South Wales, Sydney, Call No. ML A 3012. Other letters are by:

Victor Albert George Child Villiers, Earl of Jersey, 10 May 1900 (suggests G.C.M.G. for Sir F. Darley; condolence on death of brother; Federation question; appreciation of Copeland and Lyne).

Victor Daley, 1 June 1900 (apologizing for having been unable to be present); 12 September 1900 (poem to Lady Lygon on her departure from Sydney).

1

Sybil de Vere Brassey[2] *to Lord Beauchamp*

Government House,
Melbourne

Jan. 8th, 1900

Thank you very much dear Ld Beauchamp for the [illegible] photo. Please thank Mr Wilfrid for his and those of my family, they are really very good. We have just been off the [illegible]. It seems all in order & very nice. [illegible] It has been very nice meeting you here.

George Dibbs, 17 September 1900 (description of stick being sent; cup of myall for Lady Mary, thinks people will regret Federation).
Countess Feodora Gleichen (12 July 1900) will be glad to make the memorial tablet for Madresfield Chapel.
Peter F. Kempermann, Consul General for Germany, 27 July 1900 refers to an assault upon the German club at Broken Hill.
Jenico William Joseph Preston, Viscount Gormanston, 30 July 1900 (accepting hospitality).
John Adrian Hope (Lord Hopetoun) Marquess of Linlithgow, 28 August 1900 (fears his coming has hurried Beauchamp's departure; has been no willing party).
Livingston Hopkins, 28 September 1900 (forwarding a cartoon as requested; with the *Bulletin*'s compliments).
Uchter John Mark Knox Ranfurly, 5th Earl, 4 January 1899; 13 Jan 1900; 22 February 1900 (all letters refer to arrangements for Beauchamp's visit New Zealand).
George Houston Reid, 19 September 1899 (thanks for letter, colonial experience in Beauchamp's carrier, forecasts Lord Rosebery next at the Empire's helm).
Tom Roberts, 6 December 1899 (thanking Beauchamp for letter of appreciation; 21 August 1900 (thanking him for commission).
Sir John See, 9 August 1900 to Capt. Wilfried Abel Smith, Private Secretary to Governor (regarding a form used in government *Gazette* without consulting the Governor); 14 October 1900 (regarding state governorship for Lord Beauchamp).
Sir Basil Thomson, 16 June 1900 (regarding Lord Tennyson's view on the Commonwealth Bill; thanks for hospitality).
Constance, Countess of Ranfurly, 10 June 1900 (reference to plague; thanks for helping with choice of cup, has taken advice and entertained all teachers of public and private schools in Auckland); 23 October 1900 (reference to departure; reference to good passage, and common acquaintance). Source: *Ibid.*

2   Wife of Earl Brassey (1836–1918), Governor of Victoria, 1895–1900.

2

Sybil de Vere Brassey to Lord Beauchamp again

Jan. 10, 1900

The snuff box is too lovely dear Ld Beauchamp. The contents I will preserve carefully until I meet Mary. I am much obliged to you. Many thanks.

3

Lord Tennyson to Lord Beauchamp

Government House,
Adelaide

Jan 14, 1900

My dear Lord Beauchamp,

I cannot go to New Zealand at present – and I see that your boat will not after all call at Milford Sounds. Your sister wrote me a most kind letter from Sandringham in which she says: 'I have never ceased regretting leaving Sydney and should go back there tomorrow if I could!'

Whenever you can spare time remember that we are at Marble Hill, and always delighted to see you. I have just been feasting and addressing my Second Contingent. All classes are represented – many gentlemen [illegible], squatters, farmers, labourers and city-men from all parts of South Australia.

Ever yours,

Tennyson

4

Earl Ranfurly to Lord Beauchamp

Government House,
Wellington,
New Zealand

18.1.1900

My dear Beauchamp,

I have been trying to fix up my plans with a view of seeing something of you whilst over here, & have abandoned my West Coast trip, this will bring me to Government

House Auckland about February 20th, you told me you would like to see something of the real Maoris, not the town ones. I am therefore arranging a meeting with 'King' Mahuta for the end of February, it will probably be a big thing, and is fortunately very get-at-able. It being only a few hours from Rotorna in the Auckland direction. I want you to cable me date as near as possible that you expect to be at Rotorna, as these Maoris want long notice. It is my first official visit to this section of them and in fact the first invitation ever sent by these people to a governor, as in the past they have always held aloof.

I shall hope to join you somewhere about Rotorna.

Believe me,

yours sincerely,

Ranfurly

5

Henry Lawson to Lord Beauchamp

Chaplain Cottage,
Charles Street, North Sydney

Jan. 19th, 1900

Dear Lord Beauchamp,

I heard that you had spoken kindly of my books – *When the World was Wide* and *While the Billy Boils*, and as you take an interest in art and literature, I thought, as a last resource, I would confide in you and ask you to help me. The manly and independent spirit you have shown since you came to govern the colony helped to decide me. The attached article 'Pursuing Literature' speaks for itself; all that I can say is that it is true and takes the widest possible view of the situation. The English reviews and correspondence in last part of *scrap-book*, if you will kindly glance at it, will explain my present position in the literary world. (I must apologise for the appearance of *scrap-book*, which is not very presentable; it has knocked round in camps.)

The position of purely Australian literature is altogether hopeless in Australia; there is no market. The oldest and the wealthiest Daily in Australia fills its columns with matters clipped from English and American magazines. The usual answer to would-be Australian contributors is 'Very sorry Mr so and so, but we have already exceeded our allowance for outside contributions.' Nothing 'goes' well here that does not come from or through England.

I have recently been obliged to sell, or rather sacrifice, two more books in Australia and both are larger and contain better class work than my first two. I would have waited until these books came out before writing to you, but there has been a delay in the printing. I send you specimens of the work I am doing now for £1 per column. I have been contributing to a Sydney daily but the war news has crowded me out. I have to sell for £1 per col. work that is honestly worth five.

I have never been in a position to wait until my work got [its] home journal in [the] market, and the money got back. I have had splendid reviews in leading English literary journals, and letters from most of the publishers, but am tied down here because I can scarcely make a living, get some money to go home or to keep me while I do good work and get it on the English market. I am, because of the prices paid, literary new here, obliged to publish rubbish – or at least, good ideas and in hurried and mutilated form, and because of the reputation I have gained in Australia, I am forced to sign hurried work – else I couldn't get it published at all. That is the cruellest [sic] part of the business.

In short I am wasting my work, wasting my life, spoiling the reputation I have gained, and wearing out my brains and heart here in Australia. If I were single I would find my way out to England somehow, but I am married, have one child, and another one due this month, so I am tied hopelessly. We live comfortably on £2.00 per week and it takes me all my time to make that with my pen.

I am sure that I could, in six months, command my own prices in London, but how am I to get there? In order to succeed it would be necessary for me to be in London a few months to learn the ropes. We cannot deal at this distance, as it takes 9 months at least to correspond with two magazines in succession. Or if I could have 12 months out here, clear of financial worry, to do my best work and get it home, I would, I feel surely rouse myself out of this grinding, sordid life, which is killing my work and me.

I send you a book by Barcroft Boake,[3] a young Australian who, if he had lived, would have been our leading poet. While his best work was being published, he hanged himself in the scrub, down Botany way – for the same reasons that I want to raise myself out of the hole of a place.

I will not appeal to the country. I can see nothing before me but years of hack-work, of sacrificing my books as soon as written, and before it – and in the end perhaps, a big name in London and a chance to go there, and fancy prices, when I have written myself out – as was the case with Barcroft Boake. And all this for the want of a hundred pounds or so at the start. I have been obliged to sell all my rights (as you will see by the enclosed agreement, which you will kindly cause to be returned with

3   Barcroft Boake (1866–92), an Australian poet who hanged himself with a stock whip.

scrap-book) – everything except perhaps my soul; our newspaper proprietors would envy that if they could make anything on it.

I – how shall I put this? – wish you to help me out of this miserable hole I am in. I heard you were rich. All my friends are as poor as myself. I know none of our scrubby aristocracy, nor do I wish to know them. Will you – say send me enough to hang out here for a year independent of the Australian Press – or go home. I could go in about April, but could not leave my wife behind. And I'm sure that within two years I could win fame and fortune in London and repay you. If you cannot help me kindly destroy this. It is the first letter of this kind I have ever written in my life, and will be the last.

Yours truly,

Henry Lawson

Lord Beauchamp must have responded favourably to Lawson's plea. We could not locate his letter of reply, but do have Lawson's response to it:

6

Henry Lawson to Earl Beauchamp

9/2/00

Dear Lord Beauchamp,

Will endeavour to thank you in person for your generosity. It meant so much to me. I will be able to get away early in April (By the *Medea*, if I can arrange for a cabin). Your wish in keeping the matter private has, of course been respected.

Would be glad if you would let me know when it would be most convenient for you to see me.

Believe me,

Yours very gratefully,

Henry Lawson

Lawson was also advised by one of his admirers to proceed through the Authors' Society to solve his difficulties.

7

Alfred A. Grace to Henry Lawson

Nelson,
Maoriland

Jan. 7th 1900

To Henry Lawson

Dear Sir,

My excuse for writing to you is that I have read all your published work (*While the Billy Boils* and *When the World was Wide* stand in my bookshelf) which I have enjoyed exceedingly.

Your last bit of work in the *Bulletin*, 'The Story of the Oracle', however, is what causes me to write this letter. I have read all the yarns in the Xmas numbers of the English magazines, and not one of them is, in my opinion, equal to the 'Story of the Oracle'.

I ask myself, How is it that a man who can do work such as that and as *The Drover's Wife*, should be forced to relieve his feelings in such an article as 'Pursuing Literature in Australia'? And the answer is: Because he can find in Australia no proper market for his work.

London is the only market. But how are we Australians to get our work there? It is fruitless to send MSS of short yarns straight to English magazines – we are too far off. To send a book on one's own to a London publishers is to court robbery.

There is but one way – to employ an intermediary. That intermediary is the Authors' Society. It is the only straight Literary Society in the world, barring the Societé des Gens de Lettres. It is managed by a Council, on which sit Besant, Barrie, Edwin Arnold, Hall Caine, Marion Crawford, Austin Dobson, Conan Doyle, Rider Haggard, Thomas Hardy, Jerome K. Jerome, Anthony Hope Hawkins, Kipling, Henry Norman, Gilbert Parker, Pinero, G. R. Sims, in fact all the foremost fictionists.

They employ reliable literary agents, who will sell for members of the Society short yarns and books of prose or verse, on commission, and get the best terms possible. They give advice gratis, and their advice is 'good iron'. Sub. £1. 1s. per annum (which includes sub. to *The Author*, the Society's magazine).

So far as I am concerned, I look to London as the only proper publishing field, and to the Society as the best medium through which to obtain such publication. To this end I joined the Society last Sept.

I have had letters from Besant, who placed the benefits of membership before me, and I am assured that good work will find a good market in London if placed in the hands of the Society's agents.

You can do the best work produced in Australia. You are known in London; your work would succeed there. But in trying to find a London publisher, or in choosing such, I beg you not to act 'on your own'. Use the Society's knowledge of whom to submit that work to – you will make money by it. There are some straight publishers, but they are few and unknown to the general public. The Society reads the trade like a book, its agents know where to place particular kinds of work, and it is anxious to help men out here. Through it, I believe, the Australian can get all the advantages of 'going to London' without the expense of taking a passage or the inconvenience of 'stowing away'. Indeed, the best thing for a man in London to do, would be to go straight to the Society's Secretary, G. Herbert Thring, B. A., 4 Portugal Street, Lincoln's Inn Fields, London W. C.

I had promised the *Bulletin* the first refusal of my next book (which they will print shortly) or else I should most certainly have sent it to London per medium of the Author's Society. By this I do not infer anything derogatory to the *Bulletin*, but it simply can't give access to the field that is opened up by publication through a good house in London.

Yours very sincerely,

Alfred A. Grace

P. S. In applying for membership – as I hope for your own sake you will – it will be necessary to send a copy of one of your books with the sub., and your name will be entered on the Society's books straight off.

I am sending this letter to Archibald, asking him to forward it to you.

AAG

8

Earl of Ranfurly to Lord Beauchamp

Government House,
Wellington, New Zealand

22.2.1900

Dear Beauchamp,

We are quite straight here, & delighted to see you any moment & for as long as you can stay.

I wired to the Minister of Railways & asked him if he had put a special at your disposal from Rotorna, the journey even in the express is painfully slow, he replied that he was doing so & thanked me for suggestion. You can thus leave about 10.30. I fancy & arrive here before 5.

On Wednesday 28th we all go down to the Native gathering at Huntley returning the same afternoon.

On Thursday they have a Whiteman's show at Huntley, but I have excused myself, & said I thought you could not manage it either, it is hardly good enough.

You will find plenty to do here.

Believe me,

Yours sincerely,

Ranfurly

9

William Lyne to Lord Beauchamp

Premier's Office,
Sydney, N.S.W.

March 21/00

My dear Lord Beauchamp,

Thank you for your letter today. The plague has given a great deal of extra work, but I don't mind that, if only it can be grappled with.

We have quarantined a section of the worst part of the city, and declared another part an infected area. I have induced the mayor to work harmoniously with us; this morning we have nominated a committee, composed of Dr Stompson, Mr Hickeon, under secretary of works, and Mr Beakwell C. E., a member of the city corporation staff, to energetically, carry out details – about 1200 men will be employed. An area under quarantine will be dealt with from today, the infected area on Monday, in consequence of certain [illegible] required. I have moved five shipping companies from Susset st. [illegible] and nearly all the [illegible]. We shall know in a few days whether this action has the beneficial effect desired.

Yours very sincerely,

William John Lyne

10

Lady Tennyson to Lord Beauchamp

Marble Hill,

April 25th 1900

Dear Lord Beauchamp,

Thank you warmly for your most kind letter. Yes, also, you know what the sorrow is, & to both of us, our brothers meant so so much. Mine has always from boyhood been a sort of hero to me, always excelling in all he did from quite early schoolboy days & up to the time he married before he was 23, he & I had not a thought unshared. 'After our disasters,' he wrote to me the night before he sailed, 'I felt I must offer my services for dear old England & they have been accepted' – & he was off within three days notice. He was always so proud of his yeomanry & and was so beloved by his men, 3 of his stablemen belonged to his company and went out with him. His Colonel Lord Chesham sent me a message: 'was shot through head, death being instantaneous while gallantly leading company in attack on the [illegible], he had done good work & his death much grieved me & my officers.' Thank God he did not suffer is all I can say at present. As you write, one cannot find comfort in anything at present the sorrow is too keen, except that there is another world & that we shall meet again. He wrote so happily, having been made temporary galloper to General French on the famous march re-entry into Kimberley before his men arrived – he having been sent in advance by Lord Chesham to prepare for the arrival of the others. Three out of six brothers gone since I married.

...

I am so glad that you are soon going to have your sisters out, it is even worse for you than for me, for I have my Hallam to help me. Lady Mary wrote him such a nice cheery letter a few mails ago. We are looking forward to seeing her & Lady Bertha again but oh how differently we all feel to the bright day when we welcomed you all so gladly last May.

Well thank you again for your letter, it has done me good, for one feels it is written from a heart aching like one's own, and I am alone today – Hallam is down at Adelaide.

So the dear old Duke of Argyll has gone, a kind, affectionate friend to us both having known Hallam since he was born, & many happy days have we spent at Inveraray. The poor duchess has had a short-lived happiness only 4 years and a half. We are staying on up here till the end of May if the weather permits instead of moving to Adelaide as we should otherwise have done after Easter.

Believe me,

Yrs very sincerely,

Audrey Tennyson

11

Lord Beauchamp to J. Plummer[4]

Government House,
Sydney

30 IV 00

Dear Mr Plummer,

Many thanks for yr help in contradicting this rumour wh was started by the *Daily Chronicle*. I suppose it is a personal feeling of spite on his part wh made him do it.

Why do you think Mr Reid only was in attendance at the Levee? We followed the old practice as near as we could & took no steps to prevent anybody from staying. The Chief Justice was on my right & it is only from yr letter that I learn the ministers were not in the group beyond him with the Abp & other high officials. They must have left because they wanted to, & certainly not for any other reason I know of. It shows how easily misunderstandings arise. I thought the arrangements inconvenient for those attending who must have found the crowding tiresome & was anxious to try to improve things. But people are so ready to misunderstand everything that my present intention is so to leave things alone – tho' it shd be easy to allow gentlemen attending more ease & comfort.

I like yr idea about the Patriotic Cantata & after my sister's arrival will try to make arrangements. There is scarcely room under the gallery for 80 people – not even children, but I think it might be arranged somehow.

With renewed thanks,

Yours sincerely,

Beauchamp

12

William Lyne to Lord Beauchamp[5]

---

4   Source: *The Papers relating to 7th Earl Beauchamp, William Lygon.* Manuscripts in the Mitchell Library, State Library of New South Wales, Sydney, Call No. ML DOC 465.
5   There was regular correspondence with William John Lyne. See the following:
     12 March 1900 (South African troops; visit of Kang Yewwei).
     21 March 1900 (plague).

26 April/00

Premier's Office,
Sydney N. S. W

His Excellency Lord Beauchamp

Dear Lord Beauchamp,

I enclose Colonel Mackay's resignation as Vice President of the Executive Council which I received this morning.

Yours sincerely,

William John Lyne

13

William Lyne to Lord Beauchamp

May 5/00

Dear Lord Beauchamp,

In reference to Council appointments: the course followed is, I think, for me to ascertain whether the position would be accepted if offered, & then a letter to be written formally by the Governor. Before anything of a compromising nature is done, I shall of course consult you.

Yours sincerely,

William John Lyne

---

26 April 1900 (enclosing Col. Mackay's resignation as Vice President of Executive Council).
5 May 1900 (regarding Council appointments procedure).
5 May 1900 (confidential, re. honour to be conferred on William Lyne).
17 May 1900 (re. Mr See).
21 May 1900 (re. Major Gen. Hutton).
11 June 1900 (has to attend a banquet at Botany. Mr Wise will forward a copy).
19 July 1900 (forwarding copies of telegrams from the Agent General).
17 September 1900 (thanks for letter of sympathy upon his father's death).
12 October 1900 (forwarding papers).
24 March 1901 (copy of telegram re. Beauchamp's state governorship).
Source: *Beauchamp, Lord: Letters received, 1899–1901, op. cit.*

14

William Lyne to Lord Beauchamp

May 5/00

Confidential

My dear Lord Beauchamp,

I had a conversation with Mrs Lyne, and gave her your letter: she is not anxious, but feels that you have taken such a kind interest I cannot do other than accept, still I would much prefer it to be held over until the termination of war; perhaps you will please ascertain what Mr Chamberlain's views are?

Your sincerely,

William John Lyne

15

Earl Jersey to Earl Beauchamp

54 Lowndes Square,

S. W.

10.5.00

My dear Beauchamp,

I spoke to Chamberlain ten days ago about giving the Chief Justice the G. C. M. G. which he has so richly deserved. He seemed to feel that it was contrary to rule & difficult to do this till he actually retired. It will be a pity if he adheres to this view as Sir F. Darley has been a mainstay to five Governors, and has always carried out his duties in the most admirable manner. But the theory of granting honours is part explanation. One is propounded gravely and immediately it is shattered by some exception which commands no admiration. However Chamberlain ought to listen to your recommendation. We have been so sorry for you in the calamity which has befallen your family. A young promising life almost thrown away, though we may hope that your brother has set the good example which can never be without good results.

The Federation question (or rather cl.73 & 74) is exciting much interest. This is greatly stimulated by the numerous banquets & luncheons at which the Delegates fire away their unalterable determination to stand by their unchangeable Bill. It will be impossible for the government not to take some means by which the right of appeal to the Crown can be maintained.[6] Some persons think Barton, Kingston[7] & Deakin[8] too unbending, but they have no authority to accept any change. Deakin has spoken very well, though firmly. Of late I fancy Barton has spoken too long for after dinner. Within the last day or two Lamington has had a speech of his cabled over, which, as received is hardly judicious at this juncture, and has ruffled the delegates, bar Dickson.[9] Last night at the Devonshire Club dinner, at which I was present, Deakin animadverted on Lamington's speech, upon which Dickson got up and supported L.'s action with some asperity. So I expect that the delegates now form two parties. It is a pity. ...

You are sending a curious Agent-General in Copeland. A good fellow, but not exactly my idea of an A. G. I am very pleased to learn that Lyne is doing so well. I knew him very well, and always liked him. I noticed how well he has managed the matters connected with the patriotic movement. There does not seem to have been any hesitation on his part to assume responsibility & to lead the way.

Lady Jersey sends her best wishes,

Believe me,

Yours Truly,

Jersey

6   In January 1900, the Colonial Secretary, Joseph Chamberlain, invited the colonies to send delegates to discuss the Australian Constitution Bill. He had expressed certain reservations and suggested minor amendments. The delegates came to London to induce the British government to accept the draft constitution without any amendment. The delegates were: Edmund Barton (New South Wales), Alfred Deakin (Victoria), J. R. Dickson (Queensland), Charles Kingston (South Australia), Philip Fysh (Tasmania), and S. H. Parker (Western Australia). With minor alterations the Commonwealth Bill was enacted as a statute by the Imperial Parliament. It received the Royal Assent in July 1900, and the Commonwealth Act was proclaimed on 1 January 1901. For further details see: R. A. Gollan, 'Nationalism, the Labour Movement and the Commonwealth, 1880–1900', in Gordon Greenwood, *op. cit.*, pp. 192–3. The issue over clauses 73 and 74 of the bill – referred to again in a later letter in this section – was to do with whether the High Court (the supreme court of the proposed Federation) would be the ultimate court of appeal for Australians, or whether certain cases should be sent to the Privy Council in London to decide. This issue raised strong feelings.

7   Charles Kingston (1850–1908), Premier of South Australia.

8   Alfred Deakin (1856–1919), later Prime Minister of Australia.

9   Sir James Dickson (1832–1901), Premier of Queensland.

16

Lord Tennyson to Earl Beauchamp[10]

Government House,
Adelaide

Confidential

May 12, 1900

My dear Lord Beauchamp,

My Premier has committed himself in a telegram which I have forwarded to Mr Chamberlain. He much hopes that any amendments made [will be] referred to the Parliaments or Peoples of Australia for confirmation: but will be made on the authority of the Imperial Parliament alone. Can you persuade your Premier to do likewise – for a Referendum [Illegible]?

10   A lengthy exchange of letters was carried equally with Lord Tennyson:
       12 May 1899 (arrangements for Beauchamp's arrival).
       24 July 1899 (accepting an invitation to visit; Adelaide educational standards; is going to address natives at Oodnadatta; has just read Spenser and Gillen).
       14 January 1900 (cannot go to New Zealand; quotes Beauchamp's sister writing 'she has never ceased to regret leaving Sydney'; has just been feasting and addressing 2nd contingent).
       16 May 1900 (Lawson; has just opened Art & Industry Exhibition on Holland; death of 2 soldiers from N. S. W. Contingent (of typhoid) caught at the camp in Adelaide).
       7 April 1900 (Commonwealth Bill).
       20 April 1900 (Commonwealth Bill).
       5 June 1900 (Commonwealth Bill).
       8 July 1900 (forthcoming trip to Sydney and Blue Mountains; gun boat for China; Commonwealth Bill; his own unsatisfactory position; state governorship).
       19 July 1900 (arrangements re: forthcoming visit; South Africa; reactions to Hopetoun's appointment as Governor-General).
       22 August 1900 (Mrs Palmer's visit).
       5 September 1900 (does not want pony; glad Beauchamp is better satisfied with the English Church of Australia; sending extract of letter to Sir John Madden re presence of governors at swearing in of Governor-General).
       11 October 1900 (re facilities for Australians desiring to enter the Indian Civil Service; definition of a lyric).
       Source: *Beauchamp, Lord: Letters received, 1899–1901, op. cit.*

Yours ever,

Tennyson

17

William Lyne to Lord Beauchamp

Premier's Office,
Sydney N. S. W

May 17/00

My dear Lord Beauchamp,

I know I must be a trouble to you, but don't want to be so. If you can make the recommendation – should it not already be done – regarding Mr See I should be very glad. He has been 20 years in public life: been in three ministries: held office as Colonial Treasurer, & for many years held the position of President of the Royal Agricultural. He is now minister for Defence.

Yours sincerely,

William John Lyne

18

Lord Beauchamp to Sir Joseph Abbott[11]

Government House,
Sydney

28 V 00

My dear Sir Joseph,

I am rather diffident of trespassing on yr kindness in such a matter & have some doubts as to whether I shd ask you at all to help me.

But it is so difficult a matter that I must at least begin by making my excuses.

A governor has not much influence, except in such matters & it is the more necessary for him therefore to be careful in issuing invitations to Govt. Ho.

11 Source: *The Papers relating to 7th Earl Beauchamp, William Lygon.* Manuscripts in the Mitchell Library, State Library of New South Wales, Sydney, Call No. ML DOC 339.

Most unfortunately the wife of one of the Cabinet Ministers – I refer to Hassall – is said to be generally unrecognised.

Now Hassall is a man for whom I shd be glad to do all possible, but if what has been told me is true, it seems impossible to ask her.

It is a difficult and painful subject. Can you help me by any advice or information? What would Lady Abbott do?

I have been in some anxiety over another case – marriage in the Upper House about a year old – but have nearly settled to ignore the past. Once more, excuse me.

Believe me,

Yours sincerely,

Beauchamp

19

Victor J. Daley to Lord Beauchamp

31 Darling St.,
Balmain

June 1/ 1900

Dear Lord Beauchamp,

I was sincerely sorry to have been unable to accept your very kind invitation. I trust, Sir, that you will believe that nothing but very serious indisposition would have prevented me from being present yesterday evening.

When your letter arrived I was at a remote spot on the Hawkesbury. I caught a severe cold, and have been laid up. I was only back in time to send you a telegram of apology.

I am, indeed, charmed to learn that you were pleased with my lines on 'The Relief of Mafeking'. They were only rapid newspaper work – but I felt them. Which perhaps makes all the difference.

Reiterating my regrets

I trust I may still have the honour to be – Dear Lord Beauchamp,

Your obedient servant & friend,

Victor J. Daley

20

Baron Brassey[12] *to Lord Beauchamp*

Government House,
Melbourne

29th June 1900

My dear Beauchamp,

You are most kind. I shall be delighted to spend three or four days with you. I have given up Queensland. It is too far for a short stay.

You need not prepare to leave Sydney for some time. It is quite uncertain what arrangements will be made. I look forward to interesting talks on the situation and the prospects of the future.

Yours very sincerely,

Brassey

21

Sir Basil Thomson to Lord Beauchamp

'Oroya'

16 June 1900

Dear Lord Beauchamp,

Your telegram reached me when my spirits were at their lowest as the prospect of a solitary voyage home as the sequel of a most delightful week. [illegible] – I saw Lord Tennyson who is far from happy about clause 74 and would be glad to see it struck out altogether and [illegible] to the Federal Parliament. He had heard that the Government's anxiety to agree upon a compromise with the delegates is due to the fact that the delegates have been lobbying, and are sure of the support of a number of Unionists who think that the Colonies should be given all they want as a recognition of their behaviour during the war.

I also heard (not from Lord Tennyson) what you doubtless know already, though it is still to be kept an open secret, that Lord Hopetoun has accepted the Governor-Generalship. It ought to be a popular appointment.

12   Brassey, 1st Earl, b. 1836. A Liberal.

I have a ship full of West Australian miners who leave us today, and we shall then number 14 passengers! I read all about the opening of Parliament and wished that I was there, but the papers were silent about the Nonconformists who would greet the Governor coldly because they had not their share of the pomps and vanities. How did they show their injured feelings I wonder?

I cannot tell you how I enjoyed that too short week at Government House.

Very truly

Yours,

Basil Thomson

22

Julian Ashton to Lord Beauchamp

Glenview, Bondi

June 18, 90

Dear Lord Beauchamp,

I only learned yesterday from Mrs Ashton that she wrote to you in rather a heated manner concerning some slight at which she felt aggrieved.

As I would uphold any action of hers which was felt to be right, it is equally incumbent upon me to disassociate myself from responsibility in what I cannot but regard as an ill-considered impulse.

Understanding the many vexations which must beset your position here as Governor, please accept my regrets for an incident, doubtless trivial to you in itself, but marked in my opinion, by a serious lack of judgment rather than intentional discourtesy.

Yours faithfully,

Julian Ashton

23

On a visit to Woodburn[13]

19 June 1900

As Representatives of Her Most Gracious Majesty, our beloved Queen, we the undersigned, on behalf of the inhabitants of Woodburn, Richmond River, N. S. W. hereby respectfully wish to express our utmost gratification at Your Excellency's visit to this important part of N. S. W. and as loyal subjects of our Most Gracious Sovereign, beg to tender our heartiest welcome.

We have noticed with pleasure the great interest Your Excellency has evinced in distant parts of the Colony by visiting them, and we are highly pleased to see you in our midst, even though for a short time and we trust your visit to this District may be fraught with much that is pleasant and agreeable to yourself.

In conclusion we pray that the King of Kings may hold your Excellency in His Divine Keeping, and humbly subscribe ourselves,

Your Excellency's most dutiful servants,

Chairman

Members of Committee

[Signatures illegible]

Woodburn, 19th June 1900

24

Visit to Lismore[14]

19 June 1900

We the Magistrates of Lismore desire to welcome your Excellency to this District, and to express to you as the representative of the Her Majesty the Queen, our loyalty to the British Throne and our regard for the noble Lady who has so gloriously occupied it for the unexampled period of sixty-two years.

We realise the responsibility, and appreciate the privilege of administering, in a humble way, those British laws, many of which have been enacted during Her Majesty's

---

13   Source: *Beauchamp, W. Lygon, 7th Earl – Addresses, NSW, presented, 1899–1900.* Manuscripts in the Mitchell Library, State Library of New South Wales, Sydney, Call No. ML D233.

14   *Ibid.*

reign, and which have done so much to guarantee imperial justice to all classes of the community, and to protect not only British subjects, but those of every nationality who place themselves under the protection of Her Majesty's laws.

We rejoice to think that those beneficent laws will be extended without distinction of persons to Her Majesty's recently acquired Possessions in South Africa,[15] and we feel assured that British law, which has secured for us such substantial benefits in this Colony, will be recognised throughout South Africa as a blessing to all classes, and the best guarantee for the advancement and prosperity of that portion of Her Majesty's Empire.

We trust that your Excellency's tour through the Northern Rivers District will be both pleasant and profitable.

With the highest esteem, we have the honour to be,

Your Excellency's

Most obedient servants,

[Signature illegible]

And the Bench of Magistrates

25

A visit to Coraki

19 June 1900[16]

We, the Mayor and Aldermen of the Municipality of Coraki, on behalf of the residents of the town and surrounding District, deeply appreciate the honour of your presence among us to-day, and have much pleasure in tendering to your Excellency, as the distinguished representative of Her Most Gracious Majesty the Queen, a very cordial and hearty welcome on the occasion of this first visit to the Richmond River.

---

15   The reference is to developments in 'the South African War' or Second Boer War (1899–1902). In 1900, troops fighting for Britain had relieved the sieges of Ladysmith, Mafeking and Kimberley, and had then moved into the Transvaal, taking Pretoria in the month when this letter was written.

16   Source: Beauchamp, W. Lygon, 7th Earl – Addresses, NSW, presented, 1899–1900. Manuscripts in the Mitchell Library, State Library of New South Wales, Sydney, Call No. ML D233.

We much regret that owing to your present visit being a rather hurried one, you find it impossible to prolong your stay with us, as it deprives us of the opportunity of expressing in a fuller manner our appreciation of your Excellency's efforts towards advancing the interests of the Colony over which you preside: but can assure you that we fully recognise the value of a visit however short, from Her Majesty's representative.

We trust that your tour through the district may be a most enjoyable one, and that on some future occasion, we, in this particular and important centre, may enjoy the pleasure of a second and more prolonged stay.

Assuring your Excellency of our affection and loyalty to our Most Gracious Sovereign Lady, Queen Victoria, and thanking you again for this distinguished honour you have conferred upon us by your visit.

We are,

My Lord,

Yours very faithfully,

John McKinnon (Major)

[Signatures illegible]

Aldermen

Coraki, June 19th 1900

26

Countess Feodora Gleichen to Earl Beauchamp[17]

Studio,
St James's Palace, S. W.

July 12th

Dear Lord Beauchamp,

I shall be very glad to make the memorial tablet & will send you some sketches as soon as possible. Lady Ampthill very kindly showed me some photographs of the inside of Madresfield Church & she thought that you wd probably like the idea I had of using some little lapis lazuli columns that I have already got with bronze &

17   Source: *Beauchamp, Lord: Letters received, 1899–1901, op. cit.*

perhaps some mosaic. I understand you do not want any portrait in relief – I do not think the inscription is at all too long.

Lady Ampthill told me that the place for the tablet would most likely be under the west window & she is going to let me know the size of the space as before making a design it is as well to know what proportions would look best. I should imagine this shape [rectangular] wd look better than [perpendicular].

Valda sends kind remembrance & best love to Lady Mary.

Yours very truly,

Feodora Gleichen

27

From the German Consul General[18]

Kaiserlich
Deutsches General-Konsulat für Australien
Sydney,

July 27, 1900

J.N.2032

To the Private Secretary of His Excellency the Governor, Government House, Sydney

Sir,

I had the honour of receiving your communication of the 22nd inst. re. the assault upon the German Club at Broken Hill and I beg to tender to His Excellency the Governor my respectful thanks for the kind consideration he has given to my representations regarding the above affair and for the satisfactory measures that at His Excellency's command have been taken by the Government for the future protection of my countrymen at Broken Hill.

I have the honour to be, Sir,

Your most obedient servant,

Peter F. Kempermann

Consul General of His Majesty the Emperor of Germany

18   *Ibid.*

28

Baron Lamington to Lord Beauchamp[19]

Government House,

Brisbane

23rd July/ 00

Dear Beauchamp,

I have just had your wire re. Governors under the Commonwealth. Both Selborne &, I think, Sir B. Herbert spoke in accordance with my reply to you.

With reference to your cable to the S. of S. which you wired to me on the 18th inst., do you mean that you would accept a lower salary under the Commonwealth so long as you remained. I hope not; rather you should ask for an increase for consenting to remain, or as Ld Gormanston suggested, sue them for breach of contract. Seriously I regard it as a great favour for any of us to remain a day longer after the proclamation & it would be invidious were any of us to accept a lower salary than what we were entitled to. But I don't know your plans as to leaving. Personally whilst favouring Federation for definite purposes I am strong in maintaining the dignities of State Governors & they should assert their position, else men will not come from home to occupy the position. I wrote to Ld Tennyson on the subject, perhaps he would show you the letter.

I wish we could have had a meeting.

Yours sincerely,

Lamington

29

Sir John See[20] *to Captain Wilfrid Abel Smith*[21]

Chief Secretary

Sydney, 9th August 1900

Captain Wilfrid Abel Smith, Private Secretary to His Excellency the Governor

19   *Ibid.*
20   Sir John See (1845–1907), politician, state Colonial Secretary, New South Wales, 1899.
21   Source: *Beauchamp, Lord: Letters received, 1899–1901, op. cit.*

Dear Captain Smith,

I have just received your note regarding the Government *Gazette* Extraordinary of the 1st August, and desire to say that this course of action has been pursued for the last 50 years, without, as I am informed, ever consulting the Governor.

This is a mere matter of official form, and is used in the same way as 'His Excellency the Governor has been pleased to appoint Mr ...', and 'His Excellency directs it to be notified that Mr ... has been appointed'.

I am quite sure the Governor's authority has never been asked for the use of these words since I have been a Minister, which has been for many years.

However I will speak to you on the subject when next you come to town.

Yours very truly,

John See

30

Marquess of Linlithgow to Earl Beauchamp[22]

August 28, 1900

My dear Lord Beauchamp,

How good of you to write me such a kind letter of congratulation. I appreciate it very much.

Things have now shaped themselves so that I am to go to Sydney (on arrival). Your people in N. S. W., seem awfully afraid lest I should be caught by some other colony on the way. I fear from what Ampthill tells me that my coming has hurried you a little in your plans for leaving Australia. Believe me, I have been no party in any such discourteous proceeding, at least no willing party. I should have been so glad to have arrived in Sydney as your guest.

Yours sincerely,

Hopetoun[23]

22   *Ibid.*
23   Earl Hopetoun, later Marquess of Linlithgow (1860–1908), appointed first Governor-General of the Commonwealth of Australia.

31

Lionel Hallam Tennyson, 3rd Baron thanks for a stamp from Earl Beauchamp he has added to his collection[24]

Government House,
Adelaide

August 26th, 1900

Dear Lord Beauchamp,

I am so very sorry that I have not written to you before to thank you very much for the very nice stamp for our collection. It was so kind of you to think of it for us.

Mamie has asked me to thank Lady Susan Gilmour very much for her nice letter. We are all so sorry that she cannot come & stay here. Please give our love to Mary. Mamie hopes to see them on their way through Adelaide to the ship.

Your affectionate little friend,

Lionel Tennyson

Please give my love to everybody.

32

George Dibbs[25] *to Lord Beauchamp*[26]

Passy,
Hunter's Hill

[No date]

Dear Lord Beauchamp,

Many thanks for your good wishes of the 12th inst., and for the handsome present, which I shall retain in remembrance of you, when you are away from the Colony.

I am sorry that you are going [illegible].

With many thanks for your kindness to me at all times,

---

24   Source: *Beauchamp, Lord: Letters received, 1899–1901, op. cit.*
25   Sir George Dibbs (1834–1904), Australian politician.
26   Source: *Beauchamp, Lord: Letters received, 1899–1901, op. cit.*

I am dear Lord Beauchamp,

Yours very sincerely,

George R. Dibbs

33

William Lyne's reply to a condolence letter

Premier's Office[27]
Sydney, N.S.W.

Sept. 17/00

My dear Lord Beauchamp,

Thank you for your kind letter of sympathy upon my Father's death. In the condition I left him I could not wish it otherwise, though the severance of a lifelong affection is under any circumstances a [illegible] which must & does produce considerable depression.

Yours very sincerely,

William John Lyne

34

Visit to Goulburn[28]

21 September 1900

Your Excellency,

The teachers and scholars of the Public Schools in Goulburn, under the Department of Public Instruction, wish to express their gratification at your visit here, as the representative of Her Majesty the Queen.

They also desire to testify to their appreciation of the fact that during your sojourn in this land your influence and patronage have always been freely given towards the

---

27   *Ibid.*
28   Source: *Beauchamp, W. Lygon, 7th Earl – Addresses, NSW, presented, 1899–1900.* Manuscripts in the Mitchell Library, State Library of New South Wales, Sydney, Call No. ML D 233.

advancement of learning, and that your thought and endeavour have ever been for art, education, and refinement.

Whilst regretting your early departure from the colony, they would wish for you all success and happiness throughout life.

Signed on their behalf

[Signatures illegible]

35

William Lyne to Lord Beauchamp[29]

Premier's Office,
Sydney

12/10/00

Dear Lord Beauchamp,

I enclose a letter from Mr [illegible], and also other papers in reference to the Legislative Council. He will forward to me in a day or two a copy of the Lunacy Order respecting Mr White who is in the asylum; which I will submit to you on next Wednesday. I am going away tonight but will see you immediately upon my return.

Yours sincerely,

William John Lyne

Earl Beauchamp was still present in Sydney, but his mind was already roaming over the hills around Malvern. He desired to go home as early as possible.

---

29   Source: *Beauchamp, Lord: Letters received, 1899–1901, op. cit.*

CHAPTER 7

Resignation from the Governorship

On 17 September 1899 Queen Victoria announced that the people of Australia would be united in what was to be known as the Commonwealth of Australia. This new nation was to consist of six states: New South Wales, Queensland, South Australia, Tasmania, Victoria, Western Australia, and ten Australian territories outside the borders of the states. The Commonwealth would have a federal parliament, consisting of two houses, a senate and a house of representatives. The senate would be composed of equal numbers of senators from each of the states, and the house of representatives would be elected by popular vote in equal electorates.[1] There would be a federal Prime Minister, and a Governor-General, appointed by the Crown. Each state would have its own parliament, a Premier and a Governor appointed by the Crown. The Governor-General and the state Governors were required by conventions to act on the advice of the federal Prime Minister and the state Premier respectively. The Commonwealth of Australia was formally proclaimed on 1 January 1901. A new nation was thus born, with its own constitution.[2]

---

[1] See R. A. Gollan, *op. cit.*, p. 184.

[2] The Duke and Duchess of York (the future King George V) landed at Melbourne on 6 May (1901), and the next day opened the federal parliament of Australia. At the opening of the proceedings the Duke read a telegram from his father, Edward VII: 'My thoughts are with you on the day of the important ceremony. Most fervently do I wish Australia prosperity and great happiness.' Quoted in Sidney Lee, *King Edward VII: A Biography* (London: Macmillan, 1927), p. 18.

William Lyne favoured the idea that Beauchamp should continue as state Governor of New South Wales under the new constitution of 1901, and put an enquiry out to Henry Copeland,[3] the Australian Agent-General.

Telegram from the Hon. Sir William Lyne, K. C. M. G. to the Agent-General for New South Wales, London[4]

Sydney, March 24, 1901

Confidential

Interview Secretary of State for the Colonies. Ascertain whether it is likely that Lord Beauchamp will be offered position State Governor New South Wales. At my retirement he was becoming very popular. I am of opinion that appointment would be satisfactory to large majority people New South Wales.

Lyne

But Earl Beauchamp was no longer interested in remaining in New South Wales. If he had wished to remain, there is little doubt that he would have been nominated for the post by Edward VII.[5] But Beauchamp desired to enter into active politics back home in Britain. He therefore asked to be relieved from his governorship. The correspondence surrounding his resignation is reproduced below.[6]

1

Colonial Office

7 June 1901

Dear Beauchamp,

3   Henry Copeland (1839–1904); after an adventurous life as merchant seaman and miner, politician sympathetic to the working classes; Agent-General for New South Wales, 1900–4.

4   Source: *Beauchamp, Lord: Letters received, 1899–1901, op. cit.*

5   As Prince of Wales, the Duke knew Beauchamp rather well. Entry in the diary: 'Monday, April 2, 1894: York House London. Arrival at Pershare at 4:30 – tea party included Ld. Beauchamp.' Source: Royal Archives: GV/PRIV/GVD1894: 2 Apr.

6   Source: *Beauchamp, Lord: Letters received, 1899–1901, op. cit.*

I believe it is usual for governors on giving up their appt. to send in a formal resignation. If however you will send it to me privately that will do quite as well.

Yours sincerely,

Monk Bretton[7]

2

Downing Street,

29 June 1901

The Earl Beauchamp, K. C. M. G.

My Lord,

I am directed by Mr Secretary Chamberlain to acknowledge the receipt of your letter on the 9th instant, and to inform you that His Majesty has been graciously pleased to accept your resignation of your appointment as Governor of New South Wales.

I am to add an expression of Mr Chamberlain's high appreciation of the ability with which you have discharged your responsible duties as Governor.

A copy of the correspondence will be sent to the Officer Administrating the Government of New South Wales for the information of his Ministers.

I am,

My Lord,

Your Lordship's obedient Servant,

H. Bertram Cot

3

From the Hon. John See, Premier & Chief Secretary of New South Wales to Agent-General, London

Telegram

Sydney, 14th October 1901

Last week the Assembly passed a Bill authorising payment to the Governor of New South Wales of salary of Five thousand pounds per annum. Private Secretary to

7   Monk Bretton, 2nd Baron, b. 1869. A Liberal Unionist.

Governor, Three hundred and fifty pounds. Aide-de-Camp, Three hundred and fifty pounds. These are statutory obligations. The Government have leased 'Cranbrook', the residence of the late Honourable James White, containing about forty rooms altogether, and eighteen acres of ground, at Rose Bay, admirably situated and suited for a Governor's Residence. The grounds will be maintained at the Public expense. The house will be available and furnished by 1st January.

In view of the magnanimous conduct displayed by Lord Beauchamp, who vacated Government House, Sydney, to enable Lord Hopetoun to occupy same, which necessitated his retirement from State Governorship, I should be glad to know if the Secretary of State for the Colonies can see his way clear to offer the position of State Governor to Lord Beauchamp.

The Bill has not yet passed the Council, but I apprehend no difficulty whatever from that branch of the Legislature.

John See

Premier and Chief Secretary

Sydney

4

Telegram

Sydney, 15th October

Referring to my telegram of yesterday, re. Governor's Residence. Permanent official offices have been provided in Chief Secretary's Buildings, consisting of six rooms, for the Governor of New South Wales, where all business relating to public duties is transacted, also for callers to insert names in Visitors Book.

The number of rooms mentioned re. 'Cranbrook' includes Servants rooms.

Premier and Chief Secretary

5

Lord Monk Bretton to Lord Beauchamp

Colonial Office

19 October 1901

Private

Dear Beauchamp,

Mr Chamberlain desires me to send you the enclosed copies of telegrams which Mr Copeland has communicated to him.

He understood from you that you would not return to New South Wales but in view of this message he wishes to know whether you would be inclined to change your mind.

Mr Chamberlain considers that the alteration made in the position of governor of New South Wales by Federation should prevent him from pressing you to accept an office which has become of less importance than when you filled it.

Yours very truly,

Monk Bretton

[Hand written note by Beauchamp: 'It does not appear to me from yr letter or the cables that there is any reason why I should go out again. If there were any difficulty in filling the post I might think of it.']

6

Henry Copeland to Lord Beauchamp

Westminster Chambers,
9, Victoria Street,
Westminster, S. W.

23.10.01

Confidential

My dear Lord Beauchamp,

Since receiving the recent cables from Mr See having reference to your being offered the State Governorship of N. S. W. I have not seen Mr Chamberlain owing to his being out of town nor have I had any reply from him to my letter on this subject. As that personally I cannot form any opinion as to whether he is really desirous of your accepting the position or otherwise. As far however as my government are concerned I have no doubt whatever of their sincerity.

I don't know whether it has come to your knowledge that as far back as 24th March last I received a cable from Mr Lyne on the same subject; copy of which I enclose along with Mr See's cables; all of which satisfy me that whatever the views of the C. O. may be, our government are really anxious that you should be offered and accept the position.

You will notice moreover that both Sir W. Lyne and Mr See adopted the somewhat unusual course of communicating directly and confidentially through me instead of availing themselves of the usual channel of communication on such subjects through the acting governor to the Secretary of State which further convinces me of their earnest desire to succeed in obtaining your appointment.

Would you like me to see Mr Chamberlain? He will not be in Town for another week but it would be no trouble for me to run up to Birmingham and see him there; which I shall be very glad to do if you think I can be of any service in the matter.

Yours very respectfully,

Henry Copeland

7

Lord Monk Bretton to Lord Beauchamp

Colonial Office

29 October 1901

Dear Beauchamp,

I have shown your letter about the Governorship of New South Wales to Mr Chamberlain.

He must reply at once to Mr Copeland and presumes you do not wish to return to Australia on the terms offered.

Please let me know that he is right in this presumption.

Yours sincerely,

Monk Bretton

True to his conscience, Earl Beauchamp acted correctly in communicating to the Colonial Office that he was not interested in returning to New South Wales as State Governor – although it flattered him to know that he was being highly recommended by the new state Premier.

It is not possible to establish exactly when Beauchamp left Sydney, but it appears likely that he departed for England at the end of October or at the beginning of November 1901.

CHAPTER 8

Marriage

Earl Beauchamp was quite happy to return to Madresfield Court, where he could relax and enjoy the beauty of the place. He recorded his feelings in a scrapbook: 'Be it ever so humble, there's no place like home.'[1] When 'his carriage approached Madresfield, the tenants unfastened the six matching black horses and themselves hauled the vehicle up to the front of the great house, where they presented him with a silver casket containing their welcome address in manuscript on vellum'.[2]

Before Beauchamp could settle down, there were a few things connected with New South Wales that he felt obliged to attend to. One such matter was the granting of honours to Australians to celebrate the royal tour of Australia. The King was to open the first federal parliament of the Commonwealth of Australia. Perhaps the Colonial Office had not paid due regard to the number of honours being granted, and it was in this respect that a prominent member of the New South Wales legislative assembly, E. W. O'Sullivan, approached Beauchamp, asking if he would help correct the imbalance. The Earl duly responded:

Lord Beauchamp to the Hon. E. W. O'Sullivan[3]

Madresfield Court,
Malvern Link

26 XII 01

My dear Mr O'Sullivan,

---

1   Quoted by Jane Mulvagh, *op. cit.*, p. 307.
2   *Ibid.*
3   Source: *Papers relating to W. L. Beauchamp, 7th Earl, 1901–1931.* Manuscripts in the Mitchell Library, State Library of New South Wales, Sydney, Call No. Ab 150/3.

I will communicate the substance of yr letter to the Colonial Office tho' it will have little effect as compared with a recommendation made by the Governor-General. The office surprised me a good deal by granting such few honours to celebrate the Royal Tour. Indeed I was very sorry not to see more names upon the list.

Lady Mary is here now, & I heard from her with pleasure of the kindness with wh her old friends greeted her in Sydney.

At present so far as I can gather the Colonial Office do not know whom to appoint as governor of New South Wales. The position is not one of great dignity & men who have the necessary money prefer more important work. For my own part, I should be glad if it became possible for literary men to take the office. The duties do not take much time – sport cannot absorb one's whole attention & other interests are necessary. Many suitable men cannot accept the post for want of money. Altogether the question seems a difficult one.

What progress do you make with the Bridge over the Harbour? Had it not been for the Commonwealth Act, North Sydney seemed to me a very desirable place for the Federal Capital. However, that is impossible & I hope soon to see some town has been selected. The wages in the bricklaying trade will go up while they build the new City.

Pray remember me to Mrs O'Sullivan & to your daughter &

Believe me,

Yours sincerely,

Beauchamp

The immediate concern, however, was the future succession of the Lygon family tree: it was time for Beauchamp to marry. In fact, Lady Mary had been earnestly desiring it, and she took it upon herself to find a suitable match. As Lady-in-Waiting she had good connections, and she found a well fitted bride for her brother. The choice fell on Lady Lettice Grosvenor, born in 1876, the second daughter of Victor Earl Grosvenor,[4] son and heir

---

4   Victor Alexander, Earl Grosvenor (1853–84), Queen Victoria's godson, married the beautiful Lady Sibell Lumley, the Earl of Scarbrough's youngest daughter. Victor Alexander died very young because of epileptic seizures. His wife remarried the Rt Hon. George Wyndham.

of the 1st Duke of Westminster.[5] Lady Lettice was very beautiful, and well
mannered, but Lady Mary's choice was not determined by this alone. The
Grosvenors were perhaps the richest family in England: they owned land
in Scotland and in London's Mayfair and Belgravia, as well as thousands of
acres in Cheshire. There were also the Grosvenor racing stables. The family's
horses had won at the Derby three times and at the Oaks five times. It was
thus self-evident that the future Countess Beauchamp would bring with
her not only her natural talents but a rich dowry to Madresfield Court.
Earl Beauchamp was pleased to have found an appropriate life partner in
Lady Lettice. He even fell in love with her, and proposed. The proposal
was immediately accepted.

That William ('Willie') Beauchamp adored his fiancée we learn from
the letters Lady Mary wrote to her sister, Margaret Lady Ampthill. One
written from Frogmore on 23 May 1902 recounts that:[6] 'Willie is radiantly
and blissfully happy – and heavily in love ... They talk of July 17 to 30 for
the wedding and at Eton [sic, meaning Eaton, Cheshire],[7] but doubtless
we shall know more next week.' Lady Mary mentions how she is attending
the Queen in her illness and how she will go to Madresfield to entertain
Lettice:[8]

> This is rather a delightful house and a delicious garden, but it has been too cold and
> showery to enjoy it properly. Her R. H. has been in bed with a bad cold, and I have
> spent a good few hours of each day reading aloud to her. The house is comfortable
> but furnished with really hideous things, & vile pictures but somehow they all seem
> to suit the place; I feel as if I were living in 1840; and the result is rather soothing.
> We go back to London tomorrow – for a busy week of functions, and then I go out
> of waiting on Saturday; and fly down to Madresfield, to entertain Lettice.

5   Hugh Lupus (1825–99), 3rd Marquess of Westminster, created 1st Duke of
     Westminster, 1874.
6   Source: Royal Archives: VIC/ADD/U/27/99–101, 162. A copy of the typescript
     of Lady Mary's letters is located in the Royal Archives, Windsor. Every attempt was
     made by the present author to trace the copyright holder, but with no success.
7   Eaton Hall (Cheshire) was the ancestral home of the Grosvenors.
8   Source: Royal Archives: VIC/ADD/U/27/99–101, 162.

In another letter Lady Mary writes of 'Willie' 'heaping jewels' upon his fiancée.[9]

York House. May 30th 1902

I don't think there is much to tell you about *the* topic as we naturally hardly see Willie. Susan and I dined at 35 Park Lane on Tuesday: and Willie and Lettice stroked hands *on* the table the whole time. They had been down that afternoon to Fulham; and Lettice said that the Bishop had taken them into Chapel and given them a '*sweet* blessing!!' ... Willie is heaping jewels upon her: and on Tuesday gave her a delightful old set of amethysts and diamonds. I am having almost as many letters of congratulations as if I were engaged myself. I am very glad you liked the chiffons. ...

We have a weird and mixed party coming to us at Madresfield tomorrow. Lettice and the Shaftesburys, Janet Lady Clarke and Miss Clarke (of Melbourne), Lady Windsor (the Yeomanry are camping in the Penn Meadow), the Cators, Lord Westbury (who enquires tenderly after you whenever I see him), Mr Robin Lindsay, Mr Robin Clarke and Ian Smith (our Sydney Chaplain) ...

Again, at the beginning of June, Lady Mary writes:[10]

13 Belgrave Square. June 6th, 1902

How glorious it is to have peace at last – tho' it makes one very sad too, to think that there is *one* who will never come back – and that selfishly, half one's joy in it is gone. Susie writes that she can hardly realize it yet.

The Madresfield party went off well: I think I gave you the list in my last letter. It is delightful to see Willie so happy. He and Lettice walked about before the house party and all the Yeomanry with their arms round each other's waists! Imagine our William! I think Lettice more delightful every time I see her[11] – I am just off to

---

9   *Ibid.*
10   *Ibid.*
11   Lettice seems to have won the affection of other family friends. Wilfrid Scawen Blunt writes on 25 June 1902: 'Called at Dorchester House to write my name down to Princess Helene, who, with her husband, represents the King of Italy at the Coronation, and at 35 Park Lane to give Lettice her wedding gift and the Sonnet I have written her. I found her with Lord Beauchamp, her fiancé, a good looking, smooth-faced young man, who complained much of the deception that had been practised on the public in regard to the King's illness.' See Wilfried Scawen Blunt, *My Diaries, Being a Personal Narrative of Events, 1888–1914*, Part Two, 1900 to 1914

Madresfield this afternoon to enjoy a happy evening alone with the nightingales. Tomorrow we have a huge party coming. Lady Grosvenor and Lettice – Colonel and Mrs Lloyd (friends of theirs), the Arthur Pakenhams, Lady and Miss Dudley, Lord and Lady Cobham, Mr Corkran, Captain Wemyss, Sir Charles Cust and the Bishop of Worcester. As Willie is blissfully indifferent to his guests' presence – I have my hands full as you may imagine. *Such* wet weather – it rains almost every day: but I hope it will be over before the Coronation. Agnes and Maud are going out hard: and next week I am to chaperone them to Esther Smith's Cotillon and the Duchess of Newcastle's ball – a great promotion!

Beauchamp and Lettice were married on 26 July 1902.[12] The official document recorded:

(London: Martin Secker, 1919), p. 29. W. S. Blunt (1840–1922), a poet, known for his sympathies for oppressed nations; established a famous stud for the breeding of Arab horses; wrote *The Future of Islam* (1882); *Ideas about India* (1885). Sir Almeric Fitzroy, appointed Clerk of the Privy Council in 1898, was equally fascinated by the new Countess Beauchamp: 'We dined with the Beauchamps,' he writes, 'in Bryanston Square, in a house belonging to the Shaftesburys which was once the Portman family mansion. I was curious to see Lady Beauchamp, and received a favourable impression. She has an attractive manner and pretty gestures, with an evident desire to please that is very winning ...' See Almeric Fitzroy, *Memoirs*, vol. I (London: Hutchinson, 1925), entry for 16 February 1904. Even almost two decades later, Lady Lettice had not lost her charm. Fitzroy was to notice it again on 22 March 1920: 'We dined with the Beauchamps ... I found myself next to my hostess at dinner: a position I enjoyed, as I had not seen her for a long time, and her transparent beauty of character is always captivating.' See Fitzroy, *Memoirs*, *op. cit.*, vol. II, p. 726. On an earlier occasion (2 July 1914) Fitzroy writes: 'I saw Glyn Philpot's picture of Lady Beauchamp this morning. A work of marvellous technique and profound characterisation. It is not perhaps as everyone sees her, but the image that the artist's genius stamps on personality is there. It conveys no truer touch than in the way she clasps to her side the eldest girl, a charming little figure. The whole conception and treatment show how the highest interpretation is reached by the man who can put the infinite between his object and his model.' *Ibid.*, vol. II, p. 554. I am grateful to Richard Davenport-Hines for drawing my attention to these authors.

12   Viscount Mersey remembers: 'I went for a few days to Eaton in Cheshire for Beauchamp's wedding to Lettice Grosvenor. The bridesmaid's dress did not arrive until an hour before the ceremony, and the Bishop of Worcester wore a mitre, the first I had ever seen in a Protestant Church. After an immense luncheon party we went

Certified Copy of an Entry of Marriage[13]
(6 & 7 Wm. IV., cap. 86)
Given at the General Register Office, Somerset House, London

Application Number: 8387
Registration District: Chester

1902. Marriage solemnized at the Parish Church in the Parish of Eccleston in the County of Chester.

No. 125

When Married: 26 July 1902

Name and Surname: William Lygon Earl Beauchamp
Age: 30
Condition: Bachelor
Rank or Profession: Earl
Residence at the time of Marriage: Madresfield
Father's Name and Surname: Frederick Lygon
Rank or Profession of Father: Earl

Name and Surname: Lettice Mary Elizabeth Grosvenor
Age: 25
Condition: Spinster
Rank or Profession: –
Residence at the time of Marriage: Eaton Chester
Father's Name and Surname: Victor Alexander Grosvenor
Rank or Profession of Father: Earl

Married in the Parish Church according to the Rites and Ceremonies of the Established Church.

This Marriage was solemnized between us: Beauchamp, Lettice Grosvenor in the Presence of Westminster, K. Westminster, Sibell Mary Grosvenor.

Certified to be a true Copy of an Entry in the Certified Copy of a Register of Marriages in the District above mentioned.

---

round the glasshouses, one of them a quarter of a mile long.' See Viscount Mersey, *A Picture of Life, 1872–1940* (London: John Murray, 1941), p. 201.

13   Source: The National Archives (Kew) Ref.: J77/2899/9727.

The young couple began a life of luxury and self-indulgence. The enormous sum of money that Lady Lettice brought as a wedding dowry must have remained a family secret. But the guests and the estate tenants invited to the wedding could admire canteens of cutlery, silver candelabra, and jewels.[14] Over twenty servants were employed at Madresfield. The Beauchamps entertained lavishly and very often. In July 1904 alone, the butler's register recorded 2,366 guests. These included members of the royal family, cabinet ministers, close relatives, and members of the various aristocratic families whom Beauchamp knew.[15] The cook was trained to serve French delicacies. The local farms supplied fresh vegetables, game and fowl. At Madresfield there were sixty well furnished and richly decorated bedrooms to accommodate guests over the weekend.

Busy in the royal household, Lady Mary kept in touch with her brother, writing to him from time to time. For instance:[16]

I

June 23, 1906

... Lettice will be interested to hear that I am going to dine on shore to-night with Ld Chesham and his daughter Mrs Buller and Lady Constance Butler, the 2 latter are staying near here.

14   My source of information here is the invaluable book by Jane Mulvagh, *Madresfield*, *op. cit.* See especially the fascinating chapter, 'The Scrap of Paper', pp. 332–66.

15   Viscount Mersey is more specific: 'Afterwards I stayed for a few days with my friend Beauchamp at Madresfield. Lady Grosvenor, Lady Jersey, Lady Cobham and Lady Halifax, each with a daughter, Lord de Mauley, Alec Hood, Granville Somerset, Raymond Green, Victor Corkran, etc., forty guests in all. Everything was done in great style: minstrels in the gallery at dinner, numbers of footmen in powder and breeches and a groom of the chambers worthy of Disraeli's novels. Just before dinner, prayers were held in the private chapel, a very short service which we attended in evening clothes, a sort of *For what we are about to receive* ...' See Viscount Mersey, *A Picture of Life, op. cit.*, p. 190.

16   Souce: Royal Archives: GV/ADD/COPY/2/3/67,69,76,79.

2

York Cottage,
Sandringham

Dec. 6, 1906

Yesterday I made Lord Acton's acquaintance; and he told me he had been at Oxford with you. I sat next to the King at the shooting luncheon yesterday and he told me how particularly he liked all his new Lords-in-waiting and how fortunate he considered himself to have been in having them appointed to his household. He seems specially pleased to have 2 diplomats who are excellent linguists.

Both the Earl and his Countess tended their own eccentricities. He redecorated the court in neo-Gothic and Pre-Raphaelite style, collected books of art and literature, and prepared his House of Lords speeches. She read the *Book of Common Prayer* after breakfast, retreated to the Long Gallery to arrange the lists of guests to be invited, inspected the bedrooms and took her strolls about the garden.

The marriage was perfectly consummated. Lady Lettice gave birth to seven children, three boys and four girls. The firstborn was a boy, William, born in 1903; then there was another boy, Hugh Patrick, born in 1904. Next, came the four girls: Lettice in 1906, Sibell in 1907, Mary in 1910 and Dorothy in 1912. The last child was a boy again: Richard, who was born in 1916. Earl Beauchamp was devoted to his children. He regularly read them children's stories by various popular authors, among them Rudyard Kipling and Walter Scott. When they grew older, the things he read to them included Victorian novels with historical themes. He had them attend the house chapel after breakfast, and then encouraged them to go riding. The Earl was in the habit of collecting everything, even the slightest details of his children's lives, in his scrapbook – their christenings, watercolours they had painted, their coming-of-age photographs, and even court reports of his daughters' comings-out.

The children's mother, on the other hand, seemed entirely to lack any such feelings of devotion to them. Her 'delight in infants waned when they became noisy toddlers'.[17] Lady Lettice found her solace in religion. Her husband's political career interested her only in so far as she could entertain

17   After Jane Mulvagh, *Madresfield, op. cit*, p. 337.

distinguished people at Madresfield. She hardly ever read the books on art and literature that were stocked in abundance in the Madresfield Library: these meant noting to her. As the years passed, she became ever more 'sanctimonious' – which is how her children judged her. This caused her total estrangement from them. The Earl was not left unaffected. It appears that feelings of affection between the Earl and the Countess began to cool after the last child was born. From that time, there was very little conjugal affection between the two. The Earl sought satisfaction in the company of young men, and the Countess in scribbling phrases from the *Book of Common Prayer* into her scrapbook.

Earl Beauchamp's books and the gifts he made

Earl Beauchamp preserved the unbroken ancestral thread of collecting rare books. He was a man of very wide tastes and appreciated aesthetic beauty, and the library at Madresfield stocked volume after volume on such diverse fields as: ancient and modern classics, English embroidery and carving, medieval and Gothic architecture, botany, art history, Pre-Raphaelite painting, monographs on tattooing and Maori art, as well as contemporary topics like industrialism, popular democracy and government, socialism, trade unionism, education and so on.

The Earl also had a passion for making personal gifts to select and distinguished people and institutions.[18] These could be flowers from the Madresfield gardens or rare books from the Roxburghe Club. There was something unique about the books from this club. The Roxburghe Club was set up in 1812 by the bibliophile, Thomas Dibdin, a neighbour of the Lygons.[19] The club took its name from the eighteenth-century book-lover John Ker, third Duke of Roxburghe. Originally the members came entirely

---

18 Jane Mulvagh was privileged to visit the Madresfield Library, and she describes in detail her observations. See Jan Mulvagh, *Madresfield, op. cit.*, pp. 221–32.

19 For a full history see *Ibid.*, pp. 223–8.

from the nobility, and even later, only the very rich could be solicited to join. The membership, limited to forty at any one time, carried with it a specific responsibility: each member was obliged 'to reprint some scarce piece of ancient lore to be given to the members, one copy being on vellum for the Chairman and only as many copies as members'. Earl Beauchamp was invited to become a member of the club in 1898, well before his marriage. Some years later, the Earl published for the club *Songs, Ballads and Instrumental Pieces Composed by King Henry the Eighth*, a copy of which he presented to the Bodleian Library, Oxford.

Some of the following letters reflect the Earl's passions for books and for making gifts.[20] As can be seen, these went on for many years.

1

10 Downing Street, Whitehall

March 7/98

Dear Lord Beauchamp,

How very kind of you to send those lovely flowers which reached me today. Thank you very much indeed for them.

...

Alice Balfour

2

All Souls College, Oxford

15th June 1912

My dear Lord Beauchamp,

Please accept my hearty thanks for the Roxburghe Club book which I have just received. It is a most interesting addition to the Collection.

Believe me,

Yours sincerely,

William R. Anson

20   Source: Beauchamp Papers, *op. cit.*

3

Buckingham Palace

17th July, 1912

My dear Beauchamp,

I have handed to the King the book which you were kind enough to send me. His Majesty was much interested in the fact of its Editress; and was most favourable in his comments on the manner in which the work has been got up.

Yours very truly,

Stamfordham

4

Lambeth Palace

[Date illegible]

My dear Beauchamp,

I thank you for your beautiful gift. The book will be an immensely valuable addition to the Treasures of our Library & I appreciate your kindness very highly.

I am,

Yours very Truly,

Randall Cantuar

5

The Parishioners of Fairford, in Vestry assembled, desire to offer to the Right Honourable the Earl Beauchamp their hearty thanks for the magnificent gift to their Church, and especially for the beautiful and dignified Reredos which harmonizes so wonderfully with its surroundings.

Chairman and Vicar

[signature illegible]

Churchwardens

[signature illegible]

Sidesmen

[Signature illegible]

Fairford, April 5th, 1915

6

Bodleian Library, Oxford

25.6.1920

Dear Lord Beauchamp,

I find that we have not a copy of your *Songs...*, composed by King Henry the Eighth in the Library. We should very much like to have it. If you are so kind as to present it, the numbers missing from our set of Roxburghe club books will be reduced to 12, & we shall be very grateful.

Yours sincerely,

A. Cowley

CHAPTER 9

Captain of the Gentlemen-at-Arms

The Captain of the Honourable Corps of Gentlemen-at-Arms acts as chief whip in the House of Lords. It is a ministerial role. The holder of the post plays an active part at the despatch box, promoting and defending departmental policy. This task involves: 1) answering questions; 2) responding to debates; and 3) pushing through primary and secondary legislation. Earl Beauchamp occupied this post from the middle of December 1905 till the end of July 1907. We must in brief establish the background to this appointment.

In 1902 the British cabinet was in complete disarray. It was divided between the adherents of protectionism and those who stood for free trade. The situation became worse when, on 15 May 1903, Joseph Chamberlain, the Colonial Secretary, delivered a controversial speech defending imperial preference against the free trade policy. The speech caused a serious split within the government. Some prominent members of the cabinet were dismissed (C. T. Richtie, the Chancellor of the Exchequer; and Lord Balfour of Burleigh,[1] the Secretary for Scotland); and others resigned (Joseph Chamberlain himself; the Duke of Devonshire, who was Lord President; and Lord George Hamilton, Secretary for India). To stabilize the government in this crisis and to counter Chamberlain's continued agitation for imperial preference, A. J. Balfour,[2] the Prime Minister, announced a proposal to call a Colonial Conference, at which delegates would be able to air their views freely and openly without any limiting instructions. Lord

---

1   Balfour of Burleigh, 7th Baron, b. 1883. A Conservative.
2   Arthur James Balfour (1848–1930), Conservative M.P., 1874–1922; leader of the Conservative Party in the House of Commons 1891–2, 1895–1902; Prime Minister, 1902–5; leader of the Conservative Party 1906–11; First Lord of the Admiralty, 1915–16; Foreign Secretary, 1916–19; created 1st Earl of Balfour, 1922.

Balfour of Burleigh (not to be confused with the Prime Minister himself) distrusted the intentions behind this proposal. So, on 11 April 1905, he moved a motion in the House of Lords 'that in the opinion of this House it is necessary that before the constituencies of the country are asked to determine upon the desirability of such conference they should be informed (1) under what conditions the conference will be summoned; (2) what Colonies and Dependencies will be invited; and (3) how far any decision arrived at will be held as binding upon His Majesty's Government and the United Kingdom'.[3]

The House debated the motion. The Under-Secretary of State for the Colonies, the Duke of Marlborough,[4] answering for the government, stated that the government would be well advised to consult the colonies on the development of 'our colonial trade' and in what 'precise manner it can be carried out'.[5]

The Foreign Secretary, the Marquess of Lansdowne,[6] defended the government's intentions. He thought that some mutually advantageous arrangement would have 'beneficial effects upon the commerce of the Empire as a whole'.[7]

Earl Beauchamp joined in the debate. He was a staunch believer in free trade, and expressed his doubts on whether the Prime Minister (Balfour) had, at heart, views that differed essentially from what Joseph Chamberlain was arguing. The Duke of Marlborough's answer, Beauchamp asserted, did not 'afford much satisfaction to the free-trade Members of your Lordships' House'.[8] Though the government maintained that it would lay down no conditions, its leaders 'may, like the proverbial ostrich, hide its head in the sand and lay down no conditions themselves, but the conditions under which the conference will take place will be those laid down by Mr Chamberlain

3   See *Parliamentary Debates*, House of Lords, vol. CXLIV, 11 April 1905, col. 1159.
4   Marlborough, 9th Duke of, b. 1871. A Conservative.
5   See *Parliamentary Debates*, House of Lords, vol. CXLIV, 11 April 1905, col. 1172.
6   Lansdowne, 5th Marquess of, b. 1845. A Liberal Unionist.
7   See *Parliamentary Debates*, House of Lords, vol. CXLIV, 11 April 1905, col. 1229.
8   *Ibid.*, col. 1176.

himself.'⁹ Nothing could be 'more unjust', the Lord Chancellor, the Earl of Halsbury,¹⁰ retorted.¹¹ Beauchamp remained unconvinced. Mr Balfour and Mr Chamberlain, he replied, had 'the same ideas with regard to colonial preference'.¹² The Earl of Crewe¹³ said that he agreed with Earl Beauchamp. Mr Chamberlain's views, Crewe believed, were like those of the 'hide-bound political economists who deal with this question in a cold-blooded fashion'.¹⁴ After further debate the motion was, by leave, withdrawn.

The debate in the House did not in any way change the position of the Prime Minister. Further events only weakened it. The Tariff Reform League, initiated and led by Chamberlain, found wide support in the National Union of Conservative Associations. The authority of the Prime Minister continued to be damaged. Balfour now felt terribly hard-pressed.¹⁵ So he offered to resign on 4 December 1905, but did not ask for the dissolution of parliament. The King sent for the Liberal leader, Sir Henry Campbell-Bannerman,¹⁶ asking him to form the new government, which he did on 5 December .

It was the nature of the new Prime Minister to 'move persistently to the left'.¹⁷ He opened the door to the left-wing Liberals and the radical young. His period of government has aptly been characterized as 'Edwardian Liberalism'.¹⁸ Sir Henry's cabinet included such clever men

---

9   *Ibid.*

10 Halsbury, 1st Earl of, b. 1825. A Conservative.

11 See *Parliamentary Debates*, House of Lords, vol. CXLIV, 11 April 1905, col. 1215.

12 *Ibid.*, col. 1177.

13 Marquess of Crewe (1858–1945), Lord President of the Council, 1905–8; Lord Privy Seal, 1908–11; Colonial Secretary, 1908–10; Secretary for India, 1910–15; Lord President of the Council 1915–16; President of the Board of Education, 1916.

14 See *Parliamentary Debates*, House of Lords, vol. CXLIV, 11 April 1905, col. 1197.

15 For details, see Sir Robert Ensor, *England, 1870–1914* (Oxford: Clarendon Press, ed. 1968), pp. 371–81.

16 Sir Henry Campbell-Bannerman (1836–1908), Liberal M.P., 1868–1908; Secretary for War, 1886, 1892–5; Leader of the Liberal Party, 1899–1905; Prime Minister, 1905–8.

17 See Robert Ensor, *England, 1870–1914, op. cit.*, p. 384.

18 Such is the phrase used by Robert Ensor, see *Ibid.*, p. 384.

as: Lord Loreburn[19] (Lord Chancellor); the Earl of Crewe (President);
the Marquess of Ripon[20] (Lord Privy Seal); H. H. Asquith (Chancellor
of the Exchequer); Sir Edward Grey[21] (Foreign Secretary); Herbert J.
Gladstone[22] (Home Secretary); the Earl of Elgin[23] (Colonial Secretary);
John Morley[24] (Secretary for India); John Sinclair (Secretary for Scotland)
and D. Lloyd George[25] (President of the Board of Trade).[26] A place was
found for Beauchamp as well.[27] He had joined the Liberal party in 1902.[28]
A liberal at heart, he welcomed receiving a government post.[29] The Prime

19   Loreburn, 1st Earl, b. 1846. A Liberal.
20   Ripon, 1st Marquess of, b. 1827. A Liberal.
21   Edward Grey (1862–1933), Liberal M.P., 1885–1916; Foreign Secretary, 1905–16;
      created Viscount Grey of Falloden, 1916.
22   Herbert Gladstone (1854–1930), Liberal M.P., 1880–1910, chief whip, 1899–1905;
      Home Secretary, 1905–10; son of William Gladstone, the Prime Minister.
23   Elgin, 9th Earl of, b. 1849. A Liberal.
24   John Morley (1838–1923), Liberal M.P., 1883–95, 1896–1908); Chief Secretary for
      Ireland, 1886, 1892–5; Secretary for India, 1905–10; Lord President of the Council,
      1910–14; created 1st Viscount, 1908.
25   David Lloyd George (1863–1945), Liberal M.P., 1890–1945; President of the Board
      of Trade, 1905–8; Chancellor of the Exchequer, 1908–15; Minister of Munitions,
      1915–16; Secretary for War, 1916; Prime Minister, 1916–22, leader of the Liberal
      Party, 1926–1931.
26   For a complete list of the cabinet members, see: Robert Ensor, *England, 1870–1914*,
      op. cit., pp. 612–13.
27   Sir Almeric Fitzroy made a caustic comment, on 16 February 1904: 'With a view
      to coming changes, Beauchamp avowed that he was already preparing Cabinet lists,
      and had arranged one in which the holder of every office was superior to its present
      occupant. I said somewhat dryly that I should be able to form some opinion of his
      list if I knew what office he had reserved for himself.' See Almeric Fitzroy, *Memoirs*,
      vol. I, (London: Hutchinson, no date), p. 187. Sir Almeric was a clerk with the Privy
      Council.
28   Beauchamp's father, the 6th Earl, had been a thorough Tory, a loyal servant of Disraeli
      for several years.
29   Beauchamp, recorded Sir Almeric Fitzroy, 'seemed pleased with his office, which is
      to go with the representation of the Irish Government in the Upper House, so that
      he will have plenty of work'. See Almeric Fitzroy, *Memoirs*, vol. I, *op. cit.*, diary entry
      for 8 January 1906, p. 278. Beauchamp was also beginning to cultivate contact with
      other influential members of the Liberal Party. See, for instance, his letters to Lord

Minister wrote to Lord Knollys, the King's secretary on 16 December 1905 with the message that:[30]

> I have offered Lord Beauchamp the Captaincy of Gentleman at Arms ... and Lord Herschell a Lordship in Waiting.
>
> H. Campbell-Bannerman

The King gave his approval, and consistent with custom, Beauchamp was made a member of the Privy Council. On 9 January 1906 *The London Gazette* (no. 27873, p. 182) published the following notice:

> At the Court at Buckingham Palace the 8th day of January 1906
>
> Present
> The King's Most Excellent Majesty in Council.
>
> This day the Right Honourable Cecil George Savile, Earl of Liverpool; the Right Honourable Osbert Cecil, Earl of Sefton; the Right Honourable William, Earl Beauchamp, KCMG; Richard Knight Causton, Esquire, M. P.; Thomas Shaw, Esquire, M. P.; Thomas Burt, Esquire, M. P. and Sir Balthazar Walter Foster, M. P. were by His

---

Carrington (1843–1928), President of the Board of Agriculture, 1905–11; Lord Privy Seal, 1911–12; created 1st Marquess of Lincolnshire, 1912: (1) 'Madresfield Court, 31 VII 04. My dear Lord Carrington, Many thanks for yr kind & too flattering letter. It was gt fun for us, but I have tormented myself since with thoughts of what I ought to have said. It seems to me that on amendments – we ought to press on the Govt. the necessity of protecting the tenant from the big brewer. It wd help us greatly in the country as well as being just. I wish I cd accept yr kind invitation to dine tomorrow. But the Bank holiday trains prevent me from reaching London before 8.45 after wh I think of going to the H. of L. if ours is not sitting. Most unfortunately this week is always one in wh my tenants & neighbours expect to see me at home & we have local functions. With renewed thanks, Yrs v. Sincerely, Beauchamp'; (2) 'Madresfield Court 3 XI 05. My dear Lord Carrington, Many thanks. I write to say I was engaged to Fred Horne for Nov. 23, but cd go Nov. 24 if that was any use. I hope a month's rest will put you right. But even for a month we can ill afford to spare you. We are very busy round here. A big campaign against Austen [Chamberlain] & meetings even in West Birmingham, that spot hallowed to his father! Please mention me to Lady Carrington. Yours v. Sincerely, Beauchamp'. Source: Bodleian Library, Carrington (The Marquess of Lincolnshire) Papers, MS Film 1135 (2).

30   Source: Royal Archives: VIC/ADD/C/22.

Majesty's Command, respectively sworn of His Majesty's Most Honourable Privy Council, and took their places at the Board accordingly.

A. W. Fitzroy

It was now obligatory on Campbell-Bannerman to seek the approval of the country. So a general election was held on 12 January 1906. The results were a shock to the Conservatives. The Liberals were the winners by a large margin. They won 377 seats, giving them, in the House of Commons, a comfortable majority of 84 over all other parties combined. Campbell-Bannerman was now in a very strong position to introduce whatever legislation his party desired. The Prime Minister had an efficient cabinet to execute this legislation (the cabinet did not undergo change – it was the same as in December 1905). When the new Parliament met on 13 February 1906 the 'gracious speech' proposed twenty-two bills in the approaching session. With their majority in the Commons, it was now obvious that the government could with ease promote legislation in the lower chamber. The Liberal measures were certainly ambitious, but they were regarded as controversial and radical by the Conservatives. The government therefore expected trouble in the House of Lords, where nine-tenths of the peers were of a Conservative persuasion. Thus, with their permanent majority in the Lords, the Conservatives determined to destroy any bill they disliked. And indeed they proceeded to act in this unbecoming manner when the government introduced three important bills: an Education Bill,[31] a Trade

---

31   The Education Bill was designed to revise the 'vices' of the Act of 1902, which the Liberals rightly thought was strongly denominational. The non-conformists had raised objections, and the Liberals promised the abolition of state religious instruction. Now in power, they were obliged to honour their pledge. The Education Bill would establish public control over all schools maintained out of public money, but facilities were to be given for denominational teaching, though not at the cost of the state. The problem concerning this bill has been extensively described in J.A. Spender, *The Life of Sir Henry Campbell-Bannerman*, vol. II (Boston & New York: Houghton Mifflin Company, 1924), pp. 274–7, 288–313.

Disputes Bill,[32] and a Plural Voting Bill.[33] When these bills came before the Lords, the Conservatives lost no time in displaying how obdurate they could be. The government had an excellent spokesman in the person of the Lord Chancellor, Lord Loreburn. And Earl Beauchamp's performance matched the Conservative opposition with equal impenitence. His speeches were not only elegant and witty, his delivery too was weighed with facts and arguments. Yet the Conservative peers would not budge. They killed the Education and Plural Voting Bills, but let pass the Trade Disputes Bill – though even this was not without hesitation. It is beyond the scope of this book to get involved in the intricacies of these bills; but, in chronological order, we will register Beauchamp's main interventions and contributions to the House of Lords debates during 1906:

Polling Arrangements (Parliamentary Boroughs) Bill

Lord Monkswell introduced a bill on 12 March 1906 to:[34]

> abolish an inconvenient anomaly in the law. By the Local Government Act of 1888, the jurisdiction of the justices in quarter sessions to settle polling districts for counties was thrown on county councils, but at the same time, the jurisdiction of the justices in petty sessions for the same purpose was retained. The effect of that is, that in all the county districts the county council is the authority; but in regard to Parliamentary boroughs the county council is not always the authority. Where a Parliamentary borough is solely within one petty sessional district, the power still

---

32 The Trade Disputes Bill was framed to improve upon the Act of 1871. The bill concentrated on three points: 'the relaxation of the law of conspiracy, the legalisation of peaceful picketing, and the exemption of Trade Union funds'. For more details, see J.A. Spender, *The Life of Sir Henry Campbell-Bannerman*, vol. II, *op. cit.*, pp. 277–80.

33 The Plural Voting Bill aimed at removing the anomaly which 'permitted one voter to record his vote in as many constituencies as he had qualifications', and 'compelled the voter to make his choice between his various qualifications'. For more on this: see *Ibid.*, pp. 280–1.

34 See *Parliamentary Debates*, House of Lords, vol. CLIII, 12 March 1906, cols 852–3.

resides with the justices. The justices do not in the least wish to keep up their jurisdiction, and it is eminently desirable that there should be as few authorities possible to settle this matter. This Bill ... has passed this House on no fewer than four occasions, but it has never made progress in the House of Commons. I believe the reason for that is that they are non-contentious measures. It is extremely difficult to get the House of Commons to take the slightest interest in any measure that is not acutely contentious. In the other House what everybody wants nobody wants. It requires a great deal of driving power to get Bills of this description passed, and I earnestly hope that His Majesty's Government will take them up and endeavour to get them through the House of Commons.

Earl Beauchamp replied: 'My Lords, I have to say, on behalf of the Home Office, that there is no opposition to this Bill.' The bill was read the second time and committed to a Committee of the Whole House.

Administration of the Aliens Act

In a debate[35] on the Aliens Act (1906) on 22 March 1906, Lord Newton criticized the fact that the administration of the act depended 'very largely upon the views of the Home Secretary', and that his actions were founded on the Report of a Royal Commission. He would have liked to see this report, especially because the media were 'consistently' pouring 'contempt on the Act by showing how very few people have been affected by it in the sense of rejected aliens'.

The Earl of Halsbury observed that the matter ought to be treated seriously if an act of parliament 'deliberately passed by the Legislature could be set aside by indirect means at the direction of the Secretary of State'.

Speaking for the government, Earl Beauchamp rejected both charges. He sympathized, he said, with the criticism made of the defects from which the act undoubtedly suffered and he agreed that the act had not 'reached that standard of perfection' which the government expected of it. But the

---

35   See *Parliamentary Debates*, House of Lords, vol. CLIV, 22 March 1906, cols 544–68.

noble Lord, Lord Newton, had been 'misled by the extravagance of the halfpenny Press, of which, I confess, I am not so great a student as he is'. As to the actual administration of the act, Earl Beauchamp desired to point out that it had been necessary that 'certain rules and regulations should be made' before the act could be put into force. The regulations in no way interfered with 'what is considered by many people to be the most important part of the Act, the exclusion of those whom noble Lords on both sides of the House wish to see excluded, the criminal or diseased alien'. But it was never intended that the provisions of the act 'should be applied with a rigidity which excludes consideration as to whether refusal of leave to land would involve great personal hardship or suffering in the case of women or children'. And again, 'having regard to the present disturbed condition of certain parts of the Continent', the Earl trusted that the statements of a man claiming to be a political or religious refugee exposed to risk if he were to return to his country should be considered sympathetically. Although the absence of corroborative evidence frequently made it difficult for the Immigration Board to come to a decision, the act gave the benefit of the doubt, where any doubts existed, in favour of any immigrants who alleged that they were flying from religious or political persecution. Beauchamp asked the noble Lords:

> if they wish that the benefit of the doubt should not be given to those aliens who come here and say they are flying from religious or political persecution, and I should be glad to take the parallel case with regard to the Zoological Gardens. If the noble Duke who is President of the Zoological Society found that a number of children who had never had a chance of ... enjoying a day's liberty, who came from slums, and who the noble Duke knew on their return to their homes without having been admitted to the Zoological Gardens ran the risk of being severely beaten or badly treated – in those circumstance there is no member of your Lordships' House who would not approve of the action of the noble Duke in allowing them to enter the gardens.

Lord Newton was not entirely amused by this analogy, and still insisted on being able to see the Report of the Royal Commission. Earl Beauchamp refused the request, stating that he did not feel that there was any justification in alleging that the government regulations had in any way interfered with the Act of Parliament. The House adjourned.[36]

Police Superannuation Bill

On 10 May 1906, Earl Beauchamp moved what he called a 'small Department Bill' which was 'largely uncontroversial'. It was to 'give pensions to constables who continue to serve after they have qualified for pension'. After a second reading. the bill was committed to a Committee of the Whole House.[37] Here the bill was debated on 17 May. Any amendments suggested were not pressed, on Beauchamp's request. The bill was re-committed to the standing committee.[38]

The unemployed procession in London

On 15 May 1906 Lord Teynham[39] asked His Majesty's Government whether it was 'with the knowledge and approval of the Home Office that a banner inscribed "Work or Riot" was carried through the streets at the head of the

---

36   A further debate took place on the question of Aliens on 17 May 1906. Lord Weardale moved the second reading of his Aliens Bill: that an alien should not be admitted into the United Kingdom if he was 'under contract to take, or has the intention of taking, the place of a workman during a trade dispute'. This was passed by the House of Commons 'unanimously without a single comment or protest'. Earl Beauchamp, replying for the government, said that since there had been no discussion in 'the other place', they did not propose to bring up issues in the House of Lords. After a brief debate, the House divided. Contents 24; Not Contents, 96. See *Parliamentary Debates*, House of Lords, vol. CLVII, 17 May 1906, cols 593–613.

37   See *Parliamentary Debates*, House of Lords, vol. CLVI, 10 May 1906, cols 1418–9.

38   See *Parliamentary Debates*, House of Lords, vol. CLVII, 17 May 1906, cols 587–92.

39   Teynham, 18th Baron, b. 1867. A Liberal Unionist.

unemployed procession on Monday'.[40] He thought that a 'seditious banner carried through the streets with the apparent sanction of the authorities, and which may be read by thousands of people, may be productive of great mischief'. He trusted that 'in the interest of the public safety the Government will see that in future no banners of a seditious or inflammatory character are allowed'.

Earl Beauchamp agreed it was 'true that such a banner as the noble Lord has described was carried in yesterday's procession. Both the procession and the meeting, however, were perfectly orderly, and no necessity for intervention arose. ... I venture to think that the noble Lord's melancholy prognostications as to the future are not likely to come true.'

Metropolitan Police Commission Bill

On 17 May 1906, Earl Russell asked if the government was prepared to extend the scope of reference of the report of the Royal Commission to 'inquire into the duties of the Metropolitan Police in dealing with cases of drunkenness and solicitation in the street and the manner in which those duties are discharged'. There were many people who had taken 'considerable interest for some time in the manner' in which the Metropolitan Police had carried out their duties in cases of injustice and oppression.[41]

Earl Beauchamp replied stating that it was 'very important that the Royal Commission should deal promptly and finally with the special question put before them'. He agreed that there were 'few things more important than that the public should have confidence in our Metropolitan Police force; and if there is any such feeling of discomfort in the mind of the public as has been suggested, it is all the more necessary that the report of the Royal Commission should be made with the least possible delay'. To

40 See *Parliamentary Debates*, House of Lords, vol. CLVII, 15 May 1906, cols 333–4.
41 See *Parliamentary Debates*, House of Lords, vol. CLVII, 17 May 1906, cols 613–8.

this effect, Beauchamp moved a bill in the Lords on 15 June 1906, which proposed to give the Metropolitan Police Commission 'certain powers which they do not possesses at the present time'. These powers authorized the Commission to look into the complaints filed against the Metropolitan Police. The bill was debated on 15 and 19 June, and was passed.[42]

Juvenile smoking

Lord Reay moved a bill, the object of which was: '(1) to prohibit the sale of tobacco and cigarettes to children below a certain age; (2) to prohibit the sale of tobacco and cigarettes in sweet and other shops frequented by children'. Earl Beauchamp responded, saying that the speech of the noble Lord moving the bill 'contained a great deal of very interesting matter' and that he hoped the bill would 'be placed before the Select Committee'. He thought it advisable that such a committee should be 'appointed without delay'. The House sent the bill to a Select Committee.[43]

Marriages Provisional Order Bill

A Marriages Provisional Order Bill was introduced by Earl Beauchamp on 25 May 1906. It provided for the Home Department a number of provisional orders to make fully legal certain marriages about which there might be doubts. The bill was given a second reading.[44]

---

42   *Ibid.*, vol. CLVIII, 15 June 1906, cols 1249–51; vol. CLIX, 19 June 1906, cols 12–13.
43   See *Parliamentary Debates*, House of Lords, vol. CLVII, 22 May 1906, cols 1100–3.
44   See *Parliamentary Debates*, House of Lords, vol. CLVII, 25 May 1906, cols 1516–7.

Justices of the Peace (No. 2) Bill

On 14 June 1906, Earl Beauchamp moved a bill 'which abolishes the qualification by estate for Justices of the Peace'. The Earl argued that the Act of
1744 had by this qualification restricted the appointment of Justices of the
Peace, and in some places it had even been impossible to discover 'gentlemen qualified in this particular way to become justices'. Their Lordships
would agree with him 'that the best qualification for properly carrying out
the duties of a Justice of Peace is a thorough and sound qualification', and
it would be a 'very happy thing' if it were 'possible to draw more widely in
the future upon a large and deserving class of the community who possess
all the qualifications necessary for a good Justice of the Peace'. After a short
debate the bill was committed to a Committee of the Whole House.[45]

Indian Railway Act Amendment Bill

Earl Beauchamp introduced a bill on 21 June 1906 which he said was a
'small Departmental Bill', and on which he did not think there could be 'any
controversy'.[46] The original Railways Act of 1894 enabled the Indian Railway
companies, 'upon certain conditions, to pay interest on their share capital
out of capital during construction. By Section 9 of that Act the duration of
it extended only to December 31st, 1905, or to the end of the next ensuing
session of Parliament and no longer, unless Parliament should otherwise
determine. It appears desirable to make this Act permanent, and the bill
now before your Lordships has been drawn up with that object. I beg to
move that it be read a second time.' The House consented to the request
and the bill was re-committed to the standing committee.

---

45 See *Parliamentary Debates*, House of Lords, vol. CLVIII, 14 June 1906, cols 1078–95.
46 See *Parliamentary Debates*, House of Lords, vol. CLVIX, 21 June 1906, col. 320.

London County Council (General Powers) Bill

At the third reading of the above bill, on 16 July 1906, Lord Monkswell inserted an amendment giving powers to the London County Council to establish an ambulance service.[47] Earl Beauchamp argued against the insertion of this amendment. It was, he said, indeed 'within the powers of this House to take such a step, but it would be a very unusual course to take on an occasion like the present'. The Secretary of State intended to take further steps 'to improve the present condition of the ambulance service, and had therefore summoned a conference of three bodies concerned – the London County Council, The Metropolitan Police, and the Home Office – to consider what should be done in order to effect their improvement. ... It obviously would be unwise for your Lordships to interfere with any such scheme by introducing the clauses which the noble Lord wishes to restore in this Bill'. Their Lordships accepted this point and passed the bill.

The laundry industry

On 27 July 1906, the Earl of Lytton[48] asked His Majesty's government whether they would 'undertake to introduce legislation in the next session of Parliament for the effective regulation of all laundries'.[49] Earl Beauchamp answered that the government was not able to promise that facilities 'will be given to a Bill introduced by a private Member'. For that reason, the question was 'too important to be left for a private Member either of your Lordships' House or of the other House'. The government desired to introduce a bill to amend the Factory Acts in the following session, and when

---

47   See *Parliamentary Debates*, House of Lords, vol. CLX, 16 July 1906, cols 1243–69.
48   Lytton, 2nd Earl of, b. 1876. A Conservative.
49   See *Parliamentary Debates*, House of Lords, vol. CLXII, 27 July 1906, cols 13–20.

that amending bill was introduced, the position of the laundries 'shall be effectively dealt with' – and dealt with 'in a manner which will be satisfactory to all parties'.

Leckhampton Hill riots

On 30 July 1906, Earl Russell asked whether the government was prepared to reconsider the sentences passed at the Gloucestershire Assizes in connection with the rioting that had happened at Leckhampton Hill, after a trustee of the Quarry Company there had seized and enclosed common land for his own grounds and cottage.[50] Earl Russell urged that a speedy decision was desirable as the men had already been twenty-four days in prison. Earl Beauchamp said that the answer to the question was 'in the affirmative'. The matter was 'under consideration and representations with regard to it have been received by the Secretary of State. At the same time the noble Lord will not expect me to give him any hint of the decision to which the Secretary of State is likely to arrive.' However, he hoped he would be able to announce the decision 'before very long'.

Marriage with Foreigners Bill

Earl Beauchamp introduced a Marriage with Foreigners Bill on 31 July 1906. It had two main clauses.[51] The first was 'with regard to the marriage of British subjects with foreigners abroad. Some foreign countries demand that when their subjects marry a foreigner, there should be a certificate

---

50   See *Parliamentary Debates*, House of Lords, vol. CLXII, 30 July 1906, cols 327–8.
51   See *Parliamentary Debates*, House of Lords, vol. CLXII, 31 July 1906, cols 608–9.

from the country to which the foreigner belongs to the effect that there is no impediment to the marriage. In this country we have no machinery by which that certificate can be supplied. This has given rise to considerable inconvenience, and the Home Office have done what they could to enable people to get that certificate in a round-about way. Again, more than one case of hardship has occurred in respect to the marriage of foreigners with British subjects in the United Kingdom. Some foreigners come into this country and marry an English woman, and then perhaps go and live abroad. Probably not even during the lifetime of the husband is anything found out. It is only afterwards that unkind relatives intervene and point out that the marriage is illegal, and the unhappy widow is left without any provision and is deprived of the money to which she has been looking forward.' The bill was given a second reading, and was finally passed by the House on 1 August 1906.

Indian Legislative Council

Lord Ampthill asked on 13 October 1906 whether the Government was in 'a position to make a statement concerning the suggested extension of the representative element and of the limits of discussion in the Legislative Council of the Government of India'.[52] He hoped that their Lordships would agree with him that 'the growing popular interest in Indian affairs is a very striking and significant feature of the present day'. Earl Beauchamp said in reply that he could not make any such statement, because those proposals had to be 'considered by the Governor-General in Council and by the Secretary of State in Council before any statement can be made'.

---

52   See *Parliamentary Debates*, House of Lords, vol. CLXIII, 23 October 1906, cols 29–30.

Plural Voting Bill

On 10 December 1906, Earl Beauchamp moved a second reading of a bill for the abolition of plural voting.[53] The bill, he said, had passed the House of Commons by 'very large majorities'. It was not a bill in which the Lords really had 'a direct interest, because none of your Lordships are or ever possibly can become plural voters; nor does it in any way concern the constitution of your Lordships' House'. The bill itself was 'a perfectly simple one', laying 'down that no voter should vote in the course of twelve months in more than one constituency. The idea of imposing that disqualification is that it is, in the opinion of the Government, very desirable that the voter should make up his mind beforehand, so that in the event of a general election following after a bye-election it should not be possible for a large number of persons to transfer their votes without giving due notice. The penalty imposed is that to which anyone is liable who has been guilty of personation, but instead of imprisonment, which is at present the punishment for personation, power is given to impose a fine not exceeding £500.'

There were, Earl Beauchamp observed, a number of anomalies in the British electoral system. This bill did not propose to 'abolish or to add any franchise'. It was, he said, 'in the direction rather of the removal of these anomalies'.

> Nothing could be more illogical than the present system, for it is not purely a property qualification. It happens to depend upon whether an individual has all his property within a ring fence, or not. If he has all his property in one constituency, he has only a single vote; but if he has the misfortune to have his property scattered all over the place in different parts of the country, then it is that he has a number of votes. It so happens that very often those people who have many votes have less property than those who have only one vote.

This was clearly an anomaly. The government was offering their Lordships a bill 'which does introduce one single reform'. 'The proverb is that half a

---

53 See *Parliamentary Debates*, House of Lords, vol. CLXVI, 10 December 1906, cols 1487–519.

loaf is better than no bread.' But those who opposed the bill thought differently. They 'will have four loaves or none at all': that was their passion. He would, he said, like:

> to congratulate the noble Lords opposite upon this sudden passion for reform, were it not that I feel that it is not a passion which is likely to live very long, but that as soon as it has served its purpose and the debate is finished we shall hear no more about it, and the question will return to that condition of neglect in which it was left for so many years by the noble Lords opposite.

The Lords opposite ignored the warning. They displayed their 'passion' by destroying the bill. At division, the votes were: Contents 43; Not-Contents, 143.

And yet all was not lost. Earl Beauchamp had shown how skilled and energetic a speaker he was. Along with other speakers of the Liberal party he had truly impressed one very prominent observer of Parliamentary life at the time, Margot Asquith, wife of the Liberal Prime Minister, Herbert Henry Asquith. She later jotted down in her diary: 'Things started well for us in Parliament, and Henry's Colleagues were a perpetual study. Their moral and intellectual stature, as well as their appearances, manners and habits became extremely familiar to me.'[54]

A new appointment

In 1907 Campbell-Bannerman made some minor changes in the cabinet. Earl Beauchamp was appointed Lord Steward. The announcement appeared in *The London Gazette* (Supplement), 30 July/1 August 1907 (No. 28046).

---

54   See *The Autobiography of Margot Asquith*, vol. II (London: Thornton Butterworth Ltd., 1922), p. 108.

Board of Green Cloth, Buckingham Palace

1) August 1, 1907

The King has been pleased to appoint William, Earl Beauchamp, KCMG, to be Lord Steward of His Majesty's Household, in the room of Cecil George Savile, Earl of Liverpool.

2) August 1, 1907

The King has been pleased to appoint Thomas, Lord Denman,[55] to be Captain of His Majesty's Honourable Corps of Gentlemen-at-Arms, in the room of William, Earl Beauchamp, appointed Lord Steward of His Majesty's Household.

The new post drew Earl Beauchamp nearer to the royal court, where his sister had by now safely established herself as Lady-in-Waiting to the Queen. But even before becoming Lord Steward, Beauchamp had not hesitated to employ the services of Lady Mary for his own purposes; and that she readily felt bound to him we learn from her letters in return.[56]

Frogmore House,
Windsor

Whitsun Monday 1902

I will suggest to H. R. H. about luncheon if I have a chance, but she was in bed all yesterday with a bad cold and I stayed and read to her for 6 hours. I am going to try and keep her either in bed, or very quiet all this week, as she will have no more rest for the next 2 months and has a frightfully busy time before her. Perhaps I might mange to run up for a few hours one afternoon or evening.

If the Queen was not in a mood to arrange a luncheon invitation for Beauchamp at the time, it must have been primarily because the coronation of King Edward VII was scheduled to take place in August 1902. Beauchamp, as Liberal peer, attended the coronation ceremony with all the appropriate pomp and grace. As Lady-in-Waiting to the Queen, his

---

55   Denman, 3rd Baron, b. 1874. A Liberal.
56   Lady Mary Lygon to Earl Beauchamp, Whit Monday 1902. Source: Royal Archives: GV/ADD/COPY/2/3/67,69,76,79.

sister attended too. Afterwards Lady Mary wrote to her brother saying how much she had enjoyed the ceremony:[57]

Aug. 12, 1902

I longed to talk over the Service with you afterwards. I thought it far more wonderful even than I had expected and am surprised to gather from your letter to Susie that you were disappointed.

Firstly, I was immensely struck with the great reverence of the congregation, and glad to see that everyone in the Chancel, and many all over the Abbey knelt during the celebration. Then I thought the King extremely dignified – with real majesty in his movements and actions – and evidently very much moved and touched. I thought it very pretty of him to kiss the Archbishop's hand. He did gird on the sword: and wasn't one of the 2 cloth-of-gold tunics that he put on after the anointing the Colobrium sindonis [the 'shroud tunic' signifying the foregoing of worldly vanity]? The feebleness of the Archbishop made one very nervous. Especially after the Consecration when he was walking about. The music struck me as curiously ineffective, but I believe the 500 voices were overwhelming when the Abbey was empty.

How very well the Peeresses looked collectively. I was very fortunate in my place and was able to see the Altar, St Edward's chair and the theatre – whilst most people saw only one or the other. The King was none the worse and attended a thanksgiving service at the Chapel Royal on Sunday morning.

Lady Mary often updated Beauchamp on what was happening in the Palace, and recounted in detail time spent in the company of the King and Queen, when on holiday.[58]

I

March 13, 1903

I am having a most gay and un-penitential as well as busy time. On Sunday the King had a small dinner party; on Tuesday there was a dance which lasted until 3! Last night we dined with Ld Rosebery, and had a most pleasant evening, meeting Ld and Lady Cork, Ld and Lady Tweedmouth, the C. Adeans, Sir Ed. and Lady Grey, etc. My neighbours were Ld Tweedmouth and Ld Percy, and the latter was most delightful.

---

57   Lady Mary Lygon to Earl Beauchamp, 12 August 1902. *Ibid.*
58   Lady Mary Lygon to Earl Beauchamp, 13 March 1903. *Ibid.*

In the day time we visit horse shows, attend the House of Lords, go to prize givings and spend many hours at Marlborough House not to mention picture galleries etc. Sybil Primrose was in great good looks last night, and seemed very happy, she is to be married at Epsom on the 28th of this month. Her fiancé looks nice, but I did not make his acquaintance. I forgot to tell you how extraordinarily well all the men at the King's dance looked in knee breeches and stockings. It is certainly very gentleman-like and smart. Tonight there is the first Court and I am to 'chaperon' Mary Lamington at it. I must just go and dress for it.

2

March 19, 1903

I sent off a basket with blue ribbons and flowers to Princess Patricia – with a most choice assortment of Fuller's best chocolates. I am afraid my letters have been woefully empty of gossip. I haven't come across any. But here is one piece of news, which is that Bertha is engaged to be married to a Major Dawkins, a brother of Sir Clinton. Unfortunately he is very poor and is quartered at Mauritius – with a prospect of India afterwards; but she is very much in love, so one has to stifle one's own feelings about losing her, and hope that the future will make up for all the unhappiness in her past life.

H. R. H. dined with Ld and Lady Dartmouth last Monday and met the Duchess of Westminster with Lady Mary and Ld Crichton, Ld Revelstoke, Ld Hamilton, the Wenlocks, Ld Rosebery, Lady Hastings, etc. ...

3

Trondhjeim
H. M. Yacht Victoria & Albert
June 29

No! I did not wear my Coronation gown for the Ceremony and no train. I have other gowns, tho' you may hardly believe it! I think Lettice is very wise to shirk the Court. I hope you and I may meet at it. The next day I am going to have a week's holiday.

H. R. H. had a day's fishing at Steukjoen yesterday, but we returned here early this morning. We leave tonight, on our way home, spend to-morrow with Mr Bromley Davenport, Monday on some other river, and reach London at 5 on Thursday. I like the Master of Elibank very much: is he a friend of yours? He improves much on acquaintance.

4

Tregothnan. Truro. July 17th, 1903[59]

The Marlborough House Ball on Monday was a great success: and an extremely pretty sight. An enormous ballroom, to hold 1150 was built out in the garden, and with its white plaster pillars, it reminded me somewhat of the banqueting hall at Madras. The King and Queen came at 11 and stayed till 2: and we went on dancing till 3, so had only 4 hours sleep as we had to start early next morning to come here. We had a record run down here, doing 246 miles to Plymouth in 234 minutes! The ceremony at Truro on Wednesday was most interesting and impressive: and the Cornish side of me was much thrilled being there.

The party here is pleasant: Lady St Germans, St Levens, Bevil Fortescues, Clifdens, various Boscawens, the Bishop of Corea, the Pole Carews, etc. Yesterday there was a large county garden party; today we go for a motoring expedition and tomorrow we visit Marconi's station on the coast. On Monday we go to Mount Edgecombe.

These letters kept Beauchamp happy. His own interests, however, were in his government duties. Being a Lord Steward meant more work and additional responsibility.

59   Source: Royal Archives: VIC/ADD/U/27/99–101, 162.

CHAPTER 10

Lord Steward of the Household

The Lord Steward is an official of the royal household, receiving his appointment from the Sovereign in person. He is always a peer and a privy councillor with a cabinet rank. If the government representative is absent in the House of Lords, the Lord Steward usually steps in to answer for the government. But he may join in the debate of the House on his own. This Earl Beauchamp frequently did.

During the year 1907, the government introduced more bills: a Small Holdings Bill for England, an Evicted Tenants Bill for Ireland, a Small Landholders (Scotland) Bill, and a Land Values (Scotland) Bill. The Conservatives in the Lords again killed the two Scotland bills, and destroyed the other two by moving amendments that mutilated them so much as to render them valueless.[1] An answer had to be found to the destructive tactics the Lords were continually employing; and even the King expressed anxiety at the negative attitude of the peers towards the government's measures.[2] The situation had indeed become intolerable. There was now talk among parliamentarians about the composition of the second chamber, and on the possibility of limiting its constitutional powers. A purely hereditary upper chamber with a nine-tenths Conservative majority went against basic democratic principles. No one stirred discontent at this situation with fierier eloquence than that vociferous member of the Campbell-Bannerman

---

1 For details see Robert Ensor, *England, 1870–1914, op. cit.*, p. 393.

2 In a letter to the Prime Minister of 25 November 1906, King Edward made it clear that he viewed the situation as very serious if a conflict were to take place between the two Houses of Parliament, and he thought it was 'important that there should, if possible, be a compromise' in respect to the amendments. See J. A. Spender, *The Life of Sir Henry Campbell-Bannerman*, vol. II, *op. cit.*, p. 302.

cabinet, David Lloyd George. In a speech made on 1 December 1906 at the Palmerston Club, Oxford, he insisted that:

> it was essential to the good government of the country that the road from the people to the throne should be cleared. It was intolerable that every petition of right that came from the people to their sovereign should be waylaid and mutilated in this fashion ... If the House of Lords persisted in its present policy, it would be a much larger measure than the Education Bill that would come up for consideration. It would come upon this issue, whether the country was to be governed by the King and the Peers or by the King and the people.

Lloyd George was delivering a most serious warning to the peers. It irritated the King, who thought that a cabinet minister should not have brought the Sovereign's name into his criticisms: he wrote to the Prime Minister asking him to 'take the necessary steps to prevent a repetition of this violation of constitutional practice and of good taste'.[3]

Lloyd George meant what he had said. Very soon 'a much larger measure than the Education Bill' was to clip the wings of the House of Lords. However, in the meantime, Campbell-Bannerman sought to follow the evident wish of the King to find an arrangement which 'would prevent a collision between the two Houses of Parliament'.[4] He wrote an ingenious and lengthy memorandum on reform of the House of Lords. It was dated 31 May 1907, and sent to the members of the cabinet. The plan suggested a bill, the main features of which would be the following clauses:[5]

> 1. If in any Session a Bill sent from the House of Commons to the House of Lords fails to become law, by reason of the House of Lords having rejected the Bill, or postponed its consideration, or made amendments to which the House of Commons does not agree, a Conference shall, unless the Government otherwise determine, be held between Members appointed by the House of Lords and the House of Commons respectively, with the view of arriving at a settlement of the difference between the two Houses.

3   See Lord Knollys to Campbell-Bannerman (3 December 1906), *Ibid.*, p. 314.
4   King Edward to Campbell-Bannerman, 27 November 1906. *Ibid.*, p. 304.
5   The full text of the memorandum is printed in *Ibid.*, pp. 351–5.

2. If, after the Conference, the Bill is reintroduced into the House of Commons, with or without modifications, and is again sent to the House of Lords, and again fails to become law, it may, in the next subsequent Session, be again introduced in the form which it was last agreed to by the House of Commons, and if passed by the House of Commons in that form, and again sent to the House of Lords, it shall, in default of agreement between the two Houses, have effect as if passed by both Houses, and shall be enacted in the customary words accordingly.

The memorandum was discussed in the cabinet, where different opinions prevailed and no consensus was reached. But the cabinet did agree to have the Prime Minister introduce a resolution in the Commons, which declared that 'in order to give effect to the will of the people, as expressed by their elected representatives, the power of the other House to alter or reject Bills passed by this House must be restricted by law as to secure that within the limits of a single Parliament, the final decisions of the Commons should prevail'.[6] The Commons passed the resolution on 26 June 1907 by 432 votes to 147 – a great victory over the Prime Minister's opponents. This resolution was the precursor of the substantial reform of the House of Lords which took place only a few years later. It was also an enduring legacy left by Henry Campbell-Bannerman when he died on 22 April 1908.

Earl Beauchamp continued to fulfil his duties as Lord Steward.[7] It is appropriate that we print below abstracts of his speeches in the House of Lords.

---

6   For details see J. A. Spender, *Sir Henry Campbell-Bannerman, op. cit.*, p. 358.

7   Sir H. Campbell-Bannerman to Lord Knollys (1907) [Sir Francis Knollys (1837–1924), private secretary to King Edward VII, 1870–1910; joint private secretary to King George V, 1910–13; created 1st Viscount, 1911]: '10 Downing Street, Whitehall, S.W. Dear Lord Knollys, I am not sure that I was right in intimating to Lord Beauchamp that the Office of Lord Steward would shut him off from political work in the House of Lords. It appears that his father held the office under Disraeli, and answered for a Department. If this is not objected to, it wd be a convenience, and would be agreeable to him, if he was allowed to go on taking the moderate post he has recently taken. Geikie accepts the K.C.B. & I suppose could be invited on Monday. Yours very truly, H. Campbell Bannerman.' Source: Royal Archives: VIC/ADD/B/11.

Historical Manuscripts Commission

On 17 April 1907, Lord Balfour of Burleigh moved:[8]

> That an humble address be presented to His Majesty for a complete list, with dates of issue, of the Reports of the Historical Manuscripts Commission and of the appendices thereto; together with an alphabetical index of the collections examined and reported on, giving reference to the Report and appendix wherein the result of the examination may be found.

Earl Beauchamp replied: 'His Majesty's Government are quite ready to give the Return asked for by the noble Lord. With regard to the special points to which he has referred there, I know some Members of the Commission who are in favour of what he has suggested, and I have very little doubt that, with their support, the Commission will give effect to his request.'

Irish Tobacco Bill

On 7 May 1907, Lord Oranamore and Browne moved a bill, the object of which was to repeal the law prohibiting the growing of tobacco in Ireland, and to authorize the growth of tobacco for experimental purposes.[9] Earl Beauchamp replied that His Majesty's government offered 'no opposition to the passage of this Bill, which they regard with entire neutrality'.

8   See *Parliamentary Debates*, House of Lords, vol. CLXXII, 17 April 1907, cols 923–4.
9   See *Parliamentary Debates*, House of Lords, vol. CLXXIV, 7 May 1907, cols 45–6.

Employment of Women Bill

On 13 May 1907, Earl Beauchamp begged to move that 'two obsolete exemptions under the Factory and Workshop Act, 1901, and the Coal Miners Regulation, Act 1887, regarding the employment of women' be repealed. He went on: 'The International Conference at Berne last year agreed to certain limitations with regard to the labour of women, and I think we in this country may congratulate ourselves upon the fact that only these two very small alterations have to be made in order to bring the laws of this country in harmony with the general agreement arrived at by the International Conference.'[10] The bill was committed to a Committee of the Whole House.

Factory and Workshop Bill

The bill moved by Earl Beauchamp on 14 May 1907 referred to the 'unsatisfactory' state of laundries, both commercial and institutional.[11] The Factory and Workshop Acts of 1895 and 1901 had become outdated and allowed a 'great deal too much latitude'. An alteration was required. The bill would subject all laundries to inspection 'in exactly the same way as all factories and workshops are inspected at the present time; that is to say laundresses will be put on the same footing as dressmakers, milliners, and persons who follow such occupation'. Although, regarding employees, 'it was forbidden that the hours of work should consist of more than sixty-eight, including intervals for meals, there will be a certain latitude so that they may work more hours on one day, and make it up by working fewer hours on another day.' It was the intention of the Secretary of State to 'do all he can to meet the legitimate desires of the managers of these institutions, by making

---

10   See *Parliamentary Debates*, House of Lords, vol. CLXXIV, 13 May 1907, col. 565.
11   See *Parliamentary Debates*, House of Lords, vol. CLXXIV, 14 May 1907, cols 735–48.

special arrangements for them which will enable them to carry on work which is not only of an educational kind, but also of a kind calculated to improve the character and generally the welfare of the inmates of these institutions'. The motion was agreed to and committed to a Committee of the Whole House.

The Union Jack Club

On 16 May 1907 Lord Rosmead[12] asked the government if it was a fact that an arrangement was being made by the India Office 'by which an officer on leave from a regiment in the Indian Army is about to be seconded in order to take up an appointment as "Controller" of the Union Jack Club'.[13]

In reply, Earl Beauchamp stated that the noble Lord was 'perfectly accurate in saying that a request has been received from the council of the Union Jack Club for the loan of an officer on leave from a regiment in the Indian Army; but the Secretary of State for India, having given the matter full consideration, does not regard the object in view as one for which a charge should be put on the revenue of India or exceptional arrangements sanctioned'.

Advertisements Regulation Bill

On 9 July 1907 Lord Balfour of Burleigh moved a bill, the object of which was to 'enable local authorities to exercise a certain reasonable amount of control over the display of advertisement boards within their district'.[14]

---

12   Rosmead, 2nd Baron, b. 1866. A Conservative.
13   See *Parliamentary Debates*, House of Lords, vol. CLXXIV, 16 May 1907, cols 1073–4.
14   See *Parliamentary Debates*, House of Lords, vol. CLXXVII, 9 July 1907, cols 1296–8.

Earl Beauchamp replied thus: 'I am sure the object of this Bill will commend itself to every Member of your Lordships' House, and I am instructed by His Majesty's Government to say that they will be very glad to do all they can to assist its passage into law.'

Injured Animals Act (1894) Amendment Bill

On 18 July 1907, Lord Aberdare[15] moved a bill to amend and enlarge the Injured Animals Act, 1894. That Act provided for the slaughter of injured horses, mules or asses by or by order of the police. The bill proposed that the definition 'animal' include any bull, cow, ox, heifer, calf, sheep, goat or swine.[16]

Earl Beauchamp replying for the government said that its members 'will be very glad to do all in their power to assist the noble Lord in passing this Bill through your Lordships' House'.

Lights on Vehicles Bill

On 25 July 1907, the Earl of Donoughmore[17] moved a bill which contained clauses[18] to the effect that: lights were to be carried by vehicles at night (which was more or less from one hour after sunset to one hour before sunrise); these were to include a tail-light; the lights should be trimmed and kept properly; there would be penalties for failing to comply with these regulations, but power would be granted to make exceptions where

---

15   Aberdale, 2nd Baron, b. 1851. A Liberal.

16   See *Parliamentary Debates*, House of Lords, vol. CLXXVIII, 18 July 1907, cols 810–1.

17   Donoughmore, 6th Earl of, b. 1875. A Conservative.

18   See *Parliamentary Debates*, House of Lords, vol. CLXXIX, 25 July 1907, cols 4–8.

necessary (for example, if goods of an inflammatory nature were being carried and the use of a light might be dangerous); existing by-laws were to be repealed, so as to secure uniformity throughout the country.

Speaking on behalf of the Home Office. Earl Beauchamp assured the House that the government would be 'very glad indeed to see this Bill pass into law, and to assist the noble Earl in achieving that result'.

Released Persons (Poor Law) Relief Bill

Earl Beauchamp himself introduced a bill on 1 August 1907, the object of which was to 'give relief to rates of districts in which prisons are situated by giving powers for the sending of distressed prisoners, who, on release seek refuge in the nearest workhouse, to districts more properly charged with them'.[19] The bill received a second reading and was committed to a Committee of the Whole House.

Probation of Offenders (No. 2) Bill

On 5 August 1907 Earl Beauchamp moved a bill, the object of which was to 'extend a principle which has been already admitted in other Acts,[20] and which has been found to work with very good effect'.[21] The most important part of the bill was to ratify 'the permission which is given to Courts

---

19   See *Parliamentary Debates*, House of Lords, vol. CLXXIX, 5 August 1907, cols 1487–9.
20   The acts referred to were: Habitual Drunkards Act, 1879; Summary Jurisdiction Act, 1879; Probation of First Offenders Act, 1887; Youthful Offenders Act, 1901.
21   See *Parliamentary Debates*, House of Lords, vol. CLXXIX, 5 August 1907, cols 1486–7.

to provide for the payments of a salary to probation officers. ... The salary shall be paid by the authority out of the funds from which the salary of the clerk to the justices is paid.' The bill applied 'to others besides those who are before the Court for the first time. ... The more you can segregate offenders the better it is for them in the future.' The bill was committed to a Committee of the Whole House.

Cabs and Stage Carriages (London) Bill

The Cabs and Stage Carriages (London) Bill moved by Earl Beauchamp on 24 August 1907 intended 'to relieve the Home Secretary of certain restrictions which he is under at the present moment with regard to taximeters'.[22] The legislation passed 'a good many years ago' did not 'easily lend itself to modern types of locomotion'. The bill gave the Home Secretary 'powers over stage carriages which come from some place beyond London'. Owing to certain defects in previous bills, the Home Secretary had no power if the carriages started outside, and then came within the limits of the county of London. The bill would meet 'the convenience of the travelling public' by abolishing the 'privilege system'. 'A good many of us would be glad if we found, when we arrived at the great terminal station of London, taxicabs waiting to take us to our destination.' The bill did not 'in any way interfere with the control of the railway companies with their control of the cabs'. The change was 'very much desired by all the cab-men in London at the present time'. After debate the motion was agreed to, and committed to a Committee of the Whole House.

Earl Beauchamp kept up his parliamentary work, and at the beginning of 1908 was preparing for the new session of parliament when Sir Henry Campbell-Bannerman began to show increasing signs of bad health. On 12

---

22   See *Parliamentary Debates*, House of Lords, vol. CLXXXI, 24 August 1907, cols 1511–27.

February 1908 the Prime Minister spoke for the last time in the Commons. Very soon afterwards he became seriously ill, and made it clear that he wanted Herbert Henry Asquith to act as deputy leader in the Commons. On 6 April, Campbell-Bannerman submitted his resignation to the King.[23] Thereupon King Edward commanded Henry Asquith[24] to form a government. Earl Beauchamp retained his post.

---

23   Campbell-Bannerman died on 22 April 1908.

24   Herbert Henry Asquith (1852–1928), Liberal M.P., 1886–1918, 1920–4; Home Secretary, 1892–5; Chancellor of the Exchequer, 1905–8; Prime Minister 1908–16; created Earl of Oxford and Asquith, 1925.

First Commissioner of Works

For the next two years, Earl Beauchamp, as Lord Steward, proceeded to further Asquith's policies in the House of Lords.

Bishoprics Bill

The Lord Steward presented a bill to facilitate the foundation of new bishoprics and the alteration of dioceses, and to amend the Bishops' Resignation Act, 1869.[1]

Cattle drivers in Ireland

On 18 March 1909, the Earl of Donoughmore moved for a 'Return of the number and localities of cattle-drives in Ireland which had been reported by the police during the years 1906, 1907, and 1908,[2] showing the residence and occupation of the persons who had been convicted or bound-over to

---

1   See *Parliamentary Debates*, House of Lords, vol. I, 18 February 1909, col. 71.
2   Allied with boycotting, a tactic of the Irish nationalists at the time was to drive cattle off the estates of 'establishment' landlords.

keep the peace, and the quantity and Poor-law valuation of the land held by any such persons'.[3]

The Lord Steward replied, in the absence of Lord Denman, who represented the Irish Office in the Lords. There were, Lord Steward said, no cattle drives in the year 1906; they began in April 1907. The government was ready to supply part of that report the noble Earl had asked for, including the information for the years 1907 and 1908. But to obtain the statistics as desired would involve 'personal inquiries into more than 1,000 cases and reference to rate-books, which are not in the possession of the police, and it is not thought that the labour and expense involved would be justified by the results'. The motion was, by leave, withdrawn.

Boycotting

On 23 March 1909, Lord Oranmore and Browne[4] called the attention of the Government to 'the proceedings of the Clonguish Branch of the United Irish League (at which several persons were condemned by name, and the public was warned to have no dealing with them, published in the *Langford Leader* of February 27'. He further wanted to know whether the law officers of the Crown proposed to take any action in the matter.[5]

The Lord Steward said that the attention of the Irish Office had 'only recently been called to the publication referred to by the noble Lord'. They had ordered 'inquiries to be made through the police as to the circumstances of the various persons alleged to be boycotted'.

---

3   See *Parliamentary Debates*, House of Lords, vol. I, 18 March 1909, col. 495.
4   Oranmore and Browne, 3rd Baron, b.1861. A Conseervative.
5   See *Parliamentary Debates*, House of Lords, vol. I, 23 March 1909, cols 505–16.

Hops Bill

On 31 March 1909, Viscount Hardinge[6] moved a bill, the object of which was to 'prohibit the use of hop substitutes in the brewing and preservation of beer and the importation of hops except in bags properly marked'.[7]

The Lord Steward explained the position of the government. It had introduced a bill of this kind the previous year, and promised to do it again the following year. Therefore it was thought that the action of the noble Viscount was 'somewhat superfluous and likely to render legislation more difficult'. But there was an 'old phrase on the subject of dishing the Whigs'. The present intervention seemed to Earl Beauchamp to be 'an attempt on the part of the noble Viscount to obtain for those with whom he is associated some of the credit which is due to the authors of the Bill as originally introduced; and the resolutions which have been addressed to your Lordships – I myself have received a large number – asking you to support the Second Reading of this Bill, and holding up the noble Viscount as a saviour of the hop industry, represent an endeavour to ascribe to him merits which are due to His Majesty's Government, and to dress him in plumes borrowed from the Bill of last year'. However, since there was 'no practical difference between the noble Viscount and myself', the government was willing that this bill 'should be read a second time'. This was done and the bill was committed to a Committee of the Whole House.

6   Hardinge, 3rd Viscount, b. 1857. A Conservative.
7   See *Parliamentary Debates*, House of Lords, vol. I, 31 March 1909, cols 549–80.

Assurance Companies Bill

Lord Hamilton of Dalzell[8] presented a bill on 30 June 1909, the object of which was 'the consolidation and amendment of the law regarding insurance and assurance'. The word 'assurance' was used where life business was dealt with, and the word 'insurance' where other forms of business were dealt with.[9]

The bill was welcomed by their Lordships. After debate, Earl Beauchamp said that His Majesty's government had 'every reason to be gratified by the reception which has been given to this Bill', and he hoped the measure would have 'an easy passage through your Lordships' House'. The motion was committed to a Committee of the Whole House.

Cinematography Bill

The Lord Steward introduced a small bill to 'make better provision for securing safety at cinematograph and other exhibitions'. These were 'very inflammable' and special provisions were 'therefore necessary in order to safeguard the audience'.[10] The bill was committed to a Committee of the Whole House.

8   Hamilton of Dalzell, 2nd Baron, b. 1872. A Liberal.
9   See *Parliamentary Debates*, House of Lords, vol. II, 30 June 1909, cols 128–40.
10 See *Parliamentary Debates*, House of Lords, vol. III, 20 September 1909, col. 17.

Oaths Bill

The Lord Steward presented a bill on 20 September 1909. The bill dealt with a matter which, he said, was not 'very important in itself although it is one which enters very largely into the social life of the country'.[11] It was the opinion of the Home Office that an oath 'administered in the fashion prescribed in this Bill would be more welcome and would probably impress a witness more than the present rather hurried way in which it is administered in the Courts'. The officer administering the oath would be required to address the person taking the oath in the following form: 'You swear by Almighty God to tell the truth, the whole truth, nothing but the truth.' The witness would reply, 'I do.' This added 'something to the ceremony of taking the oath'. The bill was committed to a Committee of the Whole House.

The Vivisection Commission

On 26 October 1909 the Earl of Cromer[12] asked if the Lord Steward could give the House any information as to when the Vivisection Commission was likely to send in its report.[13]

The Lord Steward replied thus: 'I am afraid I am unable, in answer to the Question of the noble Earl, to fix any date. I understand that the draft of the Report is in an advanced stage of preparation, but the Chairman, Lord Selby, is unfortunately very unwell, and it is quite impossible to fix a definite date for the further proceedings of the Commission. I have no doubt, however, that the members of the Commission will take note of

---

11   See *Parliamentary Debates*, House of Lords, vol. III, 20 September 1909, cols 16–17.
12   Cromer, 1st Earl, b. 1841. A Conservative.
13   See *Parliamentary Debates*, House of Lords, vol. IV, 26 October 1909, col. 417.

the Question of the noble Earl, and accept it as an indication on the part of the public of their wish for a speedy issue of the Report.'

Police Bill

At the third reading of the Police Bill on 8 November 1909, the Lord Steward introduced the following amendment:[14] 'The power of the Secretary of State under the Metropolitan Police Superannuation Act, 1875, to make regulations respecting the grant to the officers to whom that Act applies of superannuation allowances, compensations, gratuities, or other allowances, on the like principles and conditions as were in force at the passing of that Act with respect to persons in the permanent civil service of the State, shall be extended so as to include a power to make such regulations on the like principles and conditions as are for the time being in force with respect to persons in the permanent civil service of the State, and to vary and revoke any such regulations'. The House agreed to the amendment, and the bill was passed.

The momentous years of 1909 and 1910

It was now the Finance Bill that brought about a change in Beauchamp's political career. At the beginning of November 1909, David Lloyd George, now Chancellor of the Exchequer in Asquith's first cabinet,[15] presented his first budget in the Commons. It aroused vigorous protests among the

14   See *Parliamentary Debates*, House of Lords, vol. IV, 8 November 1909, cols 533–4.
15   For a complete list of Asquith's first cabinet (formed April 1908) and changes down to August 1914, see Robert Ensor, *England 1870–1914, op. cit.*, pp. 613–14.

Conservatives, or Unionists as they were called. But, on 4 November, the bill got through in the Commons by 379 votes to 149. The bill then came before the Lords for a second reading on 8 November. Earl Beauchamp employed all his diligence to defend the budget. It was, he argued, common to both sides of the House that the subject would consist of 'a vast quantity of theory'. But there was 'also a vast quantity of fact as to which there can be no dispute, and I hope your Lordships will forgive me if I try to confine myself first to that part of the subject which deals with hard dry facts rather than with large constitutional theories'. Beauchamp exposed in detail the advantages of the budget to the country as a whole, and listed at length the successes His Majesty's Government had achieved.[16]

The Lords on the opposite benches ignored all these arguments and rejected the budget on 23 November 1909 by 350 to 75.[17] This irresponsible action infuriated both the government and the general public. The behaviour of the Lords, they rightly assumed, was unconstitutional. The control of the elected executive could not be permitted to fall in the hands of the hereditary chamber. Asquith immediately moved a resolution in the Commons, declaring 'That the action of the House of Lords in refusing to pass into law the financial provisions made by this House for the service of the year is a breach of the Constitution and a usurpation of the rights of the Commons'.[18] The motion was carried by 349 votes to 134. Asquith had pronounced a battle cry in defence of the Constitution and he went to the polls to seek the country's support.[19] The veto of the Lords became the main issue at the general election in January 1910. The Liberal party won the vast majority of seats (275). Along with Labour (40), and the

---

16 See *Parliamentary Debates*, House of Lords, vol. IV, 8 November 1909, cols 905–16.
17 See *Parliamentary Debates*, House of Lords, vol. IV, 23 November 1909, cols 821–924.
18 Quoted in Robert Ensor, *England 1870–1914*, *op. cit.*, p. 417.
19 Beauchamp 'appeared to think the only security for the Government was to strike hard against the House of Lords. No such opportunity would occur again, and it was due to their followers, and their own declaration, to make the most of it. He anticipated many changes within the Cabinet, but had no intimation of anything affecting himself. Aberdeen he thought would stay in Ireland, which, if Lord Wolverhampton [1st Viscount, b. 1830. A Liberal] goes, may open the Lord Presidency to his ambition.' See Almeric Fitzroy, *Memoirs*, vol. I, *op. cit.*, entry for 2 February 1910, p. 394.

Irish nationalists (82), both in favour of limiting the power of the Lords, Asquith could now comfortably force through his policy of reform, at least in the Commons. The House of Lords would still pose a formidable obstacle. To remove this obstacle, Asquith thought of an ingenious plan. He would ask the Sovereign to invoke his prerogative to create as many new peers (proposed by the Prime Minister) as were needed to guarantee the passage of the government legislation through the House of Lords. The cabinet entirely backed up Asquith in this plan. For the moment, the Lords were behaving decently. They passed the budget without division on 28 April 1910. Parliament then adjourned for a short recess. While the Prime Minister was away holidaying in Gibraltar, sad news reached him. King Edward VII had died on 6 May. In June Asquith slightly reshuffled his cabinet. Earl Beauchamp became, for a while, Lord President of the Council. This was for the short period till the end of the year, when a general election was to take place.

The reign of George V began with turmoil in parliament.[20] The government had introduced the Parliament Bill in mid April 1910. King George anticipated immense controversy. When the King Edward's funeral was over, the new King counselled Asquith to try to settle the problem between the two Houses by calling a round-table Constitutional Conference of the parties. Asquith took the advice, though with some hesitancy. The Conference lasted five months, holding twenty-one sittings, but its members failed to reach an agreement. The failure was announced on 10 November. Asquith now staked another election. On 18 November, he announced the dissolution of parliament. The Liberals fought the December general election on the issue of whether the country should be run by the people or by hereditary peers. The country responded giving the Liberals 272 seats, Labour 42, the Irish 84, and the Unionists (Conservatives) 272. This result enabled Asquith to form a government. In the new government Earl Beauchamp

---

20   A detailed history of the course of the Parliament Bill has been thoroughly given in Peter Raina, *House of Lords Reform: A History. The Origins to 1937: Proposals Deferred* (Bern: Peter Lang AG, 2011). Volume I: Book One: *The Origins to 1911*, chapters 24–30, pp. 459–591; Book Two: *1911–1937*, chapters 31–32, pp. 1–90.

was made First Commissioner of Works.[21] The Commissioners of Works, writes Sir Ivor Jennings,[22]

> were established by the Crown Lands Act, 1851, for the purpose of taking and holding all lands vested in them by statute or purchase. They consisted of the First Commissioner, who was generally a minister not in the Cabinet, the Secretaries of State, and the President of the Board of Trade. The Commissioners never met, and were superseded by the Ministry of Works in 1942. The Minister is not in the Cabinet, and he has a Parliamentary Secretary. The Ministry builds and maintains public buildings, including the Houses of Parliament and the Royal Palaces, and maintains the Royal Parks and Pleasure Gardens. It is also responsible for Ancient Monuments.

For the moment, the main priority of the government was the Parliament Bill, which Asquith introduced in the Commons on 21 February 1911. He

---

21 See Robert Ensor, *England 1870–1914, op. cit.*, p. 614. Sir Almeric Fitzroy noted: 'Beauchamp took the oath of Office as Chief Commissioner of Works before the Lord President. He seems quite reconciled to the change and has written me a very appreciative letter in regard to the months he spent at the Privy Council Office. He has great quickness in making up his mind, and his judgment is as a rule sound; he has moreover, considerable resolution; and is likely to prove a valuable addition to the counsels of any Government to which he may belong.' See Almeric Fitzroy, *Memoirs, op. cit.*, entry for 7 November 1910, vol. II, p. 421. Earl Beauchamp was also socially popular among the Liberal loyalists, who were often invited to Beauchamp's Belgravia house in London. Beauchamp played a willing host. Lord Crewe noted in his diary on 9 February 1910 that Beauchamp 'agrees to host one of 2 dinners for Liberal peers as proposed by Denman'. Beauchamp told him that he 'shall be very glad to do my share by giving a dinner in Belgrave Square. I shall be particularly glad because last year in mourning for little Grosvenor [the 2nd Duke of Westminster's four-year-old son had died] we did nothing for the Party & I shd like to do something.' See Crewe: *Correspondence with Ld Beauchamp ('Willie'): Madresfield Court, Malvern*, Cambridge University Library, Crewe Papers: C/2. I am indebted to Richard Davenport-Hines for this reference. Dr Davenport-Hines believes that Beauchamp's private parties 'made him much appreciated to the Liberal government of Campbell-Bannerman & Asquith' and that he became 'pre-eminently a social leader in a political environment' [private correspondence with the present author]. This can be only partly true. Earl Beauchamp was a vigorous politician.

22 See 'The British Administrative System', in Ivor Jennings, *Cabinet Government* (Cambridge: Cambridge University Press, 1951, 2nd ed.), p. 527.

could easily count on support from Labour and the Irish nationalists. The
bill was given a first reading on 23 February, having a majority of 126, a
second reading a week later with a majority of 125 and a third reading on
15 May with 121. In all these sessions Asquith had 'appeared at his best, constantly dominating debate by the dignity, clearness, and terse force of his
argument'.[23] The bill reached the House of Lords on 23 May. Here began the
crucial, but hardly elegant discourse. The Lords debated the bill for over six
weeks – perhaps one of the longest periods of debate in the history of the
British parliament. The 'die-hards', also called 'ditchers', resolved to 'die in
the last ditch' in their attempt to defend the hereditary right of the peers.
The Lords put down amendment after amendment, defiant in their attitude
of 'no surrender' all through the month of June. On the third reading of the
bill, on 20 July, the Lords passed amendments that were totally unacceptable to the government. By now, however, Asquith had secured the King's
assent to exercise his prerogative of creating sufficient peers to enable the
bill to pass into law should the Lords still reject it. Now that the Lords had
done so, the Prime Minister felt obliged to make a public announcement
revealing the agreement he had reached with King George. This was on 21
July. When, three days later, Asquith rose in the Commons to reject the
Lords' amendments, the House was in a state of uproar. Indeed, the Prime
Minister was so loudly howled down by the opposition that he was unable
to speak. These shouts from the opposition, made 'in an orgy of stupid-
ity and ruffianism',[24] had been orchestrated by Lord Hugh Cecil,[25] one of
the younger Salisburys. Such tactics proved useless. When the opposition
moved a vote of censure on the government for involving the King in the
debate on the Parliament Bill, Asquith replied with a 'masterly exposition
and defence',[26] making 'one of the most moving appeals ever addressed to

23   This is how historians have judged Asquith's performance. See Robert Ensor, *England
     1870–1914*, *op. cit.*, p. 427.
24   Margot Asquith, wife of the Prime Minister, observed the scene from the Speaker's
     Gallery. See *The Autobiography of Margot Asquith*, vol. II (London: Thornton
     Butterworth Ltd., 1922), p. 146.
25   Cecil of Chelwood, 1st Viscount, b. 1864. A Conservative.
26   See Robert Ensor, *England 1870–1914*, *op. cit.*, p. 430.

the Commons. It was a speech which will live in history.'[27] As he 'built up his case in orderly sequence, the ranks of the Conservatives looked shattered and broken'.[28] And he wound up his speech in these momentous words. He was, he said,[29] accustomed:

> to be accused of breach of the Constitution, and even of treachery to the Crown. I confess that I am not in the least sensitive to this cheap and ill-informed form of vituperation. It has been my privilege, now I think unique, to serve, in close and confidential relations, three successive British Sovereigns. My conscience tells me that in that capacity, many and great as have been my failings and shortcomings, I have consistently striven to uphold the dignity and just privileges of the Crown. But I hold my office, not only by favour of the Crown, but by the confidence of the whole people. And I should be guilty indeed of treason if, in this supreme moment of a great struggle, I were to betray their trust.

When the Prime Minister sat down, the whole Liberal party 'rose and applauded him, and it seemed as if the cheers would never cease'.[30] The Commons rejected the Lords' amendments and sent the bill back to the Upper House. Another impassioned debate took place on 9 and 10 August.[31] Here Lord Morley, then President of the Council, warned the House that if the Lords rejected the bill, His Majesty would exercise his Prerogative in creating sufficient peers to enable the bill to be passed.[32] The bill was finally passed by 131 to 114. Many Unionist peers abstained, but some

27 Margot Asquith noticed this from the Speaker's Gallery. See *The Autobiography of Margot Asquith*, vol. II, *op. cit.*, p. 153.

28 *Ibid.*, 153–4.

29 Quoted in *Ibid.*, p. 154.

30 See *Ibid.*, p. 154

31 The course of this debate has been extensively described in Peter Raina, *House of Lords Reform: A History*. Volume I, Book Two: *1911–1937* (Bern: Peter Lang AG, 2011). The chapter is: 'Ditchers versus Hedgers: 1911', pp. 23–87.

32 Asquith had prepared a draft list of some 250 outstanding and distinguished public men to be designated as peers. Many people of liberal thinking regret that Asquith did not seek the creation of these peers. Had this creation gone through, it is generally agreed, 'the Liberal government, being in control of both houses, could have passed Irish home rule, Welsh disestablishment, and a reform of the second chamber all in one session.' See Robert Ensor, *England 1870–1914*, *op. cit.*, p. 431.

even decided to join the government. The Parliament Bill considerably restricted the powers of the House of Lords – especially with respect to money bills. The most important power of the House of Commons was specified in Clause 1, which read that if a 'Money Bill, having been passed by the House of Commons, and sent up to the House of Lords at least one month before the end of the session, is not passed by the House of Lords without amendment within one month after it is so sent up to that House, the Bill shall, unless the House of Commons direct to the contrary, be presented to His Majesty and become an Act of Parliament on the Royal Assent being signified, notwithstanding that the House of Lords have not consented to the Bill'.[33] Other clauses referred to the definition and purpose of public bills. Clause 7 was significant. It related to the duration of parliaments: 'Five years shall be substituted for seven years as the time fixed for the maximum duration of Parliament under the Septennial Act. 1715.' Thus the 'most decisive step' in British constitutional development since the franchise extension of 1867 was 'consummated' during Earl Beauchamp's time in politics.[34]

In Asquith's cabinet

It appears that the Commissioner of Works was invited to attend the meetings of the cabinet. But Earl Beauchamp was one of its 'silent members'. On the activities of the Earl in the cabinet our only source is the diary kept by Charles Hobhouse,[35] who was Financial Secretary in Asquith's first cabinet,

---

33   For the complete text of the Parliament Act 1911, see: Peter Raina, *House of Lords Reform: A History*. Volume I, Book Two: *1911–1937* (Bern: Peter Lang AG, 2011), pp. 83–7.

34   *Ibid.*, p. 430.

35   Charles Hobhouse (1862–1915), Liberal M.P., 1891–95, 1900–18; Under-Secretary for India, 1907; Financial Secretary to the Treasury, 1908–10; Chancellor of the Duchy of Lancaster, 1911; Postmaster-General, 1914–15. See Edward David (ed.), *Inside*

before continuing to attend as Chancellor of the Duchy of Lancaster (from October 1911), and then Post-Master General (from February 1914 to May 1915). We produce below the entries Hobhouse made in his diary with reference to Earl Beauchamp.

1

9 June 1910[36]

There has been a sharp contest between Lords Farquhar[37] and Beauchamp over their respective duties and powers. It began when the King of Portugal came to Windsor in the autumn of 1909, and the then Queen proposed that Winston Churchill[38] should *not* be asked, as the other Ministers were – to Windsor. Lord Farquhar agreed to omit him, but Beauchamp insisted that he and the Lord Steward's Dept. regulated these things, and sent him the invitation. The dispute culminated over the King's funeral when Beauchamp was elbowed aside by the Earl Marshal and by the 1st Commissioner of Works.

2

11 November 1911[39]

[King George had proclaimed a change in site of the capital of India – from Calcutta to Delhi. The Lieutenant Governors had not been consulted. The cabinet discussed the matter on 8 November.]

The Cabinet was very uneasy about it, the only person in the secret having been Asquith, and we adjourned till Thursday Nov. 9th, but though Beauchamp, Morley, Loreburn, and self were obviously hostile, and the others except Churchill and

Asquith's Cabinet: From the Diaries of Charles Hobhouse (London: John Murray, 1977).

36   *Ibid.*, p. 91.
37   Lord Farquhar (1869–1927): Master of the Household, 1901–7; Lord Steward, 1915.
38   Winston Churchill (1874–1965), Unionist M.P., 1900–4; Liberal M.P., 1904, 1908–22; Under-Secretary for the Colonies, 1905–8; President of the Board of Trade, 1908–10; Home Secretary, 1910–11; First Lord of the Admiralty, 1911–15; Prime Minister, 1940–5, 1951–5.
39   See Edward David (ed.), *Inside Asquith's Cabinet: From the Diaries of Charles Hobhouse, op. cit.*, p. 107.

Burns,[40] frankly doubtful – still the imminent departure of the King and Crewe prevented further objection or refusal. I trust we may not suffer – as I think we ought.

3

13 August 1912[41]

[Charles Hobhouse's opinion of members of the cabinet.]

After practically a year's experience in Cabinet, I note the following characteristics of my colleagues.

Asquith, the Prime Minister carries naturally great weight, and everybody likes him, and has great admiration for his intellect and for the ease and rapidity of transacting business, and his extraordinary quickness in seizing the right point on any case. ...

Ed. Grey is clear, narrow, obstinate when convinced of the soundness of his case, but convincible up to that point. ...

Crewe is slow of thought and slower in speech, but sensible and clear headed. ...

Haldane[42] is a dangerous man, subtle, a good friend to his followers, but tricky and not to be trusted. ...

Ll. George has humour – great quickness of thought, and a powerful power of managing men for a short time. ...

Morley is useful in keeping us to constitutional precedents, and as both George and Churchill have some veneration for him, he acts as a useful check on them. ...

Churchill is ill mannered, boastful, unprincipled, without any redeeming qualities except his amazing ability and industry. ...

40   John Burns (1858–43), Labour and Liberal M.P., 1892–1918; President of the Local Government Board, 1905–14; President of Board of Trade, 1914.
41   See Edward David (ed.), *Inside Asquith's Cabinet, op. cit.*, pp. 120–2.
42   Haldane, 1st Viscount, b. 1856. A Liberal.

Birrell[43] is cynical, amusing, a bad administrator, but high principled and with plenty of courage.

MacKenna has wonderful quickness of mind, and a remarkable memory. ...

Burns,[44] Buxton[45] and Beauchamp are except on office questions silent members of the Cabinet.

Samuel[46] is industrious, a good speaker, and clear thinker. ...

Harcourt[47] has many attractive qualities: charming manners when he likes, a temper under control, a hard worker, but no one trusts him, and everyone thinks that language is only employed by him to conceal his thoughts.

Runciman[48] is able, honest, hard-working, courageous ...

More activity in the House of Lords

Earl Beauchamp might have been a 'silent member' in the cabinet, but he was certainly not reserved in speech in the House of Lords. His regular

43 Augustine Birrell (1850–1933), Liberal M.P., 1889–1900, 1906–18; President of the Board of Education, 1905–7; Chief Secretary for Ireland, 1907–16.
44 John Burns (1858–1943), Labour and Liberal M.P., 1892–1918; President of the Board of Trade, 1914.
45 Sydney Charles Buxton (1853–1934), Liberal M.P., 1883–5, 1886–1914; Postmaster-General, 1905–10; President of the Board of Trade, 1910–14.
46 Herbert Samuel (1870–1963), Liberal M.P., 1902–18, 1929–35; Chancellor of the Duchy of Lancaster, 1909–10; Postmaster-General, 1915–16; Home Secretary, 1916.
47 Lewis 'Lulu' Harcourt (1863–1922), Liberal M.P., 1904–16; First Commissioner of Works, 1905–10; Colonial Secretary 1910–15.
48 Walter Runciman (1870–1949), Liberal M.P., 1899–1900, 1902–18, 1924–9, 1929–37; President of the Board of Education; President of the Board of Agriculture, 1911–14; President of the Board of Trade, 1914–16.

interventions in the Lords' debates bear witness to his strenuously active role in the political life of the country. The following samples deserve our attention.

Census (Great Britain) Bill

Introducing the Census Great Britain Bill on 7 July 1910, the Lord President of the Council, Earl Beauchamp, explained that the bill followed the Census Acts of 1890 and 1900.[49] There were two important points in which the bill differed from its predecessors. The bill required that the 'Schedule to be filled up by the householder should include, in the case of married persons, particulars indicating the duration of the marriage and the number of children born of the marriage who are still living'. The bill also required that 'the number of rooms inhabited shall be specified in each case. It is thought that over-crowding is not confined to tenements of four rooms, and information on this subject will be useful.' The Earl supposed that 'there will be some criticism as to the omission of the religious census'. But the Government had decided that it was unnecessary to ask for those particulars. He personally thought that the census 'should apply only to matters of fact that can be easily answered and to which no individual would object'. After a brief debate, the bill was given a second reading and committed to a Committee of the Whole House.

49   See *Parliamentary Debates*, House of Lords, vol. V, 7 July 1910, cols 1150–60.

Midwives (No. 2) Bill

On 19 July 1910, Earl Beauchamp begged leave to ask their Lordships to give a second reading to a bill to amend the Midwives Act, 1902. Experience, he said, had shown that it was desirable there 'should be amendment in one or two directions'.[50] The main clauses of the bill were the following:[51]

1. The bill provided for an increase in representation on the Board. In this matter, 'I shall throw myself wholly upon your Lordships' mercy,' said the Earl, but he hoped that, if any amendment were 'discussed, it may be combined with a general scheme for the reorganisation of the Board'.

2. The bill contained 'a provision, under which the Privy Council, if after a certain length of time they find the various bodies are not sufficiently represented, take power, after bringing the matter before your Lordships' House, to alter the constitution of the Board'.

3. The bill provided for the 'imposition of an annual registration fee of a shilling upon every midwife who wishes to keep her name on the roll'.

4. The bill provided that 'where a duly qualified medical practitioner has been summoned upon the advice of a certified midwife attending a woman in child-birth to render assistance in a case of emergency, he shall be entitled to recover from the board of guardians of the Poor-law union in which the woman resides such fee in respect of his attendance as may be prescribed, and such fee may, if the board of guardians

---

50   Sir Almeric Fitzroy noted on 26 July 1910: 'The proceedings in the House of Lords upon the Committee stage of the Midwives Bill were enlivened by a prolonged duel between Beauchamp, in charge of the Bill, and Ampthill, who was charged, or who had charged himself, with a formidable list of amendments. ... Beauchamp enhanced his reputation for parliamentary skill and conciliated the Opposition by the line he took: so much so, indeed, that before the discussion had gone far Waldegrowe told me that they would support the Government.' See Almeric Fitzroy, *Memoirs*, vol. II, *op. cit.*, p. 417.

51   See *Parliamentary Debates*, House of Lords, vol. VI, 19 July 1910, cols 303–20.

think fit, be recovered summarily as a civil debt from the patient or person liable to provide the patient with medical aid'.

After a brief debate the bill was given a second reading and committed to a Committee of the Whole House.

Mines Accidents Bill

On 25 July 1910, Earl Beauchamp, moved a bill, the object of which was to 'enable the Secretary of State for Home Affairs, by Order, to require that provisions shall be made at all mines for the supply and maintenance of appliances for use in rescue work and the formation and training of rescue brigades, and also for the supply and maintenance of ambulance appliances and training of men in ambulance work'. The bill was read a second time, and committed to a Committee of the Whole House.[52]

Asylums officers' superannuation

On 21 February 1911, Lord Monk Bretton asked His Majesty's government whether the opinion of the law officers of the Crown 'had been taken on any question relating to the administration of Asylums Officers Superannuation Act, 1909'.[53] The First Commissioner of Works, Earl Beauchamp in reply stated that the law officers 'are being asked to advise as to the extent of the Secretary of State's jurisdiction to determine disputes as the right to superannuation allowance or as to the amount of such allowance'.

52   See *Parliamentary Debates*, House of Lords, vol. VI, 25 July 1910, cols 414–15.
53   See *Parliamentary Debates*, House of Lords, vol. VII, 21 February 1911, cols 93–6.

Movable Dwellings Bill

Lord Clifford of Chudleigh[54] introduced a bill, which was directed against the 'wild and free life of the gipsy'. The government, it read, could not overlook the fact that the habits of the 'gipsy' 'are not altogether suited to the refined and elaborately regulated state of community life in which we live'. The bill laid out that:[55]

1. where 'it appears to any council that the presence of movable dwellings on any special place or places within the county would be dangerous to public health, the council may by by-law prohibit any movable dwelling from being on such special place or places';
2. that it would enable a county council to 'prohibit the encampment of a movable dwelling upon any common or roadside waste or upon any land in private occupation, provided the persons who proposed to encamp there had not the necessary permission';
3. that it would give 'power to the county council to prohibit camping even upon private ground where it appears that it would constitute a nuisance to the neighbourhood'.

The First Commissioner of Works welcomed the bill on behalf of the Home Office. What was needed, he said, 'is a more effective enforcement of the existing law in cases where gipsies are guilty of offences'.

54 Clifford of Chudleigh, 9th Baron, b. 1851. A Liberal Unionist.
55 See *Parliamentary Debates*, House of Lords, vol. VII, 22 February 1911. cols 97–110.

The Territorial Army and home defence

On 6 March 1911, the Earl of Portsmouth[56] asked the government if it was in a position to state what was 'the present official view in regard to functions of the Territorial Army'.[57] The question excited a lengthy debate. Earl Beauchamp did not directly answer the question but responded in a way which gives us the flavour of the debate and acquaints us with the wit with which he expressed himself:[58]

> My Lords, I think your Lordships must have congratulated yourselves afresh this evening upon the fact that the absence of any rule of order in this Assembly permits of a number of speeches upon subjects not directly connected with the one immediately before the House. We have heard comparatively little of the discrepancy mentioned by the noble Earl in his Question on the Paper. On the other hand, we have had an interesting speech from the noble Lord who has just sat down,[59] from whose first words I had hoped we were going to discover the author of the article signed 'Master Mariner'. Then we had one of those brilliant flights of imagination from Lord Newton to which we are accustomed in the House. He told us he had not very much faith in these advisers of whom we hear a great deal. I am not surprised, because I think he belongs to that small band of members of your Lordships' House, headed by the noble Duke (the Duke of Bedford) on the Back Bench, who think that the only possible defence for this country in time of war will be an Army which shall consist of nobody but colonels of Militia, and that this Army, consisting of colonels and commanded by colonels, will be amply sufficient to repel any force which might reach this country. ...

---

56   Portsmouth, 6th Earl of, b. 1856. A Liberal.
57   See *Parliamentary Debates*, House of Lords, vol. VII, 6 March 1911. cols 290–302.
58   *Ibid.*, col. 301.
59   Lord Ellenborough.

Employment of children

On 15 March 1911, the Earl of Shaftesbury[60] proposed a bill to give 'statutory prohibition to any street-trading by boys under the age of seventeen and by girls under the age of eighteen'.[61] Earl Beauchamp replied that he was glad to 'express the thanks of the Home Office to the noble Earl for having brought forward this question'. The matter was 'ripe' for legislation, and the government would give 'general support to the provision' of the bill.

The People Bill

On 28 March 1911, Lord Balfour of Burleigh proposed that provision be made for reference to the people in the case of any difference of opinion between the Houses of Parliament: (1) in the case of rejection of a bill; and (2) in a case of a 'carried bill' (should both Houses carry a bill, it should be still possible for 200 Members of the House of Commons to ask for a referral to the people). A two-day debate followed.[62] We are interested in what the First Commissioner of Works had to say. He gave a detailed historical analysis of the problem, referring to the situation in countries such as Switzerland, Canada, Australia, and the United States. Just because the referendum had been a success in other parts of the world, he said, did not mean that it was 'likely to be a success in this country'. In his view, the bill, if passed, would 'diminish the powers of your Lordships' House in respect to the compromise and the powers of revision and of amendment which we are anxious that your Lordships' House should possess'. The

60   Shaftesbury, 9th Earl of, b. 1869. A Conservative.
61   See *Parliamentary Debates*, House of Lords, vol. VII, 15 March 1911. cols 489–508.
62   See *Parliamentary Debates*, House of Lords, vol. VII, 28 March 1911, cols 657–708; 29 March 1911, cols 711–26.

government would oppose the bill 'as far as they possibly can'. The motion
was adjourned *sine die*.

School Attendance Bill

On 4 May 1911, Lord Willoughby de Broke[63] moved that it should be made
possible for children in agricultural districts to 'obtain exemption from
school attendance'.[64] There were boys, he said, in agricultural districts who
were not 'able to pass even standard VI, and whose detention at school is
a pure waste of time and money'. In his opinion, they would be 'far better
working on the land than absorbing public money by being kept at school
for the purpose of eventually being examined in a standard in which there
is no reasonable possibility of their passing'. Earl Beauchamp replied hoping
that the Board of Education would do what was necessary and that the bill
'shall have a speedy introduction'.[65]

The Parliament Bill

With reference to the Parliament Bill, Earl Beauchamp understood, he
said,[66] that a second reading would be given. The government hoped that
their Lordships would not press various amendments to 'the ultimate issue'.
The House had after all reached 'a certain amount of agreement upon the
subject. Both parties admit the existence of a grievance. We both admit that
it is necessary to find remedies.' And, although 'we admit that this Bill is

63   Willoughby de Broke, 19th Baron, b. 1869. A Conservative.
64   See *Parliamentary Debates*, House of Lords, vol. VIII, 4 May 1911, cols 172–6.
65   See *Parliamentary Debates*, House of Lords, vol. VIII, 15 May 1911, col. 434.
66   See *Parliamentary Debates*, House of Lords, vol. VIII, 24 May 1911, cols 811–19.

not a remedy for all the defects that require remedy at present, we cannot but think it is the best method of dealing with the subject at the present time. ... We deal with relations rather than reconstitution. ... It is the relations between the two Houses which are wrong; and it is those relations which we are anxious to improve; it is that difficulty, rather, which we are anxious to solve. We hope that this Bill will be a solution of the difficulty. The futility of political prophesy is proverbial, but at any rate I would venture to say this. If this weapon were used too tyrannically or too hastily it would break in our hand, if it would be we who would be hurt rather than the noble Lords opposite who have always protested against its use.'

Indian High Courts Bill

On 16 August 1911, Earl Beauchamp presented a bill, the object of which was to 'increase the number of Judges of the High Court of India, ... there being a large number of arrears'.[67] The bill received a second reading and was committed to a Committee of the Whole House.

Government of India Act (1858) Amendment Bill

Earl Beauchamp introduced a further Indian bill, the purpose of which was to 'enable the Secretary of State to make certain allowances to members of the Staff of the government of India at home here in England'.[68] The Earl said that he was 'entirely in the hands of the House', and that he would be 'quite prepared to put off until to-morrow the future stages of

---

67   See *Parliamentary Debates*, House of Lords, vol. IX, 16 August 1911, col. 1124.
68   See *Parliamentary Debates*, House of Lords, vol. IX, 17 August 1911, cols 1140–1.

the Bill if any noble Lord desires to carefully examine its innocent provisions. But if the noble Lords are content to trust the apparent harmlessness of the Bill, I should like to get it through its remaining stages to-day.' Their Lordships negatived the Committee stage. The bill was given a third reading and passed.

London Museum

On 25 March 1912, Lord Rotherham[69] asked the First Commissioner of Works whether arrangements could be made to allow members of the House to 'inspect' the London Museum.[70] Earl Beauchamp answered that the trustees of the Museum had arranged a private view for members of both Houses of Parliament on Wednesday between 11 a.m. and 4.30 p.m. Tickets of admission could be obtained from the Lord Chancellor's secretary, and could be made to 'include the wife of a Peer, or one daughter of a Peer, if that is mentioned in the application'.

Public Offices (Sites) Bill

On 29 July 1912, the Earl of Meath[71] desired to know whether, in the building operations proposed for Whitehall Gardens, 'there is any danger of so diminishing the amount of open space lying between Whitehall Gardens and the Thames that some future Government or some future London County Council will find it very difficult indeed to extend the public

---

69   Rotherham, 1st Baron, b. 1849. A Liberal.
70   See *Parliamentary Debates*, House of Lords, vol. XI, 25 March 1912, col. 616.
71   Meath, 12th Earl of, b. 1841. A Conservative.

gardens which are now upon the Embankment, and which add so much to the beauty of our metropolis and to the health and happiness of the people'.[72] Earl Beauchamp reassured the noble Lord that 'we are not allowed under the Bill to go beyond a certain line which is even not so far forward as a continuation of the line of Whitehall Court. Therefore there will always be in front of the new buildings room for a garden quite as large as that which is now there, and to which the noble Earl referred in terms of appreciation with which I should like to associate myself.'

Temperance (Scotland) Bill

On 6 November 1912, the First Commissioner of Works proposed a bill, the object of which was to 'transfer from the Licensing Court to the voters of the district the power of reducing or abolishing entirely the licences in that area'.[73] The bill was given a second reading and committed to a Committee of the Whole House.

The Commisioner of Works' responsibilities revealed in letters

As First Commissioner of Works, Earl Beauchamp was not only active in the House of Lords. The letters below indicate some of the other areas in which he held responsibility.

---

72 See *Parliamentary Debates*, House of Lords, vol. XII, 29 July 1912, col. 752.
73 See *Parliamentary Debates*, House of Lords, vol. XII, 6 November 1912, cols 853–74.

1

Arthur Bigge to Earl Beauchamp[74]

Marlborough House,

Pall Mall, S. W.

6th July 1910

The Earl Beauchamp, K. C. M. G.

Lord President of the Council

The King has considered the list of Names which you have submitted to constitute a committee of the Privy Council to arrange the preparations for the Coronation.

His Majesty has eliminated from it the names of Lord Cholmondeley, who is no longer Lord Great Chamberlain, Lord Roberts, Lord Balfour of Burleigh, Lord Ashbourne, and Sir Edward Seymour, who are replaced by the Secretary of State for the Colonies, the Lord Chancellor of Ireland, the Earl of Selborne,[75] the Right Hon. Austen Chamberlain, and Lord Shaw.

Arthur Bigge

2

His Majesty's thanks to the Department of the Office of Works & other officials[76]

Buckingham Palace

16th May, 1911

The Earl Beauchamp, K. C. M. G.

First Commissioner of Works

I am commanded to inform you how extremely pleased the King was with the manner in which this morning's ceremony was carried out. His Majesty much appreciates the great trouble bestowed upon every detail of the work of your Department, without which it would not have been possible to have achieved a result so eminently successful, and I am desired to express His Majesty's thanks to you all concerned.

Arthur Bigge

---

74   Source: Royal Archives: PS/PSO/GV/PS/COR/56098/3.
75   Selborne, 2nd Earl of, b. 1859. A Liberal Unionist.
76   Source: Royal Archives: PS/PSO/GV/PS/MAIN/2476/71.

3

Arthur Bigge to Earl Beauchamp[77]

Buckingham Palace

28th June, 1911

The Earl Beauchamp, K. C. M. G.

First Commissioner of Works

Dear Lord Beauchamp,

I am commanded to express to you the King's entire satisfaction with the admirable manner in which the Office of Works planned and carried out their most important and heavy duties in connection with the Coronation ceremonies. His Majesty can realise what their work has been, not only in the Abbey itself, but in the arrangement for and construction of stands and other details in the Streets and Parks.

The King desires you to make known to everyone in your Department his feelings of true appreciation of their labours, which have been crowned with such successful results.

Arthur Bigge

4

Earl Beauchamp to Arthur Bigge[78]

Lieutenant Colonel, The Right Hon. Sir Arthur Bigge, G. C. V. O., K. C. B.

3rd July 1911

My dear Sir Arthur,

I have received with much gratification your letter expressing the King's gracious appreciation of the manner in which the work of this Department in connection with the Coronation has been carried out.

I shall be glad to convey to the Officials of the Department this expression of His Majesty's satisfaction.

Yours v. Sincerely,

Beauchamp

77   Source: Royal Archives: PS/PSO/GV/PS/COR/56078/952.
78   Source: Royal Archives: PS/PSO/GV/PS(COR/56078/958.

5

Lord Stamfordham to Earl Beauchamp[79]

Buckingham Palace

9th November, 1911

There has been an unfortunate delay in bringing to the King's notice the formal submission of your proposals with regard to the playing of games in Hyde Park.

His Majesty gladly approves of the first proposals, namely, that County Schools may take their classes into Hyde Park for the purpose of organised games for children under 14 years of age, including Basket Ball, Rounders and soft ball games, Hockey, Cricket, Football: but His Majesty does not approve of cricket and football being played by Members of the Young Men's Christian Association, Police and Troops from the Barracks upon the ground in front of Knightsbridge Barracks. Similar application was made in the late reign for the Royal Servants, and was refused.

Stamfordham

6

Lord Stamfordham to Earl Beauchamp[80]

Buckingham Palace

11th June 1912

The Earl Beauchamp, K. C. M. G., First Commissioner of Works

The King has settled the 29th instant at 12 noon to inspect the model of the proposed Scottish National Memorial to King Edward.

Will you be kind enough to arrange with the Lord Provost that the model is sent here by that date, and also for his attendance.

His Majesty will be glad if you will also be present on the occasion.

Stamfordham

79   Source: Royal Archives: PS/PSO/GV/PS/MAN/3742/5. The following letters are from the same Arthur Bigge, the King's Private Secretary, who was elevated to be Baron Stamfordham in 1911.
80   Source: Royal Archives: PS/PSO/GV/PS/MAIN/779/17.

7

Lord Stamfordham to Earl Beauchamp[81]

Buckingham Palace

12th June 1912

The Earl Beauchamp, K. C. M. G., First Commissioner of Works

My dear Beauchamp,

The King is much surprised to read in the newspapers that Walmer Castle has been reconverted into a residence, and that the Lord Warden is living there. His majesty can hardly believe this as it is the first intimation which he has received of any change in the use to which the Castle was assigned during the late Reign, and when the question was raised as to whether His Majesty, then Lord Warden, could reside there, the Office of Works were strongly opposed to its occupation on sanitary grounds and also on account of the large outlay necessary to meet modern requirement as to servants accommodation and comfort in general.

Will you please let me know for the King's information whether there is any truth in the report, and if so under what circumstances the Castle was handed over to the Lord Warden, also whether any arrangement has been entered into as to its again becoming the official residence of future Lord Wardens.

Yours very truly,

Stamfordham

8

Lord Stamfordham to Earl Beauchamp[82]

Buckingham Palace

June 14th 1912

My dear Beauchamp,

Many thanks for your letter of yesterday. The King has read it and now understands how the question of the reoccupation of Walmer Castle by the Lord Warden has arisen and been settled, and that, through a misunderstanding between you and McDonnell, H. M. was not informed.

81   Source: Royal Archives: PS/PSO/GV/PS/MAIN/2238/4.
82   Source: Royal Archives: PS/PSO/GV/PS/MAIN/2238/7.

I am sure the King will always be glad to see you if there is any matter which you wish to bring before him.

I see that on the 4th September 1911 you wrote that various requests had reached you asking you to make rooms and gardens at Walmer more accessible to the Public and you then asked if the place would be likely to be wanted for the Royal Children. My reply was that H. M. did not want to put any reservation upon the Castle.

Yours very sincerely,

Stamfordham

9

Lord Stamfordham to Earl Beauchamp[83]

York Cottage,
Sandringham,
Norfolk

13th October 1912

My dear Beauchamp,

I mentioned to the King the subject of our Conversation of Thursday last. His Majesty quite agrees that all questions of policy and importance should be submitted to him by the Chief Commissioner: and that nothing should be submitted in your name about which you have not been informed. But in matters of detail and routine the Secretary would, as heretofore, communicate with me; and the King would see Mr Earle in the same way as His Majesty saw Sir S. McDonnell.

At the same time the King will always be glad to see you upon such business as you desire to bring personally before His Majesty.

This is practically the system which prevails in dealing with the Lord Chamberlain's Office. Also as regards the Foreign Office the King often sees Sir A. Nicolson as well as Sir E. Grey though of course the latter, as indeed every Minister, has access to His Majesty whenever he wishes.

Yours very sincerely,

Stamfordham

83   Source: Royal Archives: PS/PSO/GV/C/O/396/2.

Other sides of Earl Beauchamp revealed in letters

If the graceful art of writing letters strengthens friendship and leads to mutual understanding, then Earl Beauchamp knew how to employ his power for this purpose. A further sample of letters should illustrate this.

First there are the letters[84] to Lord Carrington, a fellow Liberal:[85]

1

From Earl Beauchamp

13, Belgrave Square,
S. W

18 V 10

My dear Lord Carrington,

Cd you conveniently to yourself see me sometime tomorrow? I am anxious to talk over with you the question of the Lord Stewardship & the restoration of his control over the Civil List money.

Yours very sincerely,

Beauchamp

2

From Earl Beauchamp

15 III 11

My dear Carrington,

The trustees of the National Gallery are ready to lend on loan to the House of Lords their picture of the death of Chatham. I rather hope that the Nat. Portrait Gallery will follow this excellent example & that we may secure from them other pictures wh will help to decorate the H. of L. just as [illegible] has so well decorated the H. of C. But for this purpose may I hope for yr kind cooperation? – I shall hope to see you soon & talk over details with you, but meanwhile shd be very glad to know that

---

84   Source: Carrington MSS (Bod. Lib.), *op. cit.*
85   Carrington, 1st Earl, b. 1843. A Liberal.

you are benevolently inclined towards the general scheme. I hope that you are getting on all right & will soon be with us again. But the weather is cold & treacherous. So pray take care.

Yours very sincerely,

Beauchamp

3

From Earl Beauchamp

20 III 11

My dear Carrington,

I am very glad that you are getting on all right. There has been little doing in our House – but what there is has gone off without difficulty. Many thanks for what you say about the picture. I am glad that you approve.

That Com. of MPs for the Colonial guests is getting into an awful mess. They have refused to approach the Govt about it & we shall have to be very careful.

Nothing is settled further as yet about doing in our House. I fancy that Ld Lansdowne finds the Bill more difficult than he expected.

I hope this fine weather is doing you good.

Yours very sincerely,

Beauchamp

4

From Earl Beauchamp,
Commissioner of Works
Madresfield Court

4 II 12

My dear Carrington,

I must write & tell you how sorry I was to hear from you the definite news of yr retirement. Nobody could have been a kinder or more delightful Colleague than you have been to me. But I also want to tell you how much I have learnt from & how much I admire (if it is not presumptuous to say so) – the way in wh you 'play the game'.

Nobody could be more unselfish or think less of himself & more of his party than you. It has been a real lesson to me more than once. Many thanks therefore as well as very many regrets.

Do not trouble to answer, for I shall be at the Cabinet unless Lettice's confinement prevents.

Yours very sincerely,

Beauchamp

Earl Beauchamp also corresponded with Lloyd George.[86] The letters are interesting in showing his genuine concern for the lot of agricultural labourers.

1

Earl Beauchamp to Lloyd George

H. M. Office of Works, &c.,
Storey's Gate
Westminster, S. W.

15th April 1913

My dear Lloyd George,

I need hardly tell you that I have read the various memoranda with the greatest interest and with real sympathy. They seem to me to be based upon accurate information: to be quite devoid of any exaggeration: and to constitute an unanswerable argument for dealing with the various problems. I am very glad indeed that you are willing to take up the question as a whole, and shall hope to cooperate with you. On the urban question indeed I cannot pretend to any particular information, but, from the facts set forth, there is obviously need to deal with the matter, and the recommendations seem quite reasonable.

So far as the rural question is concerned, it does seem to me that the important person for whom we should in the first instance do all we can is the agricultural labourer. While we need an economic revolution with regard to his wage, a moral revolution which will give him independence (i.e. an untied cottage under fair tenure) is no less necessary. At the present moment we work in a vicious circle: the agricultural

86   Source: Parliamentary Archives, Lloyd George MSS, C/3/5/1.

labourer, insufficiently paid, is incapable of doing a good day's work, and, so long as he cannot do a good day's work, he is not worth a rise in wages. Some violent step, therefore, such as the establishment of a minimum wage is the only way to get out of this vicious circle. But I do also look upon his independence as being no less necessary if we are to make a success of any policy. One fact indeed has escaped reference, but I believe it to be of some importance. The climate in different parts of England is so different that it affects very considerably the working power of the individual, and I doubt very much if we should ever find that a labourer in some of the low-lying districts will be able to do so much work as one who lives in the more bracing North. That, however, is one of the points which the Trades Board will be able to arrange. Nor do I think that the proposals for dividing the increased expenditure at all unfair. The farmer is not so deserving of sympathy as the agricultural labourer: and, generally speaking, if you take 12 farmers and compare them with 12 tradesmen, you will find a higher level of intelligence and also greater energy amongst the tradesmen than you will amongst the tenant farmers. They are, in the worst sense of the word, conservative, and for too ready to be content with the methods of agriculture which were adequate for their great-great-grand-parents. Any grievance which they have will, I think, clearly be met by the establishment of a land court, which will have power to give them, not only fixity of tenure, but also a fair rent: and the land court would also solve the problem of game. It is always difficult to lay down a general proposition when circumstances differ so widely as they do in such a matter as this. Generally speaking, however, it is a grievance which seems to me generally to be exaggerated and which a fixity of tenure (which involves no penalty for complaints) will put right.

There is one aspect of the establishment of the land court to which no reference is made: and, as it resembles very largely a great deal of liberal legislation in other directions, it is worthy of mention. In the case of Old Age Pensions, Employers' Liability and the Agricultural Holdings Act where the State has set up a high standard and enforced that standard upon all landlords, there has been little practical difference either to good landlords or good employers. The trend of much social legislation to-day is to raise the bad landlord and the bad employer to the level which has been set already by others. So, with the land court, the good landlord has nothing to fear, but may even find his rents increased. A bad landlord will be obliged to live up to the standard which has been set for him by good landlords for many years past.

It would probably be desirable to give the land court every possible latitude and very extensive powers, because the system of agriculture is so different in different parts of the country. Some tenants prefer yearly leases: in fact, in my own neighbourhood they refuse to take longer ones; but I should not allow any landlord, whatever the terms of the lease which he grants, to contract himself out of the land court.

Lastly, let me say one word about local authorities. Their action in the past has very often been a great disappointment. For instance, so far from exercising their powers in the direction of housing, even now they often put difficulties in the way. They are too much controlled by the Landlord, the small employer and the builder. I hope, therefore, that in any legislation very considerable powers will be given to some energetic central authority to enable them to deal with matters which are neglected in the locality itself. The position of the Medical Officer of Health, to which I was glad to see reference made, shows how important it is that powers should be given to some Body which is capable of dealing with the problem with real energy.

Let me finally thank you once more for having given me an opportunity of seeing these really valuable memoranda and say how glad I shall be to help in your campaign on the lines foreshadowed. They do not go one bit beyond what the circumstances of the case demand.

Yours v. Sincerely,

Beauchamp

2

Earl Beauchamp to Lloyd George[87]

Madresfield Court
Malvern Link

September 5, 1913

My dear Lloyd George,

I am sorry that I cannot breakfast with you next week as I have people staying with me for the Gloucester Festival.

There is no doubt that the party is anxiously awaiting the campaign and is ready to rally to your support with much enthusiasm. I should like to see, as part of the general scheme, a provision for buying land compulsorily (without compensation) at an agricultural value of the land in all cases where it has been paying agricultural rates.

If we could get land with considerable gardens on roads upon such terms it would be much easier to build an economic cottage and establish the labourer upon an independent footing.

Yours very sincerely,

Beauchamp

87   *Ibid.*, C/3/5/2.

P. S. Do not be alarmed about the exaggerated statements about your house in Downing Street!

As Asquith was still the Prime Minister, we may be certain, that even he must have been quite satisfied with the work of the Earl, who had now been recommended to the office of Lord Lieutenant of Gloucestershire.

CHAPTER 12

Lord Lieutenant of Gloucestershire

Earl Beauchamp was appointed Lord Lieutenant of Gloucestershire in 1911 on the recommendation of the Prime Minister. Every county has a Lord Lieutenant, and the office dates from 1557, in the reign of Henry VIII.[1] The history of Gloucestershire itself goes back to 1016, when it was recorded that this area constituted a county. The Lord Lieutenant, the Sovereign's lieutenant, was originally responsible for maintaining local defences and civil order. Later he was expected to command the county militias and, during the Second World War, he took a leading role in organizing the Territorial Army and Home Guard battalions. Until recently, most Lord Lieutenants have been 'local landowners from the county with large houses and grand titles'. Earl Beauchamp very well fitted in this category. Again the role of a Lord Lieutenant is largely ceremonial. He welcomes the Sovereign, members of the royal family, and visiting heads of state. On these occasions he wears a general officer's uniform, complete with silver braid and sword.

We can trace the sort of work undertaken by Earl Beauchamp as Lord Lieutenant only on the basis of the records available to us. The documents, a selection of which are displayed below, speak for themselves.[2]

1

Ceremonial Department,

St James's Palace, S. W. 1.

The replies to Lord Beauchamp's questions are:

---

1   For a brief history, see 'Lord-Lieutenant and Custos Rotulorum of Gloucestershire', in Alastair Bruce, Julian Calder and Mark Cator, *Keepers of the Kingdom: The Ancient Offices of Britain* (London: Weidenfeld & Nicolson, 1919), p. 105.
2   Source: Gloucestershire Archives, Gloucester. Files: D 551/ 1–16.

1. The Lord Lieutenant as the King's representative takes precedence of the Lord Mayor, except at purely civic functions such as a dinner given by the City or a meeting of the citizens summoned by the Mayor.

It seems clear therefore that he has precedence of the Lord Mayor at a Merchant Venturers' dinner, the Merchant Venturers being an independent corporate body and not officially part of the Corporation of Bristol. It would apply also to services in the Cathedral unless there be any service which comes within the description of a 'civic function', the invitations to which are issued by or on behalf of the city authorities.

2. The Lord Lieutenant within his jurisdiction takes precedence of the County Sheriff in all circumstances under a Royal Warrant of the 20th February 1904. As the Sheriff of Bristol City is the Sheriff of the County of the City of Bristol, the Royal Warrant gives the Lord Lieutenant precedence over him in so much of the city as lies in Gloucestershire and comes within Lord Beauchamp's jurisdiction.[3] Apart from this as the Municipal Corporations Act lays down the order of precedence in Bristol as Lord Mayor, Recorder, Sheriff, the Lord Lieutenant as the King's representative has precedence over the city Sheriff throughout the City in the same way as he has precedence over the Lord Mayor.

2

House of Lords,

S. W.

The 8th of December, 1913

My Lord,

I have the honour to inform you that, in accordance with your recommendation, I have directed the 18 names mentioned in your Letter of the 16th October to be inserted in the Commission of the Peace for the County of Gloucester.

I have the honour to be,

My Lord,

your obedient Servant,

Haldane

3   The city of Bristol extended into Gloucestershire.

3

Nov. 8, 1914

'Lord Ducie[4] does not like Herbert Wilcox, he does not know him personally & has evidently had a very biased opinion given him.'

4

October 9th 14

Dear Lord Beauchamp,

Knowing all I do of ... I cannot recommend him, although I should like to do so. He may get into financial difficulties, as he has so many irons in the fire. ...

5

October 15, 1914

Dear Lord Beauchamp,

In answer to your kind letter of yesterday I shall be very willing to join the advisory Committee to assist you in the selection of magistrates.

Yours faithfully,

[Signature illegible]

6

Painswick House,
Nr Stroud,
Gloucestershire

26 X 14

My dear Lord Beauchamp,

I have at length got the information I have been seeking about candidates for the Whitminster Bench. I enclose my notes. [...]

4   Ducie, 3rd Earl of, b. 1827. A Liberal Unionist.

7

Lord Beauchamp to Sir Stafford Howard

Privy Council Office,
Whitehall. S.W.

27 X 14

My dear Howard,

I have told Hyett that the first 2 at Whitminster wd be fair & asked him if he can suggest 2 Liberals one each for Cirencester & Wooton under Edge. Otherwise we are making 3 C. to 1 L. wh is a return to the bad old system. What do you think?

Yours v. Sincereley

Beauchamp

[hand written note]

8

Cilymaenllwyd,
Llynelly,
Carm

26 October 1914

My dear Beauchamp,

Magistrates

Whitminster

J. Graham-Clarke

F. James Platt

will be all right.

I agree if more are appointed there should be one from each side of politics.

Wooton-under-Edge

I think T.E. Sherwood Hale ought to be appointed anyhow.

Cirencester

As there are 5 Liberals to four Conservatives here now I see no objection to the appointment of C. J. Maxwell.

I think we must have regard to the composition of the Local Bench in each case rather than to the balance of political opinion amongst any particular batch of Magistrates appointed at one time for various places.

Yours truly

[Signature illegible]

9

Painswick House,
Nr Stroud,
Gloucestershire

16 XI 14

My dear Lord Beauchamp,

I enclose a list of ... to three Benches for your consideration. ...

10

Cilymaenllwyd,
Llanelly,
Carm

19.11.14

My dear Beauchamp,

I am quite ready to approve the list which I return.

Yours Truly,

Stafford Howard

11

Privy Council Office,
Whitehall, S. W.

9th December 1914

Dear Sir,

Gloucestershire Magistrates

I am desired by Lord Beauchamp to inform you that all the gentlemen who were recently agreed to by the Advisory Committee have expressed their willingness to serve, with the exception of Mr Francis J. Platte of Dubridge Hill, Stroud. He states that his time is too fully occupied to allow him to undertake the duties of a Magistrate.

Lord Beauchamp is accordingly submitting the other names to the Lord Chancellor.

I am,

Yours faithfully,

[illegible]

12

House of Lords,

Dec. 12, 14

My dear Beauchamp,

I was sorry to hear that by a blunder in my office the clerk wrote Worcestershire instead of Gloucestershire in the letter for the Lord Chancellor's signature. It happens that I took the letter in to the Lord Chancellor myself, as we have a new secretary in place of Butler, and told him it was Gloucestershire; neither he nor I in fact read the letter, relying that it was right. I wish I could say that I had done it on purpose, because you ought to be Ld Lt of Worcestershire. The Gloucestershire Commission will be sent for and properly filled.

Please accept my regrets for having occasioned you any trouble or annoyance.

Yours very sincerely,

Kenneth Muir Mackenzie[5]

13

Broughtons,
Newnham-on-Severn
Glos.

---

5   Muir Mackenzie, 1st Baron, b. 1845. A Liberal.

August 12, 1914

Dear Lord Beauchamp,

Now that the actual mobilisation is complete, I thought you might like to hear how the Territorial Association & the units have got on. The mobilisation itself has gone extraordinarily smoothly, there has been no confusion. Everything happened punctually according to the scheme. And accordingly the units have played up magnificently.

14

Township of East Dean
Cinderford, Glos.

Frank Addis
Assistant Overseer
Clerk to the Parish Council

26th January 1915

[To] The Rt Hon. The Earl of Beauchamp
Madresfield Court,
Worcestershire

My Lord,

The East Dean Parish Council at their last meeting decided to ask Your Lordship to submit two names to the Lord Chancellor to be added to the Commission of the Peace for the Newnham Division of this County, which they trust Your Lordship will kindly do. Mr A. E. Dykins who was a Justice of the Peace recently died. The names they wish to submit are: Mr Martin Henry Perkins, Victoria Street, Cinderford, Glos.; Mr Ambrose Adams, Ruspidge, Cinderford, Glos.

Mr Perkins was for several years a District Councillor and a Guardian of the Poor, he is at present an Overseer of the Poor and a School Manager, he is also President of the Miners Association for the Forest of Dean and President of the Cinderford Co-operative Society Ltd., which has a Membership of 3000, he is much respected in the District and they have every confidence in submitting his name.

Mr Adams who resides at Ruspidge where there is no Magistrate, although there is a Police Station, and people requiring the Signature of a Magistrate have often the inconvenience of travelling some distance, he is a Parish Councillor and a School Manager, also Treasurer of the Cinderford Co-operative Society Ltd. and is connected with a Friendly Society of which he is Secretary and is well known and respected in the District.

Both are Members of the Miners Wage Board.

We are, My Lord,

Your obedient Servants,

Chairman

Clerk

15

Privy Council Office,
Whitehall, S. W.

To F. A. Hyett, Esq.

4th February 1915

Dear Mr Hyett,

Lord Beauchamp has been looking through a list of recommendations of names which he has received at various times to be added to the Commission of the Peace for Cheltenham, though he cannot pretend to have any intimate knowledge of the qualifications of these gentlemen. The following are some of the names on his list:

1. The Rev. W. H. Flecker, M. A.

    Principal, Dean Close Memorial School

2. Mr W. H. Horsley,

    Filey Lawn, Sydenham Road

3. Mr J. N. Hobbs,

    Concord, Moor End Grove

4. The Rev. Samuel Jackson, M. A.

    Vice-Principal, Liverpool Institute

5. Mr L. W. Montagnon,

    6, Wellington Square

6. Mr John Player,

    Thirlestane Hall

In view of the grave preponderance of Conservatives over Liberals on this Bench Lord Beauchamp does not think it would be unfair to appoint two liberals to one Conservative. He would be most grateful if you would kindly consider the names of the above and let him know your views. He is writing to Major Henry Webb with regard to Newnham.

I am,

Yours truly,

George Cunningham

16

Earl Beauchamp to Major Henry Webb, M. P.

Privy Council Office,
Whitehall, S. W.

4th February 1915

Dear Sir,

Lord Beauchamp has asked me to say that more Magistrates are wanted at Newnham. Mr McLaughlin has been recommended, and while Lord Beauchamp has no objection to this appointment, although he is a Conservative, he does not care to appoint him without adding a Liberal to this Bench at the same time. The difficulty in the matter is that what is wanted is somebody who resides in or near Newnham itself and that is the objection to the recommendations from the East Dean council. (A copy of their letter is enclosed herewith).

Lord Beauchamp is told that you are building a house near Newnham and might be willing to sit sometimes on the Bench. It would give him great personal pleasure if you would do this, and he feels sure that the Advisory Committee would unanimously endorse your appointment to the Bench. As your constant attendance would, however, be obviously impossible, perhaps you would be good enough to make suggestions of some other people who are Liberals and resident in Newnham.

I am,

Yours faithfully,

George Cunningham

17

Henry Webb to The Rt Hon. The Earl of Beauchamp, Lord President, Privy Council, Whitehall, S. W.

Dean Rise,
Newnham,
Glos.

Feb. 6, 1915

My Lord,

I am obliged for your letter of Feb. 4, Re – Making Magistrates for the Forest of Dean Division.

I have made a full inquiry about the Newnham area, and find that there is no need for another in the Newnham village. There are already four there, and all of them are Conservatives. The four are Russell Kerr, Montagu Lloyd, Spenser Shelley, and Nigel Jones. At present there is not a single Liberal in the neighbourhood. Further, McLaughlin has no record of any sort behind him to give him a qualification for the position.

I am obliged for your kind offer about myself, and can only say that if you think fit to make me one I shall esteem it a great favour and honour.

Instead of making McLaughlin I should very strongly urge that Mr James Joiner be added to the bench. I do so for the following reason. Mr Joiner is about two miles from Newnham, two miles from Blakeney and two miles from Ruspidge. He is in touch with a large number of people, and there is a large district all around him with no J.P. Nearer than Newnham or Blakeney. Mr Joiner has done a good deal of public work but is not now on any public body because he is a Contractor.

The two men recommended for Cinderford Mr M. H. Perkins, and Mr Ambrose Adams are good men for the position and I would strongly advise adding them to the bench.

I would also beg to suggest that Mr Henry Herridge Batt of Drybrook be made for Drybrook. Mr Smith has just died and there is no Magistrate nearer than Ruardean or Mitcheldean. Drybrook is a very populous district and there is great need for one.

Mr Batt is a retired butcher and much respected. He has time to attend to the work and has many years of useful work behind him.

I have the honour to be,

My Lord

Your obedient servant,

Henry Webb

18

Hyett to Earl Beauchamp

Painswick House, Nr Stroud, Gloustershire

24 II 15

My dear Lord Beauchamp,

I think your proposal for Cheltenham is a good one and I will certainly support it. ...

Hyett

19

Thirlestaine Hall,
Cheltenham

March 4/15

My Lord Beauchamp,

I thank you for your letter kindly suggesting my name as a magistrate for Gloucestershire (I am already a magistrate for County of Glamorganshire) but my age over 70 prevents my undertaking the duties.

Yours faithfully,

John Player

20

Esmond, Cheltenham

4 III 15

Dear Lord Beauchamp,

It will give me much pleasure to serve as a magistrate for the County (Glos.) should my name be approved by the Lord Chancellor. May I confess my gratitude for your Lordship's kindness in recommending me.

Yours faithfully,

Richard Gillies Hardy

21

Brightlands,
Newnham,
Gloucestershire

March 4th 1915

My Lord,

I have the honour to acknowledge Your Lordship's letter of the 3rd inst. informing me you propose recommending me as a Magistrate for the county of Gloucestershire.

Should the Lord Chancellor see fit to appoint me I shall be prepared to undertake the duties and sit at the Petty Sessional Division of Newnham. My full Christian names are: Vivian, Guy, Ouseley. My address is as above.

I have the honour to be, My Lord,

Yours obediently,

Vivian McLaughlin

22

Bradley House,
Soudley,
Nr. Newnham,
Glos.

3rd March 1915

Dear Sir,

I thank you for yours of the 3rd and beg to state I shall be very pleased to accept the honour of becoming a Magistrate in the Petty Session of Newnham, my Christian name is 'James' and address, Bradley House, Soudley, Nr Newnham.

Yours faithfully,

James Joiner

23

William Herman Flecker, M. A., D. C. L. to Lord Beauchamp

*March 4*th, *1915*

My Lord,

I thank your Lordship for your kind promise to recommend me to the Lord Chancellor as a magistrate for the county. Should your recommendation meet with the approval of the Lord Chancellor I shall be very willing to undertake the duties of the office.

I am, My Lord,

Yours faithfully,

W. H. Flecker

24

House of Lords,

S. W.

Lord Chancellor to Earl Beauchamp

March 9th 1915

To The Rt Hon. The Lord Beauchamp, K. G.

My Lord,

I am directed by the Lord Chancellor to thank you for your letter of the 8th inst. enclosing a list of recommendations for the Commission of the Peace.

His Lordship notices however the name of the Rev. W. H. Flecker & wishes me to remind your Lordship that it is not the practice of the Lord Chancellor to appoint clergyman to the Bench, unless there is such a lack of suitable persons in the district as to make the appointment a virtual necessity.

Perhaps your Lordship would be so good as to advise the Lord Chancellor whether such conditions obtain in the case of Cheltenham, & whether you consider the appointment of Mr Flecker unavoidable.

I am, My Lord,

Your obedient servant,

D. Post

25

Privy Council Office,
Whitehall, S. W.

To D. Post, Esq.

House of Lords

10th March 1915

Dear Sir,

In reply to your letter to Lord Beauchamp of the 9th instant, he desires me to say that the objection raised by the Lord Chancellor had already been considered by the Advisory Committee who were aware of the general rule on the subject. The Committee quite agree that any clergyman who holds a Benefice is placed in a very invidious position when he sits upon the Bench; however in this case they did not think that these considerations applied as the clergyman in question holds no Benefice and he is never likely to leave his present position which is of an educational character.

In view of this fact, which in other cases is held to remove the general objection, Lord Beauchamp would venture to hope that the Lord Chancellor will agree with him that it is a fitting appointment.

I am,

Yours Truly,

George Cunningham

26

House of Lords, S. W.

March 15th

To George Cunningham

Dear Sir,

Thank you for your letter which I have put before the Lord Chancellor who has decided to waive the objection which is usually made to appoint clergymen. The list will therefore be prepared as desired by Lord Beauchamp & completed as soon as I can get the Lord Chancellor's signature, I hope today or tomorrow.

Yours faithfully,

[D. Post]

27

National Committee for Relief in Belgium[6]

Trafalgar Buildings, Trafalgar Square, London. W. C.

Chairman: The Right Hon. The Lord Mayor of London
Honorary member: His Excellency The Belgian Minister

Appeal Committee:
His Grace The Archbishop of Canterbury
His Grace the Duke of Norfolk,[7] *K. G.*
His Eminence Cardinal Bourne
The Right Hon. The Marquess of Lansdowne, K. G.
The Right Rev. Thomas Nicol, D. D. (Moderator, The Church of England)
The Right Hon. The Earl of Rosebery, K. G.
The Right Hon. Sir J. Compton-Rickett, M. P. (President, The Free Church Council)
The Right Hon. Viscount Bryce, O. M.
The Very Rev. J. H. Hertz, Ph. D. (Chief Rabbi)
The Right Hon. Arthur Henderson, M. P.
John E. Redmond, Esq., M. P.
Hon. Secretary: W. A. M. Goode, Esq.
Hon. Treasurer: A. Shirley Benn, Esq., M. P.

To: The Earl Beauchamp, K. G.

9th June 1915

My Lord,

I venture to enquire if you received a letter from the Duke of Norfolk, President of our Executive Committee, dated May 25th, in regard to a County Committee to be affiliated with this organisation? If not, I should be very glad to send you a copy

---

6   This is after the outbreak of war: see Chapter 15. The German army invaded neutral Belgium on 4 August 1914 and pursued draconian policies to ensure there was no counter-offensive there, widely reported in the British press as 'the Rape of Belgium'. German occupation, together with an Allied naval blockade, caused the virtual collapse of the Belgian economy and brought about considerable hardship and shortages for the population. There was much concern in English philanthropic circles to support the Belgian people in their time of need, and this was in tune with patriotic feeling.

7   Norfolk, 15th Duke of, b. 1847. A Conservative.

of the letter; and if you did receive it, the Duke of Norfolk would be grateful for a reply to this address.

So far, in twenty-five counties the Lord Lieutenant has consented to become President of County Committees.

I am,

Your obedient servant,

W. A. M. Goode

Hon. Secretary

28

Lord Norfolk to Lord Beauchamp

May 25th 1915

My Lord,

As Chairman of the Executive of the National Committee for Relief in Belgium I wrote to ask your approval of the formation of a Gloucester County Committee in association with our National organisation, We propose to form in each county branch committees, under the patronage of the Lord Lieutenant and of the county's Parliamentary members. I sincerely hope that you will be kind enough to accept the honorary office of President of the Gloucester County Committee. This will not involve any appreciable inroad upon your time – being a Lord-Lieutenant myself I know your time is probably already well occupied – as the work of organisation in your county can be largely done from national headquarters.

If you can see your way to give a favourable reply to my request, the Honorary Secretary of the National Committee will at once communicate with the Gloucester members of Parliament, and, after hearing from them, will write to all Mayors in Gloucester notifying them that you have kindly become President of the County Committee, and asking them in your name and in the name of the Parliamentary members to open local funds, or to arrange for local committees of principal citizens to do so in order to assist the National Committee in their endeavour to save from starvation 1,500,000 people in Belgium whom the Germans refuse to feed.

All these local funds will be requested to transmit their contributions *direct* to national headquarters, therefore there will be no necessity for the establishment of any county headquarters or any tax upon time. All contributions, however, whether from towns, committees, or individuals, will be credited by the National Committee to the county from which they are received. From time to time we shall issue in the County and to the general public the results of what each county is doing.

The idea of organisation on a county basis is largely due to the numerous applications we have received from all parts of the country for authority to establish branch committees. It appeared to us that the best way to utilise this widespread response to our appeal – over £350,000 have been contributed in less than four weeks – was to adopt the County plan and to invoke the generous patronage and authority of the Lord-Lieutenant and the County members.

The proposed Committees in your county will not add to existing Belgian Relief organisations. The Belgian Minister now turns over to us all the donations he receives for the relief of distress in Belgium; therefore any local body in your county that has been sending funds to the Belgian Minister will achieve the same purpose – and save time and trouble – by contributing direct to the local funds which I hope will be opened under your auspices.

We shall be glad to support your county's efforts by arranging with the local Committees to send well-known religious or political speakers and to supply the local bodies with literature in order to emphasize the debt of honour we owe to ourselves to see to it that the bulk of the Belgian nation, still in Belgium, do not starve and die.

I enclose a copy of the appeal we issued and earnestly hope that you will give the weight of your influence to this object by accepting the Presidency of your County Committee. I should be extremely glad of an early reply.

Yours faithfully,

(signed) Norfolk
Chairman, Executive Committee

P. S. Kindly address your reply as follows:
The Duke of Norfolk,
The National Committee for Relief in Belgium
Trafalgar Building
Trafalgar Square, London. E. C.

We may safely assume that because of his devotion to the Liberal cause both in and outside parliament, Earl Beauchamp must have readily answered the call. In the meantime another accolade was bestowed upon him. He was appointed Warden of the Cinque Ports.

Alfred Emmott, 1st Baron Emmott

Edmond Warre

William Lygon, 7th Earl Beauchamp

Lady Mary Lygon

as Marie de Lorraine a lady of the Court of Marguerite de Valois.

Lady Mary Hepburn-Stuart-Forbes-Trefusis (née Lygon) as Marie de Lorraine, a lady at the court of Marguerite de Valois

Hallam Tennyson, 2nd Baron Tennyson

Sir Almeric William FitzRoy

Arthur John Bigge, Baron Stamfordham

Eton College

William Lygon, 8th Earl Beauchamp with William Lygon, the 7th Earl

'A view taken from Christ Church Meadows, Oxford', showing
James Webber and Cyril Jackson

Joe Chamberlain

Rufus Isaacs, 1st Marquis of Reading

Herbert Henry Asquith, 1st Earl of Oxford and Asquith

Francis Paget

David Lloyd George, 1st Earl Lloyd George

Victor Child-Villiers, 7th Earl of Jersey

Edward Grey, 1st Viscount Grey of Fallodon

The Education Bill in the House of Lords (The Collapse of the Archbishop of Canterbury)showing: George Wyndham Kennion; George Ridding; Francis John Jayne; Edward Stuart Talbot; Frederick Temple; Lord Alwyne Compton; Edgar Jacob; William Dalrymple Maclagan; Randall Thomas Davidson, Baron Davison of Lambeth; Arthur Foley Winninton-Ingram; and John Wordsworth

William Lygon, 7th Earl Beauchamp

Lord Warden of the Cinque Ports

Early history of the ports

The Cinque Ports have a long, complicated and intriguing history. This history has been thoroughly described elsewhere,[1] but we will outline it briefly here so as to put Earl Beauchamp's appointment as Lord Warden into context. The Confederation of Cinque Ports was the consequence of their special location. The coastline of south-east England, historically known as the 'Saxon shore' (or 'Kent shore'), commands a short sea link between England and the European continent. The narrowness of the channel caused the English to live under constant threat of attack from abroad. And such attacks indeed happened, as was seen in AD 43 when the Romans first landed on the Saxon shore. It was the Romans who first understood the strategic importance of this bit of coastline and they proceeded to build fortresses and lighthouses along it. The five ports on the Saxon shore were soon ordered to guard the coast *more solito* or 'according to the usual custom'. After the Norman Conquest, William I, following the same strategic thought as the Romans, granted a charter to these 'Cinque Ports', and the charter was confirmed by succeeding Sovereigns. However, it is a charter of Edward I [1278] that secured permanent acceptance of the Confederation of the Cinque Ports – originally Hastings, Romney,

---

1   See K.M.E. Murray, *The Constitutional History of the Cinque Ports* (Manchester: Manchester University Press, 1935). Also helpful are: Edward Hinings, *History, People and Places of the Cinque Ports* (Buckinghamshire: Spurbooks Limited, 1975); Edward Knocker, *An Account of the Grand Court of Shepway: At Dover for the Installation of the Right Honourable Henry John Temple, Viscount Palmerston* (London: John Russell Smith, 1862). Knocker was Seneschal [a 'Learned Steward'] of the Court.

Hythe, Dover and Sandwich, to which were added the two 'ancient towns' of Rye and Winchelsea. The charter gave the Portsmen various privileges. They commanded absolute control of the English Channel: no one could leave the ports without their consent. They were granted freedom from customary taxation, and also had the right to try and judge local criminals. Moreover, they were empowered to admit other towns as 'limbs' or 'members' and control even the smallest creeks and harbours along the coast. In return for these privileges, the ports were bound to keep certain obligations in the service of the Monarch. They had to furnish fifty-seven ships for fifteen days each year, each port being 'allocated a share of the total burden'. Royal interests were represented by the Lord Warden[2] of the Confederation, an office which was in the gift of the Monarch. The appointment, however, had to be upheld by the court to the Confederation. Since the ports were considered as a unit, the common court met at Shepway ['way to the ships']. The Court of Shepway 'became the means by which the King could exercise some form of control over his turbulent subjects'.[3] The Court, over which a Speaker presided, was composed of the various officers of the Ports elected for this purpose. It met at irregular times, but it could be summoned by the Lord Warden. The business of the Court was not only concerned with the settling of disputes between the Portsmen, but with safeguarding the liberties of the ports themselves. It undertook to appoint bailiffs, and to swear a new Lord Warden.

The Portsmen asserted their right to have the rank of barons. It has been suggested that the title of 'baron' goes back to the twelfth century: it was 'indicative of a man's place in society and position in the lord's court, rather than his tenure'. The barons were entitled to carry 'a canopy supported by silver staves over the heads of the King and Queen at a Coronation', and to sit 'at the chief table afterwards in the place of honour on the Monarch's

2   The origin of the office of the Lord Warden is credited to William the Conqueror, who created 'a kind of palatine jurisdiction under a *gardien* or warden'. His seat of administration was at the Castle of Dover, whence he 'exercised over the whole district the combined civil, military and naval authority'. See Knocker, *op. cit.*, p. 4.

3   It is recorded that, between the thireenth and sixteenth centuries, the men of the Cinque Ports were the 'fiercest and most rapacious pirates of the time'.

right hand'.[4] At the coronation of James I in 1603, the barons of the Cinque Ports were ordered by the King to wear 'one scarlett gowne, down to the ancle, faced with crymson satten, crymson silk stockings, crymson velvet shoes and black velvet cappes'.[5]

Of all the Cinque Ports it is the port of Dover which has retained its historical and strategic importance, because it is from Dover that there is the shortest sea passage to the continent. Dover thus represents the 'Gateway of England'. From Dover Richard I started for the Third Crusade; Hubert de Burgh led the Cinque Ports' fleet against the French; Henry VIII departed, carried by the ships of the Cinque Ports, to meet with François I of France. Charles II landed in Dover on his return from exile. And more recently plans for the evacuation of the British Army from Dunkirk were hastily drawn up in Dover Castle. The castle has its own history: the first fortifications were built after the battle of Hastings, and thereafter successive Monarchs, aware of the strategic importance of Dover, continued to strengthen the structure. Henry VIII, more than anyone else, recognized the significance of the castle's site. He had cannons mounted there to combat any seaborne enemy landing. The castles at Deal and Walmer were built with gun platforms too. Indeed, the coastal defences built in the time of Henry VIII were constructed according to an entirely new concept of design. 'With four large circular bastions around the small central keep', they had a 'wide, deep moat and parapets curved to deflect gunshots. The main armament was mounted on the outer and inner bastions and on top of the keep.'[6] It was from Deal and Walmer that English ships set out to scatter the Spanish naval force sheltering in Calais harbour at the time of the Armada. How well that bard of English history, Thomas Macaulay, put it! – 'Then it was that the courage of those sailors who manned the rude barks of the Cinque Ports first made the flag of England terrible on the seas.'

---

4   See Hinings, *op. cit.*, p. 29.
5   *Ibid.*, p. 31. William IV and Queen Victoria would have nothing to do with this self-exhibition of the Cinque Ports barons. The custom was, however, resumed during the coronations of Edward VII, Georges V and VI, and Elizabeth II.
6   *Ibid.*, p. 52.

Lord Wardens and their changing functions

The appointment of the Lords Warden of the Cinque Ports came from the Sovereign personally, and, from the very beginning, the wardenship tended to be bestowed on the Sovereign's favourite. The Lords Warden were appointed for life, with a yearly emolument. From the early eighteenth century, their official residence was Walmer Castle, built in the year 1540, but modified to be comfortable as a residence: the central keep and the tower of the castle were rebuilt as living quarters, and a large garden was laid out.

The first Lord Warden to reside at Walmer was Lionel Sackville, seventh Earl and first Duke of Dorset. He occupied the castle (with interruptions) between 1708 and 1765. Queen Anne had conferred the post upon him after the death of her husband, Prince George of Denmark, in October 1708: Prince George had been the Lord Warden for some years. In June 1713, Dorset fell into disgrace and was compelled to resign. He was replaced by James Duke of Ormonde, Commander-in-Chief of the army. Ormonde held the post for only a year, before, for political reasons, he had to flee to France. Dorset was reinstated, and, though dismissed in 1717, was returned to the office in 1727 and kept the wardenship for the rest of his life. He died in October 1765. Although Dorset lived mainly in his own residence at Knole, he made considerable internal and external alterations at Walmer Castle, which 'necessitated (a) the erection of entirely new quarters for himself [the drawing-room was designed to consist of two apartments; the dining-room was 24 feet long by 16 feet broad]; (b) the conversion of the ground floor into service-rooms for his establishment' [pantry, kitchen, washhouse, store-room and bake-house].[7] Dorset used to stay only a few weeks in the summer at Walmer. He presided over several

---

7   The Marquess Curzon of Kedleston, *The Personal History of Walmer Castle and its Lords Wardens*, ed. Stephen Gwynn (London: Macmillan, 1927), p. 17. [George Nathaniel Curzon (1859–1925), Conservative M.P., 1886–98; Under-Secretary for India, 1891–2; Under-Secretary for Foreign Affairs, 1895–8; Viceroy of India, 1899–1905; Lord Privy Seal, 1915–16; Lord President of the Council, 1916–19; created 1st Marquess Curzon of Kedleston, 1921.]

assemblies, appointed various officers to a great number of posts, and held 'the supreme command of all military forces within his jurisdiction'.

After the Duke of Dorset's death in October 1765 the next Lord Warden installed was Robert d'Arcy, fourth Earl of Holdernesse, a nobleman 'solid and steady in character but mediocre in talents'.[8] He had been a Lord of the Bedchamber to George II, and then Secretary of State in 1751, but was dismissed from this office by George III on his succession to the throne. As consolation, the King appointed Holdernesse Lord Warden, with a salary of £4,000 a year. There seems to have been 'a chorus of agreement among his contemporaries as to the insignificance' of the lord wardenship.[9] Lord Holdernesse died in May 1778, 'the least impressive Lord Warden between 1750 and 1900'.[10] The main mark he left at Walmer appears to have been the introduction of sash windows in the walls of the castle.

Holdernesse was succeeded by the acting Prime Minister, Frederick Lord North (afterwards the second Earl of Guilford), an 'easy, good-tempered, frequently witty, always well-meaning, but short-sighted statesman'.[11] There is no evidence that North ever resided continuously at Walmer. He spent the greater part of his time in London, at Grosvenor Square. North died in August 1792. There is very little to report on his wardenship during the fourteen years he held it.

On 6 August 1792, the day after North's death, the King wrote to William Pitt, his Prime Minister, anxious to take:

> the first opportunity of acquainting Mr Pitt that the Wardenship of the Cinque Ports is an office for which I will not receive any recommendations; having positively resolved to confer it on him [Pitt] as a mark of that regard which his eminent services have deserved from me. I am so bent on this that I shall seriously be offended at any attempt to decline ...[12]

8   Such was the opinion of Lord Curzon. See *Ibid.*, p. 21.
9   *Ibid.*, p. 22.
10 *Ibid.*, p. 24.
11 Qualities attributed by Lord Curzon. *Ibid.*, p. 25.
12 Quoted in *Ibid.*, p. 37.

Pitt, who was chronically in debt at the time, 'gratefully accepted an honour which both assured him of the confidence of his Sovereign and relieved his pecuniary embarrassment'.[13] The salary now amounted to £3,000 per annum. Pitt understood his job fairly well. He was a regular resident at Walmer, where he often passed his time in the company of distinguished politicians and private friends. Many of them testified to his hospitality. William Wilberforce entered in his diary on 3 October 1792 that Pitt had received him 'very kindly, and with great warmth of affection'.[14] Lord Wellesley noted that he had found his host 'playing the part of the country gentleman in a fashion which some of his successors ... enthusiastically emulated at a later date'.[15]

But, as Lord Warden, Pitt engaged himself 'in more serious pursuits'. For nearly twelve years he endeavoured to place the coast of Kent 'in a state of preparation against expected French invasion'. He raised a local volunteer corps, consisting of both horse and foot, which was called the Cinque Port Fencibles: Pitt himself was in command of this force as its Colonel. Intensive defence preparations were further undertaken to counter the imminent attack expected from Napoleon Bonaparte.[16] Cartoonists did not lose time in portraying Pitt's determination. One cartoon, entitled 'The Political Cocks', portrayed Pitt and Napoleon standing and confronting each other from the opposite sides of the English Channel. The Gallic cock says: 'Eh, Master Billy, if I could but take a flight over this Brook, I would soon stop crowing. I would knock you off that Perch, I swear by Mahomet, the Pope and all the Idols I have ever worshipped.' The English cock replies in a simple but powerful voice: 'That you never can do!'[17] Pitt's defiant stance won him the warm approbation of many distinguished men. Pitt, wrote

13   *Ibid.*, p. 38.
14   Quoted in *Ibid.*, p. 42.
15   *Ibid.*, p. 44.
16   For a lengthy, but brilliant description of Pitt's activities, see *Ibid.*, 27–142.
17   Quoted in *Ibid.*, p. 105.

Lord Muncaster, was 'doing great things as Lord Warden'.[18] Wordsworth, the great poet, felt induced to join in, addressing the Men of Kent:[19]

> Vanguard of Liberty, ye men of Kent,
> Ye children of a soil that doth advance
> Her haughty brow against the coast of France,
> ...

The critic, Peter Pindar, tried his hand at patriotic verse too:[20]

> Come the Consul whenever he will –
> And he means it when Neptune is calmer –
> Pitt will send him a d – d bitter pill
> From his fortress, the Castle of Walmer.

Pitt had other qualities. He had an astonishing interest in gardening. The moment he arrived at Walmer, he at once 'struck out improvements in his own mind' to alter the shape of the attached garden. His niece Lady Hester Stanhope, who stayed at Walmer for a length of time and thus earned the nickname 'Princess of Walmer' was herself a keen gardener. The two of them beautified the Walmer garden with 'great taste'. Pitt was so fond of his gardening that he would proudly write to invite his friends to come and appreciate his labours. He once wrote to Addington that 'I should be very glad to show you all the improvements in this place, both in beauty and comfort.'[21] And, alas, in this 'beauty' and 'comfort' Pitt sought leisure to down large quantities of port wine, which adversely effected his health. Pitt died in December 1806.

The King now conferred the wardenship upon Robert Banks Jenkonson, Lord Hawkesbury (later the second Earl of Liverpool). Hawkesbury occupied the post from 1806 until 1828. There had been, Curzon observed, a 'universal consensus that Lord Hawkesbury's abilities or services hardly justified so great an honour, and that the vacant chair required a bigger

---

18 *Ibid.*, p. 102.
19 Quoted in *Ibid.*, p. 96.
20 *Ibid.*, p. 102.
21 *Ibid.*, pp. 121–2.

man'.[22] But such was the 'generous wish of the Sovereign': George III 'overruled all Hawkesbury's objections and was determined to regard the post as one private piece of patronage'.[23] Hawkesbury did not entirely waste his time at Walmer. By an act of deed, he secured forty acres of ground around the castle, thus guaranteeing its privacy in perpetuity. Plantation of the gardens was further improved. It impressed his guests. The plantation, wrote some of the guests, was 'really very great'. It had 'grown and flourished so as to afford a great deal of shady and sheltered walking – and there is besides a sea-walk ... which for the purpose of taking sea-views into one's eyes, and sea air into one's lungs and all one's pores, is perfect'.[24] Lord Curzon complimented Hawkesbury, calling him 'one of the most public-spirited and generous benefactors to the estate of Walmer Castle, and one of the most faithful custodians of its amenities, in the long line of Lords Warden'.[25] One further distinction is attributed to Hawkesbury: he was the last Lord Warden to draw a salary from his office. In 1817 the House of Commons Select Committee on Finance recommended that the Lord Warden's salary should cease at the next vacancy. The office of wardenship would now become a distinction and honour rather than a sinecure.

After Hawkesbury's death in 1828 the King appointed Arthur Wellesley, first Duke of Wellington to the office of the wardenship. This was in January 1829. For the next twenty-three years, Wellington made Walmer his second home. He loved Walmer, and he died in the castle. The Duke entertained in abundance and was delighted to entertain children. And special guests received particularly attention. When Queen Victoria and Prince Albert decided to visit and stay at Walmer, the Duke ordered his staff to 'put out a plate-glass window, to enable Her Majesty to have a better view of the sea'. A person present at the event noted: 'A stand for a timepiece was required for Prince Albert, and the Duke sent for a village carpenter who made it of common deal and it is now a fixture in the bedroom. Her Majesty is

22   The Marquess Curzon of Kedleston, *The Personal History of Walmer Castle and its Lords Wardens, op. cit.*, p. 150.
23   *Ibid.*
24   *Ibid.*, p. 158.
25   *Ibid.*, p. 156.

stated to have been much delighted at this simplicity of the Duke.'[26] As Lord Warden, the Duke performed the following functions:[27]

1. He daily gave the countersign to the garrison of regular troops at Dover.
2. He consigned Cinque Ports debtors to a Cinque Port jail on the roadway leading to Dover Castle.
3. He still collected '*droits* of Admiralty' and appointed chartered pilots for vessels bound to the Thames.
4. He exercised, within his jurisdiction as Lord Warden, the authority of a Lord-Lieutenant and appointed Justices of the Peace having jurisdiction coincident with that of Mayor and Aldermen in a borough with a charter.
5. If Cinque Port Volunteers were raised, he would have been *ex officio* their Colonel.
6. He attended 'Courts of *lodemanage*' at Dover for the appointment and discipline of pilots.
7. He presided over the Harbour Board at Dover.
8. He made himself thoroughly familiar with matters of naval strength, especially those affecting the defence of the Channel.

On 14 October 1852 the Duke suffered a strong epileptic fit, and he died in his beloved Walmer.

In consultation with the Prime Minister, Lord Derby,[28] the Queen offered the wardenship to the Marquess of Dalhousie, at that time still Governor-General of India. Dalhousie was not too enthusiastic about the offer, but accepted it in order not to offend the Queen, who had conveyed to him that she had bestowed the wardenship on him with 'special approval'. Dalhousie's tenure of office in India had been extended until 1856, and he asked his friend, Sir George Couper, to act as Lord Deputy in

26 Quoted in *Ibid.*, p. 214.
27 Quoted in *Ibid.*, p. 256. '*Droits* of Admiralty' were rights over seized enemy ships; there were also rights over wrecks. The 'Court of *lodemanage*' had jurisdiction over pilots.
28 Derby, 17th Earl of, b. 1865. A Conservative.

his absence. Dalhousie was often sick and never visited Walmer. He died in December 1860.

Dalhousie's 'long absentee tenure' caused royal dissatisfaction with the wardenship, and it was feared that the post might be entirely abolished. However the situation was saved when a deputation from the Cinque Ports urged the Prime Minister to 'keep alive so ancient an office'.[29] Henry John Temple, Viscount Palmerston was appointed and formally installed as the new Lord Warden. Palmerston occasionally visited Walmer but made no alterations in the castle. On his death in 1865, the wardenship was given to Lord Granville. Until his death in 1891, Walmer was 'the home of this delightful person'. And perhaps, Curzon notes, no other Lord Warden 'was ever so completely domesticated there'.[30] Granville:

> built new stables and kennels and kept a pack of harriers. He planted the grounds and transferred the stones of Sandown Castle with which he erected a new tower. He purchased also the old Semaphore Station and there built the 'Villa Vita', named after his daughter.[31]

Baron Malortie recorded a fond memory of his stay at Walmer:[32]

> I shall never forget the homely cheerful look of the drawing-room when after breakfast guests and family, old and young used to congregate, each following their moment's inclination, Lord Granville as a rule selecting this moment for the despatch of official duties; he was Foreign Secretary at the time I am referring to. Dozens of red leather despatch boxes, with their respective paper labels, were piled up next to the writing table – indeed, there was only one for both Lord and Lady Granville, for the space in this, the only well-sized room, was as limited as the number of apartments available for the family and guests.

Granville died in 1891. He was succeeded by the Rt Hon. W. H. Smith, Leader of the House of Commons, as Lord Warden. Smith 'restored telegraphic

---

29   See The Marquess Curzon of Kedleston, *The Personal History of Walmer Castle and its Lords Wardens, op. cit.*, p. 272.
30   *Ibid.*, p. 277.
31   Quoted in *Ibid.*, p. 277.
32   Quoted in *Ibid.*, pp. 277–8.

communication and put in electric bells'.[33] He was the first Lord Warden to exercise the right to fly his flag on his yacht in Cinque Ports waters. Smith's tenure of office was very, very short. He died in October of the same year.

Smith's successor was the Marquess of Dufferin. He occupied the office for three years, after which he resigned. Dufferin was 'never very much attached to the place':[34] he could not afford the upkeep.

The office vacated by Dufferin was filled by the then Prime Minister, Lord Salisbury, himself. He participated in the ceremony of installation on 15 August 1896, but thereafter showed very little interest in the wardenship. On Salisbury's death, Lord Curzon, who had just returned from India as Viceroy, was installed as Lord Warden on 2 July 1905.[35] Curzon resigned from the office in November of that year. The reason was the death of his wife, who fell seriously ill at Walmer and almost died there.[36] The illness was attributed to 'defects in the dwelling'. The main contribution Curzon made during his wardenship was to write a lengthy and readable history of the Lords Wardens of Walmer Castle.[37]

Lady Curzon's death foreshadowed an unhappy turn for the continuation of the wardenship. King Edward suggested that there should be no resident Lord Warden, and that the castle be established as a national museum. Meanwhile, as a stop-gap measure, the Prince of Wales was appointed to assume the vacant post. The Prince agreed, on condition that he should have little to do with the duties of the wardenship and that he should not attend the formal installation ceremony. When the Cinque Ports men

33   *Ibid.*, p. 279.

34   *Ibid.*, p. 284.

35   For a thorough account of this spectacular procession, see: 'Lord Curzon as Ceremonial Impresario', in David Cannadine, *Aspects of Aristocracy* (London: Penguin Books, 1994), pp. 91–5.

36   There is another version of this event. According to Prof. Cannadine: 'Soon after the ceremonials, Curzon's wife became ill, miscarried and almost died. The reason given was the insanitary condition of the drains at Walmer. As a result, Curzon turned against the Castle, which he now described as a "charnel house, unfit for human habitation"'. *Ibid.*, p. 95.

37   The Marquess Curzon of Kedleston, *The Personal History of Walmer Castle and its Lords Wardens, op. cit.*

pressed for the ceremony to go forward nevertheless, the Prince resigned. This was in 1907. The Prince was succeeded by Thomas Lord Brassey. He was installed on 25 June 1908. Brassey did not reside at Walmer, but visited Dover off and on. He had 'real regard for the Cinque Ports people'. He took great joy in having the Lord Warden's flag fly on the castle. Brassey resigned from the office in 1913 because of ill health. He felt, he wrote to Curzon, 'the growing infirmities of old age. Arthritis. ... It is not well to have a disabled Lord Warden.'[38]

Earl Beauchamp honoured

When Lord Brassey resigned in the autumn of 1913, Herbert Asquith, the Prime Minister, offered the wardenship to Earl Beauchamp.[39] Asquith wrote to Beauchamp:[40]

30 October 1913

My dear Beauchamp,

... I shall be only too delighted if you were willing to take over the Warden of the Cinque Ports. Prince Arthur of Connaught has been suggested, but I doubt whether the idea would commend itself either to him or in high quarters. I leave here tomorrow and shall be in London from Monday onwards.

Yours very sincerely,

H. H. Asquith

---

38   The Marquess Curzon of Kedleston, *The Personal History of Walmer Castle and its Lords Wardens, op. cit.,* p. 287.

39   Asquith wanted to be the Lord Warden himself. Earlier Prime Ministers, Pitt and Palmerston, had set the precedent. The King discouraged him, arguing that it would cost the Prime Minister £800 a year to maintain the Walmer gardens alone. This Asquith could hardly afford, and he changed his mind. For more on this, see Roy Jenkins, *Asquith* (London: Collins, 1964), p. 347.

40   Source: Beauchamp Papers, *op. cit.*

The Prime Minister sent another note a few days later.[41]

> *10 Downing Street, Whitehall*
>
> *3 November 1913*
>
> *Private*
>
> My dear Beauchamp,
>
> The King (as I expected) won't hear of Prince A. on any terms for the Ports. So I am very gladly & gratefully recommending your appointment.
>
> Yours very sincerely,
>
> H. H. Asquith

The Earl happily gave his assent. Soon afterwards, on 23 April 1914, another mark of honour (not attached to the wardenship of the Cinque Ports) was conferred upon Beauchamp. He was made a Knight of the Garter. The Most Noble Order of the Garter is the highest order of chivalry in England.[42] It is presumed to have been founded by King Edward III in 1344, and elevations to the order were (and are) always announced on 23 April, St George's Day, St George being the patron saint of England. Membership of the Order has always been limited to the Sovereign, the Prince of Wales, and no more than 24 other members at any one time. When a vacancy occurs the Order is awarded, at the Sovereign's pleasure, as a personal gift. The Order, dedicated to the image and arms of St George, has an emblem in a garter with the motto in middle French: '*Honi soit qui mal y pense*' ('shame on him who thinks evil of it'). The membership of the Order also extends to foreign monarchs. These are called supernumerary members, and they belong in addition to the 24 companions. The installation takes place in St George's Chapel at Windsor. Along with Earl Beauchamp two other

---

41   *Ibid.*

42   For further information, see: Valentine Heywood, *British Titles: The Use and Misuse of the Titles of Peers and Commoners, with Some Historical Notes* (London: Adam and Charles Black, 1951), pp. 128–33.

recipients of the Order at the time were:[43] Christian X, King of Denmark and Albert I, King of the Belgians. Earl Beauchamp received many letters of congratulation. To these he replied gracefully. Here is one such letter of acknowledgement:[44]

Earl Beauchamp to Sir W. J. Soulsby

13, Belgrave Square
S. W.

22.VI.14

My dear Sir William,

Many thanks for yr kind message wh gave me real pleasure. It is the congratulations & good wishes wh give real savour on such occasions. But I think of throwing my ring – was this not the ancient custom to avert the evil of too great a fortune? – into the Serpentine.

With many thanks again.

Yours v. Sincerely

Beauchamp

---

43   The Letters Patent were posted to Earl Beauchamp separately: 'Lord Chamberlain's Office, St James's Palace, 31 July 1914. My Lord, I have the honour to transmit to you herewith a Box containing the Letters Patent under the King's sign Manual dispensing with your installation as a Knight of the Most Noble Order of the Garter, the receipt of which I would ask you to be good enough to acknowledge. A copy of the Statutes of the Order is also endorsed. I am, My Lord, Your obedient servant, Secretary to the Order of the Garter'. Source: Beauchamp Papers, *op. cit.*

44   Source: Senate House Library Document, University of London: 05591/1120/AL 366.

Installation ceremonies

After the installation at Windsor, there followed another, different ceremony at Dover on 18 July 1914, which is detailed in documents, supplied
to the present author by the Kent History and Library Centre, Maidstone.[45]

1

Cinque Ports

69, Castle Street,
Dover
30 June 1914

J. R. Dingle, Esq.
Grand Court of Shepway

Installation of Lord Warden

Sir,

The Lord Warden instructs me to send you as one of those who have attended a
Coronation Ceremony as a representative Baron the accompanying invitation to
attend him at the Court of Shepway to be held on the 18th July next.

His Lordship hopes that you will wear your Coronation Costume and proposes that
the Coronation Barons should form a feature of the procession and occupy special
carriages as at previous Installations.

I beg to request that you will be so good as to let me know whether you accept this
invitation. I enclose a notice as to the Luncheon. If you should be attending as an
elected representative of a Corporation I shall doubtless hear from the Town Clerk
of your Borough (if I have not already done so) as to your Luncheon ticket.

---

45   These documents are catalogued under: Fo/CPw10; Cpw/S7; Cpw/RPS8. Some of
the proceedings were appended in Curzon's volume, *op. cit.*, pp. 291–318. The local
paper extensively reported the event. See: 'Lord Warden Installed. Brilliant Scene at
Dover. Impressive Old-time Ceremonials. Interesting Speeches by the Lord Warden
and the Archbishop', *The Dover Standard*, 25 July 1914. The present author is exceedingly grateful to Dr Helen Wicker, Researcher, Kent History and Library, Maidstone
for her valuable advice.

I am, Sir,

Your obedient Servant,

R. E. Knocker

Seneschal

2.

To J. R. Dingle, Esq.
69, Castle Street,
Dover,

30 June 1914

Sir,

I am instructed by His Lordship the Lord Warden of the Cinque Ports to inform you that he has convened a Grand Court of Shepway here on Saturday, the 18th July next, for the purpose of taking upon himself the duties of his Office: and that His Lordship invites you to do him the honour of attending him on the occasion.

His Lordship proposes to meet the Members of the Court at Dover Castle, and to ride thence to the Bredenstone on the Western Heights, where the Court will be held, and he will be glad if you will accompany him.

I will hereafter communicate to you the hour and details of the Ceremony, and if I can be of any use in procuring you a carriage pray let me know.

I have the honour to be,

Sir,

Your very obedient Servant,

R. E. Knocker

Seneschal of the Court

3

Admiralty

6 July 1914

In any further communication on this subject, please quote M.14630/14, and address letter to The Secretary, Admiralty, Whitehall, London, S. W.

The Registrar of the Cinque Ports,

69 Castle Street,

Dover

4

Sir,

In reply to your letter of the 27th June I am commanded by my Lords Commissioners of the Admiralty to inform you that the Sixth Destroyer Flotilla will be at Dover on the 18th July and also H. M. S. *St George* flying the broad pendant of Commodore G. A. Ballard, C. B., A. D. as Admiral of Patrols. If it is desired that H. M. Ships should take part in the ceremonies on the 18th July at the installation of the Lord Warden, I am to request you to communicate with the Admiral of Patrols at 1 Central Buildings, Westminster.

I am, Sir,

Your obedient Servant,

[Signature illegible]

5

7 July 1914

Commodore G. A. Ballard, C. B.; A. D. C; R. N., Admiral of Patrols,
1, Central Buildings, S. W.

Sir,

The Installation of the Lord Warden of the Cinque Ports will take place here at a meeting of the Grand Court of Shepway on Saturday the 18th instant and I am informed by the Admiralty that H. M. S. *St George* flying your broad pendant and the Sixth Destroyer Flotilla will be at Dover on that date and requested to communicate with you in regard to the participation of H. M. Ships referred to in the proceedings in connection with the Installation.

I enclose a copy of the provisional programme, a formal invitation from the Lord Warden asking you to attend him on that occasion and an invitation to the Luncheon.

The Troops in Garrison will be assisting in the proceedings by lining the streets etc., and I am to enquire whether some men (and if so, what number) from the Ships under your command could assist in lining the streets and whether they could provide a

Naval Guard-of-honour to be mounted at the Town Hall at about 1.30 p. m., about which time the Lord Warden and other distinguished guests will be arriving at the building for the Luncheon.

I am directed to state that if a Guard-of-honour can be provided as suggested it is hoped that the Officers of the Guard will also accept invitations to attend the Luncheon as well as one or two other Senior Officers whose names I am to request that you will be so good as to suggest.

I am, Sir,

Your obedient Servant,

Registrar

6

Reginald E. Knocker, Town Clerk

69, Castle Street,
Dover

14 July 1914

Dear Sir or Madam,

The Installation of the Rt Hon. the Earl Beauchamp K. G., K. C. M. G., P. C. etc. as Lord Warden of the Cinque Ports will take place here on Saturday the 18th instant at a meeting of the Grand Court of Shepway, and I am directed by the Education Committee to request the Head Teachers to be so good as to arrange for the children of the Upper Departments to assemble on the bank adjoining Military Hill just above Christ Church School in order that they may see the procession on its way to the Bredenstone at the Drop Redout, Western Heights, and for this purpose to arrange for the children to assemble at the School on Saturday morning and proceed to the spot indicated at which they should arrive not later than 11.30 o'clock. It is hoped that as many teachers as possible will accompany the children. As there will be plenty of space it is not proposed to make any definite arrangements for allotting a specified position to each department. I enclose a programme of the arrangements which will show the order of procession.

The Education Committee also suggest that an opportunity should be taken on Friday next of telling the children a few facts about the Cinque Ports, their history, their connection with the Royal Navy and their great importance in that respect in former times; also with regard to the post of Lord Warden which has been held by a large number of England's most distinguished men.

For your information I may perhaps say that the Court of Shepway in olden times met at Shepway Cross near Lympne which is close to Hythe. The exact site of the Cross is however now uncertain and for some centuries the ceremony has been held at the Bredenstone which consists of the remains of what was formerly a Pharos on the Western Heights similar to that which adjoins the Castle Church.

The Cinque Ports of course are Sandwich, Dover, Hythe, New Romney and Hastings. The two ancient towns which enjoy practically equal privileges are Winchelsea and Rye and seven other towns are associated with those named as members or limbs. The limbs of Dover being Folkestone, Faversham and Margate.

The Corporations of each of these 14 towns send representatives to the Grand Court of Shepway.

Yours faithfully,

R. E. Knocker

Town Clerk

7

Installation of the Right Honourable The Earl Beauchamp, K. G., K. C. M. G., P. C., etc. etc.
As Constable of the Castle of Dover and Lord Warden and Admiral of the Cinque Ports
At Dover, 18th July 1914

Official Programme

1. The Mayors of the several Corporations, Barons, and all persons who are to take part in the Installation will be at the Keep in the Castle by 10:30 a.m.
2. A Service will be held in the Church of St Mary-in-the Castle at 11:00 a.m. (His Grace the Lord Archbishop of Canterbury and the Right Rev. The Lord Bishop of Dover, Chaplain of the Cinque Ports).
N.B. Admittance to the Castle will be by tickets issued to the Members of the Court and Visitors invited by the Lord Warden.
3. The procession will then be formed and proceed from the Constable's Gate down the New Castle Hill Road, by way of Castle Street, Market Square, Cannon Street, Biggin Street, Worthington Street, and Military Hill to the Bredenstone, Drop Redoubt, Western Heights, where the Grand Court of Shepway will be held at 12:00 (noon).
4. After the Ceremony the procession will be reformed and proceed by way of Military Hill, Worthingon Street and Biggin Street to the Town Hall, where Luncheon will

be given to the Lord Warden by the Cinque Ports. Ladies and Gentlemen having Luncheon Tickets should be at the Town Hall by 2:00 p.m. precisely.
N.B. All Mayors to wear their chains.

Grand Court of Shepway

Order of Procession
Band of the 3rd (King's Own) Hussars
Members of the Court of Shepway.
The Mayors of the Cinque Ports, accompanied by their Recorders, Town Clerks, Chaplains, and Clerks of the Peace with their Barons and Returned Men, preceded by their respective Mace Bearers and Officers

> Ramsgate
> Margate
> Tenterden
> Deal
> Flokestone
> Faversham
> Lydd
> Rye
> Winchelsea
> Hythe
> New Romney
> Dover
> Sandwich
> Hastings

The Barons who attended the Coronations of King Edward VII. and King George V in their Robes.
The Registrar of the Ports.
The Chaplain of the Ports.
The Sergeant of Admiralty bearing the Silver Oar.
The Surrogate of the Admiralty Court.
The Judge of the Admiralty Court.
The General Officer Commanding Troops Dover and Staff.
The Lord Warden, with an Escort of the Royal East Kent Mounted Rifles.
Noblemen and Gentlemen attending on the Lord Warden.
Such of the Barons of the Cinque Ports as be there.

The Route will be lined by the following:
The Royal Garrison Artillery, 1st King's Own Regiment, 2nd Lancashire Fusiliers, 2nd Inniskilling Fusiliers, and Duke of York's Royal Military School.

Guards of Honour will be mounted as follows:
Drop Redoubt – 5th (Cinque Ports) Royal Sussex Regiment.
Town Hall – Royal Navy.

Bands will be stationed at the following positions: Laureston Place, Market Square, Worthington Street and Drop Redoubt.

R. E. Knocker

8

Grand Court of Shepway

Dover, 18th July, 1914

The Lord Warden has accepted the invitation of the Cinque Ports, Ancient Towns, and their Members to a Luncheon, at the Town Hall at half-past one o'clock.

Tickets 25s. each (wines included). Each gentleman attending the Luncheon will have the privilege of bringing one lady, the price to be two pounds for the two tickets.

Applications should be made to the Seneschal of the Court, not later than Tuesday, 14th July.

R. E. Knocker,

Seneschal

69, Castle Street,
Dover

9

South Eastern & Chatham Railway

Installation of Lord Warden of the Cinque Ports Dover
Saturday, July 18th, 1914

Cheap Return Tickets
(1st, 2nd and 3rd Class)
Will be issued to
DOVER
At about a single fare-and-a-third (Minimum 1/-)
By all trains up to 12.00 noon.
From:
    Margate Sands*
    Ramsgate Town*
    St Lawrence*

Minster*
Sandwich*
Deal*
Walmer*
Martin Mill*
Canterbury West*
South Canterbury*
Bridge
Bishopsbourne
Barham
Elham
Lyminge
Hastings*
Ore*
Winchelsea
Rye
Appledore
Ham Street
Ashford*
Smeeth
Westenhanger
Sandling Junction
Sandgate*
Hythe*
Cheriton Halt
Shorncliffe
Folkestone Central

No Luggage allowed. Children under Twelve, Half-fares.
Tickets available to return by any Train on the day of issue only.
From Stations marked* the Summer Week-Day Cheap Fares will be charged.

Francis H. Dent, General Manager
London Bridge Station,
11/7/14.

10

On Saturday, the 18th July, 1914, the Right Honourable the Earl Beauchamp, K. G.,
was duly installed at Dover in accordance with the ancient ceremonies into the historic office of Lord Warden of the Cinque Ports. The ceremonial was picturesque
in every detail and attracted large numbers of visitors to Dover, who were delighted
with the pageantry of the occasion. Brilliant sunshine, gaily decorated streets, a fleet

of warships in the harbour dressed rainbow fashion, troop-lined streets, military bands at various points combined, with the brightly uniformed procession of the Lord Warden with his 'Barons and Combarons', to make a memorable day for the thousands of spectators.

Before ten o'clock the officials were wending their way up the steep Castle hill. Mace-bearers, carrying the regalia of their Ports, Mayors, Aldermen, Town Clerks, and Councillors were making their way to the Robing-Chamber in the Keep. Inside the Keep there was a quaint mixture of mediaevalism and modernity. The grey old walls, ornamented with the armour and weapons of long-forgotten men of the Cinque Ports, looked down upon the assemblage. Gorgeously-clad Coronation Barons were notable in scarlet cloaks, trimmed with blue and gold, with the arms of the Cinque Ports embroidered on the shoulder, black knee breeches and hose, and white satin embroidered waistcoats. Red- and black-robed civic dignitaries moved in and out of the throng, while frock-coated Councillors looked strangely out of place in such unusual surroundings. The Custodian of the Keep had thoughtfully relieved the cold grey cheerlessness of the walls in the Robing-Room with flags and bunting.

At half-past ten the Mayors and representatives of the fourteen municipalities – Cinque Ports, Ancient Towns and Limbs – gathered in the Royal Banqueting Hall in the Keep for a preliminary meeting to elect one of their number to request the new Lord Warden at the Court of Shepway to take upon himself the duties of his office. In accordance with ancient custom the choice of the assembly fell upon the Speaker – the Mayor of the Ancient Town of Winchelsea (Mr G. M. Freeman, K. C.).

In the Keep Yard, immediately after the meeting the picturesquely-clad Seneschal called the Roll and formed up the procession, which slowly proceeded to the venerable pile of St Mary-in-the-Castle. The black-robed Mayor of Sandwich was a conspicuous figure in the gathering, and carried a thin black rod. This dress and wand are stated to be a token of mourning for the terrible slaughter of the men of the Cinque Ports by the invading Danes, off Bloody Point, in 840 A. D.

Suddenly a musical flourish of trumpets rang out from the entrance to the Keep Yard. Troops stood at the salute, hats were raised, and through that archway of the Constable's Tower,

> Whose pond'rous grate and massy bar
> Hath oft rolled back the tide of war,

glided a motor-car containing the Earl Beauchamp, the new Lord Warden. Swiftly it ascended the slope to the Castle Yard, pulled up sharply on one side, and out stepped the hero of the hour – a fine looking figure in the full dress uniform of the Lord Warden of the Ports – wearing the blue ribbon of the Garter, the stars and emblems of many Orders glittering on his breast. A few formal greetings, and the Lord Warden, with Countess Beauchamp, and their son, Viscount Elmley, proceeded to the Church.

The Service was conducted by the Archbishop of Canterbury, the bishop of Dover, and the Senior Chaplain to the Forces. The service was short.

Special Sentence (1 Tim. ii. 1–3)
Collect for 23rd Sunday after Trinity
Versicles and Gloria
Psalm ixvii.
Lesson, Ecclesiasticus xliv. 1–15
Hymn (No. 166)
Creed
Versicles
Lord's Prayer
Versicles
Collects:
    For the Week
    For the King
First Collect for those at Sea (for the Navy)
Second Collect for Good Friday (for the Lord Warden)
Prayer of St Chrysostom
Benediction (His Grace the Archbishop of Canterbury)
Psalm LXVII, *Deus Misereatur*
    God be merciful unto us, and bless us:
    and shew us the light of his
    countenance, and be merciful unto us;
    That thy way may be known upon earth:
    thy saving health among all nations.
    Let the people praise thee, O God:
    yea let all the people praise thee.
    O let the nations rejoice and be glad:
    for thou shalt judge the folk righteously,
    and govern the nations upon earth.
    Let the people praise thee, O God:
    let all the people praise thee.
    Then shall the earth bring forth her increase:
    and God, even our own God, shall give us blessing.
    God shall bless us:
    and all the ends of the world shall fear him.

Hymn 166, Old Hundredth
    All people that on earth do dwell,

Sing to the Lord with cheerful voice;
Him serve with fear, His praise forth tell,
Come ye before Him, and rejoice.

The Lord, ye know, is God indeed;
Without our aid He did us make;
We are His flock, He doth us feed,
And for His sheep He doth us take.

O enter then His gates with praise,
Approach with joy His courts unto,
Praise, laud, and bless His Name always,
For it is seemly so to do.

For why? The Lord our God is good,
His mercy is for ever sure;
His truth at all times firmly stood,
And shall from age to age endure.

To Father, Son, and Holy Ghost,
The God whom Heav'n and earth adore,
From men and from the Angel-host,
Be praise and glory evermore.
Amen.

The Archbishop then pronounced the Benediction. Thereafter the Procession was formed on the Parade Ground and left the Castle by way of the Constable's Gate for the Drop Redoubt on the Western Heights (or Bredenstone Hill as it was formerly called) for the meeting of the Grand Court of Shepway.

The town was gaily bedecked, and everything was looking its best in the glorious sunshine. Scarlet uniformed soldiers were lining the streets, while the sides of Castle Hill were lined with the red-coated Duke of York's School-boys. On every available point on the route of the procession, crowds of sightseers had collected. The Market-square was packed, as also were the sides of Castle Street, Cannon Street, and Biggin Street, while hundreds (including a large number of children from the Elementary schools), had assembled on the slopes above Military Hill. Bands were stationed at Eastbrook-Place, Market-Square, Worthington-Street, Town Hall, and Drop Redout, while the troops guarding the streets were drawn from the Royal Garrison Artillery, the 1st King's Own Regiment, the 2nd Lancashire Fusiliers, and the 2nd Royal Inniskilling Fusiliers.

The fine mounted Band of the 3rd King's Own Hussars headed the procession on the way through Dover. Then came a long string of carriages containing the Mayors and representatives of the Cinque Ports and Limbs, preceded by their respective mace bearers and officers. The Coronation Barons made a picturesque group. ...

The Lord Warden was given a very hearty reception as he passed through the town, while the Borough Member and Lady Duncannon who were in the procession, were also cordially cheered. ...

A large marquee with annexes for the accommodation of the Court and the public, had been erected in close proximity to the Bredenstone – which is situated in the Drop Redoubt. At this point a guard of honour with colours and Band had been mounted by the 5th (Cinque Ports) Royal Sussex Regiment from Hastings, ... and saluted on the arrival of the Lord Warden who proceeded to inspect it.

The scene in the Court was an exceedingly picturesque one. On either side of the Lord Warden were seated the Mayors of the fourteen Ports and Towns represented, whilst a number of distinguished people, including the Archbishop of Canterbury, the Earl of Rosebery, the Dean of Canterbury, Lord George Hamilton (Captain of Deal Castle), Viscount Dunacannon, M.P., Lord Northbourne ... were seated in proximity to the Lord Warden. The Court was in the form of an open square, the representative 'Barons and Combarons' – many of them in their gorgeous uniforms as Coronation Barons – being seated in long rows at right angles to the position occupied by the Lord Warden and Mayors. In the centre were tables on which the maces and other emblems of office from the various ports and towns were massed, many of these being of great historical interest. ... The large assemblage of spectators evinced the keenest interest in the proceedings so reminiscent of the olden days.

First of all the Seneschal made the following Proclamation of the King's Court of Shepway:

> Oyez! Oyez! Oyez!
> All Mayors, Bailiffs, and Barons of the Five Ports and their members that be summoned and warned to appear in their proper persons before my Lord Warden at this the King's Majesty's Court of Shepway, here to be holden this day; draw ye near and answer to your names as ye shall be called, and give your attendance to the Court, upon the peril that shall fall of it

The Seneschal then read the quaintly-worded Precept of the Lord Warden summoning the Court, as follows:

> William Earl Beauchamp, Viscount Elmley and Baron Beauchamp of Powyke, in the County of Worcester, Constable of Dover Castle, Lord Warden, Chancellor and Admiral of the Cinque Ports, two Ancient Towns, and their members, one of His Majesty's Most Honourable Privy Councillors, Knight Commander of the most Distinguished Order of S. Michael and S. George, Knight of Grace of the Order of S. John of Jerusalem, First Commissioner of Works and Public

Buildings, Lord Lieutenant and Custos Rotulorum of the County of Gloucester and for the City of Bristol, Doctor of Laws:

To All and Singular the Mayors and Bailiffs of the Cinque Ports, two Ancient Towns, and Members of the said Cinque Ports and Towns, and to every one of them, GREETING.

For certain good causes and considerations me thereunto especially moving, I have thought it necessary to notify unto you by these presents, that I propose, and am resolved by God's Grace to be at His Majesty's Castle of Dover, within the Liberty of the Town and Port of Dover, one of the Cinque Ports, upon Saturday, the 18th day of July next, by Eleven o'clock in the forenoon, and thence to proceed to Bredenstone Hill, within the Liberty aforesaid, then and there to hold a Grand Court of Shepway according to the ancient usage and custom of the said Cinque Ports, and there to take upon myself the duties of the said office.

Thereupon by virtue and authority of my said office, these are, in His Majesty's name, straitly to charge and command you, and every one of you, to give good summons and lawful warning unto six, five, or four of the best and most discreet of your Combarons of every of the said Ports, Towns and Members Corporate, personally to be and appear before me at the place and time aforesaid. And that also you, the said Mayors and Bailiffs, or your respective deputies, be likewise then and there personally present to do so as to you hath been accustomed and belongeth. And that you do then and there certify to me under your hands and seals of incorporation what you shall have done in the accomplishment of the premises. Certifying me also, then and there, the names of all those persons whom you shall so have summoned and warned as aforesaid, and therewith returning back unto me, then and there, this Mandate, whereof you may not fail.

Dated at His Majesty's Castle of Walmer under the Seal of my Office, the fifteenth day of June in the fifth year of the reign of our Sovereign Lord George V, by the Grace of God, of the United Kingdom of Great Britain and Ireland, and of all the British Dominions beyond the Seas, King, Defender of the Faith, Emperor of India, Anno Domini, 1914.

BEAUCHAMP

The Mayors were then called upon to hand in their respective Returns to the Precept. ... The Seneschal having announced that the Court was duly formed, the Lord Warden said: 'Mr Speaker, Right Worshipful Sirs, Barons and Gentlemen, I have summoned this Grand Court of Shepway to take upon myself the office of Lord Warden, I desire my patent of office to be read.'.

This document, to which was attached the great seal of England, was read by the Seneschal:

> George the Fifth, by the Grace of God of the United Kingdom of Great Britain and Ireland and of the British Dominions beyond the Seas, King, Defender of the Faith, to all to whom these presents shall come, Greeting. Know ye that We of our special grace, certain knowledge and mere motion have given and granted, and by these presents for Us, our Heirs and Successors, do give and grant unto our right trusty, and well beloved Cousin and Counsellor William Earl Beauchamp Knight, Commander of our Most Distinguished Order of Saint Michael and Saint George, First Commissioner of Works and Public Buildings, the Office of Constable of our Castle at Dover with the appurtenances and also the Office of Warden and Keeper of our Cinque Ports and their Members. And moreover, We do hereby give and grant unto the said William Earl Beauchamp, the Office of Admiralty within our Cinque Ports aforesaid and their members. And We do in like manner hereby give and grant unto the said William Earl Beauchamp, all and all manner of wrecks of the sea, Jetsam, Flotsam, and Lagan, Goods, Merchandise and effects whatsoever which at any time or times during the continuance of these Our Letters Patent shall be cast away, wrecked, or lost, or which shall be taken up, gotten, or recovered by the said William Earl Beauchamp, his Deputies, or Agents in any places, ports or creeks, as well by land as by water, within the precincts of the Castle aforesaid, or the Liberties thereof, or within the precincts, limits, or Liberties of the said Cinque Ports, or any or either of them and him the said William Earl Beauchamp, Constable of our said Castle of Dover, and Warden and Keeper of our Cinque Ports and their Members aforesaid, We do make, constitute, and appoint by these presents to have and to hold the said Offices with the appurtenances and the said premises so granted as aforesaid unto the said William Earl Beauchamp, by himself or his sufficient Deputy or Deputies, for and during the term of his natural life, together with all jurisdictions, authorities, fees, and advantage due and of right belonging to the same Offices or either of them or to the said premises, hereby granted, without any account or any other thing to Us, Our Heirs or Successors, to be rendered, and we have also given and granted, and by these present for Us, Our Heirs and Successors, to give and grant unto the said William Earl Beauchamp, during the term of his natural life, full power and authority of making and deputing all and singular Officers and Ministers whatsoever to all and singular offices to be exercised and occupied in our Castle of Dover aforesaid, as fully as We ourselves can or could make within our Castle of Dover and the Cinque Ports aforesaid or the Liberties, limits, or precincts thereof if these presents had not been made. In witness whereof, We have caused these our Letters to be patent.

Witness Ourselves at Westminster, the twenty-fifth day of November, in the fourth year of our reign.

By Warrant under the King's sign manual.

Muir Mackenzie

The Speaker of the Cinque Ports then rose and made the following statement:

As Speaker of the Cinque Ports, I have been deputed by my fellow Barons to request your Lordship to take upon yourself the duties and office of Lords Warden, and to maintain the liberties, rights and privileges of the Ports. Your Lordship has filled many honourable posts during your career, but I am sure that there is no post that can give you more pleasure to occupy than that of Lord Warden of the Cinque Ports. It is a very ancient and very honourable dignity. It is associated with the names of great admirals, great soldiers, and great statesmen. To name one among so many would be invidious. Formerly the Lord Warden was required to take the oath to maintain the liberties of the Ports. That is no longer felt necessary, but we feel these liberties will be amply secured and well preserved by your Lordship. We earnestly hope that your Lordship may be spared for many years to fulfil the duties and support the dignities of the great office to the satisfaction of your faithful Barons (applause).

Earl Beauchamp replied thus:

Mr Speaker: In response to your request, I have great pleasure in taking over the duties of the ancient and the honourable office of Lord Warden of the Cinque Ports, and I undertake to maintain the franchises liberties, customs and usages of the Ports.

Thereupon the whole Court rose and did his Lordship reverence, the Lord Warden's flag was broken on the flagstaff of the Redoubt, and his salute of nineteen guns was fired by the Castle Battery – the Lord Warden had been duly installed in his office.

This was followed by a speech of cordial congratulation by Sir Frederick Pollock, Judge of the Cinque Ports of Admiralty. In reply the Lord Warden said this:

We have all of us witnessed and taken part in the ceremony of to-day with feel-ings of the deepest interest – how much deeper must be the feeling and even the emotion of a Lord Warden who finds himself for the first time meeting so many friends, so many neighbours, so many representative men of the towns to which his office is still a living reality (hear, hear). It can only be with very real emotion that any Lord Warden takes upon himself the duties of his office, and sees his name inscribed upon the roll of eminent men who have preceded him in the past (hear, hear). And deep as must be the feeling of honour of any Lord Warden, in my own case there is added to it feelings of gratification, when I think of my family associations with that post (applause). The ancient Kentish family of Stanhope has been connected in various ways with the office of Lord Warden. Mr Pitt, one of the greatest of my predecessors, was connected by marriage with that family (applause). The last Lord Lieutenant of Kent was a godson of the Duke of Wellington, and his father had for many years lived in the closest intimacy with the Duke of Wellington at Walmer Castle and elsewhere, and it was not so many years ago that his son published a most interesting book, a record of the conversations that his father had with the Duke of Wellington (applause). To-day I am glad to welcome a guest who has honoured us with his company, Lord Rosebery (applause), who shares with myself the same connection, though in different generations, with the house of Stanhope – as both our mothers came from that ancient family (applause). Let me thank Sir Frederick Pollock for his reference to his predecessor. I do not doubt that his own knowledge and legal attainments fit him completely to fulfil the duties of his office. He did not refer, as I would wish to refer, to the unique circumstances that there are living to-day three people in this country who have occupied the Lord Wardenship in turn, and it is thoroughly characteristic of the distinguished list of men who have held that post to notice how each of these three men living to-day has made a real contribution to the history of the Empire. It would be unbecoming on my part as a servant of his most gracious Majesty (who was Lord Warden as Prince of Wales) to praise him to this assembly. But it is pertinent to point out that His Majesty's connection with the Navy must always be of special interest to members of the Cinque Ports (applause). For the early history of the British Navy is the history of the Cinque Ports (applause), and the history of the British Navy is the history of the British Empire (applause). Not only is there that special connection of His Majesty's with the history of the Cinque Ports, but there is the fact that he more than any of his predecessors knows the difficulties, the economic and social and political problems of the many portions of his world-wide Empire. He has travelled as none of his predecessors have travelled (applause). Then I turn to Lord Curzon (applause). When he was made Lord Warden, Lord Curzon spoke on the problems of the Indian Empire. He has left an imperishable record as Viceroy of that great dependency, but it remains for Lord Curzon in the future to make greater contributions to the history and statesmanship of England (applause). I have the privilege of sitting opposite him and often hearing him speak. He is, with one exception [bowing to Lord Rosebery] the most eloquent orator in the House of Lords (applause), and it is a privilege to listen to the orations which he delivers in that assembly, and with which I have no fault to find except sometimes with the views and opinions to which he gives voice (laughter). Last of all, there is my immediate predecessor in the office, Earl Brassey (applause). As a yachtsman and a philanthropist,

Lord Brassey's name is known in many parts of the Empire. Whenever men go down to the sea in ships his work in connection with the Royal Naval Reserve is well known (applause), and he represents in his own person one of those great families which by their commercial integrity and by their abilities have done so much for the prosperity of the Empire (applause). And here, speaking in this place, I would make one reference to one who is no longer with us, but to who I am bound by special ties of family affection. Lady Beauchamp and I are happily intimately connected with one whose name is loved in Dover – Lady Grosvenor (applause). The death of Mr George Wyndham was a real loss, not only to Dover, but also, I venture to think, to the country as a whole (hear, hear). I do not know that I have ever met anybody in whom brilliance and charm were combined to so high a degree as they were in the character of Mr George Wyndham (hear, hear). His brilliance was charming, and his charm was brilliant (hear, hear). Everyone who met him fell a victim to that charm and recognised his brilliance. In addition to that, he possessed literary gifts of no small order; scholarship of no mean kind (hear, hear). May I say to Lord Duncannon – whom I specially thank for his presence here to-day (applause) – that I can wish for him nothing better than that he may have opportunities of service to the Empire and the country such as those which Mr Wyndham had himself (applause). Returning to the more immediate subject of my address, I say again that it is with feelings of very real emotion that I see my name enrolled upon the list of those illustrious predecessors, great in oratory, in Statecraft, in affairs, in the battlefield as well as in the study. Their talents have been many and varied, and it is a solemn moment when one sees one's name placed in succession to so much that is venerable and famous in the history of this country. I can only trust that the duties of the office – official, social, and others – such as still remain to the Lord Warden, will be fulfilled to your satisfaction (applause). We all of us know and realise that the duties have dwindled and that they are not what they used to be. But here and now, in the presence of this Grand Court of Shepway, I undertake to fulfil them to the best of my ability (loud applause).

The Seneschal then proclaimed to dissolve the Court:

All Mayors, Barons and others that have had to do at this King's Majesty's Court of Shepway, before my Lord Warden this day, you shall depart, and take your ease unto a new warning. God save the King, my Lord Warden, and the whole Court.

The Mayor of Dover on behalf of the Cinque Ports 'offered the Lord Warden an invitation to luncheon at the Town Hall, which his Lordship accepted'. The Seneschal then proclaimed:

> All Mayors, Barons and others whatsoever that be now here present are warned to proceed to the Town Hall of Dover by two of the clock and there to take such repast as is ordained.

The Lord Warden escorted by the members of the Court proceeded in procession by way of Military Hill, Worthington Street, and Biggin Street to the Town Hall.

The whole of the route was very prettily decorated with flags, festoons, and streamers connecting tall Venetian masts, erected on either side of the road, and as the multi-coloured pennants fluttered in the slight breeze the effect was most picturesque. The scheme of decoration was carried out on excellent lines. At the various points of vantage where the crowd was thickest and the military bands discoursed pleasing music during the interval of waiting, the more effective portion of the display had been carried out. At the foot of the Castle Hill a banner suspended across the road bore the salutation, 'Salve CV Custos', whilst on a similar banner at the foot of Military Hill was the Beauchamp motto, 'Fortuna mea in bello campo'. In the Market Square and at the Town Hall there were masses of bunting, floral festoons, emblazoned shields and trophies of flags in abundance. In addition to the street decoration excellent effects were created by the decoration of premises on the route.

In the beautifully decorated Town Hall 250 guests were seated to enjoy the repast 'ordained' thus:

II

Luncheon at the Town Hall, Dover, Saturday, 18th July 1914

The Mayor of Winchelsea
G. M. Freeman, Esq., K. C.
Speaker of the Ports

Toast List

To Propose	*Toast*	*To Respond*
The Speaker	The King	
His Grace the Archbishop of Canterbury	The Lord Warden of the Cinque Ports	The Lord Warden
The Lord Warden	The Speaker of the Cinque Ports	The Speaker

Vins
Gonnalez Byass & Co. Royal Pale Sherry
Laubenheimer, 1908 (Julius Kayser & Co.)
Côte de Bassens, 1911
Metropole Champagne Extra Quality, Extra Dry, Vintage 1906

Liqueurs
Des Pères Chartreuse Orange Curacao
Grand Marnier 'Cordon Rouge'
Riga Kummel et Courvoisier 'V. O.'
Liqueur Cognac
Cockburn's fine Tawny Port

Menu
Cantaloup glace
Saumon d'Écosse
Sauce Mayonnaise
Homard en Aspic à la Parisienne

Terrine de Canetons à la Clamart
Galantine de Volaille, trufffée
Jambon d'York et Langue à la Gelée
Boeuf pressé à l'Anglaise
Salade Française

Pouding 'Cinque Ports'
Gelée à la Moscovite
Soufflé glace Princesse
Éclaires au Chocolat
Café double frappé

Luncheon served by: Gordon Hotels Ltd., Lord Warden Hotel, Dover.

Programme of Music
1 March: 'Children of the Regiment': Fucik
2 Waltz: 'Count of Luxembourg': Lehar
3 Selection: 'Chocolate Soldier': Strauss
4 Barcarolle: 'Tales of Hoffman': Offenbach
5 One-Step: 'The Banshee': Kennedy
6 Morceaux: a) 'Chant Sans Paroles': Tschaikowsky
              b) 'Humoresque': Dvořák
7 Valse: 'Verschmähte Lieb': Lincke
8 Selection: 'Faust': Gounod
9 Serenade: 'O Sole Mio': Capua
10 March: 'Vive la Torero': Popy
God Save the King
Conductor: A. T. Dixon

Proposing the toast to the Lord Warden, the Archbishop of Canterbury said that he was speaking 'as a friend of a good many years'. He could say that Lord Beauchamp was 'one who has, from the culture that he has acquired and cherished from his wide experience in England and in the Antipodes, come to be among the men who has appreciated in the past, and illustrated in the present, the great traditions, civic and ecclesiastical, sacred and secular, which find in this region such marked expression (applause). May the duties be lighter – the individual responsibilities certainly will be less – than in the past, but you hold what is beyond question one of the most historic posts in England; illustrious in modern, as well as in ancient days ... It is, my Lord Warden, my belief that you will adorn that position, that you will hand on its banner unsullied, and its traditions undimmed, and we all desire to-day to wish you happiness, prosperity and Godspeed.'

The Archbishop's words received enthusiastic 'loud cheers'. With equal zeal, the toast was 'honoured with Kentish Fire'.

In response to the toast to his health, Beauchamp forewarned that his duties and responsibilities at Westminster made it impossible 'at present to make myself acquainted with the various ports and towns in the way I would wish', but he hoped he would be able to come when, with fewer responsibilities, he would be able 'to see more of the Cinque Ports and something of the municipalities comprised within their area'. The announcement brought more applause.

Earl Beauchamp at Walmer

We can only speculate on what exactly Beauchamp did during his tenure of office. The Kent County Council Archives at Maidstone have not been able to deliver any information on it. It is true that the historical responsibilities belonging to the Lord Warden had dwindled to very little by the time Beauchamp occupied this office, and yet Walmer appears to have become a place for rest and enjoyment. Even before Earl Beauchamp was installed as Warden, he and his wife began to entertain guests at Walmer.

'I must write & tell you,' wrote a friend of the family to 'dear Lettice', the Countess Beauchamp, 'how very much we both enjoyed our visit to you at Walmer & how very much we enjoyed & appreciated your kindness in having us. It was a great pleasure to me to see it all again and to feel that it is in the hands of those who care for it, for we were all so fond of the place & had so many happy years there. It is all full of recollections of my father. Lord Beauchamp was kindness itself in going over everything with me. Please tell him how grateful I was. I hope you & the boys are enjoying this delicious weather at Madresfield.'[46] Some time later, the same person wrote to thank her hosts for a gift from Walmer: 'Dear Lettice, I have received a delightful box of Walmer figs which Paramor tells me were sent by your orders. I think it is extraordinarily kind of you & Lord Beauchamp to have remembered that I was so fond of them. I never thought you would really send some. They are quite delicious & I am so glad they have reached me here as my mother is able to enjoy them also. We eat them with double relish as they come from Walmer. ...'[47] Another friend, Pamela Stewart, a member of the domestic staff at Buckingham Palace, wrote to thank the Beauchamps for an invitation to Walmer but regretted that she could not come: 'Dear Lord Beauchamp, It is awfully kind of you, and of Lady Beauchamp to have thought of asking me down to Walmer for a weekend, and thank you so much. The unfortunate part is that I am afraid I won't have the chance to avail myself of the pleasure at present anyhow, because this weekend I have got to accompany the duke of York on a visit ...'[48] Hugh Cecil too wrote to 'My dear Beauchamp', saying that he was sending him '*Broken Lights*, trusting to your sworn word. You will see on the fly-leaf in George Wyndham's hand, "Given me by Hugh Cecil", but in fact I only lent it to him in the same way as I am lending it to you. I remember thinking Walmer an attractive house; but the country round rather depressing.'[49]

46   Vita Russell to Countess Beauchamp, dated 28 April 1914. Source: Beauchamp Papers, *op. cit.*

47   Vita Russell to Countess Beauchamp, dated 31 August 1914. *Ibid.*

48   Pamela Stewart to Lord Beauchamp, dated 12 July 1914. *Ibid.*

49   Hugh Cecil to Lord Beauchamp, dated 14 June 1915. *Ibid. Broken Lights* was a collection of poems, as yet unpublished, by Glenn Hughes, b. 1894. Earl Beauchamp often

There are two brief annotations in Curzon's book.[50] In 1916, Curzon had
bought a volume of Lord Dalhousie's private correspondence at Sotheby's
and had presented it to Walmer. Lord Beauchamp 'had it bound up.'[51] And
Beauchamp, we are told, 'reverted to ancient practice and issued a precept
calling the Grand Court of Shepway to assemble at Bredenstone.'[52] Certainly
the Beauchamp children enjoyed their stays at Walmer. They were keen to
swim in the clear waters of the Channel, a striking change for them from
the muddy pool at Madresfield.

It is not out of place if we quote the impressions of a lady who once happened to be at Walmer, though uninvited. In her florid memoirs, Christabel
Aberconway remembered:[53]

> About this time I met another man whom I judged to be an eccentric, but whom I
> didn't much like: Lord Beauchamp, a brother-in-law of Bendor, Duke of Westminster,
> whom I did like. One Sunday, my host, Lord Jowitt, asked my husband if he and
> I would like to see one of the famous castles of the Cinque Ports. Delightedly we
> accepted. I don't know whether William Jowitt telephoned to ask if we might call
> on Lord Beauchamp, which would have been polite, all I recall is that we arrived

---

invited guests to spend weekends, not only at Walmer Castle but also at Madresfield.
Here is a thank-you letter for such an invitation from Herbert Warren, the President
of Magdalen College, Oxford: 'Magdalen College, Oxford, Sept. 8/1916. My dear
Lord Beauchamp, Lady Warren is writing to Lady Beauchamp. I feel however I should
like to write a line too to yourself. For you are always so specially kind & hospitable
in welcoming us when we come to Malvern and your territory. I much hoped to
have seen you again. ... But all our schemes were stopped by a most sad accumulation
of bereavements. Lady Warren lost first her sister. Then about a fortnight later her
brother-in-law was taken and then the day after we heard of the death from appendi-
citis of their daughter. ... But I fully hope to come again and pay my respect to your
Gibbon. And if it can be managed I should greatly like Bill [C. F. Bill, Keeper of the
Oxford University Galleries] to see all you have to show him.' *Ibid.*

50   Curzon, *Walmer Castle, op. cit.*
51   *Ibid.*, p. 265, n. 2.
52   *Ibid.*, 289.
53   Christabel, Lady Aberconway, *A Wiser Woman? A Book of Memories* (London:
     Hutchinson, 1966), p. 127. Lady Aberconway was a wordly woman, who accepted
     the gift of a house in Mayfair from her lover Samuel Courtauld, the millionaire con-
     noisseur. Her father was Chief of Scotland Yard.

and were shown into a garden surrounding a grass tennis-court. There I saw the actor Ernest Thesiger, a friend of mine, nude to the waist and covered with pearls: he explained that he had the right type of skin to heal pearls. Two or three other young men were introduced to me, including a nice young man who Lord Beauchamp introduced as his tennis coach. Presently the men of the party wandered away, and as I thought that they might be wanting to discuss politics I stayed behind, so did the young tennis coach. Seeing a tennis racquet on a seat, I said, 'Oh, do send me some difficult services and then tell me how to reply.' Poor young man. He couldn't even pat a ball over the net. 'I'm so sorry,' I murmured, for I can't bear seeing young people embarrassed, 'I've just re-strained my wrist, and can't play now.' Soon afterwards the men of the party returned, and we left. Some time later, I read in a newspaper that Lord Beauchamp had gone abroad 'to have mud baths'. I am almost sure that he never came back to England. Perhaps, poor man, when I saw him he was physically ill, but certainly he was eccentric.

Perhaps Lady Aberconway did not realize why in fact these 'nice' young men were being entertained at Walmer. Or, if she did, she was too discreet to convey her impressions to posterity. In any case the circumstances appear to have been generally in great contrast with the period when Beauchamp's predecessors hosted guests at Walmer. There were exceptions. Asquith and Lord Kitchener[54] did visit Walmer Castle off and on. Once King George V himself came.

Ponsonby to Beauchamp[55]

Windsor Castle

6th April 1914

My dear Beauchamp,

Stamfordham has handed me your letter as I am in charge of the arrangements for the King's visit to Paris.

His Majesty desires me to tell you that he thinks it will be perfectly correct for you to be on Dover Pier on this occasion, as he will be going to Paris in State. The King has also expressed a wish that the Lord Lieutenant should also be present on this occasion.

54　Viscount Kitchener of Khartoum (1850–1916), C.-in-C., India, 1902–9; War Secretary, 1914–16.

55　Source: Royal Archives: PS/PSO/GV/PS/SV/56079/7.

I don't know, strictly speaking, how you as Lord Warden, rank with the Lord Lieutenant, but no doubt you will be able to fix this up with Camden.

Yours sincerely,

F. Ponsonby

Annexes

There is evidence that Earl Beauchamp took care in looking after the Castle and the gardens. He was a man of aesthetic tastes. This is amply clear in the documents we enclose below as annexes.

1

Indenture declaring trusts of investments held by the said Earl upon trust for the upkeep and maintenance thereabout of Walmer Castle and the Office of Lord Warden of the Cinque Ports[56]

Earl Beauchamp K. G. To V. S. Corkan, A.J. D. C. Wilson and the Hon. L. Holland

Dated 10 September 1918

This Indenture made the Tenth day of September one thousand nine hundred and eighteen Between William Earl Beauchamp Knight of the Garter (hereinafter called 'the said Earl') of the one part and Victor Seymour Corkan C. V. O. of 40 Gloucester Terrace Hyde Park in the County of London Esquire Arthur John de Courcy Wilson of Madresfield Grange Malvern Link in the County of Worcester Esquire and the Honourable Lionel Holland of 14 Buckingham Street Adelphi in the County of London (hereafter called 'the Trustees') of the other part Whereas the said Earl is the present holder of the Office of Lord Warden of the Cinque Ports and by virtue of and during tenure of such office has an official residence at Walmer Castle in the County of Kent And Whereas Walmer Castle aforesaid is an ancient building of considerable national interest and the public are admitted during certain hours of the day to certain state rooms to view the various articles of historical interest therein and to the

---

56   Source: Worcestershire Archives & Archaeology Service, Worcester. *Deeds*, 705:99/3375/67(v).

extensive gardens moat and terrace appertaining thereto And whereas a considerable staff of gardeners custodians and other servants and attendants at Walmer Castle other than the personal attendants of the said Earl and his family And Whereas it is desirable for the purpose of maintaining Walmer Castle in a manner worthy of its importance and associations and for the purpose of providing for the adequate discharge of the official duties of the said office that in addition to all allowances from the Crown considerable sums should be available for the maintenance and upkeep of the said Castle and its gardens and appurtenances (especially during the absence of the said Earl therefrom) and other purposes in connection therewith and also for defraying the necessary costs and expenses of and incidental to the said office And Whereas the said Earl has transferred into the joint names of the Trustees the investment mentioned in the Schedule hereto to the intent that the dividends and income thereof shall during such period as is hereinafter mentioned be held upon such trusts for the purposes aforesaid as are hereinafter declared Now this Indenture Witnesseth and it is hereby and declared as follows:

1. The said Earl hereby declares that the Trustees shall either permit the said investments specified in the Schedule hereto to remain in their actual state of investment or at the request of the said Earl sell the same or any part or parts thereof and invest the proceeds of such sale in the names or under the legal control of the Trustees in or upon any of the public stocks or funds or Government securities of the United Kingdom or any of the British Dominion (that expression being herein used to mean and include any British Dominion State Colony Dependency Possession Settlement or Protectorate or any constituent part thereof respectively) or any Foreign Government or State or any securities the interest on which is or shall be guaranteed by the legislature of the United Kingdom or any of the British Dominions or by any Foreign Government or State or in or upon freehold copyhold leasehold or chattel real securities in Great Britain or any of the British Dominions or on charges registered under the Land Transfer Acts 1875 and 1897 on freehold or leasehold hereditaments in England such leaseholds or chattels real having not less than Fifty years to run at the time of such investment being made or on mortgage of or on such first registered charge as aforesaid on leaseholds having any terms of years to run together with a sinking fund policy at an annual premium securing the payment on or before the expiration of the term of a sum not less than Twenty per cent larger than the sum lent or on the security of any interest for a life or lives or a determinable on a life or lives or any other event in real or personal immovable or moveable property in the United Kingdom or any of the British Dominions or any foreign country together with a policy or policies of assurance on such life or lives or against such event or on the security of any real or immovable with or without moveable property in any of the British Dominions or any foreign country or in the purchase of freehold or leasehold ground rents in or upon the bonds debenture stock mortgages obligations or securities or any of the Stock or shares of whatsoever kind or description

respectively of and Company Corporation or any body or authority in the United Kingdom or any of the British Dominions or any foreign country whether public municipal or local or of any other description whatsoever and the Trustees shall at such as aforesaid transpose any investments into others of any nature hereinbefore authorised And further they may deposit any deeds securities or instruments including securities to bearer held by them as such Trustees with any bankers or any firm or company for safe custody or receipt of dividends and may pay out of the income of the Trust Fund any sums payable for such deposit and custody and shall not be responsible for any loss occasioned by such deposit.

2. The Trustees shall stand possessed of the said investments specified in the said schedule hereto and the investments from time to time representing the same (all of which premises are hereinafter called 'the Trust Fund') upon the trusts and with and subject to the powers and provisions following that is to say:

3. The Trustees shall during such time as the said Earl shall continue to hold the said Office of Lord Warden of the Cinque Ports and for two calendar months thereafter apply in augmentation of the moneys (if any) provided in that behalf by the Crown the whole of the income of the Trust Fund accruing due during such period in or towards maintaining in a proper state of preservation and repair the said Castle and the contents thereof and the gardens grounds and outbuildings occupied therewith and in repairing renewing or replacing the furniture carpets curtains hangings fixtures and other articles of use or ornament therein and in insuring against loss or damage by fire bombardment or aircraft risks theft or burglary such of the contents of the said Castle as the Trustees think fit to insure and in and for providing for and paying salaries wages or allowances to the necessary permanent staff of outdoor and indoor custodians servants gardeners and other persons usually employed at the said Castle and keeping up the Official establishment at the said Castle and defraying all other charges outgoings and expenses in connection with the premises or with the said establishment not being the personal expenses of the said Earl or his family and in defraying and making all proper or customary local and other subscriptions contributions and donations and in making investigations or causing investigations to be made into the records of the office of Lord Warden and providing for the acquisition and preservation of all documents relating thereto and in purchasing objects of interest relics and articles of a similar nature and such other payments and disbursements whether in connection with the said Office and the due maintenance thereof or the upkeep of the said Castle and the establishment thereof as the Trustees may in their discretion think fit. The Trustees shall whenever practicable consult the said Earl As to the manner in which the income of the Trust Funds shall be applied for the purposes mentioned in this clause and shall comply with his wishes in such respect unless in the exercise of such discretion they consider such compliance to be undesirable.

4. Any part of the income of the Trust Fund not required in any year for the purpose aforesaid shall be accumulated at compound interest by investing the same and the resulting income thereof in any of the investments hereinbefore authorised to the intent that such accumulations shall become part of and be held upon the trusts herein declared concerning the Trust Fund but so nevertheless that the accumulations of any preceding year or years may be applied by the Trustees for the purposes aforesaid in any succeeding year or years.

5. From and after the expiration of two calendar months from the date when the said Earl shall have ceased to hold the said office of Lord Warden of the Cinque Ports the Trustees shall stand possessed of the Trust Fund and the income, thereof and all such accumulations as aforesaid and all furniture and other chattels which may have been bought or acquired by the Trustees under the foregoing trusts In trust for such persons and purposes as the said Earl shall by any Deed or Deeds (executed while he shall continue to hold the office of Lord Warden or before the expiration of two calendar months after he ceases to hold such office) or in the event of the death of the said Earl while holding such office by Will or Codicil appoint and in default of and subject to any such appointment In Trust to transfer and make over the same to the Commissioners of His Majesty's Works and Public Buildings to be held and applied by such Commissioners for the maintenance upkeep improvement and generally for the benefit of Walmer Castle and the contents thereof and the gardens grounds and outbuildings used or enjoyed therewith and other purposes mentioned in Clause 3 of these presents as the said Commissioners shall think fit. Provided always that if at any time hereafter the ancient office of Lord Warden of the Cinque Ports shall be abolished or any of its ancient rights privileges or dignities (other than rights or privileges connected with the jurisdiction civil or criminal of any Court and Admiralty) shall be destroyed or abrogated or if Walmer Castle aforesaid shall cease to be used and occupied as the Official residence of the Lord Warden for the time being (or the public shall be permanently excluded from admission to the State rooms thereof) then and in any of such events the trusts hereinbefore contained concerning the Trust Fund and the income thereof and all accumulations of such income and the said furniture and chattels shall forthwith cease and determine and the Trust Fund and the said income accumulations furniture and chattels belong to the said Earl his executors or administrators.

6. The said Earl as settler hereby assigns to the Trustees all his interest in the following sums namely (1) A rent of twenty six pounds per annum payable under a tenancy agreement dated the fourth day of December one thousand nine hundred and five in respect of pasture land known as Walmer Castle Meadows or other the rent for the time being payable for the same during the said Earl's tenure of the said Office (2) The rent of one pound five shillings or other rent for the time being payable by the Walmer Urban District Council in respect of the green and beach land between

Walmer Castle and the sea (3) A yearly sum of five shillings payable by Arthur Naylor Wollaston under an agreement dated the thirtieth day of August one thousand nine hundred and five and (4) all other sums (if any) payable by any person or corporation in respect of any franchise of wreck or other franchise to which the said Earl is entitled by virtue of his said office or in respect of any user of or right or privilege of admission to Walmer Castle or any lands foreshore beach or premises thereto belonging to hold the same unto the Trustees in trust to apply the same as if the same were income arising form the investments for the time being representing the Trust Fund.

7. The said Earl hereby covenants with the Trustees that if in any year while the said Earl shall hold the office of Lord Warden aforesaid the sums mentioned in Clause 6 hereof shall not amount to two hundred pounds he will so soon as the deficiency shall have been ascertained pay to the Trustees the amount of such deficiency the moneys so paid to be applied by the Trustees as income of the Trust Fund.

8. The Trustees shall not be bound in any case to act personally but shall be at full liberty to employ a solicitor or other agent to transact all or any business of whatsoever nature required to be done in the premises (including the receipt and payment of money) and shall be entitled to be allowed and paid all charges and expenses so incurred and shall not be responsible for the default of any such solicitor or agent or for any loss occasioned by his employment And further any trustee for the time being a Solicitor or other person engaged in any profession or business shall be entitled to charge and be paid all usual professional or other charges for business done by him or his firm in relation to the execution of the trusts of these presents and also his reasonable charges in addition to disbursements for all other work and business done and all time spent by him or his firm in connection with matters arising in the premises including matters which might or should have been attended to in person by a trustee not being a Solicitor or other professional person.

9. The Trustees and each of them shall be respectively chargeable only for such moneys and securities as they shall respectively actually receive notwithstanding their respectively signing any receipt for the sake of conformity and shall respectively be answerable and responsible only for their own respective acts receipts omissions neglects and defaults and not for those of any other trustees or of any banker broker auctioneer or other persons with whom or into whose hands any trust moneys or securities shall be deposited or come and not for purchasing or lending on the security of hereditaments with less than a marketable title or for the insufficiency in title or deficiency in value of any investments or for any other loss unless the same shall happen through their own wilful default respectively And the Trustees and each of them may reimburse themselves or himself or pay and discharge out of the Trust Premises all expenses incurred in or about the execution of the trusts or powers of these presents.

10. The power of appointing a new trustee or new trustees of these presents shall be vested in the said Earl.

11. The said Earl may at any time or times hereafter by deed or deeds revoke wholly or partially the trusts powers and provision herein declared and contained of and concerning the Trust Fund.

12. The expression 'the Trustees; hereafter contained shall if the context so admits include the said Victor Seymour Corkran Arthur John de Courcy Wilson and Lionel Holland and the survivors and survivor of them or other Trustees or trustee for the time being of these presents and all the trusts powers authorities and discretions hereinbefore given to or vested in the Trustees shall devolve upon such persons or person and be exercisable by them or him accordingly.

In Witness whereof the said parties to these presents have hereunto set their hands and seals the day and year first above written.

The Schedule Above Referred To

200 shares in the London Assurance Corporation Limited.

Signed Sealed and Delivered by the above named William Earl Beauchamp Knight of Garter in the presence of [signatures illegible]

Signed Sealed and Delivered by the above named Victor Seymour Corkran C. V. O. in the presence of [signatures illegible]

Signed Sealed and delivered by the above named Arthur John De Courcy Wilson in the presence of [signatures illegible]

Signed Sealed and Delivered by the above named The Honourable Lionel Holland in the presence of [signatures illegible]

2

Deed of Modification and Appointment of a New Trustee by Earl Beauchamp of a settlement made by him on 10 September 1918 for the maintenance of Walmer Castle as the Office of Lord Warden of the Cinque Ports.

Deed dated 4 May 1928 in favour of his eldest son the Honourable William Lygon, called Viscount Elmley.

3

Deed of Revocation, dated 11 August 1930[57]

The Rt Hon. William Earl of Beauchamp K. G. and Sir V. S. Corkran and others
This Deed of Revocation made the Eleventh of day of August One thousand nine
hundred and thirty Between The Right Honourable William Earl Beauchamp K. G.
(hereafter called Earl Beauchamp) of the one part and Sir Victor Seymour Corkran
K. C. V. O, The Honourable Lionel Holland and the Honourable William Lygon
(commonly called Viscount Elmley) (hereafter called the trustees) of the other part
Supplemental to (i) An indenture of Settlement dated the Tenth day of September
One thousand nine hundred and eighteen and made between Earl Beauchamp of the
one part and Victor Seymour Corkran Arthur John de Courcy Wilson and Lionel
Holland (hereafter called the Principal Deed) of the other part and (ii) A Deed of
Modification and appointment of Viscount Elmley as a Trustee in the place of Arthur
John de Courcy Wilson dated the Fourth day of May One thousand nine hundred
and twenty eight and made between Earl Beauchamp of the First part Viscount
Elmley of the Second part and Victor Seymour Corkran and Lionel Holland of the
third part Witnesseth that in exercise of power or powers for the purpose given to
him by Clause 11 of the Principal Deed and in exercise of all other powers (if any)
Earl Beauchamp with the consent in writing (hereby testified) of the Trustee hereby
revokes clause Seven of the Principal Deed in Witness whereof the said parties to these
presents have hereto set their hands and seals the day and year first before written.

[Here follow the required signatures]

4

*Deed of Revocation of a Settlement for the Maintenance of Walmer Castle created by
Deeds dated 10 September 1918 and 4 May 1928*[58]

The Right Honourable The Earl Beauchamp K. G. and Sir Victor Seymour Corkran
and others.

Dated 27 November 1933

The Deed of Revocation is made the Twenty seventh day of November One thousand nine hundred and thirty three between The Right Honourable William Earl
Beauchamp, K. G. (hereinafter and in the Schedule hereto called 'Earl Beauchamp')
of the one part and Sir Victor Seymour Corkran of Clock Court Kensington Palace
in the County of London K. C. V. O. The Honourable Lionel Holland of Number 14

57   *Ibid.*
58   *Ibid.*

Buckingham Street Adelphi in the County of London and the Honourable William Lygon called Viscount Elmley of Madresfield Court in the County of Worcester (hereafter together called 'the Trustees') of the other part Whereas this Deed is Supplemental to (i) the two Deeds (hereinafter together called 'the Principal Deeds') which are specified in Part I of the Schedule hereto and (ii) the Deed specified in Part II of the same Schedule And Whereas Earl Beauchamp has lately ceased to hold the office of Lord Warden of the Cinque Ports Now This Deed Witnesseth that in exercise of the power or powers of revocation given to him by the Principal Deeds Earl Beauchamp with the consent in writing (hereby testified) of the Trustees hereby wholly revokes all the trusts powers and provisions by and in the Principal Deeds or either of them declared and contained of and concerning all the investments funds and property whatsoever (whether capital or income and including any furniture or chattels) now by any means subject to the trusts of the Principal Deeds or either of them.

In Witness whereof the said parties to these presents have hereto set their hands and seals the day and year first before written.

The Schedule above referred to.
Part I

Number: 1

Date: 10th September 1918

Parties: Earl Beauchamp, Victor Seymour Corkran, Arthur John de Courcy Wilson, and the Hon. Lionel Holland

Nature: Settlement or Declaration of Trust for the maintenance of Walmer Castle and the Office of Lord Warden of Cinque Ports.

Number: 2

Date: 4th May 1928

Parties: Earl Beauchamp, the Hon. William Lygon (Viscount Elmley), Sir Victor Seymour (therein called Sir Victor) Corkran and the Hon. Lionel Holland

Nature: Deed of Modification and Appointment of Viscount Elmley as a trustee (Supplemental to Number 1)

Part II

Date: 11th August 1930

Parties: Earl Beauchamp, Sir Victor Corkran, the Hon, Lionel Holland and Viscount Elmley

Nature: Deed of Partial Revocation (Supplemental to the Deeds specified in Part I of this Schedule)

[Here follow the required signatures]

CHAPTER 14

Advocate of Irish Home Rule

In the years we are considering, around 1912, the issue of Irish Home Rule was still a burning question. The two Gladstonian Home Rule bills, put forward in the nineteenth century, had been killed either by the House of Commons or by the House of Lords.[1] The Parliament Act, 1911, which had now drastically cut the powers of the upper chamber, offered new prospects of success. The Parliament Act gave the Lords a delaying period of two years to debate and decide on a bill sent up to them by the Commons, and after this delay, even if the Lords still opposed a bill that had passed the Commons through all three stages, it received the Royal Assent nonetheless. Asquith was keen to achieve Home Rule for Ireland. The problem he and his close advisers faced was whether Ireland should be treated as a single unit, or whether there should be provisions made for the Ulster Unionists who strongly opposed any Home Rule for the country. For their part, the Irish Nationalists equally resisted any concessions to Ulster. Asquith was also aware of the fact that he could not push a Home Rule bill through the Commons without Irish support. Therefore, with the backing of Lord

---

1   William Gladstone put down the first Home Rule Bill in the House of Commons on 8 April 1886. At the second reading on 8 June, the bill was thrown out by 343 votes against 313 (and these included 93 Liberals). A brief, but precise description of the bill and its fate is available in Philip Magnus, *Gladstone: A Biography* (London: John Murray, 1954), pp. 353–60. A revised second reading of the Home Rule Bill took place on the night of 21/22 April 1893. The bill was carried by 347 votes to 304. The third reading was carried by 307 votes to 267 on the night of 1/2 September. But the bill was strongly opposed by the House of Lords when they debated it on 8 September. In the division, the Lords killed the bill by 419 votes to 41. For details see *Ibid.*, pp. 412–14.

Crewe, he recommended a compromise, to which the cabinet agreed. It suggested:[2]

> a) that the Bill as introduced should apply to the whole of Ireland;
>
> b) that the Irish leaders should from the first be given clearly to understand that the Government held themselves free to make such changes in the Bill as fresh evidence of facts, or the pressure of British opinion may render expedient;
>
> c) that if, in the light of such evidence or indication of public opinion, it becomes clear as the Bill proceeds that some special treatment must be provided for the Ulster counties, the Government will be ready to recognise the necessity either by amendment of the Bill, or by not pressing it on under the provisions of the Parliament Act. In the meantime, careful and confidential inquiry is to be made as to the real extent and character of the Ulster resistance.

The government introduced the Government of Ireland Bill in the House of Commons on 11 April 1912. The debate lasted until the January of the next year. Finally, the bill received a third reading on 16 January 1913, and was passed by a majority of 109 votes. It then went to the House of Lords. Here, on 27 January 1913, the Lord Privy Seal and Secretary of State for India, the Marquess of Crewe, moved the second reading of the bill, the 'prime object' of which was 'the re-establishment of an Irish Parliament'.[3] This Irish Parliament was to consist of two Houses: the House of Commons and the Senate. The House of Commons would contain 164 members, giving an average of one representative to about 27,000 of the population. The Senate would have forty members, nominated for the first five years so as to secure the representation of different interests, but afterwards elected for the four provinces by a system of proportional representation. The objectives of the Senate were twofold. It would serve as a body to prevent too hasty legislation, and it would give a platform to some individuals

2   Quoted in Roy Jenkins, *Asquith, op. cit.*, p. 277.

3   The government also introduced the Welsh Church Bill in the Lords. Beauchamp's 'speech in moving the second reading of the Welsh Church Bill was a great success, and according to Lord Morley, placed him in the first rank'. See Almeric Fitzroy, *Memoirs*, vol. II, *op. cit.*, entry for 12 February 1913, p. 505. See also Chapter Sixteen in the present volume.

who, for various reasons, might not care to contest seats in the Commons. The Senate would be subject to 'certain disabilities in respect of Money Bills'. It would also be necessary to adopt a plan for calling a joint session of both Houses and arranging a joint vote in the event of disagreement between them.

The Crown, the army and navy, matters relating to peace and war and treaties, the law of treason etc. were to remain outside the scope of the Irish Parliament. The Imperial Parliament had a power of veto. The Lord Lieutenant was to hold office for six years; he would be bound to no party. The heads of the Irish departments would be his ministers, combined as the Executive Committee, responsible for the local government of Ireland.

The Irish representatives in the Imperial House of Commons would be limited to forty-two in number, competent to speak for Ireland as a whole. The judiciary would be composed of Irish officials, appointed by the Lord Lieutenant, and removable only by a vote of both Houses of the Irish Parliament. A judicial committee of the Privy Council would act as the Court of Final Appeal. The financial provisions of the bill put various restrictions on the Irish Parliament.

The bill roused a degree of admiration from some members of the upper chamber at Westminster, but mostly there was hostility there. It was debated by the Lords for four days, between 27 and 30 January.[4]

The Duke of Devonshire[5] said that the government was 'attempting to force this Bill through Parliament clearly without any expressed mandate from the country', and moved that the bill be given a second reading 'this day in three months'.

The Marquess of Zetland[6] said that he had the honour of seconding the late Duke of Devonshire when he moved the rejection of the Home Rule Bill of 1893. 'It is a great pleasure to me on this occasion to do the same duty for my noble friend who has just sat down.' He could not, the

---

4   See *Parliamentary Debates*, House of Lords, vol. XIII, 27 January 1913, cols 420–516; 28 January 1913, cols 517–610 ; 29 January 1913, cols 611–720; 30 January 1913, cols 721–916.

5   Devonshire, 9th Duke of, b. 1868. A Liberal Unionist.

6   Zetland, 1st Marquess of, b. 1844. A Conservative.

Marquess observed, discover what material benefit could be derived from the bill to any part of Ireland. The bill would lead to irritation between Great Britain and Ireland. There was no finality about the bill.

Lord Langford[7] supported the amendment. He would, he said, vote against the bill because it was a bill without a clear mandate from the people. It was brought in to satisfy a debt, and because the Nationalist Party had gone into the lobby and supported the budget of 1909. Now this was the 'first payment of the debt under the Parliament Act and a shattered constitution'. The bill would mean the breaking up of the United Kingdom, and it would not be a message of peace to Ireland.

Lord Aberconway[8] said he was confident that the question 'must be solved in the direction of giving Ireland a certain amount of political independence'. A practical solution was possible. Ireland had become a 'sane and sober nation'. The delirium of centuries had vanished and violence had disappeared; thus a 'moderate and reasonable measure of reform' was necessary.

Lord Kilmaine[9] thought that the bill was 'bristling with bad points'. The outstanding fact remained that the bill had been 'framed and designed entirely in the interest of one section of the Irish people and against the interests of the other section'.

The Earl of Dunraven,[10] however, said that he would not vote for the amendment. The bill was 'a workable measure'. It could 'lead to a satisfactory and therefore permanent settlement of the Irish question'. Besides, the bill was conceived in 'recognition of the principle of devolution'. He believed 'devolution to be necessary – not only for the welfare of Ireland but for the welfare of the United Kingdom, for the efficiency of Parliament, and for the permanency of representative institutions'.

Lord MacDonnell of Swinford[11] maintained that 'urgent necessity' existed for a substantial reform in the system of Irish Government.

7   Langford, 4th Baron, b. 1848. A Conservative.
8   Aberconway, 1st Baron, b. 1850. A Liberal.
9   Kilmaine, 5th Baron, b. 1878. A Unionist.
10   Dunraven and Mount-Earl, 4th Earl of, b. 1841. A Conservative.
11   MacDonnell, 1st Baron, b. 1844. A Liberal.

Earl Grey[12] said that he was a 'convinced Federalist'. The bill was based upon the 'foundation of nationalism'. It would 'promote discord and tend to civil war'.

Lord Ribblesdale[13] said that he gave 'unquestioned support to the Bill and to His Majesty's Government'. The debate was adjourned to the following day – to 28 January.

Viscount St Aldwyn[14] opened the next day's debate. His opinion on the subject, he said, 'remains the same as it was forty years ago', when 'I was Irish Secretary in 1874, when it fell to my lot on behalf of the Government of the day to oppose a Resolution for introduction of Home Rule in Ireland. I still believe that the institution of an Irish Parliament, with an Irish Government responsible to it, would weaken the United Kingdom, and therefore the Empire, would be a retrograde step in our history, would be injurious to the minority in Ireland, would add friction' to relations between Great Britain and Ireland.

The Lord Chancellor, Viscount Haldane, strongly commended the bill to their Lordships. It was, he said, humiliating to preserve the 'dependent position' in which the people of Ireland found themselves.

The Lord Archbishop of York[15] said that he agreed with the Lord Chancellor that some 'recognition must be found for the persistent and sustained desire of the majority of Irish people to have some liberty to manage their own affairs in their own way'.

Lord Clonbrock[16] looked upon the bill with the 'utmost apprehension'. He desired to remain closely united 'under the protection and control of the Imperial Parliament'.

Viscount Massereene[17] felt that the commercial relations between Great Britain and Ireland were 'endangered' by the bill. He thought the union with England, 'all things considered, is the best for Ireland'.

---

12 Grey, 4th Earl, b. 1851. A Liberal Unionist.
13 Ribblesdale, 4th Baron, b. 1854. A Liberal.
14 Aldwyn, 1st Viscount, b. 1837. A Conservative.
15 Cosmo Gordon Lang, b. 1864.
16 Clonbrock, 4th Baron, b. 1834. A Conservative.
17 Massereene and Ferrard, 12th Viscount, b. 1873. A Conservative.

The Earl of Wicklow[18] wanted to place on record his 'attitude of uncompromising hostility to any proposal for granting Home Rule to Ireland'.

Earl Brassey said he was a 'loyal follower' of Mr Gladstone in that he supported the general policy of Home Rule for Ireland.

Lord Farnham[19] said that the bill was 'really more obnoxious than the two previous Home Rule Bills'.

Lord Ellenborough[20] believed that the 'chief fault of this Bill is that there is no finality about it. It is a dangerous stop in a slipping slope, and will ultimately make our position in war untenable'.

The Under-Secretary of State for the Colonies, Lord Emmott,[21] observed that Home Rule was not only 'advisable but must inevitably come'.

Viscount Midleton[22] ventured to submit that the bill was not 'progressive but reactionary, and must lead to disorder and trouble'.

Lord Charnwood[23] said that the bill was a 'long step forward'. He was convinced that the bill was a measure 'too long delayed', and that it 'will bring about a great appeasement of the existing state of feeling in Ireland, that sharp severance of religion from religion, and class from class, of which, I believe, the Union is not the remedy but one of the fundamental causes'.

The debate was resumed on 29 January.

Lord Ashby St Ledgers[24] submitted that 'we have authority from the constituencies on this subject; and armed with the authority from the British electors and in response to a demand from the great majority of the Irish people, the Government have framed a Bill calculated to give as great a measure of autonomy to Ireland as is consistent with the Imperial supremacy, with the protection of the minority, and the financial harmony and equilibrium'.

---

18   Wicklow, 7th Earl of, b. 1877. A Conservative.
19   Farnham, 11th Baron, b. 1879. A Liberal Unionist.
20   Ellenborough, 5th Baron, b. 1841. A Conservative.
21   Emmott, 1st Baron, b. 1858. A Liberal.
22   Midleton, 9th Viscount, b. 1856. A Conservative.
23   Charnwood, 1st Baron, b. 1864. A Liberal.
24   Ashby St Ledgers, 1st Baron, b. 1873; afterwards 1st Viscount Wimborne. A Liberal.

The Marquess of Londonderry[25] contended that the government was endeavouring to carry the bill through parliament, not 'only behind the backs of the people of this country but against the will of the people'. The bill was 'unconstitutional'.

The Marquess of Lincolnshire[26] thought that Lord Londonderry's speech was 'destructive'. 'Why do we support Home Rule?' he asked. The answer was simple. All 'those of us who have gone out into the wide world would support Home Rule, because we are convinced, we are absolutely positive ... that self-government in Ireland is a necessity if we wish to continue a great and a growing British Imperial confederation'.

The Earl of Selborne observed that there were two possible forms of Home Rule in Ireland, and two only: one was the colonial form, and the other was the federal form. The bill was not of the colonial form. The government had rejected that, and 'rightly'. To introduce the colonial form of Home Rule would be an 'irreparable disaster'. But the government had not introduced the federal form either. What they had introduced was a 'bastard' bill.

Lord Welby[27] believed that the course the government had pursued – namely, that of 'handing over the Government of Ireland to the new Irish Government, and giving them time to make good each step as they go along' – 'is the most reasonable plan of administration that could be devised'.

Lord Oranmore and Browne said that he objected to the bill on three grounds: first, the bill 'is injurious to Ireland'; secondly, it 'is injurious to England'; and thirdly, it 'is fatal to the Empire'.

Viscount Peel[28] said that, as an Englishman, he felt this measure was not 'the free outcome of English opinion or of English feeling'.

The Earl of Kenmare[29] opposed the bill for two reasons: first, the proposal to set up a separate parliament in Dublin was 'against the best

25   Londonderry, 6th Marquess of, b. 1852. A Conservative.
26   Lincolnshire, 1st Marquess, b. 1843. A Liberal.
27   Welby, 1st Baron, b. 1832. A Liberal.
28   Peel, 2nd Viscount, b. 1867. A Unionist.
29   Kenmare, 5th Earl of, b. 1860. A Liberal Unionist.

interests of Ireland'; secondly, it was an 'experiment which will be fraught with peril to the Empire'.

The Earl of Kilmorey[30] said that he wanted to draw attention to the 'cruel injustice' the bill did to the 'loyalist minority' in Ireland. He considered it 'the biggest of the many blots to be found in its voluminous pages'. The loyalists of Ireland acknowledged 'one flag and one flag only as the national emblem of the British Empire, on which the sun never sets'.

Lord Killanin[31] said that the bill was of 'supreme and vital importance to my native land', and he considered the 'special exemplification of Home Rule which we have in the shape of this Bill is in itself most unjust and most unfair to Ireland'.

The First Commissioner of Works, Earl Beauchamp, then rose to deliver one of his most eloquent speeches, a portion of which we print below:[32]

> If I may be pardoned a personal reference, I am, I sometimes think, one of the few members of your Lordships' House who were in this House in the year 1893, and it does seem to me that a great change has come over, not only the constitution of this House but also the way in which this matter has been discussed. I remember being dragged from somewhat fruitless undergraduate studies at Oxford to swell the majority which defeated the bill on that occasion. No doubt my vote added one to the immense majority, but I do not know that it added anything to the moral influence of your Lordships' House when the bill was rejected. But at any rate I see a very real and a very great difference between the way in which this matter has been discussed during these last few days and the way in which it was discussed then. We have discussed far more points of detail during these three days and far fewer points of real underlying principle than were discussed in those great days of 1893. We have not really discussed tonight what was discussed then – the question as to whether Ireland was entitled to self-government or not, and I suppose that one of the great reasons for that is that the attitude of the people in this country towards self-government has changed, because wherever they have seen it tried, they have found that it has been proved to be a success. There are twenty-eight Parliaments, I believe, within the British Empire, and the noble Lords opposite wish us to believe that the twenty-ninth will work destruction to the whole Imperial system. ... After all, My Lords, we all of

30   Kilmorey, 3rd Earl of, b. 1842. A Conservative.
31   Killanin, 2nd Baron, b. 1867. A Conservative.
32   See *Parliamentary Debates*, House of Lords, vol. XIII, 29 January 1913, cols 698–712.

us in this country believe in government by and with our own consent, and I believe that the noble Lords opposite would rather be governed, perhaps misgoverned, by Radicals than governed by Conservatives if only those Conservatives were foreigners. They would prefer misgovernment by their own fellow-countrymen rather than what they would think good government by aliens. That is really the position so far as it applies to Ireland. We are anxious that they should have the privilege which we have ourselves. We wish to know why that privilege should be denied to the Irish which we have ourselves. ... Home Rule is the one subject to which through all these years you have opposed a resolute negative. ... The only obstacle is the small minority in one corner of Ireland who persuade your Lordships to refuse to the rest of Ireland what four-fifths of her people want. We say that such a claim on the part of so small a minority is an intolerable claim, and one which we cannot allow. ... Your Lordships may delay, but you cannot prevent the passage of Home Rule. ... The passage of this Bill would heal the old sores and strengthen Ireland and the United Kingdom and the whole of this Empire.

The Earl of Mayo[33] ended the day's debate, pronouncing that this was a 'bad bill' and one that 'will not bring contentment to Ireland'.

The discussion was recommenced on the afternoon of 30 January. Again a lengthy debate took place, and the House divided: Contents, 69; Not-Contents, 326. The Devonshire amendment was adopted. It was resolved that the bill should be read 'this day three months'.

The Government of Ireland Bill was brought before the House of Lords once again on 14 July 1913. The Lord Privy Seal, the Marquess of Crewe, moved that the bill be given a second reading. The Marquess of Lansdowne rose to move the following amendment: 'That this House declines to proceed with the consideration of the Bill until it has been submitted to the judgement of the country'. The House debated this motion for two days.[34] On 15 July the House divided: Content: 64; Not-Contents, 302. The House agreed to the amendment, thus pitching out the bill – it was the third time the House of Lords had killed a bill on Home Rule for Ireland. The government would not give up, though. It waited until the

---

33 Mayo, 7th Earl of, b. 1851. A Conservative.
34 See *Parliamentary Debates*, House of Lords, vol. XIV, 14 July 1913, cols 869–960; 15 July 1913, cols 965–1033.

next session of parliament, which opened on 10 February 1914. The King's Speech contained the following reference:[35]

> The measures in regard to which there were differences last Session between the two Houses will be again submitted to your consideration. I regret that the efforts which have been made to arrive at a solution by agreement of the problems connected with the Government of Ireland have, so far, not succeeded. In a matter in which the hopes and the fears of so many of My subjects are keenly concerned, and which, unless handled now with foresight, judgement, and in the spirit of mutual concession, threatens grave future difficulties, it is My most earnest wish that the good-will and cooperation of men of all parties and creeds may heal discussion and lay the future of a lasting settlement.

His Majesty's 'Most Gracious Speech' was debated in the House of Lords on 11 February.[36] Viscount Midleton put down an amendment that there should be a dissolution of parliament on the question of Home Rule for Ireland. Earl Loreburn, speaking for the government, said that he 'sufficiently' regretted that in two consecutive years their Lordships had refused to go into Committee upon the Government of Ireland Bill. He pleaded that 'this trouble should be settled now and by friendly arrangement'. The Marquess of Lansdowne argued against the setting up of a Home Rule parliament. The question must be referred to the electors of the country. Viscount Haldane, the Lord Chancellor, wished that 'we can get something like a common principle on which it is possible to negotiate'. Viscount Peel observed that if concessions to Ulster would have to be limited, and Ulster was to 'have her liberties guarded by various changes and concessions', he feared that that 'will not carry us any further in the path of compromise, concession, or agreement'.

Earl Beauchamp, supporting the government motion,[37] began by welcoming a new member of the House, Lord Crawford,[38] whose participation in the debates of:

---

35   See *Parliamentary Debates*, House of Lords, vol. XV, 10 February 1914, cols 1–4.
36   *Ibid.*, 11 February 1914, cols 56–144.
37   *Ibid.*, cols 132–8.
38   Crawford, 26th Earl of, b. 1847. A Conservative.

this House for the first time I am sure was heartily welcomed by members on both sides. It is a special pleasure, if he will allow me to say so, to an old college friend of his, as I am myself, to offer him that welcome, and I think I heard in some of the strictures which he addressed to His Majesty's Government some echo of the strictures which he addressed to me while we were members of the same club in Oxford when he thought my views were far from the orthodox Conservative character. And if, My Lords, I venture to think that it is no small gain to your Lordships' House that talents and ability of no small order should be contributed by him to our discussions, he will perhaps allow me to express the regret that they are added to a Party which in our view at any rate already possesses almost a superabundance of them, and which is able to bring into discussions in this House controversial abilities with which we sometimes find it difficult to cope with our attenuated numbers. I congratulate the noble Earl also upon having already assimilated one common custom in this House. He has already found that the rules of order which strictly govern debate in another place do not apply to this Assembly, and it was only in the latter portion of his speech that he turned to the Amendment which we are nominally discussing. ...

Earl Beauchamp then referred to the Amendment:

My Lords, we are anxious, naturally, to make the most of everything which has been said by the noble Lords opposite which tends towards any settlement of the question. We notice with the greatest pleasure the fact that the mere discussion of the exclusion of Ulster from an Irish Parliament is itself an admission that the noble Lords opposite have so far departed from the standpoint of years ago that they now are ready to contemplate the existence of an Irish Parliament in Dublin. ...

I only regret, when the noble Marquess who leads the Opposition went a little further and spoke of the safeguards which he would demand for the South and the West and the East and the middle parts of Ireland – safeguards which evidently might be obtained, in his opinion, and which if they were obtained would be sufficient for their welfare – that he did not think apparently that it was possible that similar safeguards might be introduced for the North-eastern province at the same time. ... While the Amendment which is before your Lordships' House has dealt chiefly with Dissolution, the debate has turned very largely upon the exclusion of Ulster. That is a point from which I wish to turn in order to discuss the Amendment. And here we have the three alternatives which have been mentioned by more than one of the speakers in this debate. First of all, the possible result, supposing there was a General Election, of a tie. In the event of a tie, then the noble Marquess opposite contemplated the passage of a measure which reasonable men of all parties might agree to. I wish I could think the noble Marquess thought that there was a large number of reasonable men who sit on the benches behind His Majesty's Government. I fear that he thinks these numbers are very much larger on the other side of the House, and that we might not agree upon what he thought was a reasonable measure to be submitted to the House of Parliament. But there were the other two possibilities. First, that the noble Lords opposite would be returned, in which event they would be faced by administrative and financial difficulties of the very gravest and most serious kind; and I suppose that if they won they would also introduce without delay into another place measures which would bring about a system of Tariff Reform in this country. But if, on the other hand, His Majesty's Government were to win, let me ask the noble Lords opposite to contemplate exactly what would happen. In the first place, under the provisions of the Parliament Act His Majesty's Government would lose the whole of the advantage of the two years which have passed. Noble Lords opposite, I think, are apt to forget what are the exact provisions of the Parliament Act with regard to measures such as this which we are now discussing. Suppose there was a General Election and we were returned to office. We should have once more to begin with the whole dreary business of these bills being introduced and passed three successive Sessions. ...

If we came back into office and then brought in our proposals for the reconstitution of the Second Chamber, I can imagine that they would be rejected by this Chamber, and it would be only after we had got through our suggestions for the reconstituted Second Chamber that we should get on with the Home Rule Bill. Well, supposing there was a General Election this year, there would be no possibility of bringing it to a final conclusion until the year 1916. That seems to me to be a very large demand to make. The noble Earl, Lord Curzon was anxious last night to make his meaning plain with regard to the way in which the noble Lords opposite would deal with the Home Rule Bill if it was introduced by His Majesty's Government after they were returned to power. The manner in which he has dealt with that question has been made plain by his use of the word 'palatable'. Unfortunately there will be two points of view in regard to the Bill when it is once more introduced. Amendments which the noble Earl might quite honestly and fairly think dealt with small matters, points of detail, might seem to us to deal with matters of very real importance, matters which affect sentiment, things to which he, perhaps, attached less importance. We should therefore once more be reduced to the point at which we were two years ago, and that, we say, is a position which we are not to accept.

One result, as we understand, of a successful Government Election from our point of view would be that the noble Marquess who leads the Opposition, and the Unionist Party would reconsider their attitude with regard to Ulster resistance. I wish I could think that the people of Ulster would have as much respect for the opinion of the noble Marquess who leads the Opposition as we have who sit upon the Front Bench opposite him every day during the Parliamentary session. I think it is very doubtful indeed if the people of Ulster would be seriously moved in their determination to resist the Home Rule Bill by the attitude which was taken up in the matter by the noble Marquess. We know that they say today that their opposition to the Bill will be determined, resolute, and formidable. I think, even if the noble Marquess were to withdraw his contingent approval of their action, that it would be no less formidable or no less resolute than it promises to be today.

After all, we have had some experience of the effect of a General Election upon the noble Lords opposite. I must remind the noble Lords, especially may I say the Front Bench, of what happened on a previous occasion. We had a General Election on the Parliament Bill, but even that General Election upon that particular Bill scarcely secured the passage of the bill through your Lordships' House. Who is there who had any responsibility in the matter who can forget the anxiety of that night when the Parliament Bill came up for its Second Reading in this Chamber? Who is there who can possibly forget the anxiety with which we watched as noble Lords issued from the one or the other Division Lobby? Was the advice of the noble Marquess going to be followed, or was the Parliament Bill going to be rejected, and with it the consequent creation of a large number of Peers forced upon His Majesty's Government?

My Lords, those of us who remember those anxieties are not likely, having gone through that experience, to welcome or even to put ourselves into such a position as to go through a similar experience again. We know that a General Election on one particular Bill does not necessarily involve the passage of that Bill in the form in which it is introduced by His Majesty's Government. Why, my Lords, we need not only refer to the second election of 1910, we can go to the General Election and see how small an effect they have had upon the legislative action of your Lordships' House. We all know the large majority with which the Government was returned in 1906. They came back and I suppose that of those election addresses, to which noble Lords pay now so much attention, there was hardly one which did not deal with plural voting or with education. The Education Bill perished before it left this House; the Plural Voting met with even shorter shrift; the Licensing Bill two years afterwards was secretly murdered, not in this Assembly, but in a private house in London. Having had this experience of the effect of a General Election upon your Lordships' House, we are, not unnaturally I venture to think, unwilling to entrust ourselves once more to such a course and on this occasion without further explanations from the noble Lords opposite. I would venture to hope, rather than urging upon your Lordships a course to which His Majesty's Government is opposed, that the Home Rule Bill may yet be considered by your Lordships' House in the light of the passage from the gracious Speech from the Throne to which I have already referred. As I went through the streets of London last night I noticed, as most of your Lordships, I am sure, did, the posters on which were printed the words: 'Grave Words in the King's Speech'.

My Lords, they were grave words; and having heard those read I venture to hope
that we may mark them, learn them, and inwardly digest them. I am no pessimist in
this matter. I venture to hope that, by the good will of men of all Parties, we may still
see the Home Rule Bill passed into law, and that it may bring peace with honour to
both political Parties in Ireland, and in this country, too.

The full debate ended on 12 February. Their Lordships then divided on
Lord Midleton's amendment: that 'it would be disastrous to proceed further with the Government of Ireland Bill until it has been submitted to
the judgment of the people'. Contents, 243; Not-contents, 55.[39] The Lords
had again killed the bill.

The government tried to come to some compromise with the
Opposition. The attempt failed.[40] Since the Commons had passed the
Ireland Bill in all three stages, the government now proposed a Suspensory
Amendment Bill on 16 September 1914, declaring a moratorium: it read that
the Act would come into operation after the expiration of twelve months
from the date of its passing in the Commons. The Commons passed this
amendment, but the Lords rejected it. The Ireland Bill was passed under
the provisions of the Parliament Act 1911.

---

39   See *Parliamentary Debates*, House of Lords, vol. XV, 12 February 1914, cols 148–217.
40   These events have been brilliantly portrayed in 'The Irish Imbroglio I and II', in Roy
     Jenkins, *Asquith, op. cit.*, pp. 274–323.

CHAPTER 15

Man of Peace

While Walmer Castle remained a place of repose, Earl Beauchamp spent most of his time attending to his ministerial duties in the House of Lords with the utmost regularity and conscientiousness. What his engagements actually were and what he was obliged to do we learn from the parliamentary records.

Party honours

On 23 February 1914, the Earl of Selborne rose to move: 'that a contribution to Party funds should not be a consideration to a Minister when he recommends any name for an honour to His Majesty; that effectual measures should be taken in order to assure the nation that Governments, from whatever political Party they are drawn, will act according to this rule; and that this House requests the concurrence of the House of Commons in the foregoing Resolution'.[1]

The First Commissioner of Works, Earl Beauchamp, said that his Government offered 'no opposition to this Motion', and the House agreed to it.

---

1   See *Parliamentary Debates*, House of Lords, 23 February 1914, vol. XV, cols 252–96.

School provision at Warrington

Lord Sheffield[2] asked Earl Beauchamp what steps the Board of Education was taking to prevent overcrowding in schools and hasten the provision of more places.[3] The Earl responded, stating that the Board was pressing the local education authorities to expedite the provisions of more places in the new schools.

The roof of Westminster Hall

Lord Southwark[4] asked the First Commissioner of Works whether he could give any information to the House as regards the condition of the roof of Westminster Hall, and an estimate of the time its repair was likely to take. Earl Beauchamp answered in detail:[5]

> We have gone lately at some length into the question of the stability of the roof, and many authorities on the historical and archaeological side have been consulted. ... The problem may be stated in the following terms. It is necessary to ensure the stability of the present roof structure and to take such steps as will prevent, or at least diminish, further depredations of the larvae of the *Xestobium tessellatum*. The most obvious means of securing these objects would be to replace throughout the roof the decayed beams in structure. But the decay has progressed so far, and is of such serious dimensions, that if this method were adopted it would be necessary practically to reconstruct the whole roof. Apart from the great cost involved by such an undertaking, it is highly questionable whether such a new structure would be of any historical interest. It has therefore been decided to attempt a scheme of strengthening which will preserve every vestige of sound timber now existing in the roof, and only to cut and piece the timbers in so far as cavities and perished wood occur. To

---

2   Sheffield, 4th Baron, b. 1839. A Liberal.
3   See *Parliamentary Debates*, House of Lords, 3 March 1914, vol. XV, cols 361–2.
4   Southwark, 1st Baron, b. 1843. A Liberal.
5   See *Parliamentary Debates*, House of Lords, 10 March 1914, vol. XV, cols 444–8.
     Xestobium tessellatum is Death Watch Beetle.

adopt this method it will be necessary to carry out a scheme of steel reinforcement. By this means the great stress carried by the present structure will be transferred to the steel reinforcement, which in turn will transmit such stresses in the form of dead loads on to the walls. The steel structure will be made so as to be practically invisible from below, and will not only carry the stresses of the roof, but will secure for a vast number of years every separate timber in the present structure. The system of steel reinforcement proposed will also permit of the removal of the modern oak struts and strengthening pieces, and also the steel rods and bars inserted in the roof from time to time, which break across and upset the original lines of the trusses.

The work will be of considerable difficulty of execution and is certain to be costly, but until one bay has been successfully treated it is impossible to frame a firm estimate for the whole of the proposed works of strengthening. While the works of strengthening are being carried out, it is intended to arrange for the removal of the modern cast-iron flèche, and to provide for a system of ventilation throughout the whole of the upper portions of the Hall roof, including the re-erection of a ventilating flèche on the lines of the original one instead of the one which is now there. A sum of £10,000 has been inserted in the Office of Works Estimates for the coming financial year, which are about to be considered in another place. With reference to the question of the preservation of the rest of the timbers from further attacks by the larvae of the *Xestobium tessellatum*, a small Committee of experts in chemistry and entomology have been assisting the Office of Works with their advice, and they have made a series of elaborate and most interesting experiments with various chemical subjects. Various methods of treatment have been suggested and considered, and it is expected that the results of the deliberations of this Committee will give us a method of treatment which will satisfactorily deal with the difficult problem of this insect. I am hoping before long to lay a White Paper before both Houses of Parliament embodying the reports dealing with the roof. ...

Movable Dwellings Bill

This bill, to be read a second time, allowed a county council to declare certain places, on grounds of health, improper for encampment.[6] Earl Beauchamp expressed 'the general approval of His Majesty's Government of this measure'.

6   See *Parliamentary Debates*, House of Lords, 25 March 1914, vol. XV, cols 684–7.

Poor Law relief

The Earl of Selborne rose to ask His Majesty's government, whether the Local Government Board 'will issue, before the Poor Law Institutions Order, 1913, comes into actual operation, an explanatory circular, explaining the legal duties and powers of guardians of the poor as to the relief of necessitous married women, widows and children'.[7] Earl Beauchamp assured the House that the matter 'shall be brought to the personal attention of the President of the Local Government Board'.

Midwives (Scotland) Bill

On 1 April 1914, Lord Balfour of Burleigh presented a bill to 'secure the better training of midwives in Scotland and to regulate their practice'.[8] Earl Beauchamp welcomed the bill admitting that he could not 'doubt' that there was 'need for legislation of this kind in Scotland'.

Elementary Education (Defective and Epileptic Children) Bill

Earl Beauchamp presented a bill which contained the following clauses:[9]
    Clause 1 imposed on the local education authority the duty to educate mentally defective children over the age of seven.

7   See *Parliamentary Debates*, House of Lords, 26 March 1914, vol. XV, cols 73–46.
8   See *Parliamentary Debates*, House of Lords, 1 April 1914, vol. XV, cols 877–86.
9   See *Parliamentary Debates*, House of Lords, 23 July 1914, vol. XVII, cols 107–13.

Clause 2 provided that if the number of children in the day school fell below 15 the authority could discontinue the school and make some alternative provision for the children.

Clause 3 provided that the authorities must consult the parents and give effect to their wishes as far as possible in determining how the child should be educated.

Clause 4 allowed the local education authority in cases where the area was too small for many children to need provision, to hand over these powers to another authority so that they might provide for their own children and those of the smaller authority at the same time.

Clause 5 made a distinction between day schools and boarding schools.

Clause 6 provided that a head teacher was to be consulted upon the condition of the child and the best way of educating him.

Clause 7 provided that when a certificate had been granted, it was not to be brought up against the child in later life.

Clause 8 determined which authority should be responsible for the education of a child who moved about from place to place.

The bill was read a second time and committed to a Committee of the Whole House.

Exportation of Horses Bill

On 30 July 1914, Lord Leigh[10] presented a bill to 'seek to put an end to a traffic which has been the cause of intense and abominable cruelty, and which has roused much public indignation. A large trade in worn-out and decrepit horses exists between this country and Belgium, the fact that a vast majority of these horses are unfit for further work proving that they are intended to be slaughtered on the other side for human consumption.'[11]

10   Leigh, 3rd Baron, b. 1855. A Conservative.
11   See *Parliamentary Debates*, House of Lords, 30 July 1914, vol. XVII, cols 294–6.

Earl Beauchamp, speaking for the government, said that it gave 'cordial approval' to the bill, which was read a second time, and committed to a Committee of the Whole House.

The coming of war: An issue of conscience

As their Lordships were expressing their indignation at the export of decrepit horses to Belgium for human consumption, the cabinet was debating whether and how to defend Belgian sovereignty, soon to be threatened by the German armed invasion. War appeared to be imminent in Europe in July 1914. The crisis had been caused by the assassination of the Archduke Franz Ferdinand, heir-apparent to the Austro-Hungarian Empire, on 28 June in Sarajevo. The murderers turned out to be Serbian fanatics, and the conspiracy had been contrived in Serbia. Enraged at this crime, Vienna was determined to take vengeance by attacking Serbia. But before he ordered such an action, the Emperor Franz Josef wrote to Wilhelm II, Emperor of the German Second Reich, to seek his approval. This the German Emperor willingly gave. So, on 23 July, Austria presented an ultimatum at Belgrade, demanding an apology and punishment of the criminals. Although, on 25 July, Belgrade accepted most of the demands, the answer was rejected by Austria. She broke off diplomatic relations with Belgrade and ordered the mobilization of her army. On 28 July, Austria declared war on Serbia and bombarded Belgrade. At this, Russia prepared to mobilize. Great Britain was now alarmed. If Russia went to war, so would France. Russia would call on France to honour the Franco-Russian Treaty of 1894, which guaranteed mutual assistance in case of aggression. On 29 July, the British Foreign Secretary, Edward Grey, warned Germany that Britain could not stand neutral in any European armed conflict. But Grey also gave France to understand that she should not count on British intervention. However the British attitude slowly changed when it became increasingly clear that Germany was about to violate Belgian neutrality. On 31 July, Germany sent a twelve-hour ultimatum to Russia, demanding that the Russian mobilization must stop. Russia refused to obey. Germany declared war against Russia on 2 August, and against France on 3 August.

During the last week of July – that is from 25 to 31 July – the British cabinet had been split on whether Great Britain should remain neutral or intervene. A 'peace party' composed of ten ministers (half of the cabinet) was against British involvement in a European war.[12] These ten (Morley, Lloyd George, Beauchamp, Simon,[13] Harcourt, Pease,[14] Samuel, McKinnon Wood,[15] Runciman and Burns) met privately at Beauchamp's house in London to coordinate their policy.[16] Morley was the most dedicated pacifist, but the others opposed war too. Asquith suspected that it was Lloyd George who was leading this dissent, and he sought the assistance of Churchill to persuade Lloyd George to give up his opposition. Churchill willingly agreed to do this. He wrote to Lloyd George: 'I implore you to come and bring your mighty aid to the discharge of our duty.'[17] On 1 August, Churchill read a letter he had received from F. E. Smith, the Conservative leader, that the government could 'rely upon the support of the Unionist Party' if Germany contemplated a violation of Belgian neutrality. This assurance 'produced a profound impression' in the cabinet.[18] But Morley, Simon and Beauchamp were not convinced. 'If we have to fight', Morley said, 'we must fight with single-hearted conviction. There is no place for me in such affairs.'[19] Simon and Beauchamp took the same view. They detested militarism, and all three

---

12   See Roy Jenkins, *Asquith, op. cit.*, p. 327.

13   John Simon (1873–1954), Liberal M.P., 1906–18, 1922–31; Solicitor-General, 1910–13; Attorney-General, 1913–15; Home Secretary, 1915–16, 1935–7; Foreign Secretary, 1935–7.

14   Joseph Pease (1860–1943), Liberal M.P., 1892–1900, 1901–10; Chancellor of the Duchy of Lancaster, 1910–11; President of the Board of Education, 1911–16; Postmaster-General, 1916.

15   T. McKinnon Wood (1855–1927), Liberal M.P., 1906–18; Under-Secretary, Foreign Office, 1908–11; Secretary for Scotland, 1912–16; Chancellor of the Duchy of Lancaster, 1916.

16   See Roy Jenkins, *Asquith, op. cit.*, p. 327 n.

17   Quoted by Martin Gilbert, *Churchill: A Life* (London: Minerva, 1992), p. 271.

18   *Ibid.*, p. 270.

19   Quoted in *Ibid.*, p. 273.

submitted their resignations. This absolutely shocked Asquith. The pathos of the situation is recorded in the diary kept by Charles Hobhouse, who was present at the meeting:[20]

> We have had daily Cabinets since Thursday last [30 July] with two on Sunday and Monday. At each we discussed what should be our attitude to France and Germany. We had and have no engagements to France, and Cambon in an interview he had with E. G. never suggested that we in any way were bound to her. But he pleaded hard for assistance. Grey had from Lichnowsky the most definite assurances that as Germany and in particular the Emperor were working hard for peace, we ought to remain neutral, which Grey was inclined to do. But on Thursday despite the telegrams of Henry of Prussia and the Emperor William ... it became clear that Germany meant to invade France and violate Belgium and that to hoodwink us, she had kept Lichnowsky deliberately in the dark as to her real intentions. From that moment Grey who is sincerity itself became violently pro-French, and eventually the author of our rupture with Germany.
>
> At first Ll. G. was very strongly anti-German, in memory no doubt of their attempts to Declasse him in 1909 [sic], but as the Liberal papers were very anti-war, he veered round and became peaceful. Churchill was of course for any enterprise which gave him a chance of displaying the Navy as his instrument of destruction. McKenna was for war if Belgian territory was invaded, but against the despatch of an expeditionary force. Harcourt, Beauchamp and Simon were for unconditional peace. The P. M., Haldane and I for war if there was even a merely technical breach of the Belgian treaty. Pease and Runciman were strongly against war but not for unconditional neutrality. Burns on Sunday morning was saying that this meant either unconditional neutrality or (leaning over the table shaking his clenched fists) war with both hands, naval and military. He was interrupted by McK. And Ll. G. saying 'But which is your policy?' He hesitated, they repeated the challenge, and with a gulp said 'Neutrality, under circumstances', and turned very white. John Morley then said: 'You all know my views, those of a lifetime, I cannot renounce and if you persevere in intervention, I cannot return to this room.' ... At the end of our meeting J. B. lent forward and in a few words of deep feeling said he must separate from his colleagues with whom he had lived in friendship for 9 years and from a P. M. whom he loved. He was moved to tears. J. Morley said he too could not continue. The P. M. begged them to wait at events till our evening meeting. When we met at 6.30 to continue the pros and cons

20   See Edward David (ed.), *Inside Asquith's Cabinet: From the Diaries of Charles Hobhouse* (London: John Murray, 1977), entry for August (undated), 'War-Lords under Strain, July–December 1914', pp. 179–80.

of neutrality or intervention we the majority came to an understanding that E. G. should tell the H. of C. that we could not stand aside if Belgium were invaded, and that would give France maritime protection, and so inform Germany. The minority – Burns, J. Morley, Beauchamp, Simon said they could not agree and they must retire. On Monday August 3, after settling what Grey should say, the P. M. said he had the painful duty of telling us he had received the resignations of J. M., J. B., and Simon. Beauchamp leant forward and asked to be included. The P. M., whose eyes filled with tears, said that it was the first time in his 6 years of leadership; they were men for whom he had regard and friendship; the party was still hesitating, the country was in danger and unity of counsel was essential. So they agreed except Burns, who had undoubtedly been trapped by Ll. G., to stay, until after Grey had spoken and the H. of C. had indicated its opinion – not very brave conduct. In Simon's case almost despicable because he pretended to a special and personal abhorrence of killing in any shape. ...

On the afternoon of 3 August, the Foreign Secretary, Edward Grey, told the Commons that the events had moved 'so rapidly that it is exceedingly difficult to state with accuracy the actual state of affairs, but it is clear that the peace of Europe cannot be preserved.' And he outlined the position of the government. 'We feel strongly,' he said, 'that France was entitled to know – and know at once! – whether or not in the event of attack upon her unprotected northern and western coasts, she could depend upon British support.' He was authorized to assure France that 'if the German Fleet comes into the Channel or through the North Sea to undertake hostile operations against the French coasts or shipping, the British Fleet will give all the protection in its power'. Britain had also 'vital interests in the independence of Belgium. If she is compelled to submit to her neutrality being violated, the situation is clear.' His Majesty's government would safeguard the integrity of Belgium. Grey's announcement was received with 'a hurricane of applause'.[21] Grey 'made a most remarkable speech', observed Asquith. It was 'extraordinarily well reasoned & tactful & really *cogent* – so

---

21   Noted by Margot Asqutih, who listened to the speech in the Commons' gallery. See *The Autobiography of Margot Asquith*, vol. II, (London: Thornton Butterworth Ltd., 1922), p. 191.

much so that our extreme peace-lovers were for the moment reduced to silence; tho' they will soon find their tongues again.'[22]

They did. Grey's speech terribly disturbed Beauchamp's conscience. Alone at 13 Belgrave Square he jotted down a few lines:[23]

> It is very difficult to sit down calmly in the middle of a crisis to record events as they fly by. But the decision wh was taken at yesterday's Cabinet – in the morning – to provide France defence of her coast & shipping against Germany was so momentous that I wish to fix it.
>
> Grey proposed it as a definite step in favour of France. For that reason I & others objected. There was however the overwhelming argument that we had tacitly allowed France to concentrate in the Mediterranean in virtue of those unfortunate naval conversations wh were to pledge no one to any thing. It was obviously unfair to leave her in such circumstances unprotected. At the end of the Cabinet Burns protested in a moving speech & said he must resign. Everybody formed in a chorus of dissension & the PM spoke forcibly on deserting colleagues etc. Eventually he promised to return for the evening Cabinet at wh we expected a great fight [illegible]. Grey however has gained his point & avoided a conflict. A form of words was agreed to – we all jaded & exhausted. Burns renewed his protest & was to see the PM this morn. I cannot but feel that our promise to France is a *casus belli* to Germany. Alas for this country.
>
> Beauchamp

Beauchamp then wrote the following letter to Asquith.[24]

> *13 Belgrave Square,*
> *S. W.*
>
> *3 VIII 14*
>
> My dear Prime Minister,
>
> It is with the greatest regret that I write to confirm my resignation. By successive acts the Cabinet has passed to a position at wh war seems to me inevitable. That is not a responsibility wh in present circs. [sic] I cd share.

22   Quoted in Roy Jenkins, *Asquith, op. cit.*, p. 329.
23   Source: Beauchamp Papers, *op. cit.*
24   *Ibid.*

At some earlier moment it is possible that I shd have taken this step. But my fault – if fault it is – is due to a real anxiety to cooperate as long as possible with colleagues & a chief for whom I have a great admiration & respect.

For all yr kindness to me I can never thank you enough. You must please realise that I wd gladly do any thing I can to mitigate any inconvenience wh this step may cause.

Believe me always,

Yours very sincerely,

Beauchamp

The Prime Minister must definitely have replied to Beauchamp, but it has not been possible to locate the letter. However, it can be assumed that Asquith answered in the same spirit as he did in response to John Simon's resignation. It is therefore worth citing the letter he wrote to Simon:[25]

10 Downing Street,
Whitehall, S. W.

3 August 1914

My dear Simon,

I have thought over what you said this afternoon, I fully realise your point of view. And I am most anxious that, whatever I ask you to do, should not in any way compromise your future. In that respect, I think I can fully safeguard you. After full reflection (in which I have in every respect had regard to your strong convictions), I am clearly of opinion that, at such a moment as this you have something that nearly approaches to a public duty for the time being at any rate, to remain. I cannot say more. Whatever decision you come to, I shall always most gratefully and affectionately recognise and remember your invaluable service to the Government, and your loyal and devoted attachment to myself.

Believe me always,

Your most sincerely,

H. H. Asquith

25   *Ibid.*

On the morning of 4 August, the Belgian government informed London that German forces had 'penetrated' into Belgian territory. Thereupon Asquith informed the Commons that His Majesty's government had sent a telegram to the German government requesting that Germany should respect Belgian neutrality. 'We have asked,' Asquith said 'in a slow, loud voice,'[26] 'that a reply to that request, and a satisfactory answer to the telegram of this morning – which I have read to the House – should be given before midnight.' These 'fateful and terrible words, "should be given before midnight"', were, Margot Asquith entered in her diary, 'greeted by wave upon wave of cheering, which continued and increased as Henry rose and walked slowly down the floor of the House.'[27]

Asquith's personal appeals to the dissidents in the cabinet had an effect on two of them.[28] Simon and Beauchamp agreed to stay in the government.[29]

26   Noted by Margot Asquith, who listened to the speech in the Commons' gallery. See *The Autobiography of Margot Asquith, op. cit.*, p. 193.

27   *Ibid.*, p. 194.

28   The peace-lovers presumably unsettled Margot Asquith's mind more than they agitated the Prime Minister's. She drove herself to make some rash and absurd comments. 'It is always interesting,' she writes, to 'speculate on the motives that move men, and after considerable experience I have come to the conclusion that self-love or self-consciousness of some kind lies at the root of most resignations. At every stage in life men are to be found on the point of resigning. They start in the nursery, and continue in the servants' hall. ... Unself-centred people do not suffer from the same temptations: they are simple and disengaged, willing to help and ready to combine or stand aside. Threatening to resign is a mild form of blackmail equally common to both sexes.' See *The Autobiography of Margot Asquith, op. cit.*, pp. 167–8. It is very odd that such an intelligent woman should have thought that those who hated war were motivated by 'self-love'.

29   C. P. Scott (editor of the *Manchester Guardian*, 1872–1929) recorded on 3/4 September 1914: 'Had some talk with Simon in another room and went on with him to law courts where he was to open first prize court. He explained his position as a member of the government. He and Lord Beauchamp and Morley and Burns had all resigned together on the Saturday before the declaration of war (August 1) on the ground that they could not agree to Grey's giving pledge to Cambon (the French Ambassador) to protect North Coast of France against Germans, regarding this as equivalent to war with Germany. ... On urgent representation of Asquith he and Beauchamp agreed on Monday evening to remain in the Cabinet without in

Morley and Burns remained 'obdurate'.[30] Morley replied in a very humble and affectionate tone:[31]

August 4th, 1914

My dear Asquith,

Your letter shakes me terribly. It goes to my very core. In spite of temporary moments of difference, my feelings for you have been cordial, deep and close, from your earliest days. The idea of severing these affectionate associations has been far the most poignant element in the stress of the last four days. But I cannot conceal from myself that we – I and the leading men of the Cabinet – do not mean the same thing in the foreign policy of the moment. To bind ourselves to France is at the same time to bind ourselves to Russia, and to whatever demands may be made by Russia and France. With this cardinal difference between us, how can I honourably or usefully sit in a Cabinet day after day, discussing military and diplomatic details, in carrying forward a policy that I think a mistake? Again, I say divided counsels are a mistake.

I am more distressed in making this reply to your generous and most moving appeal than I have ever been in writing any letter of all my life.

Ever yours,

Morley

Morley's letter definitely moved Asquith, who spoke of him to his wife 'as one of the most distinguished men living'.[32] But Asquith was quite happy to record that 'a slump in resignations'[33] had now taken place. The Prime Minister was also able to inform His Majesty about the latest developments in the cabinet. Accordingly he wrote to Lord Stamfordham:[34]

---

the smallest degree, so far as he was concerned, withdrawing his objection to the policy, but solely to prevent the appearance of disruption in face of a grave national danger ...' Trevor Wilson, ed., *The Political Diaries of C. P. Scott, 1911–1928* (London: Collins, 1970), p. 103.

30 For more on this, see Roy Jenkins, *Asquith, op. cit.*, p. 329.
31 Quoted in *The Autobiography of Margot Asquith, op. cit.*, p. 182.
32 Quoted in Roy Jenkins, *Asquith, op. cit.*, p. 329.
33 *Ibid.*, p. 329.
34 Source: Royal Archives: PS/PSO/GV/C/K/731/1.

10 Downing Street,
Whitehall. S. W.

4 Aug. 1914

My dear Stamfordham,

I have persuaded Simon and Beauchamp to withdraw their resignations. The others will not: so that our total losses are Morley, Barnes, and Charles Trevelyan.

There can be no doubt that Runciman is the right man to succeed Barnes at the Board of Trade. For the other vacancies, I suggest for the King's consideration:

President of the Council – Lord Emmott

President of the Board of Agriculture: Lord Lucas

Secretary to the Board of Agriculture: Sir Harry Verney, MP

Secretary to the Board of Education: Mr Gladstone, MP or Dr Addison, MP

Yours very truly

H. H. Asquith

The Prime Minister forgot to mention that Earl Beauchamp would succeed John Morley as Lord President of the Council.[35] But *The London Gazette* (Supplement) to 4 August 1914 noted the following:

35   Sir Almeric Fitzroy made the following entry in his diary on 6 August 1914: 'Four days of feverish activity have passed, each signalised by two Councils, the business of which traced the progress of preparation up to and in pursuance of the declaration of war. ... The hesitants in the Cabinet, which three days before had constituted a majority, were now reduced to four, whose resignations were rumoured: Lord Morley, Beauchamp, Burns, and Sir J. Simon. Lord Morley was present at the Council in the afternoon, but would not admit his resignation, though he said oracularly that the Cabinet might lose the presence of three Johns. Up to this point Beauchamp was certainly one of the leaders of dissent, his house having been the rallying-point of the disaffected, but the personal appeal of the Prime Minister, to which Lord Morley with grave emphasis turned a deaf ear, appears to have modified his objection. He had attended the Cabinet that afternoon from which Lord Morley was absent, and at the evening Council certainly showed a changed disposition. ... At the second Council Beauchamp was declared Lord President, the Prime Minister having offered him the opportunity of returning, which he gladly seized, and Runciman was sworn President of the Board of Trade.' See Almeric Fitzroy, *Memoirs*, vol. II, *op. cit.*, pp. 560–1.

At the Court at Buckingham Palace, the 5th day of August, 1914

Present

The King's Most Excellent Majesty in Council.

His Majesty in Council was this day pleased to declare the Right Honourable William, Earl Beauchamp, K. G., K. C. M. G., Lord President of His Majesty's Most Honourable Privy Council, and his Lordship, having taken the Oath of Office, took his place at the Board accordingly.

Almeric FizRoy

Beauchamp returned to the House of Lords again as a member of the cabinet. When, on 4 August, the Marquess of Lansdowne desired to ask His Majesty's government whether it would impart information 'of the most momentous character relating to the present European situation', Earl Beauchamp answered for the government. He quoted verbatim the statement the Prime Minister had made in the Commons.

The British ultimatum to Germany was to expire at midnight on 4 August. The King held a privy council (also attended by Earl Beauchamp)[36] at Buckingham Palace before the expiry of the ultimatum. Germany made no reply and the council sanctioned the proclamation of a state of war with Germany.[37] The first signal to 'commence hostilities against Germany' were sent from the First Lord of the Admiralty, Churchill, to all British ships. Lloyd George noted that when Winston came to 10 Downing Street at midnight, 'You could see he was a really happy man.'[38]

---

36   See A. J. P. Taylor, *English History, 1914–1915* (Oxford: Clarendon Press, 1965), p. 2.
37   *Ibid.*, p. 2.
38   Quoted by Martin Gilbert, *Churchill, op. cit.*, p. 275.

CHAPTER 16

Lord President of the Council

Earl Beauchamp and the war

We do not have records of Earl Beauchamp's attitude to the war, as it progressed. A decade-and-a-half previously, while he was in Australia, Lady Tennyson and he had exchanged letters revealing their heartache over family members who had fallen in the South African War. In the years 1914–18, almost every family in England was to experience the same.

The Earl had opposed entry into the war and had failed in this endeavour. He had relinquished the post he held as a way of saying he did not want to be part of the business of war. Yet, by nature, he was an intensely loyal man and his main loyalties lay towards the Liberal party, which had achieved such great things in the years before this great catastrophe. A man of peace, Earl Beauchamp continued to work hard in the capacity left to him – as Lord President of the Council.

The office of Lord President of the Council

The office of the Lord President of the Council is a cabinet post, filled by the Prime Minister. The holder is by convention a member of one of the Houses of Parliament, usually a statesman whose advice in the cabinet is desired, but who is 'unwilling or unable to undertake heavy administrative work'.[1] His duties are not department-specific, but he may undertake special office work for about two hours a week.

Getting bills through the House of Lords

Earl Beauchamp was admitted to the office of the Lord President of the Council on 5 August 1914.[2] Only a few days later he began his activity in the House of Lords. On 10 August, he introduced the *Housing (No. 2) Bill* to enable the government to deal with the building of cottages in rural areas. It was intended that there should be voluntary purchase of land and no attempt at compulsory powers. The House passed the bill without discussion.

Then, on 15 September, Earl Beauchamp proposed resumption of debate on the *Welsh Church Disestablishment Bill* with a second reading.[3] This bill had suffered the same fate as the Irish Home Rule Bill. Asquith, had first introduced the Disestablishment Bill (also called The Welsh Church Bill) in the House of Commons when he was Home Secretary in Gladstone's government back in 1893/4. It was slaughtered by the House of Lords.[4] In April 1912 Asquith, re-introduced the Welsh Bill in the Commons along with the *Irish Bill*. The Welsh Bill aimed to enable members of the Church in Wales to make rules for their own constitutional self-government. By its terms, the Church of England would be separated and disestablished in Wales, leading to the creation of a 'Church of Wales'. As from the date of disestablishment, the bishops and clergy of the Church in Wales would

---

1   See Ivor Jennings, *Cabinet Government* (Cambridge: The University Press, 1951, 2nd ed.), pp. 52, 65.

2   It was the second time that Earl Beauchamp was appointed to this office. He had previously filled it for a short period from 21 June till 7 November 1910.

3   See *Parliamentary Debates*, House of Lords, 15 September 1914, vol. XVII, cols 661–93.

4   See Jenkins, *Asquith, op. cit.*, p. 66.

cease to be members of, or be represented in, the House of Convocation of the Province of Canterbury; and the disestablished Welsh dioceses would form a separate ecclesiastical province.

Both bills went through a 'laborious' committee stage in the Commons until mid January 1913, before they were given a third reading and passed. In July 1913, however, when the bills were debated in the House of Lords, they were thrown out – the Irish bill on 15 July, the Welsh bill on 22 July.[5] Now, Asquith was never a party to underhand scheming: he assured his cabinet colleagues that there would be no 'jiggery-pokery' this time over either bill.[6] He intended to execute the provisions of the Parliament Act, 1911. The House of Lords had had at its disposal two delaying years, and the time had now run out. In September 1914 the Commons passed a Suspensory Bill which declared a moratorium stating that the Welsh Church Act 'shall come into operation six months, or not more than twelve months, to be fixed by Order in Council, after the date of its passing'. The Suspensory Bill was sent to the Lords, who debated it on 15 September. Naturally the bill excited, as it had in the past, considerable resentment. This came from both the English bishops and the Lords opposite. The bill, the Lord Archbishop of Canterbury complained, was being debated at a time when the country 'is rightly and patriotically absorbed in a vast struggle involving the life and honour of the Empire'; and the postponement of its 'operation at this moment is probably universal except on the part of a small clique in Wales'. This earned a deserved retort from the President of the Council. 'We have to learn,' he said, 'that the vast majority of those who represent the people of Wales in the House of Commons can be called "a small clique". I deprecate this way of speaking of those who represent the vast majority of Wales.' Earl Beauchamp observed that he regretted the action of their Lordships with regard to the Welsh Church Bill. It would allow the spiritual affairs of the Church in Wales in future to be 'entirely within her own competence, and she will no longer be subject to the necessity of coming to Parliament in order that she may make such arrangements as she thinks desirable. The temporal arrangements will be completely under

5   *Ibid.*, pp. 278–9.
6   *Ibid.*, p. 329.

her own control, and if at any time she desires to meet Church people of England in consultation, there is nothing of which I know which will prevent the representatives of Wales from sitting with the representatives of the Convocations of Canterbury or York.' Was it not possible then, the Earl appealed to their Lordships, that 'by accepting the verdict of the people of this country, by ceasing to resist the wishes of the people, by believing that their elected representatives properly represent their wishes and their wills, you may find a better means to national unity than the way which has been suggested to us by the noble Lords opposite?' He hoped that their Lordships would give their agreement.

The Earl of Selborne moved the adjournment of the debate. The Lords divided: Contents, 89; Not-Contents, 27. The debate was adjourned *sine die*. Thus began a ping-pong game: the bill went back and forth between the two Houses.

The government agreed to meet half way. They introduced an amendment to the Suspensory Bill on 16 September 1914 which provided that 'no steps shall be taken to put these Acts [the Government of Ireland Act 1914 and the Welsh Church Act 1914] into operation until the expiration of twelve months from the date of the passing of these Acts respectively'.[7] The Lords opposite were indignant, especially with regard to the Ireland Bill. Earl Curzon of Kedleston accused the government of a 'breach of faith with us'. The treatment of the Opposition by the government he regarded as 'humiliating and unfair'. The Lords opposite had believed, Curzon observed, that the whole of the controversy about these bills would be postponed until the end of the war. Earl Beauchamp spoke for the government. His tone was very conciliatory. The fact, he argued, that:[8]

> we have had these discussions during the last two days we are glad to think will not, from what the noble Lords opposite have told us, prevent their continued support in matters relating to the war whenever His Majesty's Government call upon them for support. But I hope at the same time, much as we appreciate the action of the noble Lords, they will allow me to add that we should have been still more grateful

7   See *Parliamentary Debates*, House of Lords, 16 September 1914, vol. XVII, cols 704–32.

8   *Ibid.*, cols 719–20.

had they seen their way to extend it in other directions, in directions where they do not support His Majesty's Government so warmly as they do in connection with the war. ... Is it not perfectly evident that when the end of this war comes, there will probably be a very different state of things in Europe? There will be a new era. It is not too much to imagine that, as things change in Europe, so also things will be very different in Ireland. [A noble Lord asked: Why?] It seems to me inconceivable, when men have been fighting side by side together in the British Army, encountering bullets in company with one another, that when they go back to Ireland their feelings will be as bitter as they have been in the years gone by. ... When men go out from Ireland, when Ireland is in great excitement over the question of Home Rule, to meet a common foe, it is inconceivable to me that their feelings towards one another when they come back will not be far better and less acute than they were before they underwent that common experience. As it is inconceivable to me that men who have been fighting together, should on their return, fight against one another, I think things must be, when the war is over, very different indeed from what they are at the present time. ...

These pleas had no effect on the mood of the Lords opposite. They put down amendments, read and passed them, and returned the Suspensory Bill to the Commons. On 18 September 1914, the Deputy Speaker announced in the House of Commons that the following Acts were passed under the provisions of the Parliament Act 1911: (1) The Government of Ireland Act 1914; (2) The Welsh Church Act 1914. It was also announced that the bills received Royal Assent the same day.[9]

There were now other bills that Earl Beauchamp had to look after. On 16 September, he moved the Superannuation Bill, which dealt with 'a number of anomalies and small matters connected with the superannuation of Civil Servants, and the passing of the Bill during the present Session will allow the relatives of a Civil Servant who falls in the war to have certain advantages'.[10] The bill was read a second time and Committee negatived; it was then read a third time, and passed.

---

9 See *Parliamentary Debates*, House of Commons, 18 September 1914, vol. 66, col. 1017.
10 See *Parliamentary Debates*, House of Lords, 16 September 1914, vol. XVII, cols 703–4.

From now on until the end of the year 1914, the House of Lords sat to proceed with general business that did not require the interventions of Earl Beauchamp. These, however, were required again at the beginning of the new year.

When, on 7 January 1915, Lord Southwark called attention to the loss of life and destruction of property caused by the German bombardment, and urged that the state should assume liability for all losses sustained to property in this way, Earl Beauchamp, speaking for the government, said that their Lordships 'would wish an expression of concurrence with the feelings of the country generally of deep sympathy for those afflicted towns which suffered so greatly from senseless and wanton bombardment form the German ships, deep sympathy with them in the loss which they suffered both of civilian life and civilian property'; but he was unable to tell the House the exact lines upon which His Majesty's government was prepared to proceed. However the government was 'resolved to provide relief from the Imperial funds in respect of damage to persons and property sustained in the recent bombardment'. He assured the House that the government would make public the exact details 'without undue delay'.[11]

It would be appropriate here to list and quote extracts of Earl Beauchamp's statements made with reference to various topics discussed in the House of Lords, and these are detailed below.

Sir John French's despatches

The Earl of Derby asked the noble Lord who represented the War Office whether 'he can tell us when we may expect the publication of Sir John French's[12] Despatches? It is common knowledge that they have been for some considerable time in this country, and I do not think the delay in

11   See *Parliamentary Debates*, House of Lords, 7 January 1915, vol. XVIII, cols 313–7.
12   Field-Marshal Sir John French (1852–1925), C.-in-C. Expeditionary Force in France, 1914–15.

publishing them is quite understood.'[13] Earl Beauchamp replied that he was unable to commit the Secretary of State for War to any course of action by giving an answer. However, he understood that 'there is reason to believe that a Despatch will very soon be published'.

Admiralty courts-martial

On 24 February, the Earl of Selborne rose to move: 'That this House is of opinion that the established custom of the Navy by which a Court-Martial is held to investigate the loss of any of His Majesty's ships is founded on the best interests both of the Navy and the public, and that it is expedient that it should be maintained'.[14] Again replying for the government, Earl Beauchamp referred to the 'disadvantage' under which their Lordships' House suffered 'from the absence of any direct representative of the Board of Admiralty when we discuss Naval matters'. He hoped that the House would 'therefore realise all the more readily the difficulty when I am asked at somewhat brief notice to accept an amendment of or an addition to a Resolution of this important kind'. He could only suggest that the mere passage of the resolution in the House 'would probably not of itself affect in any way the practice of the Board of Admiralty. It would be necessary for a similar Resolution to be passed by the House of Commons before it could become operative.' He personally thought that the decisions the Admiralty had so far arrived at were 'without prejudice', and the course adopted by the Admiralty was 'a proper and wise one'. The debate was adjourned *sine die*.

13   See *Parliamentary Debates*, House of Lords, 10 February 1915, vol. XVIII, cols 505–6.
14   See *Parliamentary Debates*, House of Lords, 24 February 1915, vol. XVIII, cols 557–90.

The Order of the Bath

Lord Latymer[15] asked His Majesty's government whether they would be willing to approach His Majesty the King 'with a view to the amendment of the Statutes governing the appointment to the First Class of the Order of the Bath so as to admit thereto officers of the Royal Marines'.[16] Earl Beauchamp agreed that, under the statutes of the said order, officers of the Royal Marines were not eligible for the Grand Cross, but he assured the noble Lord that 'this matter will be considered, together with a whole lot of difficult questions of a similar kind'.

British prisoners in Germany

Lord Newton asked what steps were being taken by the government to obtain an independent report on the treatment of British prisoners in Germany.[17] Earl Beauchamp answered thus:

> In view of the conflicting reports which had reached His Majesty's Government, mainly from private sources, as to the conditions of internment of British prisoners of war, a proposal was made some time ago through the United States to Germany that United States officials, lent by their own Government for the purpose, should be in permanent touch with the commandants of the various camps, and they should generally supervise the distribution of relief to the British prisoners of war. As no answer could be obtained from the German Government to the proposal, His Majesty's Government then suggested the United States Government to obtain permission from the German Government for an American representative, selected by the United States Embassy in London, to proceed to Germany and visit camps in which British prisoners were interned.

15   Latymer, 5th Baron, b. 1852. A Conservative.
16   See *Parliamentary Debates*, House of Lords, 2 March 1915, vol. XVIII, cols 598–602.
17   See *Parliamentary Debates*, House of Lords, 15 March 1915, vol. XVIII, cols 745–58.

There was 'now reason to hope that the German Government will accept the proposal of His Majesty's Government for the adoption of the permanent scheme which has been outlined'.

Defence of the Realm (Amendment) No.3 Bill

On 13 May, Earl Beauchamp presented a bill, the object of which was to 'provide more munitions of war for war armies in the field'.[18] The bill also empowered the government by Order in Council to make such regulations as 'may be necessary for transferring the control of the liqueur traffic in the area to the prescribed government authority'. This included not only the ordinary public houses, but also clubs, grocers' shops, and such methods of distribution as railway bars. The new government authorities, when they were set up, would be representative. They would consist of representatives of the Army and the Navy, and it would be their duty to put themselves in touch with local committees in the various areas. The regulations of the bill were not to be of a permanent character. Introducing the bill, Earl Beauchamp hoped that it would not be a 'bone of contention' between the Lords opposite and the government, and that the noble Lords opposite were 'as anxious as we are' to see the bill passed into law. The Earl then flattered the noble Lords opposite by expressing his acknowledgement for the 'assistance which they have so far given us in this direction', and said he expected that the bill 'which we are now discussing may receive the same treatment from this afternoon'. Thereupon the Leader of the Opposition the Marquess of Lansdowne responded with some irony. He did not think, he said, that 'upon this occasion we are likely to show ourselves more niggardly than we have upon former occasions'. The bill was given a second reading, and committed to a Committee of the Whole House.

18 See *Parliamentary Debates*, House of Lords, 13 May 1915, vol. XVIII, cols 989–97.

Fishery Harbours Bill

Earl Beauchamp introduced a bill to provide for the improvement of small fishery harbours.[19] The bill was limited to two years and its passing was strictly within the definition of emergency legislation. The bill was given a second reading, and Committee negatived; it was then read a third time and passed.

Housing (Rosyth Dockyard) Bill

On 19 May, Earl Beauchamp introduced another emergency bill, which dealt with the building of houses at Rosyth and the running of tramways so that there could be access between the houses and the dockyard. The bill was read a second time, Committee negatived, then read a third time, and passed.[20]

No place in the new cabinet

With the management of these two bills on 19 May, Earl Beauchamp ended his duty as a member of the cabinet. On this very day Asquith announced the formation of a Coalition Government, which now consisted of twelve Liberals, eight Unionists and one Labour member.[21] The new cabinet did

19   See *Parliamentary Debates*, House of Lords, 19 May 1915, vol. XVIII, cols 1052–3.
20   See *Parliamentary Debates*, House of Lords, 19 May 1915, vol. XVIII, cols 1055–61.
21   Lord Kitchener entered the cabinet as Minister for War. See Roy Jenkins, *Asquith*, *op. cit.*, p. 370.

not include certain members of the previous cabinet: Haldane, Samuel, Pease, Emmott, Lucas, Hobhouse, Beauchamp and Montagu.[22] The list of

22 *Ibid.* p. 370. Asquith's rating of his cabinet stood on 26 February 1915 as follows: '1. Crewe; 2. Grey; 3. McKenna; 4. Ll. George, Winston, Kitchener; 5. Harcourt, Simon; 6. Haldane, Runciman; 7. Samuel; 8. Pease, Beauchamp, Emmott, Lucas, Wood.' See Roy Jenkins, *Asquith, op. cit.*, pp. 340–1. See also Charles Hobhouse's diary entry for 23 March 1915: 'The Cabinet has lost or gained so much in personnel since last I tried to note its members' characteristics that I will do so again. We sit round the table thus: Asquith, Harcourt, Beauchamp, Montagu, Emmott, Simon, Birrell, Pease, Samuel, Haldane, Grey (opposite the P. M.), George, Crewe, McKenna, Runciman, Hobhouse, Lucas, Wood, Churchill, Kitchener. The P.M.'s abilities are transcendent as ever ... Loulou Harcourt, subtle, secretive, adroit, and not very reliable ... Beauchamp is a nonentity of pleasant manners, a good deal of courage, and a man of principle, but with no power of expression. Montagu has a power of speech, clever, even brilliant ... Emmott is honest, slow, laborious ... Simon, a most attractive personality; a ready wit, a persuasive advocate ... Birrell, Pease, and Samuel do not seem to have changed. ... Haldane has always repelled me. ... Grey, we all like, admire, and respect, for his transparent sincerity and honesty ... Ll. G. is in council as in every other relation wonderfully versatile, adroit and quick, with an unrivalled, indeed miraculous, power of picking other people's brains. ... Crewe is liked and respected by everyone. ... McKenna has one of the best and quickest intellects in the Cabinet ... Runciman carries considerable weight. ... Lucas, between whom and Runciman I sit, has not yet found his legs ... Churchill, as always, in a hurry to be conspicuous ... Kitchener who sits on the P. M.'s left has gained the undoubted confidence of the nation, the unquestionable dread of the British Officer, for qualities not really his own. ...' Edward David (ed.), *Inside Asquith's Cabinet, op. cit.*, pp. 229–31. On Beauchamp's work, Sir Almeric Fitzroy noted differently on 9 March 1915: 'The settlement of the controversy with the Opposition on Welsh Disestablishment was effected today, largely owing to Beauchamp's persistence, by which he won the support of both Crewe and the Prime Minister. It was not done, however, without violation of all established parliamentary practice, the Bill, for the purpose of being carried, went through all the stages in the House of Lords when nine-tenths of the Peers had not seen its text; a few copies were brought in by Beauchamp while the Committee stage was being hurried through. McKenna, too, in an interview with Beauchamp's Private Secretary, assumed the part of outraged importance; but his anger was not impressive.' See Almeric Fitzroy, *Memoirs*, vol. II, *op. cit.*, p. 586.

the new cabinet members was made public on 25 May.[23] On the same day
Asquith sent a brief confidential note to Beauchamp.[24]

> *10 Downing Street,*
> *Whitehall*
>
> *25 May 1915*
>
> *Confidential*
>
> My dear Beauchamp,
>
> I greatly regret that, in the reconstruction of the Government, I have not for the
> moment been able to find you a place. I am most grateful for your loyal & devoted
> service in the past, and I hope and believe that our severance will be short-lived.
>
> Yours always sincerely,
>
> H. H. Asquith

Earl Beauchamp replied immediately:

> *The Rt Hon. H.H. Asquith, M.P.*[25]
> *Privy Council Office,*
> *Whitehall S. W.*
>
> *25 V 15*
>
> My dear Prime Minister,
>
> Many thanks for the kindness of yr note. I shall always be proud to have served under
> you during these last years & to have received for so long yr confidence & trust.
>
> Yours v. sincerely,
>
> Beauchamp

23   For Asquith's coalition cabinet, see: A. J. P. Taylor, *English History, 1914–1945, op.
      cit.*, pp. 640–1.
24   Source: Beauchamp Papers , *op. cit.*
25   Bodleian Library. MSS Asquith 27 (fol.188).

The very next day Beauchamp received a private letter that must have enormously pleased him.[26]

Marlborough Club,
Pall Mall

26.5.15

My dear Lord Beauchamp,

This is a good moment, perhaps, for reminding you, as I really have no need to remind myself, how solid and broad is the political position you have built up for yourself in the last six or seven years. It has been my great pleasure to see it from a near point of view. No one of your age has done so much in the times.

This is what I think today, when I see your name omitted – as I have known that it was your wish it should be omitted – from the Coalition list. But I do not forget this is no defeat or decline, it is simply a provisional pause. You remain stationary for a little while, ready to start again from the same point.

Your old friend and constant admirer,

Edmund Gosse

Earl Beauchamp was never to become a government minister again. His political passion was now dedicated entirely to the work done by a hereditary peer in the House of Lords, where he could speak as he wished and not as a spokesman for the government. 'I shall greatly miss you on the Bench if indeed I stay there', wrote Lord Sandhurst[27] to Beauchamp on 28 May 1915, and: 'If I may so say, your work has been so good and thorough since you have been there. I hope the rest, at any rate for a time, may not be unacceptable.'[28] On 3 June 1915, Lord Stanmore[29] gave Beauchamp his impression of the new atmosphere in the Lords:

The new ministers are to sit on the front bench; otherwise everyone is to keep his old place. Crewe & Lansdowne have made short speeches each calling the other

26 Source: Beauchamp Papers, *op. cit.*
27 Sandhurst, 3rd Baron, b. 1857. A Liberal.
28 Source: Beauchamp Papers, *op. cit.*
29 Stanmore, 2nd Baron, b. 1871. A Liberal.

'my noble friend' a great number of times. Selborne sat the other side of Crewe. The others have not put in an appearance. Buckmaster[30] looking very uncomfortable sat on the extreme edge of the Woolsack. Crewe proposes that the Ld Chairman should ask the regulation questions as to war etc. I had a very happy time at Madresfield.[31]

---

30   Buckmaster, 1st Baron, b. 1861. A Liberal.
31   Source: Beauchamp Papers, *op. cit.*

CHAPTER 17

Maintaining the Liberal Cause in the House of Lords

David Lloyd George tricked Asquith out of office at the beginning of December 1916, and took over the premiership himself on 7 December. The course of events that led to Asquith's resignation has been ably, and in detail, described elsewhere.[1] Many who had worked closely with Asquith, or were in one form or another devoted to him, mourned his departure. When Asquith placed his resignation in the King's hands on 5 December, the King himself recorded how he 'accepted' it 'with great regret'. It was 'a great blow to me', the King entered in his diary.[2] Margot Asquith, the Prime Minister's wife felt 'shocked and wounded by the meanness, ingratitude and lack of loyalty shown' to him. 'My husband,' she wrote, 'fell on the battle-field surrounded by civilians and soldiers whom he had fought for, and saved; some of whom owed him not only their reputations and careers, but their very existence.'[3] Earl Beauchamp expressed the loss to the nation in a private letter to Asquith:[4]

> *Madresfield Court,*
> *Malvern*
>
> *10 xii 16*
>
> My dear Mr Asquith,
>
> I cannot forbear inflicting a letter upon you in order to say how deeply I regret – for the country's sake – yr resignation. You were & are still the man in whom most Englishmen believed. The difficulties have been caused – not for the first time

---

1   See 'A Palace Revolution' I & II in Roy Jenkins, *Asquith, op. cit.*, pp. 421–63.
2   See Harold Nicolson, *King George the Fifth: His life and reign* (London: Constable, 1953), pp. 287–8.
3   See *The Autobiography of Margot Asquith*, vol. II, *op. cit.*, pp. 246–7.
4   MSS Asquith (fol. 223), *op. cit.*

– by a small clique of men in London singularly unrepresentative of public opinion throughout England.

You cd not fail to be pleased if you cd hear as I do the general appreciation of sober men who realise something of what you have done for the country.

I hope that for many years to come you will enjoy the affectionate esteem wh those who have been privileged to serve under you will always feel.[5]

Meanwhile Lettice and I will hope that you will have fine weather at Walmer now that you have more leisure to be there.

Believe me,

Yours very sincerely,

Beauchamp

P. S. This atmosphere of intrigue is not auspicious for the new Government.

The later war years

Lloyd George found no place for Earl Beauchamp when, as new Prime Minister, he constructed his War Cabinet. But as a Liberal peer, Beauchamp's services were still welcomed in the Lords. And his ardent zeal for the Liberal cause showed no sign of weakening, even if he was no longer a minister. He was ever-present in the House of Lords, and intervened in debates whenever he felt he could make a positive contribution. Some of these contributions we detail below. At places we have inserted brief remarks, where special points were raised in the Earl's delivery.

Re-examination of Rejected Men (24 February 1916).[6]

5   Asquith liked to spend weekends at Walmer castle. Lord Beauchamp 'had been lend-
     ing Asquith the Walmer Castle for use at weekends since 1914'. See John Grigg, *Lloyd
     George: From Peace to War, 1912–1916* (London: Penguin Books, 2002), p. 454, n. 2.
6   See *Parliamentary Debates*, House of Lords, vol. XXI, 24 February 1916, cols 198–202.

South Eastern and London, Chatham and Dover Railways Bill (8 March 1916).[7]

The Price of Barley (13 November 1917).[8]

Statue of Abraham Lincoln (11 December 1917).[9]

Representation of the People Bill (23 January 1918).[10]

Sexual Offences: In debate, Beauchamp pointed out that the underlying principles were two: first, to assist and to protect young soldiers from difficulties and temptations which came not only from within but also from without; and secondly, to deal as far as possible, with both sexes on an equal footing (7 May 1918).[11]

The War – Pacifist Activities: The Earl of Denbigh called the Lords' attention to pacifist activities in the country, and to general ignorance regarding the German war aims and the causes of the war. He thought that there was certainly 'plenty of oratorical talent in the House, and a great many Peers would be rendering very useful service to the country if they would come out and do some of this strenuous work, in endeavouring to bring these matters home to the public' (8 May 1918).[12] Earl Beauchamp responded by saying that he would like to make two remarks: 'One is with regard to the question of the men who are now fighting in our Army. We have got now, as there has never been before in the history of the world, an Army of educated men, men who can read, who have read the history of the causes which led to the war and who may read in their daily newspaper for the first time in the history of the world exactly what is going on – what Statesmen are doing, what they have been saying to one another. [Another was] that with an educated Army of that kind I do not believe that anything could make them more determined to go on fighting than

---

7 See *Parliamentary Debates*, House of Lords, vol. XXI, 8 March, 1916, cols 295–301.

8 See *Parliamentary Debates*, House of Lords, vol. XXVI, 13 November 1917 cols 958–64.

9 See *Parliamentary Debates*, House of Lords, vol. XXVI, 11 December 1917, cols 111–24.

10 See *Parliamentary Debates*, House of Lords, vol. XXVII, 23 January 1918, col. 1031.

11 See *Parliamentary Debates*, House of Lords, vol. XXIX, 7 May 1918, col. 988.

12 See *Parliamentary Debates*, House of Lords, vol. XXIX, 8 May 1918, cols 1009–51.

the knowledge that it is inevitable that they should go on fighting for the honour of their country, and it is an admirable thing to remove from them any impression that the continuance of the war is unnecessary.'[13]

Small Holding Colonies Bill (10 July 1918).[14]

Summary Jurisdiction (Ireland) Bill (16 July 1918). Earl Beauchamp registered his objections at the offhand way in which this bill was introduced into the House of Lords: 'This is not a proper way of treating your Lordships' House. It is a very clear want of respect. The Lord Privy Seal, who put down the Notice on the Paper, neither attended in his place to explain the Bill nor asked any other noble Lord to do it on his behalf. It is quite true that we are living in difficult times, but that is no reason why for the first time, I think, your Lordships should be treated with such scant respect as on this occasion. I hope your Lordships, if you do give a Second Reading to the Bill, will make it quite clear that you will not tolerate such treatment on any subsequent occasion, and that, if Bills are moved, they should be moved by the noble Lord who is in charge of them, or by some other noble Lord who has had an opportunity of getting up the question beforehand.'[15]

Economic Policy (7 August 1918).[16] Referring to the government's preferential scheme of trade within the Empire, Beauchamp said: 'My object is not so much to initiate a debate as to try and elicit some information, if it is possible to get it, and if necessary, to register a protest. My first criticism must be directed to the method in which the announcement was launched upon the country. Here is a matter which has been the subject of discussion between two political parties for fifteen years. It has already divided people in this country; it has frequently been made a matter of discussion both in this House, and in another place. I venture to think that Parliament is the proper place in which the announcement should first have been made; instead of which the Secretary of State for the Colonies, at a casual luncheon somewhere in the City, made a reference to this, and the matter

13   *Ibid.*, col. 1031.
14   See *Parliamentary Debates*, House of Lords, vol. XXX, 11 July 1918, col. 760.
15   See *Parliamentary Debates*, House of Lords, vol. XXX, 16 July 1918, col. 856.
16   See *Parliamentary Debates*, House of Lords, vol. XXXI, 7 August 1918, cols 622–48.

was so ill-understood by the people of this country that since then there has been more than one explanation issued on behalf of the Secretary of State for the Colonies to try and explain what exactly was meant. ... I think there is yet another point of fair criticism. His Majesty's Government is a Government for conducting the war. As I understand – and I hope I am right in saying so – this is a policy which is not to be carried out during the war, but is only to be adopted when the war is over.'

The war was very soon over. It had been a calamity. In hindsight, it is easier to appreciate the stance Earl Beauchamp took, as one who opposed hostilities but who nevertheless maintained his loyalty to the party that had once held such progressive ideals.

The course of post-war politics

Earl Beauchamp was ever a convinced Liberal, but to hold this line was no easy task in the complex turns of post-war politics, which split his party and eventually saw the Liberal ascendancy fade away. The general background needs to be sketched.

The December 1918 general election was fought on a joint Conservative-Liberal ticket. The Conservative leader, Bonar Law,[17] and Lloyd George had jointly signed a letter called the 'coupon', to those Liberals who had supported the Coalition during the war, making them the official coalition candidates. This arrangement divided the Liberal party. Those who supported Lloyd George were now known as 'Coalition Liberals', and the Asquithian

---

17   Andrew Bonar Law (1858–1923), Unionist M.P., 1900–6, 1906–10, 1911–18, 1918–23; Leader of Unionist Party, 1911–21; Colonial Secretary, 1915–16; Chancellor of the Exchequer, 1916–18; Leader of the House of Commons, 1916–19; Prime Minister, 1922–23.

Liberals[18] (nicknamed 'Wee Frees')[19] formed a separate group. The election results were a landslide victory for the Coalition: the Conservatives won 332 seats and the Coalition Liberals 127. Lloyd George retained the office of Prime Minister up to October 1922, when he resigned. In the general election that followed, 344 Conservative MPs were returned and there was a great reduction in the Liberals. The Labour party was now the second largest party in the Commons with 142 MPs. Asquithian Liberals gained 62 seats and Coalition Liberals 53. The Conservatives formed the government, with Bonar Law as Prime Minister.

At this moment when the influence of the Liberals was declining in the country, Lord Beauchamp attempted to save the party from complete disintegration. He succeeded in bringing Asquith and Lloyd George to agree to unite their groups to fight future elections as a united party. A Liberal Campaign Committee was set up under the chairmanship of Earl Beauchamp to adopt candidates to stand simply as Liberals 'without any prefix or suffix'.[20] The endeavour proved a success. The May 1923 general election results gave the Conservatives 258 seats, Labour 191 and the Liberals 158. Labour and Liberals together could have dislodged the Conservatives, but this did not happen. So Stanley Baldwin headed a Conservative cabinet.[21] Disagreement on various social questions, including the debate on Free Trade and Protectionism, caused the Liberal party to decline yet further. Many Liberals felt ideologically closer to Labour – so much so that, when on 21 January 1924, a Labour amendment was carried by 328 votes

---

18   See Lord Beaverbrook, *The Decline and Fall of Lloyd George: And Great was the Fall Thereof* (London: Collins, 1963), p. 14.

19   Such members of the Free Church of Scotland who refused to merge with the United Free Church of Scotland in 1900 had been given the nickname, 'Wee [very small] Frees' and the term was now used again.

20   See Chris Cook, *A Short History of the Liberal Party, 1900–2001* (Hampshire: Palgrave, 2002, sixth edition), p. 91.

21   Stanley Baldwin (b. 1867. Conservative M.P., 1908; President of the Board of Trade 1921; Chancellor of the Exchequer 1922; agitated against coalition with Lloyd George; Prime Minister 1923–4, 1924–9; 1935–7). For Baldwin's first Conservative cabinet, see A. J. P. Taylor, *English History, 1914–1945, op. cit.*, pp. 643–4.

to 256[22] and Baldwin was forced to tender his resignation, the King invited the Labour leader Ramsay MacDonald[23] to form a government.[24] Thus a first Labour government was installed with the help of the Liberals. This certainly made the ultimate condition of the Liberal party ruinous. The general election results of October 1924 were disastrous for the Liberals. They won just 40 seats. The Conservatives booked 412 seats, and Labour with 151 seats now became the Official Opposition.[25]

The decline of the power of the Liberal party in the Commons really disturbed Earl Beauchamp. He bent his efforts to at least saving the situation in the House of Lords. Here all the Liberals, he declared, should put up a united front. To achieve this aim he arranged meetings and corresponded with those who might bring about this unity.

22 The King's Speech to both Houses of Parliament on 15 January 1924 referred to the number of people still unable to find work, which caused the King the 'greatest concern'. Under such circumstances, 'your assent will be invited to an extension and amendment of Trade Facilities and Export Credit schemes, to the proposal of the Imperial Economic Conference for expediting and assisting the execution of certain public enterprises throughout the Empire by the grant of financial aid from public funds, and to an extension of the contributions towards the cost of Public Utility Works, whether undertaken by local authorities or promoted by statutory and private corporations.' See *Parliamentary Debates*, House of Lords, vol. LVI, 15 January 1924, cols 6–9. To many, the announcement smelt of Protectionism and Imperial Preference. Labour and Liberal MPs, staunch Free Traders, joined hands on 21 January 1924 to vote Baldwin out of office.

23 James Ramsay MacDonald, b. 1866, Labour Prime Minister, January to November 1924; 1929–35.

24 For MacDonald's first Labour cabinet, see A. J. P. Taylor, *English History, 1914–1945, op. cit*, p. 644.

25 For a valuable and detailed analysis of the fate of the Liberal party at this time, see Chris Cook, *A Short History of the Liberal Party, op. cit*., pp. 77–105.

Earl Beauchamp's activities up to 1924

Earl Beauchamp continued to assist in the passage of bills through the House of Lords.

Justice of the Peace – Qualification of Women Bill (20 May 1919).[26] Beauchamp said he believed that women should be made eligible to carry out the duties of a Justice of the Peace.[27]

Criminal Law Amendment Bill (15 August 1921).[28] Beauchamp said that he was responsible for introducing the Act of 1908 – an act providing for cases of incest to be tried *in camera*: 'I am convinced that it was a mistake to make that enactment. I welcome the opportunity of repealing it in the Criminal Law Amendment Bill.'

Law Lords and Party Politics (29 March 1922). In the debate on whether Law Lords should show party loyalty, Beauchamp pointed out: 'The fact of the matter is that it is well-known that it is exceedingly rare, almost unknown, for members of your Lordships' House who are Law Lords to take part in political debates.'[29]

26   See *Parliamentary Debates*, House of Lords, vol. XXXIV, 20 May 1919, cols 734–6.
27   The following letter is worth quoting: 'July 16th, 1919. Dear Lord Beauchamp, I think you have been made aware of the conversation we have had with Lord Weardale regarding the Women's Emancipation Bill now in the House of Lords, and if you can do anything to help the passage of the Bill we shall be very obliged. We had already spoken to Lord Kimberly on the matter, and our idea was that perhaps you could co-operate, and now Lord Kimberly informed me that he has got the Bill put down for Thursday of next week. Lord Weardale has informed me that you will not be in attendance here until the week after next, but if the Bill survives on Thursday week and you can render assistance in its further stages it will be very good of you. Yours sincerely, W. F. Wilson.' Source: Beauchamp Papers, *op. cit.*
28   See *Parliamentary Debates*, House of Lords, vol. XLIII, 15 August 1921, col. 582.
29   See *Parliamentary Debates*, House of Lords, vol. XLIX, 29 March 1922, cols 957–9.

Correspondence with Buckingham Palace

Earl Beauchamp was by nature a cordial and hospitable person. He paid attention to his acquaintances and preserved good relations with people who were important either in the Palace or in his own Liberal party. And although he might have been critical of Lloyd George because of his behaviour towards Asquith, the Earl chose to maintain good contacts with the new Prime Minister. It will be proper to quote a few letters for this purpose. Here, first, are some written to Buckingham Palace:

1

Earl Beauchamp to Lord Stamfordham[30]

13 Belgrave Square, S. W.

16. 2. 22

Confidential

Dear Stamfordham,

Only with a great deal of hesitation do I venture to write to you, and indeed it is only that I know you will throw it in the waste paper basket if it is presumptuous that I do it at all. The question is the Lord Ltcy. of Oxfordshire. Glos. is contiguous and my friends in that county talk a good deal about it. They are intimate with Oxfordshire folk and tell me what they hear and feel themselves. The ambiguous position of the Duke and Duchess of Marlborough[31] creates a good many difficulties and evidently the fact that he represents His Majesty must go far to break down that hatred of divorce which is one of the foundations of Society. God knows that none of us here have the right to cast a stone, and this accounts for so much silence. Their Majesties' opinions are well-known to resemble in this matter those of Queen Victoria whose constant insistence upon a high standard in this matter won her so great a respect. The

---

30   Royal Archives: PS/PSO/GV/C/O/480/45.
31   The ninth Duke of Marlborough had succeeded Lord Jersey as Lord Lieutenant of Oxfordshire in 1915, and was under pressure to resign after his divorce and re-marriage. He remained in post until his death. His new wife was a Parisian with a colourful history: her sad biography has been written by Hugo Vickers.

feeling at present is one of surprise that he continues in office. Personally of course I note the difference between this case and that of my brother-in-law Westminster.[32]

Pray forgive me for writing to you, but after long consideration it did not seem to me right as Lord Lieutenant in Gloucestershire to take the easier course and refrain from letting you know that the matter is being much discussed in the neighbouring Counties.

Yours sincerely,

Beauchamp

2

Lord Stamfordham to Earl Beauchamp[33]

Buckingham Palace

17th February 1922

Private

Dear Beauchamp,

Please rest assured there was no inclination to consign your confidential letter of the 16th instant to the waste-paper basket.

I am sorry to say that the question it raises has occupied the serious attention of the King for upwards of the last two years; and His Majesty is not surprised to hear of the feelings entertained by you and your friends in Gloucestershire upon the subject.

Would you have any objection to your letter of the 16th being forwarded to the Prime Minister?

Stamfordham

32   Beauchamp's brother-in-law, the 2nd Duke of Westminster, had been appointed Lord Lieutenant of Cheshire in 1905 (at the early age of 26) on the death of Earl Egerton of Tatton; but had been asked to resign in 1920 as the result of his divorce. He was succeeded as Lord Lieutenant by Sir William Bromley-Davenport.

33   Source: Royal Archives: PS/PSO/GV/C/O/480/46.

3

Lord Stamfordham to Earl Beauchamp[34]

Buckingham Palace

28th November 1922

Private

The Right Honble. the Earl Beauchamp, K. G.,

Madresfield Court,

Malvern

Dear Beauchamp,

All you express in your letter of the 24th instant is practically reciprocated by the King. When the Prime Minister has got a little more into the saddle, and the Irish question is settled, he will be approached on the subject.

Yours very truly,

Stamfordham

4

Lord Stamfordham to Earl Beauchamp[35]

Windsor Castle

22nd June 1923

Dear Beauchamp,

In reply to your letter of the 15th instant: of course I realised that you and I had previously corresponded about the Duke of Marlborough; but the question you raised in the letter which I sent on to the Lord Chamberlain was about the Duchess of Marlborough – and as the matter of her presence at Court was entirely out of my province I naturally sent it to the Lord Chamberlain, as he alone could give you the information which I assumed you required when she was presented at Court.

Yours very truly,

Stamfordham

34   Source: Royal Archives: PS/PSO/GV/C/O/480/56.
35   Source: Royal Archives: PS/PSO/GV/C/O/480/62.

5

Earl Beauchamp to Lord Stamfordham[36]

Walmer Castle, Kent

24. 6. 23

Dear Lord Stamfordham,

I am obliged to you for your letter. The reasons for and against the invitation of the lady in question to Royal functions – whether to the Duke of York's wedding or to Evening Courts are to my mind exactly those which govern her husband's position as the King's representative in Oxfordshire. No doubt some reference in my last letter to our former correspondence would have made this plainer and it is my fault to have omitted such a connecting link. I confess that I am not prepared to begin any literary controversy with the Lord Chamberlain on the subject. The better course seems to me – if he desires it – to be a discussion in the House of Lords on the whole matter. This is however entirely a matter for you to decide. It would not be [a] pleasant debate altho' he would probably secure a large majority. I should initiate it only with the greatest reluctance. But if (he) wishes it and in view of your unwillingness to receive my last letter this appears to be the best course.

Perhaps you will be good enough to let me know what you think about this. Obviously it cannot be done without your approval.

Yours sincerely,

Beauchamp

6

Lord Stamfordham to Earl Beauchamp[37]

Buckingham Palace

The Right Honble the Earl Beauchamp, K. G.
Walmer Castle, Kent

25th June 1923

I hasten to reply to your letter of the 24th instant, which only reached me at Windsor this morning.

36   Source: Royal Archives: PS/PSO/GV/C/O/480/65.
37   Source: Royal Archives: PS/PSO/GV/C/O/480/66.

I do not imagine that the Lord Chamberlain wishes to raise in the House of Lords the question of either the Duke or Duchess of Marlborough's position vis-à-vis the Court: indeed I expect he would be as reluctant to do so as you are. Personally I should think that the best course would be to leave the matter alone: though it is for the King to decide with the Prime Minister what is done about the Duke's position as Lord Lieutenant of the County of Oxford. As I think you are aware, it was brought to Mr Lloyd George's notice more than once by His Majesty.

Yours very truly,

Stamfordham

Correspondence with David Lloyd George

Earl Beauchamp wrote a series of letters to Lloyd George,[38] and they show his anxiety to heal the split in the Liberal party.

1

Earl Beauchamp to Lloyd George

In our anxiety to end the differences between Liberal Peers, wd. it be of any use to leave the choice of both whips to the national Liberals?

B.

14 XII 22

2

Earl Beauchamp to Lloyd George

13 Belgrave Square, S. W.1

14. 5. 1923

My dear Mr Lloyd George,

38   Parliamentary Archives: Lloyd George MSS, LG/ G/3/5/1–13.

Can you conveniently see me one day this week before 4 p.m.? I want you to be good enough to sign an autograph book in which I hope that Dame Margaret Lloyd George will also be good enough to write her name.

Our meeting at Birmingham was not unsatisfactory.

Yours sincerely,

Beauchamp

3

Earl Beauchamp to Lloyd George

13 Belgrave Square, S. W.1

13 XII 23

The Rt Hon. D. Lloyd George, O. M., M. P.
18 Abingdon St.
London, S. W. 1

Confidential

My dear Lloyd George,

It was very good of you to ask me to luncheon tomorrow but I cannot leave London engagements. What I wanted to say to you was that I hope some occasion will offer for a gathering of all Liberal ex-ministers.

Reunion ought to mean something more than you & yr friends meeting in 18 – while Mr Asquith meets us at 21. Joint consultation wd be much more effective. You I feel sure wd welcome it & perhaps will suggest it when you meet on Tuesday. It wd give you the chance of meeting all yr old colleagues. I discussed it with Mond this aft. & he urged me to write to you about it.

Lady Beauchamp has offered a party here on the eve of the King's opening, wh will mean a reunion. That afternoon we might have the smaller meeting of ex-ministers – or the next morning.

I want to avoid separate meetings in the future & there is a danger of them.

Pray forgive me for troubling you, but you know my anxiety for a complete reunion.

Yours v. sincerely,

Beauchamp

4

From Lloyd George's Personal Assistant to Earl Beauchamp

19th December 1923

Dear Lord Beauchamp,

I am desired by Mr Lloyd George to thank you very much for your kind confidential letter of December 13th which he safely received.

Yours sincerely

[Signature illegible]

5

Earl Beauchamp to Lloyd George

5 IV 24

My dear Lloyd George,

Mond[39] & I have been talking over the situation & we think it might be useful if we cd meet this eve.

If it is not inconvenient to you therefore I will come to yr Room in the H. of C. at 6 this eve.

The party seems to me to be drifting & to need leadership. We want yr help & advice.

Yours v. Sincerely,

Beauchamp

6

Earl Beauchamp to Lloyd George

Madresfield Court,
Malvern

12 VIII 24

My dear Lloyd George,

---

39 Sir Alfred Mond, b. 1868; industrialist and founder of ICI; Liberal M.P., 1906–1926; First Commissioner of Works 1916–21; Minister of Health 1921–22; eventually fell out with Lloyd George. Baron Melchett from 1910.

These enclo. will interest you. The party in the H. of L. is rather in pieces & will need a good deal of trouble to get it together again.

Yours v. Sincerely,

Beauchamp

P. S. I admire more and more your successive speeches.

B.

7

Post card: Earl Beauchamp to David Lloyd George

The Rt Hon D. Lloyd George M. P.
Criccieth
North Wales

Our best wishes for Christmas & New Year.

Beauchamp

Elmley

[December] 1924

A photograph of Beauchamp and his son Elmley was enclosed with this postcard.

Correspondence with Lord Emmott

It was however with Lord Emmott,[40] an eminent member of the Liberal party and former associate in the Asquith cabinet, that Earl Beauchamp corresponded[41] with regard to the course the Liberals should adopt in the House of Lords. He was searching for a way to reunite and strengthen the party he loved.

40   Alfred Emmott, b. 1869; Liberal M.P. from 1899; Chairman of Ways and Means 1906–11; Secretary of State for the Colonies 1911–1914; First Commissioner of Works 1914–15; Director of War Trade Department 1915–19. Baron Emmott from 1911.
41   Nuffield College Library Archive, Oxford: Emmott MS, box no. 3, 5–7, 9.

I

Earl Beauchamp to Lord Emmott

2 VII 16

My dear Emmott,

I had hoped to see *you* again in the House on Thursday to ask you about Free Trade[42] & whether you wd feel yourself able to help in any way an attempt to defend it. The danger seems to me that unless we back up the Free Traders in the Cabinet, the case will go against us by default. You will see that I have a motion down – but I wondered if you wd join in a general manifesto wh ought to be widely signed, re-affirming our adherence to Free Trade. You will have seen the danger of the Paris resolutions. A temporary tariff, for 5 years is impossible. It is just an attempt to get us to change our fiscal system after the war is over by means of a sham war necessity!

Yours v. sincerely,

Beauchamp

2

Lord Emmott to Earl Beauchamp

4th July 1916

I am making enquiries as to how far my position here ought, or ought not to cripple any action I may desire to take in regard to Free Trade. As soon as I can get that settled I will either write to you or see you. The latter course would be the best as there are a good many questions I may want to ask.

Generally speaking, I may say that the tendency to throw over Free Trade in a hurry and to tie ourselves to action [which] would seem to me to point in the direction of another war is most regrettable.

3

Earl Beauchamp to Lord Emmott

26 XII 22

My dear Emmott,

42   Advanced especially by Lloyd George, there was a move to control the economy in order to make sure the war effort had sufficient backing. There had been an economic conference at Paris approving Protectionism.

Buckmaster suggests that I shd ask a few Peers to discuss the position in our House on Jan. 25. I hope very much that that date will suit you & that you will join us at the Reform Club that eve. at 8.

Stanmore has given us a conciliatory answer from Ll. G. about the whips – saying that he wd be content with one, but suggesting that while we shd appoint a Leader – a deputy Leader might be chosen from the Nat. Libs. This does not seem to me unfair, & at any rate shows that with a little good will we ought to be able to arrange something.

It is not only a question of reunion but of preventing the erection of fresh barriers wh may end in he & his – like the Lib. Un. – joining the Cons. We ought to stop that.

With all the compliments of the Season to you and Lady Emmott.

Yours v. Sincerely,

Beauchamp

4

Earl Beauchamp to Lord Emmott

28 XII 22

My dear Emmott,

Many thanks for yr letter. I am very glad you can come. Frankly I did not like the system last Session. Grey attended seldom & was encumbered by railway meetings at York. There was no one with authority to speak for us on two or three important occasions. Liberalism was dumb & Birkenhead[43] took the field. If Grey wd really do the work it wd be the best thing. But I don't like the idea of going on as we did. Ll. G. answered conciliatory wise & wd like to have one whip. The Nat. Libs are pressing for a party meeting before Parliament meets & then we must either come to terms or separate. They want to appoint a deputy Leader – not altogether unreasonable – & if Grey wd attend, there wd not be any great harm. But he comes seldom, then the Nat. Libs take over the whole party. What in these difficult circumstances do you advise? Can you talk it over with Stanmore or Pentland?[44] I think they are both in London & it is only by discussing it that we can come to any good conclusion.

Once more every good wish to you & Lady Emmott for the New Year.

43   F. E. Smith took the title Lord Birkenhead in 1921. He was a Conservative and a persuasive orator.
44   Pentland, 1st Baron, b. 1860. A Liberal.

Yours v. Sincerely,

Beauchamp

5

Earl Beauchamp to Lord Emmott

8 I 23

My dear Emmott,

Many thanks for yr letter. I am glad you have had a talk with Stanmore. I don't feel that reunion is at all impossible. The alternative is a second Liberal party in the H. of L. wh will be a fresh hindrance to fusion later on.

Denman tells me that he thinks Grey wd take the leadership if some one else wd do the day by day work. This seems to make it difficult if not impossible for us to refuse to the Nat. Libs the appointment of a Deputy sympathetic to them. We cannot well take Leader & Deputy L. The arrangement of last Session worked badly. A party meeting early (if it does not come to an agreement) at any rate wd allow us to appoint a Com. say 3 from each side. They might hammer out a solution wh is very difficult while we are separated as at present & allow us to present a united front when Parliament meets. Do talk it over with Buckmaster. We need good will on both sides to effect our reunion. Grey, assisted by a Nat. Lib. might be a solution accepted to all. What do you think?

Yours v. Sincerely,

Beauchamp

6

Lord Emmott to Earl Beauchamp

January 19th 1923

My dear Beauchamp,

I went to see Grey yesterday and I found that you had seen him on Wednesday. In these circumstances, I need not write at length, for having seen him, you will know what he thinks, and probably you will have seen Buckmaster also.

I may say, however, in reference to the main question, that I gravely doubt whether there is sufficient similarity of opinion either on foreign policy or on fiscal policy to make a Coalition other than a dangerous experiment. Matters would be far worse, for instance, if a Coalition were arranged (they having the deputy leadership) and some question turned up, as in all probability it will, which made division in the Coalition.

This being my view, I think it would be far better to run our own show and act in the most friendly manner with them, so far as we can.

Yours sincerely,

E.

7

Earl Beauchamp to Lord Emmott

20 I 1923

My dear Emmott,

Your letter was a sad surprise. Some kind of arrangement with the National Liberals really seems to me essential if we are to survive as a Party. Nor do I feel that there is any very great dissimilarity in opinion between the two Wings. Certainly there is no such acute division as existed in the Liberal Party from 1900–1905. The Party in the country certainly expects and hopes for a re-union and if the pundits of the Party look askance, I feel sure that we ought to do what we can in the House of Lords to consider the alternative. The National Liberal Peers, unofficially led by Birkenhead might even outnumber the faithful Wee Frees. In that case we shall find ourselves no longer the official opposition, ousted from the Front Bench and exercising less and less influence upon public opinion. Surely it is worth some effort to avert all this.

Yours very sincerely,

Beauchamp

Lord Emmott died in 1926. Beauchamp had lost one of his closest associates in the Party. His pain he expressed in a letter to Lady Emmott.

Earl Beauchamp to Lady Emmott

14 XII 26

My dear Lady Emmott,

Nothing we say can soften the dreadful blow wh has fallen upon you. But I send you the report of what took place last night in the House of Lords where private conversations all emphasized their sense of the great loss we all suffer. I wish that with more time I cd have given a better & more eloquent account & estimate. But it cd not have been more sincere.

We shall miss him very greatly on the Front Bench where we valued his wise advice. Please accept my deepest sympathy in this irreparable & sudden loss.

Yours very sincerely,

Beauchamp

Liberal spokesman during the first Labour administration

When the first Labour government came to office under Ramsay MacDonald, it was against general distrust from the establishment. But King George V wanted the new ministers 'to be given a fair chance'. As spokesman of the Liberal party, Earl Beauchamp carried on with his work in the House of Lords, standing up for the principles of his own party. Diverse were the subjects on which he addressed the House.

The government's policy

The new Labour administration came in at the start of January 1924, and in February, Ramsay MacDonald made a statement of policy. In the House of Lords, many hoped for a detailed debate about it. Here Beauchamp expresses general dissatisfaction that this was evaded:[45]

> My Lords, the rules of debate in the House are proverbially lax, but I doubt whether we have ever before departed so far from the usual course. The government yesterday made a statement of policy. Questions were put to them, so far-reaching and urgent that the noble and learned Lord, the Lord President of the Council, asked special leave to adjourn the debate until to-day, in order that he might prepare a sufficient answer to the Questions. He then, as I understood, wound up for the Government the discussion upon that point. The House then proceeded to listen to Earl Russell, who asked a Question on a totally different subject. He received no answer, and I

45   See *Parliamentary Debates*, House of Lords, vol. LVI, 13 February 1924, cols 152–3.

understand that the defence which is being made by the noble and learned Lord, the Lord President, is that he had no right to intervene again in the discussion. But I understood that these were separate Notices upon the Paper, and therefore there is every reason why, had he wished to do so, he could have given a complete answer to the noble Earl who sits alone on the seats behind the Government. Then we had a most valuable contribution from the noble Viscount (Lord Cecil) – to whom we always listen on this particular subject with attention – which I think was also worthy of a more detailed answer than the noble Viscount received from the Lord President.

It is customary in this House, when a noble Lord puts down a Question on the Paper, for a full answer to be given by the Government, which should attempt at any rate to deal with the Question that has been raised. I confess that this new view, that the noble and learned Lord, the Lord President, is unable to intervene again in the course of the discussion this evening, is an unfortunate one for the future, because there are not many members of the House probably who will be prepared to support the action of the Government, and if they are only to speak once in the course of the evening it will be very difficult for them to carry out their duties. For my own part I regret the fact that the Lord President terminated the discussion on the policy of the Government so soon.

I also have found a great reform which has been carried out by the Government, and which has not yet been mentioned. The noble Earl, Lord Balfour, mentioned the provision of a room in the Foreign Office for the Lord President. The newspapers have told us for three weeks of the arduous days and nights worked by every member of the Government. His Majesty's Cabinet went early to their offices and stayed there till late at night, although I doubt if they ever worked longer hours than did the noble Marquess, Lord Curzon. Then, at the end of several days, at last one great reform was announced – the clothes of which they were to wear at State functions were to be different from those worn by their predecessors. Whether they are to be congratulated upon having substituted far more ugly costumes I will not venture to enquire.

I regret the fact that the debate has been cut short for another reason – namely that it prevents me from giving an answer to a question put to us by Lord Birkenhead on the Question of the Popular Order. He directly challenged us on this Bench, and as I have been led astray by so admirable a leader as Lord Balfour, perhaps I may say, in answer to Lord Birkenhead, quite briefly, in regard to the action of the Poplar Guardians,[46] that in so far as it is intended to be, and is, an attempt to break down the system of local government in London, we are entirely and heartily opposed to it. But what is quite a separate question, and about which we ought to have more information in this House, is the action of the Minister of Health in rescinding the

46   See below.

Mond Order.[47] We want more information before coming to a definite decision. If the noble Lords opposite are not prepared to put down a Question on the matter soon, perhaps they will allow us to do so, and when it is raised I hope we shall get a great deal more than the formal unsatisfactory answers which we have received from the Lord President in reply to the two Questions on the Paper to-day.

Preferential tariffs

The issue of 'Imperial Preference' was still rumbling. On 20 February 1924, Earl Beauchamp rose to call attention to the high duties levied upon British goods under the preferential tariffs when they enter the self-governing Dominions and to the Indian tariffs; and to move for the papers:[48]

> In calling the attention of His Majesty's Government to this Question I am anxious not to make a speech which could in any sense be called controversial. The fact of the matter is that before very long your Lordships will probably be asked to discuss the general question of Imperial Preference, and it is very desirable that when we do so, we should have all the figures available for a full and frank discussion. These figures are very difficult to get at. A few of them are to be found in official Papers but comparatively few. I have thought that it would be to the general advantage that before the discussion took place, we should have these figures actually available. I have no doubt that the noble Lords who represents the Colonial Office in this House will tell me in what way he thinks it most convenient that they should be circulated – whether it will be sufficient that they should appear in the report of his speech or whether he thinks it more desirable that a White Paper should be issued. I should be quite ready to fall in with whatever he suggests. ...

The Under-Secretary of State for the Colonies, Lord Arnold,[49] replied for the government. Thereupon Earl Beauchamp asked leave to withdraw his motion. He expressed his thanks to the Under-Secretary 'for the

47　As Minister of Health and in response to the rates revolt in Poplar, Mond had announced a change to the Metropolitan Poor Fund in favour of poorer boroughs.

48　See *Parliamentary Debates*, House of Lords, vol. LVI, 20 February 1924, col. 209.

49　Arnold, 1st Baron, b. 1878. Labour.

very full reply which he was good enough to give. It amply satisfied my requirements.'⁵⁰

Poor Law relief in Poplar

On 21 February 1924, Earl Beauchamp rose to call attention to the administration of Poor Law relief by the Poplar Guardians. Poplar was a poverty-stricken area of East London, with high unemployment; and a concerned local Labour administration raised higher rates in order to relieve the population. It also held back the rates (or 'precepts') formally due to the various London central bodies, and this raised a furore. Inevitably, critics could find fault with some of the things the Poplar Guardians had done. In the House of Lords, Beauchamp wanted to ask 'His Majesty's Government if the action of the Board is approved by them; to call attention to the rescission of the special Order by the Minister of Health; and to move for Papers.'⁵¹ He continued:

> My Lords, it will be seen that this Question, of which I have given notice, is really divided into two parts. It may be for the general convenience of your Lordships' House if I say at once that the first part of the Question is that to which I attach the greater importance, and it is that part to which chiefly I shall direct my remarks. The facts in this matter are admitted. Nobody denies them. The system of Poor Law relief, as administered by the Poplar Guardians, was reported upon by a Special Commissioner appointed by the ministry of Health, in May, 1922, and the White Paper which was issued contains, in various parts, a series of condemnations of the way in which they carried out their duties. ... There were insufficient deductions in respect of children's earnings in calculating the allowances of relief, resulting in the granting of relief in cases in which no real destitution existed. Again, relief was allowed in excess of the earnings of an independent workman who maintained himself by his labour. ... What we want know is whether these methods of the Poplar Board of Guardians are approved by His Majesty's Government or not. That is, I

50   See *Parliamentary Debates*, House of Lords, vol. LVI, col. 227.
51   *Ibid.*, 21 February 1924, cols 267–73.

think, a quite plain and simple issue which I venture to put to the noble and learned Viscount on the Woolsack. ...

Work for the unemployed

Earl Beauchamp criticized the Labour government for its initial failure to announce measures that might make real change for the people. It was a time of seriously high unemployment. On 19 March 1924, he rose to say:[52]

> The noble Lord, the Secretary of State for India, will not be surprised if his extraordinary and unusually provocative speech induces me to make some reply. I do not deny the educative influence of the Labour Party. It has had a considerable influence upon the Liberals. Is not the noble and learned Viscount on the Woolsack an example of the educative influence of the Labour Party on the Liberals? And has not their influence been equally effective upon the ranks of the noble Lords who sit on the front Opposition Bench? Two of the noble Lord's chief colleagues, the Lord President of the Council and the first Lord of Admiralty, have equally been educated by the Labour Party as recruits from the ranks of the noble Lords who sit on the Opposition Benches. But whilst the noble Lord plumes himself on the influence he has had in educating other people, he forgets, sometimes at any rate, what has been done by the Liberal Party. It was the Liberal Party which passed the first Unemployment Insurance Act, and, naturally enough, having regard to the general tone of the noble Lord's speech, he omitted to make any reference to that Act.
>
> I listened with very deep disappointment to the speech which we heard from the noble and learned Lord, the Lord President of the Council. I subscribe to the opinion of the noble and learned Viscount who spoke from the front Opposition Bench that not one new proposal have we had from His Majesty's Government on this occasion. And we are entitled to be disappointed in view of the high hopes which the Labour Party raised in the country and the way in which they spoke of the problem of unemployment. The Prime Minister himself said that Labour had a programme and a power which no other Party possessed. I have a very keen recollection of having made, on more than one Liberal platform during the last General Election, special reference to the hopes which we in the Liberal Party entertained of being able to do

---

52   *Ibid.*, 19 March 1924, cols 890–3.

something to restore trade if once the foreign policy of this country led to a considerable measure of pacification in Europe. Members of the Liberal Party continued
to emphasise that. It was the chief remedy which we proposed, but we were not like
the noble Lord and his friends opposite, who said they had a programme which
no other Party possessed. We did not put before the country high hopes which we
should not be able to carry out when we came into office. We said that there was no
royal road to the getting rid of unemployment, and we certainly did not boast that
we had a programme and a power which no other Party possessed. ...

It is perfectly true that they have adumbrated, and, I think, introduced into another
place, proposals by which there will be a certain amount added to what I think is
wrongly called the dole. And I have a distinct recollection of members of the Labour
Party saying – and I agreed with them – that what the unemployed wanted was not
money, but work. His Majesty's Government have, so far, done something to assist
those who are unemployed in the way of maintenance, but in regard to work, in
spite of their professions, they have not produced a single measure which has given
real employment. ...

Unemployment Insurance Bill

By 9 April 1924, when we hear Earl Beauchamp speak again, the unemployment issue was still being discussed. In some ways, matters had moved on;
in some ways they had not. The Marquess of Curzon of Kedleston asked the
government about the course of business with regard to the Unemployment
Bill. The Lord Chancellor answered, stating that he desired to meet the
convenience of the noble Marquess who led the Opposition, and of Lord
Beauchamp, who 'speaks for the Liberal Party'. This was a matter, Earl
Beauchamp replied which could only be reached by 'general agreement'.
The bill, he said, was 'a Money Bill', and therefore 'it is not one of those
measures on which your Lordships generally spend very much time. For
my own part, and speaking for noble friends who act with me, I see no
objection, in these special circumstances, to meeting on Friday at twelve

o'clock and carrying the bill through all its remaining stages after it has been read a first time tomorrow.'[53]

In the debate that followed, Earl Beauchamp observed that he hoped that His Majesty's Government, in 'bringing forward these Unemployment Insurance Bills, of which we heartily approve, will not forget the really urgent need there is of giving to these unfortunately unemployed people work as well as opportunities of drawing unemployed rates of pay. We wholly agree with what has been said frequently by members of the Government, that what these men really want is work, and therefore we hope that before very long these large schemes of which we have heard a great deal in the past will be introduced with the approval of both Houses.'[54]

Correct procedure

In these times of great political change, Earl Beauchamp was a stickler for correct procedure in the House of Lords, as bills were debated. We can see Earl Beauchamp trying to control how the Lords conducted their debates in the following extract from March 1924:[55]

> My Lords, I confess that I intervene with a great deal of reluctance in this most irregu-lar discussion. It is only a short time ago, I think, that a protest was made against questions and answers following one another in your Lordships' House, and I regret to think that in spite of the protest then made by the noble Marquess, the Leader of the Opposition, we should once again have fallen into the custom, and also another which is unusual in this House – namely, the reading of Long quotations from dis-cussions in another place. A new terror will be added to life if, in future, we should have column-long extracts from the debates in another place read to this House. I hope that it will not be a custom extensively followed in the future.

53   *Ibid.*, vol. LVII, 9 April 1924, col. 224.
54   *Ibid.*, vol. LVII, 11 April 1924, col. 264.
55   *Ibid.*, 12 March 1924, cols 726–7.

This was not the only time he had to step in. When it was moved that the House resolve itself into Committee on the *National Health Insurance (Cost of Medical Benefit) Bill*, Earl Beauchamp expressed reservations. He ventured to say that:[56]

> as a general rule no Bill should be taken in Committee of this House on the next sitting day after it has been read a second time. That is a good sound rule, and if I may be allowed to refer to my own experience, I remember that when I sat on the Government Bench, and there was a vigilant Opposition, I was never allowed to do anything of that kind except under duress and occasionally, of course, in regard to Money Bills. In the ordinary way that rule was enforced, and I think it is very desirable that we should return to that principle in this House. If this House is to do its duty as a Legislative Chamber it must be given time to think over these things. It is nothing to do with this House that a Bill has been agreed outside. Indeed, I have a good deal of suspicion of these bargains which are entered into by people outside this House, and possibly it is more necessary to consider bargains of that kind than it is to consider Bills not founded upon any such agreement between interested parties.

The question of correct procedure came up again over the *Education (Scotland) Supperannuation Bill*, brought to the Lords on 28 May 1924. Viscount Chelmsford[57] while introducing the above bill to be committed to a Committee of the Whole House warned their Lordships that the Act 'for which we are obtaining an extension of one year will expire unless this Bill is passed tomorrow or Friday, and I shall have to move to-morrow the suspension of Standing Orders in order to enable the Bill to be taken through its remaining stages in your Lordships' House in one day. I know how strongly your Lordships feel on this question of the suspension of Standing Orders, and I only pray that the noble Earl, Lord Beauchamp, will not be too severe on this request of mine. I can assure him that the position is not due to any delay in this House, but because the Bill came up so recently from another place.'[58] Earl Beauchamp responded thus:

---

56   *Ibid.*, vol. LVII, 13 May 1924, cols 389–90.
57   Chlemsford, 1st Viscount, b. 1864. A Conservative.
58   See *Parliamentary Debates*, House of Lords, vol. LVII, 28 May 1924, cols 733–4.

> My Lords, I think that some explanation is due to your Lordships' House as to why the Bill came so late to this House. It seems to me that the explanation of the noble Viscount is very incomplete. How was it that the Bill came so late to this House? Was it not introduced into another place early enough, or was it introduced early and then entirely neglected with the idea on the part of the noble Viscount's friends that they might treat this House with complete disrespect and not regard our Standing Orders? I should be glad to hear from the noble Viscount, Lord Chelmsford, or from the noble and learned Viscount on the Woolsack, some explanation of the matter.

The Lord Chancellor replied, stating that the bill was introduced 'in another place some time ago and was discussed and was then put aside to make way for other business in the House of Commons. The unfortunate Secretary for Scotland tried hard to bring it forward from day to day but was not able to do so, and it was only very lately that it passed through the House of Commons. That is the explanation, though not perhaps a very good one, of how the position has arisen.'

Again with the ***Local Authorities (Emergency Provisions) Bill,*** taking its passage through the House of Lords on 4 June 1924, we find Earl Beauchamp insisting on adherence to the rules. The Lord Chancellor moved that the bill be read a third time. Lord Strachie[59] had put an amendment, which the Lord Chancellor declared was out order because the bill was 'a Money Bill', and so the question of privilege applied. Lord Beauchamp answered in the absence 'of his noble friend', Lord Strachie.[60] The government, he said, insisted on a point of privilege and was asking their Lordships not to consider the amendment 'simply on that ground'. And yet the 'merits of the Amendment were never discussed at all by any speaker on behalf of His Majesty's Government. Whether the Amendment was, on its merits, good or bad really was not touched upon ... I think that was, if I may so, rather a mistake.'

> We all know that Amendments of this kind are frequently introduced in your Lordships' House, and that a question of privilege is frequently waived in another place. Amendments exactly like this are admitted, even though there may be technical questions of privilege in the way. The real danger which will follow if His Majesty's

---

59 Strachie, 1st Baron, b. 1880. A Liberal.
60 *See Parliamentary Debates*, House of Lords, vol. LVII, 4 June 1924, cols 911–12.

Government, on similar Bills on future occasions, abstain from arguing the question on merits, is that a Bill will run the risk of being rejected even on Second Reading. If a Bill is rejected on Second Reading no question of privilege arises at all. If Amendments which in themselves are sound are not to be considered on their merits but are to be rejected without discussion merely on the ground of privilege, it may make legislation in this House of a somewhat summary character, because noble Lords who have Amendments which are sound, if they realise that His Majesty's Government will not consider them on their merits but will simply dismiss them without a further word on the question of privilege, will be tempted to ask your Lordships' House to reject a Bill on Second Reading. That, I think, would be a very great misfortune, and it is in order to prevent that happening in future – there is no question of it being done on this Bill – that I venture to make this appeal to His Majesty's Government.

Earl Beauchamp was much respected for his knowledge of the workings of the House of Lords and it is not surprising that, before long, he achieved promotion.

CHAPTER 18

Liberal Leader in the House

The Liberal leadership in the House of Lords

There was another problem that earned Earl Beauchamp's attention, as he strove to defend the Liberal cause. It concerned party discipline and the official Liberal leadership in the House of Lords. The Earl was not himself leader: from 1923 Earl Grey fulfilled this task – but the elder statesman was losing his sight and had become tired and somewhat disinterested, since he was unable to read all the official documents. He seldom showed up in the Lords, and often the work there was entirely left to Beauchamp. Some action needed to be taken. We trace correspondence over the problem back to 1919 and follow it through:

1

Lord Crewe to the Marquess of Lincolnshire (formerly Earl Carrington)[1]

38, Berkley Square,
W.1

10 January 1919

Private

My dear Charlie,

Many thanks for your letter of the 7th January. I have been considering for some time the reorganisation of our party in the House, in view of the changed circumstances, and am proposing to appoint a whip, or perhaps two, on the old lines. I am thinking also of calling a meeting of Liberal Peers before Parliament meets, to which I think

---

1   Bodleian Library, Carrington Papers. MS. Film 1135 (2).

most could be invited, though, of course, it would not be fair to ask those who hold any Government or Household appointments. There will be a certain number who will prefer to receive the Government whips, but there will be others who prefer to retain their independence, – all the more as we hope to give general support to Government measures, and sometimes even to save them from the excessive attentions of their own friends.

I am happy to say that Rosebery[2] makes steady progress, and regains strength, but it is a very slow business. I hope he may come South before the end of next month.

Ever yours,

Crewe

2

Stanmore to Beauchamp[3]

186 Ebury Street, SW1

27.12.22

Private

My dear Beauchamp,

I have heard from Wimborne[4] suggesting that he and I should meet after the holidays to discuss the question of the opposition leadership in the H. of Lds.

I quite agree with you that it is important we should have the joint meeting before the beginning of the Session.

I am just back from the country & shall now try to see Pentland & one or two others.

I see difficulties in the place of [illegible] of 3 from each group, but would like to talk it over with you.

Yours very sincerely,

Stanmore

2   Crewe was Rosebery's son-in-law.
3   All the letters are packed in the Beauchamp Papers, *op. cit.*
4   Wimborne, 1st Viscount, b. 1873. A Liberal.

3

Beauchamp to Grey

29 XII 22

Madresfield Court, Malvern

Dear Grey,

Many thanks for your letter. I am very glad that you can come on the 25th. Meanwhile however I am ashamed to hear that you did not know about the whips. I asked Buckmaster to tell you but I ought to have written to you myself.

Denman owing to ill health has resigned & his place is very difficult to fill. Stanmore or failing him Colebrooke[5] are the best persons available. Buckmaster and I talked it over & we agreed in asking Stanmore whether his friend wd consider the question of filling up the whips. My letter to you a week ago carrying his answer must have puzzled you.

We promised to hold another party meeting when we met at Denman's house & I understand that they are pressing for this meeting to be held – in accordance with the understanding – before Parliament meets. The whole question of Leadership & Deputy will have to be discussed there & it will be most convenient to have it in good time. Buckmaster is strongly opposed to the appointment of any Deputy in our House. I have told him that a very good solution wd have been his appointment as yr Deputy. [illegible] Stanmore is now waiting for an answer & I wd be very glad to let him know what you think on this point.

We ought to be able to reunite without any great difficulty in the Lords – very much to the advantage of Free Liberalism.

Yours sincerely,

Beauchamp

4

Beauchamp to Buckmaster

Madresfield Court

20 I 23

Dear Buckmaster,

5   Colebrooke, 1st Baron, b. 1861. A Liberal.

Many thanks for your letter. I told Grey that my chief opposition to a Deputy from the N. L. P. [New Liberal Party] was it passed over you, whose abilities & powers of speech surpassed the other members of the party. He agreed with this & so I am sure wd others. Gladstone[6] also writes to me protesting against a Deputy – as does Maclean. Naturally they do not know how the Party's affairs were managed in the H. of L. from 1906–1914, & others have forgotten.

But what is of immediate importance is the alternative. Denman has no substitute as a whip & the band of Wee Frees – 10 or 12 will be left without an organisation while probably the Nat. Libs will elect a leader who will become the representative of the opposition. The Liberals in the country will be disappointed & our influence decrease in the House and elsewhere. That is not a pleasant prospect. I don't believe in the newspaper canard that Birkenhead will lead the N. Libs. Anyhow all these considerations must be in our minds when we meet to consult next week. With a little good will I feel sure that some arrangement is possible wh will sacrifice no Liberal principle. You & I can remember how from 1900–1905 the party was rent in twain while in opposition. Therefore now it does seem unnecessary to insist on complete union. We want to prevent things becoming worse.

Beauchamp

5

Beauchamp to Maclean

Madresfield Court

20 I 23

My dear MacLean,

Many thanks for your letter & enclosure from Gladstone. As he may be back next week perhaps this letter will do as an answer to you as well as to him. I am very sorry he seems so much opposed to any rapprochement with the Nat. Libs in the H. of L. The fact that Ll. G. does not sit there enables us to do more than is possible in the H. of C. Up & down the country the rank and file are urging us to unite again & the loose organisation in the H. of L. makes it easier.

Failing some arrangement of some kind it is not unlikely that the majority of peers will go to N. L. & dispossess us of the Front Bench. I wish that Gladstone came oftener to the House & took part in our proceedings.

6   Herbert Gladstone, 1st Viscount Gladstone, b. 1854. William Ewart Gladstone's son.

Denman cannot find us a whip & we shall be left – perhaps 10 in number, while the prestige of Liberalism in our House passes over to Ll. George & his friends. Surely it is worth making some small sacrifice to prevent that. A 'Deputy' Leader wd have no influence if the Leader attended regularly. Last Session's arrangement seemed to be thoroughly ineffective. To those who helped in the Party's affairs in the H. of L. 1905–1914 it really was melancholy to see how little we counted. If we can co-operate with the N. L. Peers in the House we ought gradually to detach them from the evil influence under which they have lately suffered & certainly the differences between them & us are no greater than those in the Liberal Party 1900–1905. So that I cannot yet give up hope of some measure of reunion however slight. With good-will it really is possible.

Beauchamp

6

Stanmore to Beauchamp

Brooks's
St James's Street SW1

22 I 23

My dear Beauchamp,

I met Colebrooke & Denman this morning. We decided that the meeting should be at the Reform at 4 p.m. on the 31st; the hour has been made later as the Poynder-Grigg's[7] wedding is at 2.15 that day.

Will you be so kind as to write to the authorities at the Reform about engaging a room for the meeting? Denman tells me that he has seen the Steward & said that it was hoped you would write on the subject.

I had a long & satisfactory talk with Pentland last Thursday. He thinks that every consideration should be shown to Buxton, if Grey is not at the meeting, he Buxton should be asked to take the chair.

Yours very sincerely,

Stanmore

7   Joan Dickson-Poynder, daughter of Lord Islington; married a Liberal M.P., Edward Grigg, later Lord Altrincham.

7

Stanmore to Beauchamp

22 January 1923

Dear Beauchamp,

Many thanks for your letter telling me that Grey is not prepared to lead the opposition in the H. of L. & his hope that Buckmaster would be elected.

In my opinion Buckmaster is the ablest man & most effective speaker in the House but I doubt if he would be acceptable to many of the National Liberal peers owing to the very strong line he has taken against Lloyd George and the Coalition.

I understand that Colebrooke has already asked Wimborne [illegible] to the preliminary meeting on the 30th. He will probably ask one more, as one of the whips will also be present.

Yours sincerely,

Stanmore

8

Buckmaster to Beauchamp

1, Porchester Terrace,
Hyde Park, W.

22 I 23

Dear Beauchamp,

You wrote to me in far too generous terms. My objection to the Deputy Leader is what I have already stated. [illegible].

I agree people do not look back now so far as I can see nor do they look forward. Our real strength lies in the fact that the L. G. people cannot elect a Liberal Leader who would be anything but a jest. [illegible]

Buckmaster

9

Earl Beauchamp to Lord Grey of Fallodon[8]

8   Nuffield College Library Archive, Oxford: Emmott MS, box no. 3, 5–7, 9.

8. 8. 1924

You were good enough early last year to ask me to help you in leading the House of Lords and I have been glad to do my best since then. I cannot, however, but feel that the position is unsatisfactory. I am unable, for reasons which you know, to be present this week, and in your absence at home, the Party remains without lead. Such as it is, it cannot hope, so it seems to me, to maintain any influence in the Lords without constant & consistent leading. The position has gone from bad to worse. The other day when Denman issued a whip on London traffic, 12 of our small band voted against Buxton. We are apparently quite out of touch with the members of the Party and the neglect with which both Government & Conservatives seem to wish to treat us is altogether inconsistent with our position in the Country. We cannot expect our followers to make sacrifices by attending regularly unless we show ourselves ready to do the same. Apart altogether from the earlier weeks of the Session, the last few days are always specially important. Even if the Bills themselves deal with small matters there are difficult points arising out of differences of opinion between the two Houses & they need to be carefully watched. This year we have failed to deal with them adequately and so we have lost a real opportunity of helping our friends in the Commons & in the Country.

Will you therefore be good enough to excuse me from further service in this respect and make other arrangements for October?

Yours sincerely,

Beauchamp

10

Lord Grey to Earl Beauchamp[9]

9. 8. 1924

My dear Beauchamp,

I agree that the position is unsatisfactory. As you know I only took the place of leader with great reluctance at a time of peculiar difficulty in the Party. I did so because it was pressed upon me that my doing so might ease the situation. That was at the beginning of the Session of 1923.

A few months ago I told you that I thought I could not continue in the position much longer. The reason is that I have other work which is a first charge upon my time and often prevents me from being in the House of Lords.

9   *Ibid.*

Besides another disability is that I cannot with impaired sight do more than keep in touch with some of the more important questions such as those of Foreign Affairs which I have been in the habit of following. It was for this reason that I was reluctant to take the place of leader for I felt sure that I must sometimes be absent when an important debate took place and that I must often be unable when some new and intricate subject came up to give the lead that would naturally be expected.

I feel that the moment has come to hand over the place to someone who can give full time to its duties and is better qualified to discharge them. The change should be made before the House reassembles. Perhaps you could arrange for some consultation with Liberal Peers as to choosing my successor.

I must add a line to express my gratitude to you for all you have done. Without your help I should not have attempted to fill the place at all.

Yours sincerely,

Grey of Fallodon

11

Beauchamp to Grey

Madresfield Court, Gt Malvern

12.8.1924

My dear Grey,

Many thanks for what you say so kindly. It has been a real pleasure to serve you, who have so great a claim upon every real Liberal. Had I been able to do better, the system might have worked successfully, but unfortunately it has broken down. Liberals in the Lords are always in a difficult position.

I have duly written to Denman as you desired and have suggested a meeting on the eve of our reassembly.

Yours v. sincerely,

Beauchamp

12

Asquith to Beauchamp

The Wharf,
Sutton Courtney,
Berks

14 August 1924

My dear Beauchamp,

Grey has already sent me a copy of his reply to you. I have replied expressing my extreme regret at his decision, and at the same time admitting my inability to controvert his arguments. I agree with you that the present situation is an impossible one, & ought not to continue. I hope you may be able – as Grey suggests – to arrange for consultation with the Liberal Peers.

Yours very sincerely,

H. H. Asquith

13

Denman to Beauchamp

Balcombe Place,
Balcombe, Sussex

14 August 1924

My dear Beauchamp,

Am much relieved to get your letter of the 11th, which eases the situation. I take it as certain that you will now have to lead, but I suppose a meeting will have to be called as you say, before Parliament meets. Do you think that I ought to send out the notice for the meeting, also the time and place must be fixed soon. How would 2.30 in the afternoon of the 30th Sept. do? It is usual to hold such meetings at a private house; as you are to be elected perhaps it would be better not to have it at yours. I think ours would be available if it were thought suitable. ... Judith loved her time at Madresfield. Thank you so much for having her.

Yours v. sincerely,

Denman

Before the next session of Parliament started in October 1924, the Liberal peers elected Earl Beauchamp as their Leader in the House of Lords.

The 'front bench' issue

It was a difficult time to take on such a leadership task. The elections of 1924 had been disastrous to the Liberals – indeed, so much so that the main party of opposition to the victorious Conservatives was now Labour. This posed a problem that had never come up before: which party should sit on the Opposition front benches in the House of Lords, where there were many Liberals but very few Labour peers?

I

Muir Mackenzie[10] to Beauchamp

11 November 1924

My dear Beauchamp,

It was very good of you to write to me, & a great pleasure to receive your letter. I had been meditating a letter to you. Shall we dine together one night next week? Either here or at the Atheneum or [illegible]?

I don't know yet how we stand, still less how we sit, as opposition. I believe that the orthodox view is that the outgoing party is the opposition, but there never has been such a situation as the present. Can the formal opposition (Her Majesty's opposition) be different with two Houses? MacDonald will undoubtedly lead the official opposition in the Commons. As for myself, I shall hope to find myself able to serve the House in some way or other. If I may take your friendly letter as an invitation to act with my lifelong associates, I am very much obliged to you, but I felt at the beginning of the year that I was not wanted, and though I did not the least resent it. I think I can be of most use to those who are woefully short-handed in our House & who made a great deal of use of me while there was occasion. ... Please give my love to your most dear wife,

and believe me always

sincerely & affectionately yours,

Muir Mackenzie

10   Kenneth Muir Mackenzie (First Baron Muir Mackenzie), b. 1845; the Labour admin-
      istration's chief whip in the House of Lords.

2

Stanmore to Beauchamp

Goldings Manor, Loughton, Essex

16 November 1924

My dear Beauchamp,

Muir Mackenzie's contention that the opposition in both Houses must belong to the same party is too absurd in view of the 1923 Parliament. Colebrooke tells me that he thinks we should be the official opposition in that he was quoting Crewe on the question when he talked to Mackenzie. I'm very sorry to hear that Curzon's letter is also unsatisfactory. When do you come to London?

Yours sincerely,

Stanmore

3

Lloyd George to Beauchamp

18 November 1924

Dear Lord Beauchamp,

Mr Lloyd George has asked me to thank you for your letter of the 12th. Lord Stanmore duly reported to Mr Lloyd George that Labour were claiming the Front Opposition Bench and he agrees with you that it is a ridiculous claim. Lord Stanmore was informed by Mr Lloyd George that if necessary he would certainly fight any such claim. Perhaps you will kindly keep Mr Lloyd George informed on any developments.

Yours sincerely,

[Secretary to Lloyd George]

4

Muir Mackenzie to Beauchamp

27 Cumberland Terrace

17 November 1924

My dear Beauchamp,

On returning from Brighton I hear that you have phoned asking me to dine on Wednesday, & that my kitchen maid has accepted for me. If I don't hear from you to the contrary, I will turn up on Wednesday at 8.15. It is very good of you to have me to dinner, especially if it means that I shall see her most dear Ladyship.

Ever yours,

Muir Mackenzie

5

Muir Mackenzie to Beauchamp

27 Cumberland Terrace

20 November 1924

My dear Beauchamp,

I have had a very satisfactory talk with Parmour, and I have no doubt that you & he would come to terms if he saw you. But I am not quite clear that he is exactly in a position to speak for Haldane yet, and so I have suggested that he should ask you to see him as soon as you return to town next week, instead of tomorrow morning. I shall have had a talk with Haldane by that time, and shall have shown him Crewe's letter which I return for that purpose. Shall you be in town next Wednesday?

Yours ever,

Muir Mackenzie

I hope her Ladyship's cold is better.

6

Beauchamp to Curzon

14 XI 1924

Dear Curzon,

Many thanks for your letter. I shall be glad to do as you suggest & go to see you one day next week. I will telephone on my return and find out what time will be convenient to you. There may often be difficulties in the future if once we depart from the criterion of numbers which Labour has accepted up till now. Last year the opposition was different in the two Houses without the public interest suffering in any way. Labour in the Commons & Liberalism in the Lords. Nor should I offer any difficulty if we being the official opposition, Labour wished to sit on the Front Bench. But one or two of my friends seem to object to our joining Labour there and think we should do much better to remain where we are. I am inclined to agree with this point of view if Labour became the official opposition. But we could talk this over.

At present Haldane has not communicated with me & I have no reason – except rumour – to suppose that he will want to alter the custom of the House.

Yours sincerely,

Beauchamp

7

Haldane to Beauchamp

28 Queen Anne's Gate,
Westminster

21 November 1924

My dear Beauchamp,

Muir Mackenzie has told me of your claim to the Leadership of the opposition in the Lords, and to the room. Now I am not an egoist, and personally do not trouble about these things. But the question raised is one of principle, and of high importance. The late Government which will be led as an opposition in the Commons by the late Prime Minister, has asked me to lead its opposition in the Lords, and I have agreed to do so.

I am quite unable to see how there can be two official opposition parties, one in each House. It was not so in the Commons in 1918, nor can any analogy arise. Half of your 80 odd peers support the Conservatives, and some of your men in the Commons depend on Conservative votes for their seats. This may not continue to be so. I hope not. But it is so to-day.

Under the circumstances the late Government claims to be the official opposition, and I am bound in duty to put forward and press their claim. The question is of course one which the House of Lords will decide, but I may have to refer to public opinion as the justification for the claim to fair treatment which I am making for the Labour Party.

Forgive an unpleasant letter.

Yours v. sincerely,

Haldane

8

Haldane to Beauchamp

24 November 1924

My dear Beauchamp,

I shall be very glad to have a friendly talk with you. 2.30 on Wednesday at your house would suit me well. Let me have a line to say whether that will do. ... I have had a visit from Ramsay MacDonald. He is clear that there will be a tremendous row in the provinces if the Labour Government (that was) is refused her official position in the Lords. Labour have 70 members against the Liberal 30. The question is in reality a constitutional one.

Haldane

9

From Earl Buxton to Beauchamp

Newtimber Place, Hassocks, Sussex

27 November 1924

My dear Beauchamp,

I was afraid, as you know, that Curzon would take that line. In fact I rather doubt if he really had any other option, under the circumstances, but you made a good fight, and it will at all events have the advantage, that it will show that we do not intend to be ignored as an Opposition.

You will have seen from my letter to you of yesterday, that we agree in reference to where we shall sit. I hope you will impress on our fellows at the meeting the necessity and advantage of their all sitting behind us (the Tories I take it, will sit the other side) and that they should attend as regularly as they can, in order that we may show that we constitute really a stronger and more effective Opposition than Labour.

Yours ever,

Buxton

Irish Free State Bill

The October session was strained with several important bills, and Earl Beauchamp's contributions to the debates bear witness to his utmost efficiency and talent.

An example is his speech made on 5 October 1924 concerning an Irish Free State Bill. After a bitter war of independence, twenty-six of the thirty-two counties of Ireland had achieved Dominion status through the Irish Free State Constitution Act 1922 (though there had been further civil war over the compromises this entailed). The President of the Executive Council of the Irish Free State was W. T. Cosgrave.[11] The remaining six counties comprised Ulster, or Northern Ireland, which, with Sir James Craig[12] as Prime Minister, had opted to remain part of the United Kingdom. There was still much animosity. The issue in the Irish Free State Bill of 1924 was whether the two countries could take territory from one another. Earl Beauchamp's view of the matter was as follows:[13]

> I think what we need in this matter is a general atmosphere of good will. What we need perhaps more than anything else is to try to bring the pressure of public opinion here in England to bear upon those responsible statesmen in Ireland so that they may feel that it is the unanimous wish of the public opinion of this country that they should come to an arrangement among themselves for the settlement of this question. Therefore I do not bandy about the words 'honour' and 'honesty' which have been used, perhaps too much, in this connection. As it appears to me, this is an unforeseen contingency which has arisen, and in these circumstances I shall certainly do my best to support His Majesty's Government in this connection. I regret the necessity for any legislation at all, as the legislation is necessary, I shall certainly vote for the passage of this measure.
>
> The Amendment which we are more particularly discussing at this moment is an interesting innovation. Let me say something on the subject of the matter contained in it. I confess that I deplore the introduction of the Amendment more on the score of the matter which it contains than its actual manner. Surely the introduction of an Amendment of this kind is almost a direct incitement to the other Parliament, which is passing a similar Treaty, to pass an Amendment of the same kind; putting forward perhaps a very different point of view to that contained in the Amendment of the noble Marquess. I cannot help thinking that incitement of that kind is not calculated to settle the matter. I regret it, therefore, on that ground. It is, further,

---

11   W. T. Cosgrave, b.1880. A Dubliner; Chairman of the Provisional Government of the Irish Free State 1922; First President of the State Executive Committee 1922–32.

12   James Craig, b. 1871. Belfast Orangeman; Leader of Ulster Unionist Party 1920; First Prime Minister of Northern Irelan 1921–40. Made Viscount Craigavon 1927.

13   See *Parliamentary Debates*, House of Lords, vol. LIX, 8 October 1924, cols 644–7.

surely an attempt to prejudge what has been left quite deliberately by Parliament to the judgement of the Commission. I need not remind your Lordships – you have been reminded of it already to-night by others – how important it seemed to be at the time when the Treaty was passed that this matter should be left to the judgement of the Commission itself. We leave, therefore, entirely to the Commission the duty of interpreting the Treaty, and of carrying it out the way that they think best. I should greatly deplore the consequences if, as the result of the passing of this Amendment by your Lordships' House, there were to prevail in any part of Ireland an idea that there is a desire on the part of your Lordships' House to alter in any way the contents of the Treaty.

With regard to the manner of the Amendment, which has been somewhat severely commented upon by other Lords, I confess that I find myself in no state of quarrel with the noble Marquess. I rejoice in our freedom from Standing Orders in this House, and the Amendment seems to me to be a very amusing and highly ingenious method of expressing an opinion which certainly would not be open to the House of Commons to adopt. But I do not regard the contents of the noble Marquess's Amendment with the same equanimity. It seems to me an illustration of the old saying: 'Willing to wound, yet afraid to strike'. It will have, in itself, no practical effect. I wish to say nothing which is provocative. I should blame myself if I thought anything I said could be held by moderate men on either side to be in any way intended, or likely, to lead to a continuance of highly acute controversy on this matter. I prefer to confine myself, therefore, to praising the statesmanship of those who were responsible for the introduction of the Treaty and especially those Unionist members of the Coalition, the noble Marquess the Leader of the Opposition and the noble and learned Earl, who with rare courage and sagacity signed the Treaty and induced your Lordships to accept it.

We want no talk of coercion or surrender, no warlike talk or any rattling of sabres. We want this matter to be settled in a different atmosphere altogether from that. We realise the difficulties of the problem. It commands the co-operation of men of good will, and especially of moderate men. Have we not in India an example of the misfortune which follows when things get too much into the hands of extremists? One of the underlying ideas at the base of the Indian reforms was that they would secure the co-operation of men of all classes. Unfortunately, they have not succeeded in doing that; some have stood outside and are wrecking measures which we introduced. That is one of the chief causes of the unfortunate position which exists there. We need to avoid the same mistake in regard to Ireland. We want the more moderate men to get together, settle the matter and impose their settlement on the whole country. If it were generally understood in Ireland that the chief wish of the people of this country is that there should be a settlement by Irishmen among Irishmen it would go a long way towards settling the matter.

During the discussion too much stress has been laid upon the question of the actual pledges which have been given in the past by the Parliament of this country. None of us like the idea that pledges should be broken, but I wonder what some noble Lords who have taken part in this debate would have said in regard to a certain Act to which I should like to draw their attention. In the year 1783 an Act of Parliament was passed for 'preventing and removing all doubts which have arisen', and one of the clauses reads as follows:

'That the said right claimed by the people of Ireland to be bound only by laws enacted by His Majesty and the Parliament of that Kingdom ... shall be, and it is hereby declared to be established and ascertained for ever and shall at no time hereafter be questioned or questionable.'

If ever there was a pledge directly given that seems to me to be one. I wonder what would have been the action of the noble Lords when the Act of Union came to be discussed and they were told that they were unable to deal with the matter because so many pledges had been given by the Parliament of this country.

One of the most hopeful features of the discussion was the latter part of the speech made by the noble Marquess, Lord Londonderry, who insisted upon the desirability of direct negotiations between Mr Cosgrave and Sir James Craig. We do need something of that kind; I hope it may take place. It is quite evident that the Commission may not be, in itself, conclusive of the whole matter. Many alternatives may present themselves. There may be one Report, there may be two Reports, or even three Reports, but I hope that at the very worst these Reports will form the basis of an agreement between the two sides to this controversy.

What we need in England is to have more information on this question. That is the tendency of the day. When there is an industrial dispute in this country we set up a Court of Inquiry, not only in order that the President of the Court may give an award but that the information gathered in the course of the Inquiry may be given to the public. Public opinion is thus focused upon the very heart of the matter, and is able to bring all the weight it possesses in order to secure a settlement of the dispute in the best possible way. This does not apply only to industrial disputes at home. It is relevant here to draw attention to the fact that His Majesty's Government have been a party to a discussion in Geneva – I am not sure how far they have gone in agreement – to decide that in all cases of international disputes the aggressor shall be the person who has refused to take part in arbitration on the point. That is a warning which those who are unwilling to take part in arbitration under this Commission may very wisely take to heart. Public opinion throughout the world seems to be focusing itself on the point that the man who refuses to submit his case to arbitration commits a general offence and puts himself in the wrong, and he is not likely to be supported by public opinion if he determines to proceed with the dispute.

Lastly, may I say this to the representatives of the Irish Free State? I can imagine nothing would be more likely to injure their *status* than the inclusion within their borders of large numbers of people who wish to be governed by Ulster. All history is an example of that. Alsace-Lorraine may be quoted as a particular example. The presence of a hostile population within your own borders is a constant sore which can only hurt the country in which it occurs. That is what I say to the Free State, and I hope I shall not be considered guilty of partiality if I say that it applies equally to Ulster. I cannot imagine for either one or the other country anything more likely to retard development than the presence of an unwilling population within the borders of these respective States. Though this would be admitted in regard to every other country, there may be controversialists in this particular case who might say that it did not apply to them. Whether that is so or not, I believe that in this matter our chief hope lies in bringing public opinion in this country to bear on the controversy in Ireland and impressing upon Irishmen the desire we have that they should, by themselves, settle their own disputes.

Leading the Liberal Lords in opposition

As we have seen, The Liberals, who had ridden on such a surge before the First World War, had found their numbers in the Commons collapse, so that Earl Beauchamp's leadership in the House of Lords was for a party in opposition – indeed one that was sometimes almost side-lined. During the debate on the Address in Reply to the King's Speech on 9 December 1924,[14] a peer asked what exactly his position as Leader of the Liberals in the House would be. The Earl retorted that he would represent those noble Lords with whom he had the 'honour to act'. There was 'no difficulty, no doubt and no hesitation in our minds. We are out to oppose His Majesty's Government, and on every appropriate occasion we shall not hesitate to oppose their actions in so far as we think them wrong, with all the forces in our power.'[15]

14   This was for the opening of parliament under a government led by the Conservative Stanley Baldwin.
15   See *Parliamentary Debates*, House of Lords, vol. LX, 9 December 1924, col. 46.

Earl Beauchamp's interventions took various forms: introducing motions, putting down amendments or giving notice to ask his Majesty's government to clarify its policy.

In 1925 the Earl intervened more than forty times in the House.[16] He had things to say on the following topics: the Peers' War Memorial (24 February); The Air Force (11 March); a British Sugar Subsidy (19 and 24 March); Protection of Birds (28 March, 7 May); Agricultural Returns (7 May); Performing Animals (14 and 21 May); the British Film Industry (14 May); the Church of Scotland (19 May); Agricultural Wages (23 June); London and Home Counties Electricity (24 and 29 June); Honours:

---

16   Earl Beauchamp's presence was welcomed in various other places. See for example Lord Newton's (Newton, 2nd Baron, b. 1857. A Conservative) letter to Beauchamp, dated 18 December 1925: 'My dear Beauchamp, Winston Churchill (who evidently welcomes the idea) has agreed to receive a deputation on Betting taxation on Tuesday next at 12. ... It is rather short notice, but could you manage to come? Your presence would be very useful, and Churchill would probably want to hear your experience. Please let me know on Friday.' Also: 'Oxford, 30th October 1925. Dear Lord Beauchamp, The Union Society would be extremely gratified if you could see your way to taking part in the presidential debate on November 26th as our principal guest. There will be a Liberal standing against a Conservative and I thought that a motion on the Government's ... programme might afford an excellent debate. ... Even at the Centenary Banquet you were unable to be present on account of illness. I know however that you do visit Oxford for I remember being discomfited by you when I spoke on the question of Imperial Preference when you addressed the New Reform Club on the Fiscal question! I therefore venture to hope very much that you will be able to come on the 26th and of course you will dine with me before the debate. I am asking Mr Davidson, the Civil Lord of Admiralty to speak on the other side. Yours very truly, A. H. E. Molson, President, Oxford Union Society.' Also: 'Buckingham Palace, 24 November 1924: *St George's Chapel Windsor Restoration Fund*. Dear Lord Beauchamp, I have been asked by the Duke of Devonshire to call a Meeting of the Committee at 11 a.m. on Wednesday, December 10th, at Buckingham Palace (Privy Purse Entrance). I trust that this date will be convenient to you. F. H. Mitchell, Hon. Secretary.' Also: '10 Downing Street, Whitehall, 23 November 1927. My dear Lord Beauchamp, Many thanks for your letter. I really must congratulate you on your speech on the subject of the Worcestershire Regiment. It was a very moving tribute and I was extremely glad to have an opportunity of reading it. Yours sincerely, Stanley Baldwin.' Source: Beauchamp Papers, *op. cit.*

Prevention of Abuses (29 June); Former Enemy Aliens (8 July); Fire Brigade
Pensions (9 July); Arable Cultivation (9 July); Claims for Cultivation in
Ireland (15 July); Teachers' Superannuation (21 July); Allotments (22 July);
Summary Jurisdiction (27 July); Contributory Pensions (28 and 31 July);
Sandwich Port and Haven (29 July); Public Health (3 July); the Coal Mining
Industry Dispute (6 August); Army Accounts (25 November); Railway
Administration (26 November); Rating and Valuation (8 December);
Ireland: Confirmation of Agreement (9 December); a Draft Convention
on Slavery (16 December); Education: Scotland (17 December); Horley
Electricity Special Order (21 December). This long list shows us just how
active Earl Beauchamp was.

During the year 1926 Earl Beauchamp addressed the House forty-
five times on: the Address in Reply to the King's Speech (2 February);
the League of Nations (24 February); Agricultural Wages (25 February);
Compulsory Voting (17 March); Land Drainage (18 March); Criminal
Appeal: Scotland (23 and 24 March); Public Health: Smoke Abatement
(22 and 29 April); Ancient Monuments and Historic Buildings (29 April);
the Economy: Miscellaneous Provisions (5 and 11 May); the University of
London (29 June and 8 July); Coal Mines (6 July); Disorder in the House (13
July); Procedure of the House (14 July); the Boards of Guardians: Default
(14 July); Business of the House (15 July); the Mining Industry (29 July);
Adoption of Children (29 July); a Clergy Pensions Measure (3 August
and 2 December); Regulation of Railways (17 November); Lead Paint:
Protection Against Poisoning (18 November); Business of the House (30
November and 1 December); Merchandise Marks: Imported Goods (2
and 13–14 December); Church Measures (8 December); Small Holdings
and Allotments (8 and 13 December); Expiring Laws Continuation (10
December); Judicial Proceedings: Regulation of Reports (13 and 14
December); the Patrington Small Holdings Colony (15 December).

There were thirty interventions during 1927 on the following topics:
Address in Reply to the King's Speech (8 February); Railway Administration
(16 February); House of Lords Procedure (1 March); Business of the
House (8 March); National Expenditure (16 and 22 March); the Second
Ballot (29 March); Tribute to the Late Marquess of Lansdowne (16 June);
Overseas Trade Department (16 June); House of Lords Reform (22 June);

Agriculture (29 June); Trade Disputes and Trade Unions (12–14 July); Empire Marketing Board (18 July); Police: Appeals (20 July); Crown Lands (20 July); Finance Bill (26 July); Protection of Animals (26 July); an Indian Church Measure (28 July); Business of the House (23 November, 5 and 6 December); Cinematograph Films (28 November); Landlord and Tenant (8 December); a Prayer Book Measure (12 December); Nursing Homes Registration (19 and 21 December); Road Transport Lighting (20–21 December).

In 1928 the Earl rose to speak twenty-five times on: the Address in Reply to His Majesty's Most Gracious Speech (7 February); a Tribute to the Late Earl Haig (8 February); Judicial Vacancies (14 February); Export of Sugar Beet Pulp (21 February); the Basle Trading Company (22 February); the Lords and Government Bills (1 March); a Road Fund (6 March); Patents and Designs: Convention (14 March); Irish Free State Civil Servants (25 April and 21 June); Rating and Valuation: Appointment (1 May and 24 July); Petroleum Amendment Bill (17 May and 11 June); Representation of the People: Equal Franchise (21 May); National Health Insurance (7 June); the Deaf and Dumb (18 June); Slums (20 June); Reports Under Merchandise Marks (2 July); Business of the House (17, 26, 30 and 31 July); Marriages: Prohibited degrees of Relationship (23 and 30 July); Finance Bill (31 July).

He rose thirteen times in 1929 in debates on: Select Vestries (2 July); Road Traffic Regulation (11 July); Procedure: Mover's Right to Reply (18 July); Business of the House (18 July, 3 December, 9 December, 12 December and 17–19 December); Empire Free Trade (19 November); Private Members' and Government Bills (5 December); Mental Treatment (10 December).

The Earl almost exhausted his energies, speaking twenty-seven times in 1930. The topics covered: the Optional Clause (29 January); Business of the House (12 February, 8 April, 10 April, 3 June, 16 July and 22 July); Resignation of the Clerk of the Parliaments (27 February and 4 March); a Tribute to the Late Earl of Balfour (20 March); the Royal Fine Art Commission (3 April); Coal Mines (29 April, 15 May and 15 July); Land Drainage (19–20 May and 27 May); a Tribute to the Late Archbishop Lord Davidson of Lambeth (27 May); Hairdressers' and Barbers' Shops (27 May); Work of the Session (4 June); Ministry of Health Provisional Orders (24 June); British North American Bill (2 July); Housing (15 and

21 July); Adoption of Children: Scotland (24 July); Public Works Facilities
(28 July); Finance Bill (29 July).

In 1931, for personal reasons, he was in the House of Lords far less.
But even so, he spoke thirteen times on: a Tribute to the Late Princess
Royal (27 January); Ancient Monuments (3 February); Education: School
Attendance (18 February); British Representation in the Dominions (26
February); Unemployment Insurance (26 February); Agricultural Land
Utilisation (4 March, 22 April and 7 May); Business of the House (19
March); the Chairman of the Committees (21 April and 28–29 April); a
Pharmacy and Poisons Bill (28 April).

In addition, Earl Beauchamp acted as a member of the Special Orders
Committee (21 July 1925); a member of the Select Committee considering
the Gas Light and Coke Company Bill (15 July 1926); and a member of
the Select Committee on the House of Lords Offices (22 February 1927).

Continued correspondence with Lloyd George

As Leader of the Liberal peers in the House of Lords Earl Beauchamp
selected every favourable opportunity to stay in contact with David Lloyd
George: he was unshakeably loyal. Lloyd George responded with equal
cordiality.[17]

1

Earl Beauchamp to Lloyd George

25. 9. 1924

My dear Lloyd George,

I was very much vexed by a misleading report of a speech which I made the other day
at Nuneaton. I, therefore, venture to trouble you with the enclosed cutting from the

---

17   Parliamentary Archives: Lloyd George MSS (correspondence with Beauchamp,
     William Lygon): LG/G/3/5/1–37.

Nuneaton paper which shows how far from adequate was the report in the London papers. The Chairman of the Meeting has also written to me deploring the report and saying of my speech: How this can be construed into an antagonistic attitude being taken up by you to that of Mr Lloyd George and other members of the Liberal Party I am at a loss to understand. Pray do not trouble to answer, and

Believe me,

Yours v. Sincerely,

Beauchamp

2

Lloyd George to Earl Beauchamp

26th September 1924

Dear Lord Beauchamp,

This is merely to acknowledge your letter of September 25th addressed to Mr Lloyd George. He is at present in the country but I am forwarding it on to him by bag to-night.

Yours sincerely,

[Illegible]

3

Earl Beauchamp to Lloyd George

6 XI 24

My dear Lloyd George,

I am ordering a platform wh. will hold 3. for Monday eve.

Yours,

B.

4

Earl Beauchamp to Lloyd George

12 XI 1924

My dear Lloyd George,

I have told Stanmore to let you know that we are threatened with a little difficulty in the House of Lords. Rumour says that Lord Parmour[18] wishes to claim the front opposition bench in view of the fact that they formed the last Government. It is obviously a ridiculous claim especially as they are quite unable to carry out the work if only because of their numbers. I have written to their whip and also to Curzon. After all, these things will be decided in the end by the majority of the House. I do not think that Tories wish to see Parmour at the task.

I trouble you with this letter as I think you ought to know what is going on and think that perhaps you may be able to help us in our fight.

I return to London next week and shall be there until the House meets.

Yours very sincerely,

Beauchamp

5

Lloyd George to Earl Beauchamp

18th November 1924

Dear Lord Beauchamp,

Mr Lloyd George has asked me to thank you for your letter of the 12th.

Lord Stanmore duly reported to Mr Lloyd George that Labour were claiming the Front Opposition Bench and he agrees with you that it is a ridiculous claim. Lord Stanmore was informed by Mr Lloyd George that if necessary he would certainly fight any such claim.

Perhaps you will kindly keep Mr Lloyd George informed on any development.

Yours sincerely,

[Signature illegible]

6

Earl Beauchamp to Lloyd George

18 XII 24

My dear Lloyd George,

18   Lord Parmour, 1st Baron, b. 1852, Socialist. Labour leader in the House of Lords.

A thousand congratulations to you on last night's speech. It just hit the nail on the head!

We owe many thanks to Baldwin! He did much to bring us together last year, & now he makes our path easy again. Preference goes into the background & Protection emerges. This will all help to unite the Party again.

I wish I cd have seen you to talk things over. We are holding our own in the Lords.

Yours very sincerely,

Beauchamp

7

Lloyd George's secretary to Earl Beauchamp

22nd December 1924

Dear Lord Beauchamp,

Mr Lloyd George has asked me to thank you for your letter. He would have liked to have spoken to you personally, but found that you had left town.

Yours faithfully,

[signature illegible]

8

Earl Beauchamp to Lloyd George

Walmer Castle, Kent

23 IX 25

My dear Lloyd George,

Herewith the paper & my friend's letter. You will see that he takes a serious view of it. I wish that you wd take some action on organisation. Indeed you are the only person who can. A promise of money on conditions wd make you master of the situation. Precious time is being lost, & tho' the failure will be more evident next year, the machine ought to be at work now.

You know that I will gladly help.

Yours v. Sincerely,

Beauchamp

9

Earl Beauchamp to Lloyd George

13 Belgrave Square, S.W.1

29 XI 25

My dear Lloyd George,

I am very much distressed & alarmed by what I see in the papers & hear of what is going on in the Party.[19] It looks as if what I did for reunion was in danger again & am quite certain that all through the country Liberals wd look upon it as a disaster. Lord Oxford has not told me anything of what is happening so that my knowledge is small.

Can I not do something? Do pray! let me know if I can be of use. I wd gladly come to see you at yr convenience any time on Monday between 5 & 8, or on Tuesday except from 1.30–3 or from 4–7 p.m. when the H. of Lords will be sitting.

I had hoped to have a chance of speaking to you at the funeral on Fri., but we were separated as we went out.

Yours v. Sincerely,

Beauchamp

10

Earl Beauchamp to Lloyd George

2 XII 25

My dear Lloyd George,

Lord Oxford has not answered my letter but I had a useful talk with Mander this morn. Before he went to his meetings. I am much pleased with what I hear of things this morn. Godfrey Collins told me in the Lobby that he felt sure the N. L. F.[20] wd do nothing foolish this aft. Please do not hesitate to let me know if I can be of service. The chairman's speech at last night's dinner was described to me as a model.

---

19   The reference is to the election of October 1924, when the Liberals suffered devastating losses. The catastrophe exacerbated the split between Asquith – elevated to be Lord Oxford – and his supporters and those loyal to Lloyd George. One of the issues was between free trade and protectionism.

20   The National Liberal Federation (NLF) had remained loyal to Asquith.

At present it seems to me that this opportunity might well be taken to draw the claws of the anti-unity party.

Yours sincerely,

Beauchamp

11

Earl Beauchamp to Lloyd George

13 Belgrave Square, S. W.1

31 1 1926

My dear Lloyd George,

I am just returned this afternoon from Italy where I got a cable asking me to preside at the Land Convention. I accepted at once thinking it better that I should be in the Chair than that it should be by someone opposed to you. I do hope that you will approve of this. May I come and talk to you about it some time on Thursday if that suits you? Morning for choice.

Yours very sincerely,

Beauchamp

P. S. Lady Beauchamp & I are much vexed by the form of card for her party. It was done in my absence by 21 Abingdon St. But I hope to see you tomorrow eve all the same. B.

12

Earl Beauchamp to Lloyd George

Confidential

31 V 26

My dear Lloyd George,

I feel so much bound to secrecy that misunderstanding wd at once arise if I came to see you. Pray forgive me for not keeping the appointment. I am more disturbed than ever. There never was any hope of any meeting, nor any wish for compromise. I was alone.

Yours very sincerely,

Beauchamp

13

Lady Beauchamp to David Lloyd George

Trianon Palace – Versailles

2nd June 1926

Dear Mr Lloyd-George,

I feel moved to write to you from Here – as you have been, & are, continually in my thoughts – I wish you well in yr present gt responsibilities in this momentous crisis.[21] Every evening during our dinner Here, I look up & see yr Name in shining gold letters – wh record all you were enabled to do in that crisis. Then again, in La Galerie des Glaces, au Palais.

What you accomplished then, you will be enabled to accomplish now. It has seemed especially interesting to Me, to be Here during these days, when you are again called to face such difficulties.

Believe Me, to remain,

with best wishes,

Yrs sincerely,

Lettice Beauchamp

P. S. Please may I send many kind messages to Dame Margaret Lloyd-George. L. B.

14

Lloyd George to Countess Beauchamp

25 Old Queen Street,
Westminster,
London, S. W.1

June 9th, 1926

My dear Lady Beauchamp,

I thank you from my heart not merely for the encouraging letter you sent me but even more for the kind thought that prompted you to send it at that trying and worrying moment. It cheered me more than I can express in words.

21   The Liberals were irrevocably divided over the legality of the General Strike which had taken place between 4 and 13 May 1926.

Lord Beauchamp has behaved throughout like the great English Gentleman he is. I wish I could say as much for my other colleagues. I never thought Oxford capable of this kind of thing.

Ever sincerely,

D. Lloyd George

15

Lord Inchcape[22] to Earl Beauchamp

Glenapp Castle
Ballantrae, Ayrshire

1st September 1926

My dear Beauchamp,

I think you know I have never been a politician but I have sat on the Liberal side of the House of Lords since I was made a Peer because I was and am still in favour of Free Trade. But in reading the speech of Mr Lloyd George at Holyhead on 23rd August I find my views so divergent from those of one who is supposed to be the leader or the nominal leader of the Liberal Party I feel compelled to take my seat on the other side. Not that it matters much but I feel I cannot associate myself with the doctrines now promulgated by the Liberal Leader. They are not mine.

Yours sincerely,

Inchcape

16

Earl Beauchamp to Lloyd George – forwarding on a letter from Lord Inchcape

3 IX 26

My dear Lloyd George,

I think you ought to see the enclo. at once. He has never been much use to us in the Lords, so that it won't really make much difference. But I can't think what there was to object to in yr speech. I shd – if present – have cheered loudly all through.

Yours v. sincerely,

Beauchamp

22   Inchcape of Strathnaver, 1st Viscount, b. 1852. A Liberal.

17

Lloyd George's secretary to Earl Beauchamp

6th September 1926

Dear Lord Beauchamp,

Mr Lloyd George asked me to acknowledge with many thanks your kind letter to him of September 3rd with the enclosure from Lord Inchcape. Mr Lloyd George quite agrees with you when you say that you are unable to appreciate what there was to object to in his speech at Holyhead.

Yours sincerely,

[illegible]

18

Earl Beauchamp to Lloyd George

27 V 27

My dear Lloyd George,

Just a line to thank you for the enquiries & kind messages you have been so good in sending. I escape to Walmer on Monday & return to London for the Land & Nature meeting on the 14th by wh time I shall be as well as ever & all the better for the rest.

Let me congratulate you on the way things are going now & on yr speeches. Each one emphasises yr position as the only Leader of the Party.

Yours very sincerely,

Beauchamp

19

Lord Elmley Beauchamp to David Lloyd George

20/6/27

Dear Mr Lloyd-George,

As you probably know, my Father recently underwent an operation. Though he has recovered, he has been left very much pulled down, & we are very anxious that he should get right away & travel for two or three months.

Therefore, I'm venturing to write to you as his Leader, & ask you to suggest such a course to him next time you see him, because we are afraid that the good which the operation & the rest did him will be undone if he goes on working as hard as he is now. I write with the full approval of my Mother, who would be very glad to see you in London when you are next there, & explain matters more clearly to you.

Your sincerely,

Elmley

P. S. It has occurred to me that there might be some Liberal Mission to U. S. A, or elsewhere, which he might possibly undertake. E.

20

Lloyd George's secretary to Rt Hon. Viscount Elmley, Walmer Castle, Kent

23rd June 1927

Dear Lord Elmley,

Mr Lloyd George asks me to thank you for your private letter of June 20th. When Mr Lloyd George had the pleasure of seeing Lord Beauchamp in his room at the House of Commons he tried to get a chance to make the point you suggested, but the room was full of other people and he did not have an opportunity to do so. Mr Lloyd George is hoping, however, to see Lord Beauchamp again next week and he will then try to seize an opportunity.

Mr Lloyd George hears from all sides splendid reports of the first rate speech which Lord Beauchamp delivered in the House of Lords yesterday.

Yours sincerely,

[Lloyd George's secretary]

21

Lloyd George to Earl Beauchamp

7th September 1927

Dear Lord Beauchamp,

Mr Lloyd George asked me to let you know how sorry he was that he could not be at the Executive Meeting this afternoon as he had an appointment out of town which it was essential he should keep. He asked me, however, to let you know that, after reading the documents which you will have before you at this afternoon's meeting, he hopes very much that nothing will be published in a hurry in spite of all that was said yesterday. There are some aspects presented in these memoranda which Mr Lloyd George feels will have to be considered very carefully. For instance, there is the bitter attack upon the Farmers' Union in the paper on Marketing, which he thinks is extremely unwise coming as it does at a time when the Farmers' Union is actually doing our work in attacking the Government. All this will be pabulum for the Tories and it is quite unnecessary to do it.

Then there is another point about setting up a Board consisting of men at £5,000 a year which Mr Lloyd George considers is a mistake. That will be fastened upon by all the Tories as an illustration of the creation of fresh officials at high salaries.

There is the further point with regard to income tax that Mr Lloyd George is definitely against.

He suggests that if the meeting is so inclined they might approve the proposals in part, but they should be referred to, say, yourself, Sir Francis Acland and Mr Lloyd George to be gone through fully before anything is published.

Yours sincerely,

A. F. S.

22

Earl Beauchamp to Lloyd George

19 VI 28

My dear Lloyd George,

I have been to the N. L. C. [National Liberal Club] where we thought of Allendale[23] as a possible Chairman. Gilpin who is a Vice-chairman returns from the [illegible] next week & will be consulted at once. If he agrees I think we might get the whole thing settled during the holidays. It wd be a good solution altho' A. is not at present a member of the Club, but that can easily be put right. I think you will agree that this is a possible solution.

Yours v. Sincerely,

Beauchamp

23

Earl Beauchamp to Lloyd George

26 XII 1929

23   Allendale, 2nd Viscount, b. 1890. A Liberal.

My dear Lloyd George,

The Midland Liberal Federation meets on 11th January and I want very much to know what you think should be said about the votes of Mander and Edge on the Coal Bill. I need not remind you that at the last election the division amongst ourselves was the most damaging thing against us, and here it is again. They are both of them members of the Federation and Mander indeed was chairman until he was elected to Parliament. Elmley tells me that he is in rather close touch with Trevelyan and some of the other Labour people. Personally, I do deplore tremendously this division in our ranks which will once more give the enemy an opportunity to mock. Ramsay Muir is our chief orator and we have a double function – first there is a private lunch with speeches (not reported) and then the Annual Meeting later. At one or other of these occasions something might be said by Ramsay Muir or me if you think well.

Christmas Day was wretched yesterday with a gale blowing all the time. To-day, however, is better.

Yours very sincerely,

Beauchamp

24

Earl Beauchamp to Lloyd George

With all good wishes for Christmas & the New Year. 1929. B.

[Enclosed is a photo of Beauchamp in his University of London Chancellor's robe.][24]

25

Earl Beauchamp to Lloyd George

3rd January 1930

Both Edge and Mander behaved very stupidly. Edge, having regard to the fact that he is the Second Whip of the Party, behaved in defiance of all tradition and there is no doubt at all it will weaken his authority in future.

It would be desirable to say something in general terms about the importance of the Party acting together once it comes to a decision on important issues, but I am doubtful whether it would be wise at this stage to single out by name the Coal Mines recalcitrants. I think an appeal from you for unity and co-operation will have a great effect especially as you are likely to get a good response from the audience.

24 See Chapter 19.

The power and influence of the Party in this House will depend upon its cohesion. It does not matter how well we do in Debate if in the Division Lobby we are divided into fragments.

Wishing you all a very Happy New Year,

Ever sincerely,

Beauchamp

26

Earl Beauchamp to Lloyd George

21 I 30

My dear Lloyd George,

How wise of you & clever – as usual – to treat Grey so.[25] He will dislike it far more than anything else & will write under yr reproach that he had no good word to say for those who were doing the work of the Party.

Last night & again here there is nothing but praise of yr speech. Really I think the way to treat him is as a naughty little boy who wants spanking.

The function here was funereal. Fog hardly dissipated by a ghastly blue light. Black coats did nothing to relieve the appearance of the Gallery. However the loud speakers obscured the King's accent. I fled before the five speakers & five interpreters.

Yours very sincerely,

Beauchamp

27

Earl Beauchamp to A. J. Sylvester[26]

I VII 30

Dear Sylvester,

25 In a speech at the National Liberal Club, Lloyd George had rebuffed criticisms made of him by Lord Grey of Falloden. Reckoning that cooperation between the different Liberal factions was now impossible, he had recommended independent action for his own group.

26 Albert James Sylvester, b. 1889; Principal Private Secretary to Lloyd George from 1923 on.

I have come across a most interesting little pamphlet called *German Agriculture* by J. Dunlop. It bears out everything said in the Liberal Land Enquiries & seems to me so good that Mr. Lloyd George might like to read it – if it has not yet reached him. I do hope he is recovering from his chill.

His speech on Saturday – as usual – met with my admiration. Baldwin is a bubble & he ought to be pricked. No one can do it better.

Yours v. sincerely,

Beauchamp

28

Earl Beauchamp to Lloyd George

19 VII 30

My dear Lloyd George,

If you can spare the time, I shd be glad to see you & say good-bye before starting off on Aug. 1.

The House of Lords has been rather dull – but Mersey[27] has promised to help Stanmore in whipping.

Unfortunately when we do send out a whip, a number – usually away – come down & vote against us!

I am very glad to see Gwillim[28] is better.

Yours v. Sincerely,

Beauchamp

29

A. J. Sylvester to Earl Beauchamp

22nd July 1930

My dear Beauchamp,

---

27   Mersey, 1st Viscount, b. 1840. A Unionist.
28   Later 1st Viscount Tenby.

This is merely to acknowledge your letter to Mr. Lloyd George of the 19th July, and to say that he is just leaving for Wales, and when he returns he will fix an appointment with you.

Yours sincerely,

A. J. S

30

A. J. Sylvester to Earl Beauchamp

9th March 1931

Private and confidential

Dear Lord Beauchamp,

Mr Lloyd George is desirous of having a discussion on the subject of the organisation of a Liberal Speaking Campaign and also as to any deficiencies in our machinery which may be considered to have been revealed by the recent by-elections.

Mr Lloyd George would, therefore, be glad if you could make it convenient to attend a meeting at the above address on next Wednesday week, March 18th, at 11.30 a.m.

Yours sincerely,

A. J. S.

31

Earl Beauchamp to A. J. Sylvester

10.3.1931

Dear Sylvester,

I hope to be with you on the 18th at 11.30 a.m.

Yours sincerely,

Beauchamp

While Earl Beauchamp was successfully attending to his duties in the House of Lords he was soon to attain another mark of distinction. He was elected Chancellor of the University of London.

Chancellor of the University of London

The chancellorship of the University of London has been the domain of eminent British statesmen. More recently, however, members of the royal family have also been elected as Chancellors. The first Chancellor was Sir William Cavendish, 7th Duke of Devonshire (1836–56). He was followed by Granville George-Leveson Gower, 2nd Earl of Granville (1856–91), Edward Henry Stanley, 15th Earl of Derby (1891–3), Farrer Herschell, 1st Baron Herschell (1893–99), John Wodehouse, 1st Earl of Kimberley (1899–1902), and Archibald Philip Primrose, 5th Earl of Rosebery & 1st Earl of Midlothian (1902–29). Rosebery died in May 1929, and Earl Beauchamp was elected as the next Chancellor. The role of the Chancellor is largely ceremonial. He is required to attend conferment of degrees, and other ceremonies of the colleges and institutes of the university.

Election and installation

The election and the installation of the Chancellor is of particular inter-est. We document below the course of this event with regard to Earl Beauchamp.[1]

---

1   Source: Senate House Library Archives, University of London. File – 05591: 1120 (AL 366); 1121 (UoL/VP 1/4); 1123 (UoL/CF 1/30/1502); 1124 (UoL/CF 1/31/1502); 1125 (UoL/CN/4/8/1).

University of London
Deed of Appointment of the Chancellor

KNOW all Men by these Presents that in accordance with the Statutes for this purpose made and provided by the Commissioners appointed under the University of London Act 1926, We, the Convocation of the said University, at a meeting duly convened and holden on the eighth day of October in the year of our Lord nineteen hundred and twenty nine, the office of Chancellor then being vacant by the death on the twentieth day of May last of the Right Honourable the Earl of Rosebery and Midlothian, K. G., did, on the nomination of Sir Thomas Gregory Foster, B. A., Ph.D. (Vice-Chancellor), Sir William Henry Beveridge, K. C. B., M. A., B. C. L., LL. D., Sir William Job Collins, K. C. V. O., M. D., M. S., B. Sc., Rev. Canon John Albert Douglas, B. D., B. A., Ph. D., Prof. Louis Napoleon George Filon, M. A., D. Sc., F. R. S., Dame Helen Charlotte Isabella Gwynne-Vaughan, G. B. E., D. Sc., LL. D., Rev. John Scott Lidgett, M. A., D. D., Ernest Gordon Graham Little, M. D., B. A., M. P., Sir Philip Magnus, Bart., B. A., B. Sc., and Thomas Franklin Silby, D. Sc., duly elect

The Right Honourable
SIR WILLIAM LYGON, EARL BEAUCHAMP, K. G., K. C. M. G., P. C.

to be the Chancellor of the University.

Given at our Meeting of Convocation holden this eighth day of October in the year of our Lord nineteen hundred and twenty nine.

In witness whereof the Common Seal of the University has been affixed in the Presence of

S. L. Loney, Chairman of Convocation.

[Signature illegible], Clerk of Convention.

Harold Claughton, Secretary to the Senate.

Declaration of Election of Chancellor

I, SIDNEY LUXTON LONEY, Bachelor of Arts of the University of London and Master of Arts of the University of Cambridge, Chairman of Convocation of the University of London, hereby declare that at a meeting of Convocation of the University duly convened and holden at the University Building South Kensington on the eighth day of October in the year of our Lord nineteen hundred and twenty nine the Right Honourable

SIR WILLIAM LYGON, EARL BEAUCHAMP
Knight of the Most Noble Order of the Garter
and a member of his Majesty's most honourable Privy Council,

was, upon the proposal of ten members of Convocation in accordance with the Statutes and Standing Orders made and provided for the purpose of such elections, duly elected to be Chancellor of the University in place of the Right Honourable the Earl of Rosebery and Midlothian, lately deceased. I therefore by Authority of Convocation and on behalf of the whole University duly admit him, the said Right Honourable

SIR WILLIAM LYGON, EARL BEAUCHAMP

to the said office and all its rights and privileges.

Earl Beauchamp made a special request concerning the style of the oath.

Earl Beauchamp to Dr Deller

13, Belgrave Square, S. W. 1

18 XI 29

My dear Principal,

If I am too late pray tear this up. But happening to see the speech of the Public Orator, I thought he might like to call me 'de Bello Campo' – a title wh goes back at any rate to 1120 in a Latin document of that period. Beauchamp sounds odd in Latin, especially when there is authority for the other wh has never died out in the family & wh connects up with the motto: 'Fortuna mea in bello campo'.

My lot has fallen unto me in a fair ground. Rather a pretty pun.

But this is probably too late.

Yours sincerely,

Beauchamp

Don't answer!

B.

His wish was observed:

Dr Deller to Earl Beauchamp

19 November 1929

Dear Chancellor,

There was just time, and 'Bello Campo' it shall be.

Yours sincerely

[signature]

The Vice Chancellor addressed the following invitation to the guests invited to attend the ceremony:

The Vice Chancellor
requests the honour of your Company
at Dinner, on Friday the 22nd of November, 1929,
at 6.45 for 7 p. m. in the
University Building, South Kensington.
To meet The Chancellor of the University,
The Right Honourable the Earl Beauchamp, K. G., K. C. M. G., P. C.
Decorations.
Please reply forthwith
to The Vice Chancellor,
The University of London, South Kensington, S. W. 7

The installation was conducted with great ceremony.

Installation of the Chancellor
The Right Hon.
Sir William Lygon, Earl Beauchamp,
K. G., K. C. M. G., P. C.,
In The
Great Hall, South Kensington,
22nd November, 1929.

Order of Proceedings

While the guests and members of the University are assembling, the Orchestra, under the Direction of Dr P. C. Buck (Mus. Doc.), King Edward Professor of Music in the University, will play a selection of music.

9 p.m. The following Procession will enter the Hall:

Deans of Faculties
Members of Senate
Members of Court
The Principal – The Public Orator
The Chairman of Convocation – The Chairman of Court
Esquire Bedell

Vice-Chancellor

The Vice-Chancellor

My Lords, Ladies and Gentlemen – We are assembled and gathered together for the installation of the Chancellor and for the conferment on him of the Honorary Degree of Doctor of Literature.

I invite the Chairman of Convocation to read the Deed announcing his election which has been duly sealed by order of the Senate.

University of London
Deed of Appointment of the Chancellor

Know all Men by these Presents that in accordance with the Statutes for this purpose made and provided by the Commissioners appointed under the University of London Act, 1926, We, the Convocation of the said University, at a meeting duly convened and holden on the eighth day of October in the year of our Lord nineteen hundred and twenty nine, the office of Chancellor then being vacant by the death on the twentieth day of May last of the Right Honourable the Earl of Rosebery and Midlothian, K. G. did duly elect

The Right Honourable
SIR WILLIAM LYGON, EARL BEAUCHAMP, K. G., K. C. M. G., P. C.
to be the Chancellor of the University.

The Vice-Chancellor

I request the Chairman of Convocation, accompanied by the Clerk of Convocation and the Esquire Bedell, to conduct the Chancellor to the Hall.

A Fanfare of Trumpets will be sounded as the Chancellor enters the Hall.

The Chairman of Convocation

Mr Vice-Chancellor, I have the honour to present to you, for Installation, the Chancellor, The Right Honourable Sir William Lygon, Earl Beauchamp, K .G., K. C. M. G., P. C., who has been duly elected by Convocation in accordance with the Statutes of the University.

The Vice-Chancellor

My Lord – The Deed of Election appointing you Chancellor of the University of London has been read by the Chairman of Convocation.

On behalf of the University, I accordingly install you, Sir William Lygon, Earl Beauchamp, Knight of the Most Noble Order of the Garter, Knight Commander of the Most Distinguished Order of Saint Michael and Saint George, Member of His Majesty's Most Honourable Privy Council, as Chancellor of the University of London: I invite you to take the Chair which I now vacate.

A Fanfare of Trumpets will then be sounded.

The Vice-Chancellor

My Lord – You have been elected Chancellor by the unanimous vote of Convocation in succession to the late Earl of Rosebery, who had held the office since 1902, whose memory will ever be kept in honour and in affection in this University.

On behalf of the University as a whole it falls to me to convey to you a warm welcome and to express to you the great satisfaction of the University at your election.

Your tenure of the great office of Chancellor begins at a time of changes when the Statutes, sealed on 21st March last by Our Visitor – His Majesty the King in Council – are in process of being carried into effect. It is our hope that the new constitution will promote the unity and effectiveness of the University for the great purposes set forth in Statute 4, which is as follows:

'The purposes of the University are to hold forth to all classes and denominations, both in the United Kingdom and elsewhere, without any distinction whatsoever, an encouragement for pursuing a regular and liberal course of education; to promote research and the advancement of science and learning; and to organise, improve and extend education of a University standard.'

It is my duty to invite you at all times and seasons to uphold and defend the privileges and rights of our University.

The Chancellor

I, Sir William Lygon, Earl Beauchamp, hereby declare that I will at all times and seasons fulfil the duties of Chancellor as required by the Statutes of the University, and will loyally uphold and maintain the privileges and rights of our University and will endeavour to promote the great purposes for which our University exists.

The Vice-Chancellor

It is the desire of the Senate that there shall be conferred upon you the Degree of *Doctor of Literature, honoris causa.*

I invite the Public Orator to present you for the Degree.

The Public Orator

Quoniam Vniuersitatis Londinensis Graduatis Conuocatis Cancellarium eligere placuit, Gulielmum Lygon Comitem de Bello Campo, Equitem nobilissimi ordinis Garterii, cursu honorum amplissimo insignem, antiquissimae Australiae prouinciae quondam Proconsulem, Consilii Regii olim Praesidem, quinque Portuum Custodem, eundem Senatus Vniuersitatis decreuit summo academico honore decorandum et ad gradum Doctoris Litterarum honoris causa accipiendum.

Duco, igitur, ad te, Domine Procancellarie, virum optime de patria meritum, quem Vniuersitati speramus felicissime praefuturum, ut in numerum Graduatorum, auctoritate tibi a Seantu commissa, rite admittas.

The Vice-Chancellor

By the authority of the Senate I confer upon you the Degree of *Doctor of Literature, honoris causa.*

The Chancellor will reply.

Mr Leyland White will sing:

(i) Concinamus, O Sodales
(ii) The University Song
(iii) God Save the King

Guests and members of the University are asked to sing in unison the chorus of the two songs and 'God Save the King'.

The rest of the evening will be informal during which there will be incidental music under the direction of Dr P. C. Buck (Mus. Doc.).

Concinamus, O Sodales

By A. H. Cruickshank
Music by J. C. Bridge

Concinamus, O sodales,
Vias ite triumphales
Novo Cancellario
Doctus clarus sancta vita
Dignus est quem exquisita
Ducat acclamatio.

Doctores et discentes
Tibi adsunt, dux, faventes

Tam iustae gloriae;
Io, io, canemus
Quos pila, quosque remus
Iuvant, quos litterae.

Triplex Almae Matris forma
Sed cor unum una norma
Diem celebrantium.
Hinc sit aetas fortunata,
Sint piorum vota rata
Erga nostrum Studium.
Doctores et discentes, etc.

University Song

Poem by John Drinkwater
Music by John Ireland

Pilgrims from many paths we came
To where the roads of Empire meet,
Our lives to kindle at the flame
Of Schools wherein a million feet
Have trod the years, or with a fame
That yet along the years shall beat.
O London maids and London men
Bring in the golden age again.

In no seclusion pastur'd round
As where the Cam and Isis flow,
Our cloister'd learning have we found,
Where loud the tides of traffic go.
Our nightingales have been the sound
Of London bells from Fleet to Bow.
O London maids and London men
Bring in the golden age again.

Life calls us, and we bid farewell
To this the latest of our springs,
But on our travels we will tell
How fellowship of gentle things
Is kept for ever where they dwell
Who know the song that England sings.
O London maids and London men
Bring in the golden age again.

In field or market-place or mill,
Beneath a dear or alien Sun,
We'll build a generation still
Of faith and honour here begun,
That sires of the old English will
Shall know their own and cry: Well done!
O London maids and London men
Bring in the golden age again.

Programme of music given by Students of Trinity College of Music, under the direction of Dr P. C. Buck, Mus. Doc., King Edward Professor of Music in the University

Overture 'Prometheus' *Beethoven*
March 'Imperial March' (Vice-Chancellor's Procession) *Elgar*
Scherzo 'Midsummer Night's Dream' *Mendelssohn*
Fantasia 'Die Meistersinger' *Wagner*
Two Hungarian Dances *Brahms*
'Molly on the shore' *Grainger*
Minuet from 'London' Symphony *Haydn*
First Selection from Operas *Sullivan*
Cortège de Noces from 'Coq d'Or' *Rimsky-Korsakoff*
God Save the King

Earl Beauchamp's interest in the University

That Earl Beauchamp fully intended to fulfil his duties as the Chancellor of the University we learn from the following correspondence:

I

Earl Beauchamp to Sir Gregory Foster, Acting Principal

Madresfield Court,
Gt Malvern

12 X 1929

My dear Sir Gregory,

You will not I hope think that I have become King's Stork writing so soon after my formal appointment. But Parliament is meeting on 29th October and I shall only be in London next week before that happens. Would it be convenient for me to see round the rooms at the Imperial Institute on Wednesday or Thursday morning next? I do not want to trouble you but perhaps Dr Hurd could spare the time to show me over. I expect to reach London late on Tuesday night after Quarter Sessions are over at Gloucester.

Yours sincerely,

Beauchamp

2

Earl Beauchamp to Dr Deller

Madresfield Court,
Gt Malvern

29 XI 1929

My dear Principal,

Many thanks for your letter. I will duly come as you suggest but hope to see the staff and students in their Academic costume. It will certainly make the scene a brighter one. One ought to go gradually in this matter and find out what other people prefer.

Yours sincerely,

Beauchamp

Other business

In addition to the Chancellor's responsibilities, Beauchamp had various other duties to attend to. The following correspondence, especially with Lord Reading,[2] guides us as to what these were:

2   Rufus Daniel Isaacs, 1st Marquess of Reading (1860–1935), Solicitor General, 1910;
     Attorney General, 1910–13; Lord Chief Justice, 1913–21; Viceroy of India, 1921–6;
     Secretary of State for Foreign Affairs and Leader of the House of Lords, 1931.

1

Earl Beauchamp to the Marquess of Reading[3]

5 VII 28

My dear Reading

I have to go down home to prepare a welcome for H. R. H of Gloucester on Thurs. 12th next.

Cd you very kindly be here [in the House of Lords] that aft. in my place? The business is likely to be over I think quite soon tho' the Chancellor has a Bill on Northern Ireland.

I wd not trouble you but that Buxton is not in London. It wd be very kind of you if you cd come. As you know, I never trust the Tories & if we have no one here, some important matter is sure to arise.

I see Lady Reading is back & hope she feels some benefit from her visit to Berlin.

I doubt if H. R. H of Gloucester will excite more attention in that City than Mrs Pace!

Yours very sincerely,

Beauchamp

2

Earl Beauchamp to the Marquess of Reading

Madresfield Court,
Gt Malvern

9 X 1929

My dear Reading,

I hope that you got some message to you through Erleigh and Lady Erleigh, saying how sorry we were not to see you at Deal during the summer and how still more sorry we were for the cause.

3   Source: The British Library: MSS Eur F118/3/3–22: 1928–1931 [Title: Beauchamp, William Lygon, 7th Earl]. Personal and semi-official papers of 1st Marquess of Reading.

I should not trouble you now but for the enclosed letter. I am not anxious to go to London next week though I expect to be there for a few hours tomorrow afternoon. I do not know whether you think it even a good thing to see these people.

Pray forgive me for troubling you, and

Believe me,

Yours very sincerely,

Beauchamp

[Enclosure]

3

Sir Arthur Crossfield to Lord Beauchamp

41, West Hill,
Highgate, N.

7th October 1929

My dear Beauchamp,

You may possibly have seen in the papers some reference to the arrival in England 10 days ago of a Delegation from Cyprus. They have come to plead for a Union of Cyprus with Greece. As four-fifths of the population of the Island are Greek and ardently desire a re-union with the Motherland, I have little doubt that your sympathies in this matter will be with the Islanders, and I think that if some day you had time to meet the Delegation and discuss the whole position with them, you would probably then feel the more strongly in favour of a policy that would be so in accord and in keeping with that policy Gladstone adopted when he brought about the cession of the Ionian Islands to Greece.

During the years 1919–1921 a concentrated effort was made to get the re-union carried out, and perhaps I may add confidentially that for reasons I will mention when we next meet, I have really no doubt that but for a certain election in Greece in the late Autumn of 1920, and the overthrow of the Coalition here in 1922, the Union of Cyprus with Greece would have been an accomplished fact years ago.

At different times during the years 1920 and 1921 I wrote to the then *Westminster Gazette* and to the *Manchester Guardian* and in some other ways took a hand in the movement for re-union. Perhaps that is why the Delegation came out here to see me the other day. We had a long discussion and it was agreed that the Delegation should first seek an interview with Lord Passfield[4] and afterwards – with the Colonial Secretary's assent and approval – with the Foreign Secretary.

It was suggested that it might then be advisable for the Delegation to endeavour to see Snowden as acting-Prime Minister, Baldwin and Lloyd George as the respective leaders of the Conservative and Liberal parties, and Churchill on his return from abroad.

Special hope was expressed during the Conference here that you might be able to spare time for an interview with the Delegates and should you see your way to that, and favour the policy of re-union, perhaps you would also advise the Delegation to endeavour to arrange an interview with Lord Reading as well.

I will not trespass on your time with a longer letter on the matter at this moment, but I will report to you some further information very shortly and then I would very gladly bring the Delegation to see you at some time convenient to yourself – say for instance some day next week if you were likely to be available then and could kindly give me a choice of dates.

The Delegation will be remaining in England until some time after the Prime Minister's return from America – of course in the hope that more at his leisure Mr McDonald [sic] may be able to give the Cyprian question his consideration.

Yours sincerely,

[signature]

4

Lord Reading's Private Secretary to J. Wilson Tylor

May Thirteenth, 1930

J. Wilson Taylor Esq.,
The Pilgrims
Hotel Victoria. W. C. 2

Dear Mr Wilson Taylor,

Lord Reading has asked me to write and inform you that Lord Beauchamp is anxious to become a Member of the Pilgrims. I understand he is shortly going over to America and imagine that Membership in England is identical with Membership in the United States. Would you kindly let me know if this is so.

4   Passfield, 1st Baron, b. 1859; a Socialist.

In the event of Lord Beauchamp requiring a proposal, Lord Reading would of course be only too pleased to act as such.

Yours truly,

Private Secretary

5

Sir Arthur Crosfield to the Marqess of Reading

41, West Hill, Highgate. N.

26th May 1930

Most Hon. the Marquis of Reading, K. C. B., K. C. V. O., P. C.
32 Curzon Street, W. 1

My dear Reading,

The other day I suggested to Beauchamp that it might be worth his while to join the 'Pilgrims'. He readily agreed, and I mentioned the matter to the Secretary and intended writing to you to ask if you would kindly propose Beauchamp for membership and let me second your nomination. Wilson Taylor, the Secretary, has, it seems, anticipated me, and I hear you have kindly agreed to do this. I therefore enclose the form of nomination. I have filled in my signature as seconder, and perhaps you won't mind filling in your own name and having the form returned to the Honorary Secretary, addressed, as you will see, to the Pilgrims, Hotel Victoria, W. C. 2.

I hope before long we may be seeing you out at Highgate, which looks its best at this time of the year.

I don't know whether you are lunching out now, but we have some friends coming here to lunch on the 11th, and Domini asked me to say how delighted we should be if you felt inclined to join us then at 1.15.

Vy sincerely yours

A. Crosfield

6

Lord Reading to Sir Arthur Crosfield

May Twenty-seventh, 1930

My dear Corsfield,

Many thanks for your Letter.

I have filled in and forwarded the form to Wilson Taylor.

It is very good of you to ask me to lunch on the 11th and I should have liked to have come had it not been for the fact that I have to attend a Board Meeting which prevents my accepting.

Yours sincerely,

[Reading]

7

Lord Reading's Private Secretary to J. Wilson Taylor

May Twenty-seventh, 1930

Dear Mr Wilson Taylor,

I enclose herewith the nomination form for Lord Beauchamp.

Yours very truly,

Private Secretary

8

J. Wilson Taylor to the Marquess of Reading

The Pilgrims
Hotel Victoria, W. C. 2.

President: Filed Marshal H. R. H. The Duke of Connaught, K. G.
Chairman: The Rt Hon. The Earl of Derby, K. G.
Vice-Chairman: The Rt Hon. Lord Hewart, P. C (Lord Chief Justice of England)

28th May/30

Dear Sir,

I beg to acknowledge and thank you for your letter in support of the candidature of The Earl of Beauchamp, K. G., which I will place before the Committee when his name comes up for consideration.

Believe me,

Yours faithfully,

J. Wilson Taylor

Hon. Secretary

9

Earl Beauchamp to Lord Reading

British Embassy,
Washington

19 XII 30

My dear Reading,

The papers tell me that the House meets again on Jan. 20, & I am arranging to reach London on the 19th (Southampton 18th) I shall be able to thank you in person for yr kindness in looking after the Liberal Peers these last two months.

This house is fine & spacious with marble halls & a great portico wh is never used! But it looks more magnificent than its predecessor.

You know how deceptive cables can be, but it looks as if L. G. had accomplished a most useful task in persuading the govt. to adopt the A. V.

I do hope that so good a habit as regular attendance in the House will not be dropped!

With every good wish,

Yours sincerely,

Beauchamp

Revisiting Australia

One of the responsibilities of a university Chancellor is to pay ceremonial visits to various countries. Soon after his election Earl Beauchamp set upon an official tour of Australia as Chancellor of London University. Australians well remembered him from the days when he came as Governor of New South Wales. The Chancellor was given a hearty reception everywhere he went. And there were still old friends whom he gladly met:

Earl Beauchamp to the Marquess of Reading

R.M.S. *Niagara*
Off Vancouver

4 XII 30

No answer

My dear Reading,

I expect to leave New York about the middle of January & to be back in London on Tu. the 26th – hoping that the House does not meet before that day. I have often thought with gratitude of your kindness meanwhile & hoped it was not a constant or great nuisance to you, especially as the Round Table Conference has been added to yr other work.

My time in Sydney was delightful. I enjoyed every moment of it & found myself welcomed & entertained almost as Royalty. Every sort & kind of person – the gov. & the P. M., the Lord Mayor & the C. J. Business men & artists gave me functions. Sydney is a most amusing place now-a-days & Australia is in an interesting condition. [Sir Otto] Niemeyer is on board this boat & you will no doubt see him soon. The financial position seems to me particularly bad because there are so many people out there who want repudiation & are working for it – behind the backs of Saellin (?) & of Lang.

My plans are San Francisco, Washington, New York (Pilgrims alas!) Harvard & so home.

Once more a thousand thanks & all the wishes of the Season.

Yours very sincerely,

Beauchamp

A file that recorded Beauchamp's visit to Australia has disappeared from the London University archives, so it is not possible to narrate in detail his exact itinerary.

After Beauchamp's arrival back in London, he had little time to meet the Chancellor's obligations. Unforeseen circumstances awaited him. His vivacious and lucrative life came to a sudden end. He was thrown into a state of torment.

CHAPTER 20

Divorce

On 14 May 1931 Lady Beauchamp filed a petition for divorce: that by reason of the conduct of her husband, Earl Beauchamp, the petitioner had 'suffered acute mental agony and misery and her health was undermined'. Earl Beauchamp was accused of being a homosexual, the details of which were specified in the petition. That Earl Beauchamp cherished intimate contact with young men was no secret among his close friends. He very seldom had a permanent lover. It was mere sexual lust that drove him to make physical love to men. But it disturbed nobody. His children did not care about their father's sexual preferences, nor did his political allies worry themselves.[1] Even his own wife, Lettice, had been aware of it for a long time. Years later she confessed to this in a letter to her daughter, Dorothy. 'Now you should know,' she wrote, 'that for many years, I had strongly suspected that [with Daddy] all was not as it shld be and that one side of his life and desires went contrary to everything that is Natural. It was for your sake, when you were all very young, I deliberately refrained, thro' many years of anguish, from converting my suspicions into actual knowledge, but, as I once told Daddy, there were times when I welcomed the sufferings of illness, so as to escape from my great agony of mind.'[2] We do not doubt the agony of mind that Lady Lettice must have suffered. But why should this agony have taken so radical a shape in 1931? Earl Beauchamp's conduct

---

1 But of course you could find people in society who raised their fingers out of pure malicious pleasure, or owed their proclivity to what A. L. Rowse sensibly calls 'absurd Victorian prudery'. See his fascinating work, *Homosexuals in History* (USA: Dorset Press, 1983), p. 126. Rowse has made an extraordinary study of many distinguished people, who were homo-erotic, and shows that there was nothing unnatural about it nor were these people in any way eccentric.

2 Quoted in Jane Mulvagh, *Madresfield, op. cit.*, pp. 396–7.

had not changed. But Lady Lettice's 'agony' had. Why? We have to look for an answer somewhere else. It is not that Lady Lettice suffered more in 1931 from what she thought was her husband's unnatural conduct. She was simply forced to file the petition. And the person who exerted strong pressure upon her was her own brother, the degenerate playboy, the 2nd Duke of Westminster. The Duke did so, because he was pathologically jealous of his brother-in-law and desired to destroy him. Extreme jealousy does lead to a state of mind tending to the exercise of cruelty upon others. The Duke may have inherited a deranged mind from epileptic ancestry. He also inherited vast riches, which enabled him to gratify his licentious appetite and to seduce women whom he met. He procured the means of perversion and blackmail by practising bribery. What then was the source of this jealousy?

With particular splendour, Earl Beauchamp had established himself in high society, in high politics, and in high church circles. He had won the affection and respect of royalty (the Earl had carried the Sword of State[3] at the coronation of the King George V). He often hosted members of the great families of the English aristocracy. He appeared at official receptions wearing the Garter ribbon. He occupied ancient offices of state and had lately had the chancellorship of a distinguished university conferred on

---

3   The Sword of State, the insignia of royalty used at coronations, symbolizes the power of the monarch to use the might of the State against its enemies, and thus to preserve right and peace. It is a high privilege to carry this sword. Earl Beauchamp was thought to be the deserving candidate. He also had a good knowledge of Coronation arrangements. Sir Almeric Fitzroy, clerk of the privy council from 1898, recorded this on 18 March 1911: 'I received from the Archbishop the draft of the Order of Service for the Coronation. Most of the changes are improvements, but the net result will not shorten the Office. The Archbishop found it comic that the instruction to abridge the service was reiterated time after time, a procedure which, if followed, would by this time have whittled the service away. I told him in reply, that the injunction was intended as a warning against prolixity. I sent a copy to Beauchamp, who is the only member of the Committee qualified to express an opinion upon such matters, and from him some interesting and erudite comments, on the whole favourable to the alterations.' See Almeric Fitzroy, *Memoirs*, vol. II (London: Hutchinson, no date), p. 440.

him. He had proved an important member of the House of Lords, where his frequent interventions were welcomed and appreciated both by the front benches and by the Lords opposite. When Lloyd George learnt that Beauchamp might be temporarily absent from the Lords, he at once wrote to the Earl that his partial retirement 'from the very hard work you have done for us will be a real loss to the Party', and that 'we have come to rely so much upon your ready and very effective help in all our difficulties, that we shall miss it more than I can tell you ...'[4] Further to that, Beauchamp had three sons, and the Duke had no successor.

The Duke, by contrast, was a person of no importance. True, he was the richest man in England; he owned elegant houses, race horses and expensive motor-boats. True he hosted aristocratic families and enjoyed upper-class company. But that was all. Basically he was an 'apostle of viciousness'. One of his wives spoke of his 'pathological jealousy' and said that he was a 'despotic husband'.[5] Another wife complained that he 'suffered from overwhelming fits of jealousy'.[6] This vacantly silly and unfulfilled man sought vengeance on his brother-in-law in 1931. His anger flared up when the *Church Times* published an article tarnishing the Duke's reputation.[7] Since Earl Beauchamp was at the time President of the English Church Union, the Duke assumed that Beauchamp himself must have been behind the article. There is no evidence that such was the case. The Duke set about getting information concerning Beauchamp's homosexual activities. The Duke learnt that certain male servants at Madresfield, at Halkyn House (Beauchamp's residence in London) and at Walmer Castle had been involved in various 'amours' with the Earl. Most of the servants were loyal to Beauchamp, but a few agreed to give evidence against their master. It is not so much the general evidence as the content of the testimony that sounds incredible. Earl Beauchamp was a refined and delicate person; his tastes were aesthetically highly developed. We simply cannot imagine that

---

4   Quoted in Jane Mulvagh, *Madresfield, op. cit.*, p. 379.
5   Leslie Field has given us an authentic portrait. See her *Bendor: The Golden Duke of Westminster* (London: Weidenfeld & Nicolson, 1983), p. 256.
6   Quoted in Jane Mulvagh, *Madresfield, op. cit.*, p. 374.
7   See *Ibid.*, p. 376.

his erotic habits would have been as coarse as how they were portrayed by the people with whom he had sexual contacts. The descriptions are simply revolting. We venture to advance our suspicion that the Duke managed the evidence on purpose. He must have paid enormous bribes to induce these persons to swear testimony for legal purposes. Our suspicion is strengthened by the fact that the box marked 'The Beauchamp Papers' in the Grosvenor family archives was destroyed in 1960.[8] The testimony was weighty, the object of which was to shock Lady Lettice so considerably that she would execute her brother's commands. The testimony also answered the Duke's ulterior purpose: to bring Beauchamp down. Let us then quote below the full text of the 'Humble Petition' from Lady Lettice. It reads as follows:[9]

In the High Court of Justice
Probate, Divorce and Admiralty Division
(Divorce)

Beauchamp Lettice Mary Elizabeth Countess
v
Beauchamp William Lygon Earl

Court Minutes
Petition Filed 14 May 1931

In the High Court of Justice
Probate Divorce & Admiralty Division
(Divorce)

---

8   See Paula Byrne, *Mad World: Evelyn Waugh and the Secrets of Brideshead, op. cit.*, p. 136. 'The fact,' writes Paula Byrne, 'that the Beauchamp Papers were held in the family offices in Davies Street shows that he [the Duke] was the man who took it upon himself to gather the evidence. And the fact that the fifth Duke of Westminster ordered a senior employee to burn those papers suggests that the family were long embarrassed by the extreme lengths to which Bendor [second Duke of Westminster] was prepared to go in his determination to bring Beauchamp down.' *Ibid.*, p. 136. Beauchamp's children, particularly his daughters, were convinced that 'it was not their father's proclivities but their uncle's [the Duke's] malice that ruined everything.' *Ibid.*, p. 136.

9   Source: The National Archives (Kew), Ref.: J 77/2899/9727 (C 632718). A fragment of this document was first published in Paula Byrne, *Mad World, op. cit.*, pp. 144–5.

To the Right Honourable the President of the Said Division
The 13th day of May 1931

The Humble Petition
of Lettice Mary Elizabeth Lygon Countess Beauchamp
for dissolution of marriage,

Sheweth:

1. THAT on the 26th day of July 1902 Your Petitioner then being Lettice Mary Elizabeth Grosvenor Spinster was lawfully married to William Lygon Earl Beauchamp (hereafter referred to as the Respondent) at the Parish Church in the Parish of Eccleston in the County of Chester.

2. THAT after the said marriage Your Petitioner lived and cohabited with the Respondent at Halkyn House, 13 Belgrave Square in the County of London, Madresfield Court, Malvern Worcestershire, and Walmer Castle in the County of Kent, and there has been issue of the marriage seven children to wit William Viscount Elmley born on the 3rd day of July 1903 The Honourable Hugh Patrick Lygon born on the 2nd day of November 1904 Lady Lettice Lygon now Lady Lettice Cotterell born on the 16th day of June 1906 Lady Sibell Lygon born on the 10th day of October 1907 Lady Mary Lygon born on the 12th day of February 1910 Lady Dorothy Lygon born on the 22nd day of February 1912 and The Honourable Richard Edward Lygon born on the 25th day of December 1916.

3. THAT Your Petitioner is at present residing at Saighton Grange, Chester, aforesaid, and the Respondent resides at No. 13 Belgrave Square in the County of London. Both your Petitioner and the Respondent are domiciled in England.

4. THAT there have been no previous proceedings in this Honourable Court with reference to the said marriage either by or on behalf of your Petitioner or the Respondent.

5. THAT the Respondent is a man of perverted sexual and unnatural practices, has committed acts of gross indecency with the male servants and other male persons and has been guilty of sodomy.

6. THAT throughout the married life at 13 Belgrave Square, Madresfield Court, and Walmer Castle, aforesaid, the Respondent habitually committed acts of gross indecency with certain of his male servants, masturbating them with his mouth and hands and compelling them to masturbate him and lying upon them and masturbating between their legs. The said servants with whom the Respondent committed the said acts of gross indecency were John Scown, Samuel John Scown, Redvers George Rolfe, Edward Hyatt, George Roberts, Frank Webb, William Cann and Ernest Edward Tippel.

7. THAT from the month of May 1909 to the Month of April 1912 in the chauffeurs room at 13 Belgrave Mews, West, the Respondent frequently committed sodomy with the said Samuel John Scown.

8. THAT on an occasion in the month of January 1911 at 13 Belgrave Square, aforesaid, the Respondent attempted to commit sodomy with one Frederick Moore.

9. THAT from the year 1922 to the year 1925 at the Garage 13 Belgrave Square, West, the Respondent frequently committed sodomy with Redvers George Rolfe.

10. THAT in or about the month of October 1924 in the Library at 13 Belgrave Square, aforesaid, the Respondent committed sodomy with a man named Cook.

11. THAT in or about the month of November 1927, in the Library at 13 Belgrave Square, aforesaid, the Respondent committed sodomy with a man whose name in unknown to Your Petitioner.

12. THAT by reason of the aforesaid conduct of the Respondent Your Petitioner suffered acute mental agony and misery and her health was undermined.

WHEREFORE YOUR PETITIONER PRAYS

that your Lordship will decree:

THAT her marriage with the Respondent may be dissolved.

THAT she may have the custody of the said Lady Dorothy Lygon and the Honourable Richard Edward Lygon.

SUCH further and other relief as may be just.

[Signed] Lettice Mary Elizabeth Lygon Beauchamp

The Court sent the following intimation:

To WILLIAM LYGON EARL BEAUCHAMP of 13 Belgrave Square in the County of London.

TAKE NOTICE that you are required, within eight days after service hereof upon you, inclusive of the day of such service, to enter an appearance either in person or by your Solicitor at the Divorce Registry of the High Court of Justice at Somerset House, Strand, in the County of London, should you think fit so to do, and thereafter to make answer to the charges in this Petition, and that, in default of your doing so, the Court will proceed to hear the said charges proved and pronounce judgment your absence notwithstanding.

The Petition is filed and this notice to appear is issued by MESSRS LEWIS & LEWIS of 10, 11 &12 Ely Place Holborn in the County of London.

Dated at London the 14th day of May 1931.

[Signature illegible]

Registrar

NOTE: Any person entering an appearance must at the same time furnish an address for service within three miles of the General Post Office London.

Earl Beauchamp did not appear, nor did he contest the petition in the Court. Thereupon the marriage was dissolved.

In the High Court of Justice
Probate Divorce and Admiralty Division
(Divorce)

In the matter of the Petition of Lettice Mary Elizabeth Lygon Countess Beauchamp
for dissolution of Marriage.

I, Lettice Mary Elizabeth Lygon Countess Beauchamp of Saighton Grange Chester in the County of Chester the lawful wife of William Lygon Earl Beauchamp and the above named Petitioner make oath and say as follows:

1. That the statements set forth in Paragraphs 1, 2, 3, 4 and 12 of my Petition dated the 13th day of May 1931 are true.

2. That the statements set forth in paragraphs 5, 6, 7, 8, 9, 10 and 11 of my said Petition are true to the best of my knowledge, information and belief.

3. That there is no collusion or connivance between me and the said William Lygon Earl Beauchamp in any way whatsoever.

Sworn at Eaton Hall
in the County of Chester
this 13th day of May 1931

Lettice Mary Elizabeth Lygon Beauchamp

Before me

(W.I. Richardson)
Commissioner for Oaths

In the High Court of Justice
Probate Divorce & Admiralty Division (Divorce)

Sworn 13th May 1931

*In the Matter of the Petition of Lettice Mary Elizabeth Lygon Countess Beauchamp
for dissolution of Marriage.*

Affidavit verifying Petition.

Lewis & Lewis

Ely Place, Holborn, E.C,.1.

Beauchamp	v	Beauchamp
Lettice Mary Elizabeth Lygon		William Lygon
Countess		Earl

WD Lewis & Lewis	Hasties
14 May 1931	Filed petition for Dissolution and affidavit in support.
27 May 1931	Hasties, 65 Lincolns Inn Fields, W.C. 2 Appeared for Respondent

The dissolution of the marriage did not satisfy the Duke of Westminster. He demanded a public trial on criminal acts of indecency. The Criminal Law Amendment Act 1885 provided that 'Any male person who in public or private commits or is party to the commission, or attempts to procure the commission by any male person, of any act of gross indecency with another male person, shall be guilty of this mis-demeanour and being convicted thereof, shall be liable at the discretion of the Court to be imprisoned for any term not exceeding two years, with or without hard labour.' This Act, still in force in 1931, could, on the evidence available, have easily sent Beauchamp to prison for such a term.[10]

What happened next is obscure. It is believed that when King George V heard about the Beauchamp affair, he felt he should intervene. And it appears that he did. The King was against a trial, which he feared would bring a curse upon the whole Beauchamp family. In June, so the story goes, the King privately delegated three of Beauchamp's fellow Knights of the Garter to go to Mandresfield and persuade the Earl to go into exile so as to

---

10   It was under this Act that Oscar Wilde was sentenced to two years' in prison, a turn which ultimately ruined his life.

escape a public trial. Beauchamp was also given to understand that there was a police warrant to arrest him if he did not leave the country forthwith.[11] Under this pressure, the Earl is supposed to have signed a declaration never to return to his native land.[12]

Earl Beauchamp acted wisely and left England. He crossed the Channel on 9 June 1931. On 10 June *The Times* noted that: 'Earl Beauchamp, accompanied by his son, the Honourable Hugh Lygon, left for Nauheim yesterday to take a cure. His daughters will join him later.'[13]

11   This information appeared first in Jane Mulvagh, *Madresfield, op. cit.*, pp. 369–71. The author portrays the situation in flowery language: 'On a warm evening in June 1931, the fifty-nine year-old William sat dozing in a chair in the Moat Garden. The embroidery he was completing had dropped into his lap. He could hear, just behind him, the unripe grapes tapping against the mullioned windows in the breeze. Before him water trickled in the old iron well ... Suddenly four car doors slammed shut. A black, chauffeur-driven saloon had entered the estate, driven down the Gloucester Drive, over the cattle grid and had drawn up on the gravel beyond the moat. Three formally dressed men crossed the bridge into the Court ...' And so on. This makes a good fairy-tale, but is not good enough for historical narrative, which needs to be substantiated by documentary evidence. No such evidence is produced: the episode is repeated without a supporting source. See Paula Byrne, *Mad World, op. cit.*, p. 146; Leslie Field, *Bendor, op. cit.*, pp. 246–7.

12   Hugh Dalton writes: 'On Thursday night I dined with Ponsonby at the House, and he told me all about the sad case of Lord Beauchamp, who has had a persistent weakness for footmen, and has been finally persuaded by Simon and Buckmaster to sign an undertaking not to return to England. The King didn't want a scandal because he was a Knight of the Garter!' See Ben Pimlott, ed., *The Political Diary of Hugh Dalton, 1918–40, 1945–60* (London: Jonathan Cape Ltd', 1986), entry for Thursday 16 to Friday 17 July 1931, pp. 148–9. [Hugh Dalton, b. 1887: Labour politician, Under-Secretary at the Foreign Office, 1929–31; Arthur Ponsonby, b. 1871: Leader of the Labour Party in the House of Lords, 1931–5; John Simon, b. 1873: Home Secretary, 1935–7; Stanley Buckmaster, b. 1861: Solicitor-General, 1913–15; Lord Chancellor, 1915–16, legal adviser to the King.]

13   Quoted in Paula Byrne, *Mad World, op. cit.*, p. 147.

Exile

Earl Beauchamp was still Leader of the Liberal peers in the House of Lords when he went into exile. Later, he would resign from such state offices as Warden of the Cinque Ports and Lord Lieutenant of Gloucestershire and also from the chancellorship of London University. But the House of Lords did not yet provide any such option. As a hereditary peer, he was obliged to be a member of the House of Lords until his death. However, he could resign from the leadership of his party which he had taken on in the Lords. This he did in a letter to Lloyd George[1] shortly before his departure from England. Lloyd George replied, saying how sorry he was to hear that the Earl was 'suffering from cardiac fatigue' and assuring him that 'a period of comparative rest' was essential for his recovery. The Liberal party, Lloyd George wrote, had 'come to rely so much upon your ready and very effective help in all our difficulties'. However, he hoped that 'you will consider your health as first and foremost, so that that you may have a full chance of an early restoration to complete vigour'.[2]

Beauchamp was also obliged to make appropriate arrangements for his absence from the House of Lords. With this in mind, he approached the Marquess of Reading, a senior Liberal peer:

Earl Beauchamp to the Marquess of Reading[3]

13 Belgrave Square,
S.W.1

---

1   David Lloyd George succeeded Asquith as Leader of the Liberal Party in 1926.
2   Quoted in Paula Byrne, *Mad World, op. cit.*, p. 146.
3   Source: The British Library: MSS Eur F118/3/3–22: 1928–1931 [Title: Beauchamp, William Lygon, 7th Earl]. Personal and semi-official papers of 1st Marquess of Reading.

4 VI 1931

My dear Reading,

You will not be surprised to hear that I really am obliged to go abroad for a cure at
Nauheim on Tuesday next. I am afraid that I am, therefore, once more deserting my
place in the House of Lords, leaving it to you and Buxton. I know that I can rely on
your kindness in the matter, nor do I think there is much to do between now and
the end of July when I hope to return.

It is kind of you to have seen Stanton,[4] an old friend of mine whom I met when I was
made Lord Lieutenant of Gloucestershire twenty years ago and in whose judgement
I have a great deal of confidence.

Yours very sincerely,

Beauchamp

Now that the Earl had arranged an at least temporary retirement from the
House of Lords, it became indispensable that he should resign from the
chancellorship of the University of London. It required lengthy correspondence, the publication of which is appropriate here. It not only exposes the
laborious bureaucracy which such a resignation involved at the time but
shows how the Earl had not as yet extricated himself from business and had
not, indeed, really come to terms with his situation. Also shown is how, in
certain circles, news gradually got out of the Earl's disgrace.

1

Fredrick W. Price to the Principal, University of London, Dr Edwin Deller

133, Harley Street. W.

14th May 1931

Dear Sir,

---

4   Having met Beauchamp abroad Stanton wrote to Reading: '35 Spring Gardens,
    Trafalgar Square, London S. W. 1. Dear Lord Reading, Might I come and see you one
    day about Lord Beauchamp whom I saw when I was abroad last week? Yours very
    truly, A. W. Stanton.' Source: The British Library: MSS Eur F118/3/3–22: 1928–1931
    [Title: Beauchamp, William Lygon, 7th Earl]. Personal and semi-official papers of
    1st Marquess of Reading.

I am writing to you with regard to Earl Beauchamp, whom I saw in consultation with his doctor two days ago. He is suffering from cardiac fatigue, and consequently should be relieved from work in every possible way until at least the end of the present Session.

Yours faithfully,

Fredrick W. Price

2

The Principal, University of London to Frederick W. Price

15th May 1931

Dear Sir,

Thank you for your letter of the 14th instant. I have had a talk with Lord Beauchamp and you can be sure that we shall not make more demands upon him than are absolutely necessary.

Yours sincerely,

Edwin Deller

3

Lord Beauchamp to Edwin Deller

Jeschke's Grand Hotel, Bad Nauheim

13 VI 31

My dear Principal,

This letter is in the first place meant to apologise for my absence from the dinner on Wed. & hope that all will go well. I wish I cd say I was better, but have had another of these fainting fits since I got here. I am sure that the Vice Chancellor will take my place more than adequately & hope that we will meet at Prague about July 20.

The silly *Daily Mail* did me no good![5] We have our family difficulties as do many others but here there is no question of a divorce. If there was I shd of course reconsider my position in relation to the University. Greiffenhagen has nearly finished

---

5   On 11 June 1931, the *Daily Mail* printed 'Special News' under the heading 'Countess Beauchamp's Divorce Suit'. It stated that a 'Petition for divorce by the Countess Beauchamp against her husband, the seventh Earl Beauchamp, K.G., has been placed on the files at Somerset House'.

the portrait. Do go & see it. He wd appreciate a visit. I got thro' Westfield – I hope all right but it was a great effort & was very glad to get home to bed.

My second boy brings this back & will soon be replaced here by one of my daughters.

Yours v. sincerely,

Beauchamp

4

Edwin Deller to Earl Beauchamp

18th June 1931

*The Right Hon. the Earl Beauchamp, K. G., K. C. M. G., P. C., D. Litt, LL. D.,
Jeschke's Grand Hotel,
Bad Nauheim, Germany*

My dear Chancellor,

Thank you for your letter. I am sorry that you are finding progress slow but I hope that with the rest you will soon be yourself again.

The Vice-Chancellor has written to you about the Dinner and I need not repeat what he has said. It was most kind of you to have allowed us in this way to make the better acquaintance of the representatives of the Home Counties. Your steward was most helpful in making arrangements.

A date about the 20th July will suit President Masaryk's[6] convenience. I understand he will not be in Prague at that time but that he will go to Topolcavky, his official Slovak residence. I will let you have further details later.

I hope you will let me know if there is any matter in which I can be of assistance.

Yours sincerely,

Edwin Deller

5

Earl Beauchamp to Edwin Deller

Jeschke's Grand Hotel, Bad Nauheim

6   Tomas Masaryk (1850–1937), first President of Czechoslovakia, 1918–35. The University of London had conferred an honorary degree on him.

My dear Principal,

I am much obliged to the V.C. & yourself for yr kind letters about the dinner. Bradford is an excellent fellow & wd I know do his best. Topolcavky is nearer Vienna than Prague & it might be better for me to join you from here in that way if the President receives us there rather than in Prague. But I put myself entirely in yr hands & will join you in either place as the President decides. Will you bring my robes? I have evening dress & Garter ribbon etc. with me in case there is a dinner. We are within motoring distance of Frankfurt wh is a very convenient city centre. The doctor (tho' I don't yet feel very different) promises me that I can join you anywhere about that time. This is a little confusing but the Continental Bradshaw is a gt help.

Yours sincerely,

Beauchamp

What about the hon. degree? Do I write to them & when? What dates? Sept. 29 is it or Nov.26?

B.

I am glad to say that the proceedings of wh I wrote to you are 'stopped' & when the lawyers have finished wrangling are to be withdrawn altogether.

B

6

The Vice-Chancellor to Earl Beauchamp

24th June 1931

Confidential

My dear Chancellor,

I am sorry to say that an unexpected hitch has occurred in connection with your nominations for the conferment of Honorary Degrees on Foundation Day next.

It was necessary, of course, for the Senate to pass a resolution before your nominations could become operative, since the actual conferment of degrees is a matter which the Senate only is legally competent to do. When the resolution came up it was obvious that there were some members present who were extremely apprehensive as to the wisdom of the policy of conferring Honorary Degrees on any of the leaders of political parties. Some again seemed to think that it would be invidious to include the two mentioned and omit the one not mentioned. Although it is difficult to speak with certainty I should say that the former opinion was more strongly held than the latter.

After considerable discussion the list was referred back in order that we might talk it over again. We had a meeting of the Honorary Degrees Committee yesterday and we unanimously came to the conclusion that it would be wise on the whole to postpone further action until your return, when we could have the great advantage of discussing the matter personally with you.

In your absence and in order to avoid troubling you during your cure, as well as to avoid delay, I communicated with other persons on whom it is proposed to confer honorary degrees and up to now I have received very pleased and appreciative acknowledgements.

I hope you are continuing to make satisfactory progress and that you will soon be restored to perfect health. The Principal to whom I have shown this letter is, I understand, writing to you about the visit to Czechoslovakia.

Believe me, my dear Chancellor,

Yours sincerely,

J. L. S.

7

Earl Beauchamp to Vice Chancellor

Jeschke's Grand Hotel, Bad Nauheim

27 VI 31

My dear Vice Chancellor,

I am much obliged to you for yr. letter about the difficulty of the hon. degrees. You will of course remember that my chief interest was to repay the compliment offered me at Cambridge by Mr Baldwin & that we all agreed that if one party was represented, so shd the others. Perhaps however we were wrong in this last consideration. I feel sure that, if it were so represented to them the Senate wd agree to him. Otherwise I have no particular feelings in regard even to these wh were supposed to be more personal nominations. I shd have no objection at all to withdrawing the other two politicians & substituting others whose names wd in your opinion command a more general support. I fear you said that Czechoslovakia was out of the question for you or we might have discussed it then.

This place is hot & relaxing & I look forward to an 'after cure' when we have been to President Masaryk. I hope you will have a pleasant holiday & return refreshed for another year's hard work. We shall meet at least for General Smuts.

Yours very sincerely,

Beauchamp

P.S. I will not trouble the Principal with a letter until he writes again about President Masaryk. My passport is all correct. I shall have a valet with me. B.

8

The Principal to Earl Beauchamp

25th June 1931

My dear Chancellor,

The position about President Masaryk is that we have been assured by the Legation that the proposal to confer an honorary degree will give very great pleasure. A formal letter has gone and we are expecting a reply any day. Colonel Brooke is making the necessary enquiries as to dress etc. but I am assuming that evening dress will be required. We will see that your robes are on the spot. I will communicate with you again when things are a little more advanced. I don't know whether your own passport is available for Czechoslovakia but if it is not and you will let me know I will arrange matters through the Legation.

I hope by this time that you are better in health. I am glad to hear that the matter about which you wrote is coming to a satisfactory conclusion.

Yours sincerely,

E. D.

9

Earl Beauchamp to the Principal

Jeschke's Grand Hotel, Bad Nauheim

30 VI 31

My dear Principal,

The doctor is sending me next Wed 8th on to Freudenstadt-Hotel Wandlust. Before then however I hope to hear when & where President Masaryk will receive us. If at his country place I shall probably join you at Bratislava via Vienna for Freudenstadt is near Baden Baden. My final after-cure will probably be in Italy with my children bathing. For economy's sake we shut up my houses & they will join me there for a month or so. But plans cannot well be fixed till I hear from you.

I am a little disturbed about Baldwin – the others don't worry me, but I think it shows that the Chancellor had better not attend the Hon. Degree Com. in future. Do you not agree?

Yours very sincerely,

Beauchamp

10

The Principal to Earl Beauchamp

3rd July 1931

My dear Chancellor,

Thank you for your letter which I am glad to interpret as meaning that you are continuing to make progress. I hope most sincerely that you are making a satisfactory recovery.

I am sorry that I cannot be more definite about President Masaryk. A conversation I had the other day with the Minister (Mr Jan Masaryk) leads me to think that there is a strong probability that the President may ask us to postpone the proposed visit: he is, as you know, advanced in years and needs the complete rest which he gets in July. However, I have not yet heard officially. I am going to Edinburgh on Monday night but I will arrange for you to be informed of the position at the earliest possible moment.

Yours sincerely,

E. D.

11

Earl Beauchamp to the Principal

Hotel Waldlust
Freudenstadt

10 VII 31

My dear Principal,

Many thanks for yr letter about President Masaryk. Not having heard any more, I presume the date will be postponed, but shall still hope to come with you.

My own plans are uncertain. Professor Groedel did not give me a clean bill of health at the end of my cure, & tho' I have come here for a change, think that instead of Italy I shall be obliged either to return to Nauheim or go to a specialist in Lausanne. For the moment my plans are uncertain, but I shall be very sorry to give up the Italian plans.

I am not sure that my day here is not pleasanter than if I were in Edinburgh today!

What day is the Smuts degree?

I am especially sorry that our visit to the President is postponed as I was particularly anxious to talk to you about the hon. degrees.

The 3 objected to are my 3 political ones & it amuses me to think that they were – as to two – really suggested to me by the Com. Mr Baldwin, as you know I do rather cling to, & the others I accept readily tho' without enthusiasm. What do you advise?

At present so far as I can tell I expect to be here for 10 days or a fortnight & shall then know whether to return to Nauheim or try Lausanne.

Yours very sincerely,

Beauchamp

My youngest boy is also going to Westminster as a day boy next Sept. aged 15. B.

12

Edwin Deller to Earl Beauchamp

The Right Hon. The Earl of Beauchamp, KG.
Jeschke's Grand Hotel,
Bad Neuheim,
Germany

My dear Chancellor,

Thank you for your letter which I am glad to interpret as meaning that you are continuing to make progress. I hope most sincerely that you are making a satisfactory recovery.

I am sorry that I cannot be more definite about President Masaryk. A conversation I had the other day with the Minister (Mr Jan Masaryk) leads me to think that there is a strong probability that the President may ask us to postpone the proposed visit: he is, as you know, advanced in years and needs the complete rest which he gets in July.

However, I have not heard officially. I am going to Edinburgh on Monday night but I will arrange for you to be informed of the position at the earliest possible moment.

Yours sincerely,

[E. D.]

13

Edwin Deller to Earl Beauchamp

13th July 1931

My dear Chancellor,

We have now had an official intimation that it would be preferable to postpone the visit to Czechoslovakia and of course we have agreed to this course. I am sorry to gather that your cure is proving a slower business than you expected, but I hope that with care and freedom from worry you will make a good recovery.

The Congress at Edinburgh passed off very well; the informal business being perhaps, as is often the case, more useful than the formal. But the weather was unkind and rain abundant.

The ceremony of conferment of Honorary Degrees in connection with the Centenary of the British Association takes place on September 28th. The recipients are, in addition to General Smuts, Lord Rutherford, Sir Joseph Thomson, Sir Charles Sherrington and Sir Gowland Hopkins. If you are still precluded by absence from England from being present at the Ceremony the Vice-Chancellor will of course act in your place. As to the other Honorary Degrees I don't think anything can be done at present. The Committee are recommending to the Senate, which meets on Wednesday, that in view of your absence abroad, the question should be deferred until your return.

I am leaving on the 28th for the South of France and shall be absent from England about six or seven weeks. I will arrange for any urgent letters to be sent on to me.

Yours very sincerely

E. D.

P. S. I am interested to hear that your boy is going to Westminster, and I hope you will let me know if I can help him in any way..

14

Edwin Deller to Jan Masaryk, Czechoslovak Legation in London

21st July 1931

Jan Masaryk, Esq., C.B.E.
Czechoslovak Legation,
8, Grosvenor Place, S.W.1

Dear Mr Masaryk,

I shall be going away on Wednesday next for a holiday. If there is anything that you would like to discuss with me before then, perhaps you will give me a ring and I will come along. I am most grateful to you for your timely help the other day. Everything is now in order and we shall be sending along to you shortly the diploma signed and sealed, and asking you to be good enough to transmit it to His Excellency.

Believe me,

With kind regards,

Yours sincerely,

[E. D.]

15

Edwin Deller to Jan Masaryk

21st July 1931

Your Excellency,

I have the honour to enclose a Diploma for the Degree of Doctor of Laws conferred by the Senate on the President of the Czechoslovak Republic, and I beg that you will be good enough to cause it to be transmitted to His Excellency.

I am,

Your Excellency's most obedient servant,

Edwin Deller

16

Edwin Deller to Sir Clive Wigram

Col. Sir Clive Wigram, K. C. V. O., C. B., C. S. I.,
Buckingham Palace,
S. W. 1

23rd July 1931

Dear Sir Clive Wigram,

I am leaving London on Wednesday morning next for the South of France. We are not going direct and shall take a few days getting there and the journey will not come to an end until August 3rd. From then onwards for about a month my address will be Hotel Surmer, Cavalaire, Var, France. I don't suppose you will want me but I promised to let you know my address in case you might do so.

Yours sincerely,

Edwin Deller

17

Sir Clive Wigram to the Principal, University of London

Buckingham Palace

23rd July 1931

Private

Dear Mr Deller,

Many thanks for your letter of today's date.

I need hardly say how sorry I am about the acknowledgement of the Report of the University of London but, as I explained to you, at one time certain Reports were acknowledged by the King's Private Secretary. Now, however, *all* are dealt with by the Keeper of the Privy Purse and, as I am sure you will understand, the number received is so great that it is impossible to do more than send a formal acknowledgement. I have spoken to the Keeper of the Privy Purse and said I felt that the University of London was rather in a special category and he said he would make a note and see whether something more than the ordinary letter could not be sent in the future.

Yours sincerely,

Clive Wigram

18

Dr Maxwell Simpson to the Principal, University of London

8, Grosvenor Street, W. 1

24th July 1931

Sir,

I am asked by Earl Beauchamp to write to inform you as to his state of health. I have received a report from Professor Groedel, under whose care Lord Beauchamp was during his Cure at Nauheim, telling me that while the Cardiac condition responded satisfactorily to the treatment the patient's general health still gives cause for anxiety.

It is necessary for Lord Beauchamp to undergo further special treatment before contemplating the resumption of any Official work.

I am,

Yours faithfully,

G. Maxwell Simpson

19

Earl Beauchamp to the Principal

Schwarzwaldhotel Waldlust
Freudenstadt

24 VII 31

My dear Principal,

Many thanks for yr letter of the 13th. It raised a question in my mind on wh I shd much like yr opinion.

Who ought to give these degrees? What is the custom at Oxford, Cambridge, St Andrews etc.? I am fearfully ignorant of these things but vaguely have an idea that generally it is the Vice C. Now I shd hate to impinge on the privileges of the V. C. & hope you will tell me without hesitation what you think. Stupidly enough it never occurred to me before.

The South of France sounds too far from Prague to allow you to go there before returning to London. But my children motor out to me in Lausanne in August & they may want me to take them to the Riviera. Cd we, if so, by some happy chance meet?

The doctor here confirms Groedet's report of wh. I believe a copy has gone to you.

I think 'to be forwarded' & Madresfield is my best address.

Yours very sincerely,

Beauchamp

20

The Principal, University of London to Sir Clive Wigram

27th July 1931

Private

Dear Sir Clive Wigram,

Many thanks for your letter. I quite understand the position, and if anything can be done we shall, I am sure, greatly appreciate it.

Yours sincerely,

E. D.

21

The Principal, University of London to Sir Clive Wigram

28th July 1931

Private

Dear Sir Clive Wigram,

I think you may be interested to see a copy of a letter I have had from Dr Maxwell Simpson.

I am leaving London tomorrow for, I hope, bluer skies and sunnier days, and I shall be back about the middle of September.

Yours sincerely,

E. D.

22

Edwin Deller to G. Maxwell Simpson

28th July 1931

G. Maxwell Simpson, Esq., M. D.

8, Grosvenor Street, W.1

Dear Sir,

I write to thank you for your letter of the 24th instant, informing me of Professor Groedel's report on Lord Beauchamp's state of health.

Yours faithfully,

Edwin Deller

23

The Principal to Earl Beauchamp

The Right Hon. the Earl Beauchamp, K. G
Schwarzwaldhotel Waldlust,
Freudenstadt

28th July 1931

My dear Chancellor,

I have your letter of the 24th instant. I am not very familiar with the practice at Oxford and Cambridge, but from enquiries I have made I gather that it is the general practice for the Vice-Chancellor to confer honorary degrees, and only in very exceptional circumstances does the Chancellor himself officiate. In the present case, especially in view of Groedel's opinion, it would, I think, be best to proceed on the assumption that the Vice-Chancellor will act on this occasion.

We are not staying on the Riviera proper but in a much quieter place, in the Côtes des Haures district, which is a good deal more to the west. Our address will be Hotel Surmer, Cavalaire, Var, France, and if by any chance you could come so far, needless to say we should be delighted to see you. Dr Simpson's letter in which he refers to Professor Groedel's report came after yours. I am sorry to gather that your progress towards recovery is so slow. You may be sure that we shall not trouble you more than is absolutely necessary.

I am giving instructions for any letters to be sent to Madresfield to be forwarded.

Yours very sincerely,

Edwin Deller

24

Earl Beauchamp to the Principal

Berlin W.9
Bellevuestrasse

1 VIII 31

My dear Principal,

You will I believe & hope be sorry to hear that I have found myself obliged to resign the Chancellorship & have so written to the Vice Ch. Today – tho' not sure if he was the right person. But I cannot do it without a line to you of thanking the Principal of London University for having done so much to make my time of office so delightful. A thousand thanks! I need not repeat to you my regrets – you will understand that they are very real.

Yr letter found me here – where I am expecting a visit from my boy & then I go back to Nauheim to see Groedel again before Lausanne wh he advises. I feel really very seedy & unwell. It wd have been delightful to watch the new buildings rise in close cooperation with you but there it is!

Yours sincerely,

Beauchamp

25

Lord Beauchamp to the Vice-Chancellor, The Rev. J. Scott Lidgett, D. D.

Bad Nauheim

1st August 1931

My dear Vice-Chancellor,

In more than one interview my specialists have insisted upon a great reduction of my public work, and I feel bound in these circumstances to tender to you my resignation of the Chancellorship of the University of London.

The experience of two years has taught me something of the great work of the University and of the services which could be rendered to it by an active Chancellor, especially at this important moment of its history.

I cannot feel that in these circumstance it would be fair to stand in the way. It is with the deepest regret that I take this step. My election was an unexpected and tremendous honour which I have never failed to appreciate most highly. Let me take this chance of expressing to you and to the other officials of the University my profound thanks for all the help they have always been so ready to give me and to the many friends who in many of the Schools or Colleges of the University have always shown me unvarying kindness.

Nauheim unfortunately has failed to effect a cure and I must look forward to a much less active life.

Believe me,

Yours very sincerely,

Beauchamp

26

From the Principal to the Vice Chancellor

Hotel Surmer,
Cavalaire, Var, France

4th August 1931

My dear Vice Chancellor,

I have today received a letter form the Chancellor stating that he has found himself obliged to resign the Chancellorship, and that he has so written to you. I am writing a personal letter to him and I am writing, as I promised to do, to Sir Clive Wigram. That is all, I have done.

You will I suppose send a notification to the Chairman of Convocation although of course no action can be taken until next term to appoint a successor.

As to the Press. Might I not be able to send an announcement without waiting for the October Senate? The grounds are, I suppose, stated as ill health? (He says to me 'I feel really very seedy and unwell'.)

The new Calendar & other publications will be going to press during the Vacation. I suggest to your consideration that the word 'Vacant' should be inserted under 'Chancellor'. If you so determine, perhaps you would give instructions to Mr Worsley or Miss Forman?

We had a very pleasant and interesting journey across France and arrived here yesterday to find the sun awaiting us. I hope you will have a good & restful holiday.

My wife joins in sending greetings & kindest regards.

Forgive paper & ink! [Perhaps the author should have added: illegible script!]

Yours sincerely,

Edwin Deller

27

From the Vice Chancellor to Earl Beauchamp
University of London

South Kensington, London, S. W. 7

(N. Wales)

7th August 1931

My dear Lord Beauchamp,

Your letter of the 1st instant, in which you forward to me your resignation of your office as Chancellor of the University of London has reached me here. In accepting it on behalf of the University I write to express my deep regret that you have been obliged to take this step & for the reasons that have made it necessary. I hope that medical attention & rest may restore you to health.

I shall convey your resignation to the proper university quarters in due course & give your message of thanks to the Staff. Owing to the holidays some delay is unavoidable.

In conclusion, I would express to you my personal thanks for your services to the University during your term of office & for the consideration with which you have always treated me.

Believe me,

Yours very sincerely,

J. Scott Lidgett

28

Sir Clive Wigram to Edwin Deller

H. M. Yacht Victoria & Albert

7th August 1931

Edwin Deller Esq., LL. D.,
Hotel Surmer,
Cavalaire, Var, France

Dear Dr Deller,

Thank you very much for your letter of the 4th instant, informing me that Earl Beauchamp has resigned the Chancellorship of the University of London. I should think he is wise to have done this on account of his health and I have duly informed His Majesty.

Yours sincerely,

Clive Wigram

29

The Vice-Chancellor to Mr Loney

N. Wales

Confidential

10th August 1931

My dear Loney,

Best thanks for yours. It will be well to take, as you suggest, no further steps till we meet in September.

I have no University books here, but I think I am right in thinking that the Statutes do not provide for the *resignation* of a Chancellor. Beauchamp evidently thought that the resignation should be sent to the V. C. & when we meet we may find a means of communicating his resignation to you, without further proceedings with him.

When I see you I will make a confidential statement as far as I am permitted to do so, which will show that I had no alternative but to accept the resignation on behalf of the University *without delay*. The urgency of certain situations may be, & in this instance was, imperative, as I will explain to you.

Yours very sincerely,

J. Scott Lidgett

30

Maurice Webb to the Vice Chancellor

University of London,
South Kensington, London, S.W.7

Aug. 10th

Dear Vice Chancellor,

As a matter of courtesy, I have informed Mr Loney of the contents of your letter about the Chancellor, both because he is the Chairman of the electing body & because I knew you had been in communication with him. I understand that he holds the view that no communication to the Press should be made until he has received formal notice of the Chancellor's resignation; & that then it should be made not through the Secretary to the Senate but through the Clerk to Convocation. Of course I must take my instructions from you & carry out whatever you wish me to do; but under the circumstances, I have ventured to hold up the communication, until I have explained the position to you & received your further instructions.

Yours sincerely,

Maurice Webb

31

The Vice Chancellor to Maurice Webb

N. Wales

12 Aug. 1931

Most confidential

Dear Mr Webb,

Your letter reached me this morning. I heard also, yesterday from Mr Loney & have written to him.

Please show him this letter & confer with him. But do not show it *to any one else* & do not put it among the official correspondence. It is very difficult to write about highly confidential & perplexing matters, &, if this letter be insufficient, the matters must stand over till September. But the following statement may be sufficient. Lord Beauchamp has, probably in [error] though the Statutes do not provide for the resignation of a Chancellor, sent a formal resignation of his office to me, as Vice-Chancellor, & I, from knowledge of the facts, lost no time in accepting it.

I propose, on my return to London, *formally* to convey his resignation to the Chairman & Secretary of Convocation.

I do not think that it would be well, if it can be avoided, to trouble Lord Beauchamp further in the matter. Both the Principal, who has written to me, & I think what in view of the facts known to us, early publication of the resignation, is, for several reasons highly desirable in the interest of the University. I must add, *in very strict confidence*, that the connection of the late Chancellor with the University has been the subject of serious concern in very high quarters.

Further information must await conversation with Mr Loney, when the Principal and I return.

Yours sincerely,

J. Scott Lidgett, V. C.

P. S. I ought to add that in my letter to Lord Beauchamp I said, 'I shall convey your resignation to the proper University quarters in due course.'

32

Maurice Webb to the Vice Chancellor

University of London,
South Kensington, London, S. W. 7

August 12th

Dear Vice Chancellor,

I have shown your letter to Mr Loney & he has explained his position to me. He is anxious that nothing should be done which would make it obligatory on him to hold an election at the October meeting of Convocation; & for that reason he would prefer that no communication should be made to the Press & that he should not receive official information of the Chancellor's resignation until September, when, as you suggest in your letter, the matter can be further discussed. When that time comes – I say this on my own responsibility – he would, I think, possibly be prepared to take the Chancellor's letter to you, if handed to him officially, as an official communication to Convocation of his resignation.

I shall of course mention the contents of your letter to nobody; I am keeping it at my own house & will give it back to you when you return.

Your sincerely,

Maurice Webb

33

S. L. Loney to the Vice Chancellor

Aug 12, 1931

My dear Vice Chancellor,

In your letters of Aug 7 and 10 you proposed that no action should be taken re. the Chancellor until we meet in September. In this I entirely agree, especially as I do not want to put a new Election down for the meeting of Convocation on Oct. 13 (or to have a meeting at all on that day) wh. I am afraid I should be obliged to do if I had official notice of the vacancy before Sept. 8. But to my surprise I learn from Webb, and from an interview with him this morning, that you are proposing to send a notification to the Press at once.

I should deprecate any such action on your part for the reason I have given above, and also because I submit that no resignation of the Chancellor is legal and complete until it has reached me under the Chancellor's own hand. At any rate I could take no action for filling the vacancy, until I had received this formal notification. I am quite willing to write to the Chancellor saying that you have informed me that you have received a communication from him, and asking him to formally communicate with him, so that I may be legally in the proper position. But I would prefer that no action of any kind should be taken until we meet in September.

All being well, I shall be away in the car next week from Monday morning to Sat. night, and shall have no address, as we shall be moving on from day to day. I am intending to start with the Derbyshire [illegible].

I am, Very faithfully Yours,

S. L. Loney

34

Sir Clive Wigram to Edwin Deller

Buckingham Palace

1st October 1931

Edwin Deller, Esq., LL. D.
Principal, The University of London, S. W. 7

Dear Dr Deller,

This is to let you know that Lord Beauchamp has resigned the Lord-Lieutenancy of Gloucestershire, but has not as yet sent in his resignation as Warden of the Cinque Ports.

Yours sincerely,

Clive Wigram

35

Edwin Deller to Sir Clive Wigram

2nd October 1931

Private

Dear Sir Clive Wigram,

Many thanks for your letter. We shall be announcing Lord Beauchamp's resignation of the Chancellorship in the course of a few days.

Yours sincerely,

Edwin Deller

36

Vice-Chancellor to the Chairman of Convocations, University of London

5th October 1931

Dear Chairman of Convocation,

During the vacation I received a letter from Lord Beauchamp (of which I enclose a copy) tendering his resignation of the office of Chancellor in consequence of the state of his health. I have accepted it on behalf of the University and expressed my deep regret that he has been obliged to take this step.

I shall report the matter to the Senate at their next meeting. Clause 8 of the Statutes provides that

'Upon any vacancy in the office of Chancellor, Convocation shall, at a meeting held not later than six months after the occurrence of such vacancy, elect, under the provisions hereinafter contained, a fit and proper person to be Chancellor',

and I therefore send you this notification in order that you may take the proper steps for the filling of the vacancy created by Lord Beauchamp's resignation.

I am,

Yours sincerely,

Vice-Chancellor

37

The Principal, University of London to S. L. Loney

8th October 1931

Dear Mr. Loney,

I send the original of Lord Beauchamp's letter to the Vice-Chancellor. Will you please let me have it back when you have done with it? I send also a copy of the Vice-Chancellor's reply.

Yours sincerely,

E. D.

38

S.L. Loney to Edwin Deller

Parkside,
172 Kew Road,
Richmond, Surrey

Oct. 10, 1931

Dear Deller,

When I returned the Chancellor's letter to you yesterday, I meant to have told you that I received a formal resignation from him on Thursday aft., but after I had telephoned to you. By this mornings post I have received 25 nominations, sent through the V. C. (!!!), of Lord Moynihan. As I now know *officially* of his nomination, I feel that I cannot do anything more about a Conference but that the election must go through in the normal way with voting papers etc. if there is another Candidate nominated. It will not do much harm if one is nominated though I would have preferred no contest.

Faithfully yours,

S. L. Loney.

39

Nomination of the New Chancellor

At the request of a number of graduates of the University of London, Lord Irwin has accepted nomination for election to the office of Chancellor.

Among the graduates who have already signified their support of Lord Irwin for this office are:

Prof. H. G. Arkins

Sir William Beveridge (Director of the London School of Economics)

Prof. Winifred Cullis

Mr H. L. Eason

Dr W. McAdam Eccles

Dr John Fawcett

Prof. L. N. G. Filon

Sir John Gilbert

Dr A. H. M. Gray

Professor T. E. Gregory

Professor H. C. Gutteridge

Professor Dame Helen Gwynne-Vaughan

Miss E. C. Higgins (Principal of Royal Holloway College)

Prof. G. B. Jeffrey

Canon W. R. Mathews

Professor Sir Frederick Maurice

Sir Percy Nunn

Lord Passfield

Mr Frank Pick

Prof. A. W. Reed

Mr E. J. Sainsbury

Dr George Senter (Principal of Birkbeck College)

Mr Roger T. Smith

Sir Josiah Stamp

Sir Holburt Waring

In addition to the heads of colleges named above among the graduates, he is supported also by the following heads of colleges who are not graduates of London:

Miss D. Chapan (Principal of Westfield College)

Dr W. R. Halliday (Principal of King's College)

Miss G. E. M. Jebb (Principal pf Bedford College)

Dr Allen Mawer (Provost of University College)

Mr H. T. Tizard (Rector of the Imperial College)

The person elected to the office of Chancellor was Alexander Cambridge, 1st Earl of Athlone (1932–55).

From splendour to a state of mental agony

Earl Beauchamp began to recover slowly from cardiac fatigue. Yet the mental agony did not disappear. It heavily pained him that his wife, with whom he had enjoyed such a glorious life when they were first married, should have lowered herself to demolishing all they had. Beauchamp had lived in grandeur, with dozens of servants attending him. He had held grand receptions and luscious dinners in the company of people proficient at politics and literature. Sir Almeric Fitzroy, a close associate, had recorded some of these events in his diary:[7]

1

16 February 1904

We dined with Beauchamps in Bryanston Square, in a house belonging to the Shaftesburys which was once the Postman family mansion.[8]

2

7 March 1906

... Afterwards I went to a small party at the Beauchamps' to welcome the Ampthills. Lady Ampthill showed the effects of more than five years in India, but the sweet courtesy of her manner had undergone no change, and she bore herself with the same stately grace ...[9]

3

16 November 1906

... The Lord President, Beauchamp, and I went down to Windsor this afternoon for a Council, Althorp and Sir D. Probyn being there. We got down about 5.15 and found a large party of the Household and guests at tea at three round tables. I was next to a very pleasant Norwegian lady in attendance on Queen Maud. Her impressions of Windsor were almost overwhelming. She was eloquent on the popularity

---

7   See Almeric Fitzroy, *Memoirs, op. cit.*
8   *Ibid.*, vol. I, p. 187.
9   *Ibid.*, vol. I, p. 285.

of the King and Queen in Norway, their taste for a simple life having won them universal good will ...[10]

4

22 March 1908

We dined last night with Beauchamps, Princess Louise of Schleswig-Holstein, the Austrian Ambassador, two Russians who are here with the Empress, the Halsburys, Londonderry, Lord Fitzmaurice, Lady Kenmare. ...[11]

5

7 March 1911

Last night dined with the Beauchamps, the Italian Ambassador and his wife, the Prime Minister and Mrs Asquith, R. Cavendish and Lady Moyra, the Dowager Lady Granville, the Northcotes, Nicolsons, and Jack Lesties [?].[12]

6

12–15 April 1912

At Madresfield. A small party: George Peel and Lady Agnes, Professor and Mrs Stuart of the University of Sydney, and Beauchamp's Private Secretary. The gardens were looking lovely in the rich blossom of this remarkably early spring.[13]

7

30 April 1913

Dined with Beauchamps. The Austro-Hungarian Ambassador, Lalaings, Brasseys, Grimstons, Chelmsford, Lady Stanhope, Lady Leconfield, Lady Harcourt, Hugh and Lady M. Morrison, Erringtons, and P. Ralli.[14]

8

13 July 1913

---

10   *Ibid.*, vol. I, p. 305.
11   *Ibid.*, vol. I, p. 343.
12   *Ibid.*, vol. II, p. 438.
13   *Ibid.*, vol. II, p. 484.
14   *Ibid.*, vol. II, p. 509.

Dined with Beauchamps: Lady Leconfield, Victor Corkran, and the Archdeacon of London were there.[15]

9

22 March 1920

We dined with the Beauchamps. ... I found myself next to my hostess at dinner: a position I enjoyed, as I had not seen her for a long time, and her transparent beauty of character is always captivating.[16]

We also get a glimpse of these past times in letters Earl Beauchamp wrote to Earl Carrington:[17]

I

From the Lord Steward
Madresfield Court
Malvern Link

Whitsunday 1908

My dear Lord Carrington,

We have an annual Agricultural Show here wh will bring 10 to 11 thousand people. This year it is to be on Aug 7. I venture to ask you to come.[18] If you were to do us the favour I shd still further venture to ask for a speech at the luncheon where the farmers congregate. It wd be an immense service to the party tho' the occasion is nominally non-political. Lots of Tories wd be here & wd gladly listen to you.

Lady Beauchamp & I wd be still more pleased if Lady Carrington came too & stayed here for it. I send you a catalogue of last year to show the kind of thing it is. Farmers – cottagers & the whole neighbourhood cooperate to make it a success. But if you cd come it wd be the greatest help of all.

Yours v. Sincerely,

Beauchamp

15   *Ibid.*, vol. II, p. 517.
16   *Ibid.*, vol. II, p. 726.
17   Bodleian Library, Carrington (the Marquess of Lincolnshire) Papers, MS. Film 1135 (2).
18   The point of this invitation was that Carrington was Minister of Agriculture.

2

From Earl Beauchamp

Madresfield

3 viii 11

My dear Carrington,

I have arranged with Colebrooke to invite all Liberal peers to dine at the N.L.C. on Wed. – following a hospitable example you set.

I hope that you will come!

Yours

Beauchamp

All this splendour of living was now lost. The Earl was in exile. He was given to looking back at the past, and he might even have been disposed to commit suicide. At least the children thought so. And they decided never to leave him alone. During the five years of Beauchamp's exile, his children took turns to spend time with their father. Beauchamp was much too restless to stay at one place for more than three weeks; he travelled a lot, visiting Italy, France, Australia and the Americas.[19] His second son, Hugh, of whom he was extremely fond, often travelled with him. When very young, all the children had been devoted to their father, and they proved even more so when he was in exile. Beauchamp himself was never wanting in affection for his children. He made it a point to write to each one of them every Sunday.[20] The letters disclose his worries and his sentiments. In August 1931 he wrote to his daughter Dorothy from Sydney

19 Much later, presumably after his exile was over, Beauchamp appears to have turned up in Algeria. Here is what Vita Sackville-West told her husband Harold Nicolson: '26 January 1937, Touggourt: Darling, I think Touggourt is one of the most magical places I ever struck! ... But the best of all was last night. We gave, rather unintentionally, a party. It included Lord Beauchamp, who has turned up here accompanied by a sulky, embarrassed and bored young man called George, whom I take to be a footman ...' See Nigel Nicolson, ed., *Vita and Harold: The Letters of Vita Sackville-West and Harold Nicolson* (London: Weidenfeld & Nicolson, 1992), p. 292.

20 See Jane Mulvagh, *Madresfield, op. cit.*, pp. 390–1.

that 'the detectives in Paris [perhaps hired by his brother-in-law] annoyed me a great deal. When will she [Lady Lettice] relax her hatred of us all?' Earlier, he wrote from Berlin to ask her about Hugh's health: 'He will be the centre of fashion again when the manoeuvres begin. I want to see a photo of the new bowler hats.'[21] In November, Beauchamp wrote from Singapore, saying that 'My plans after Sydney remain vague. There seems to be no use in coming back if yr mother is still implacable.'[22] At one time Beauchamp wrote to Hugh, worried because of the strikes going on in Britain at the time and hoping that his brother, Elmley, would be able to find a job: 'if not he may become Labour!'[23] Beauchamp often wrote to Dorothy, and wanted her to share his letters with her sisters and brothers. Once at Avignon in France, he wrote: 'Imagine my excitement on seeing the Pont d'Avignon of wh I had so often sung to the family one after another. So there is a picture for each of you.'[24] He wished he could be with them at Madresfield to share their joy and happiness. And indeed he regretted the 'happiness your mother misses'.

Lady Beauchamp

The children's mother, Lady Lettice, had left Madresfield just after the divorce and gone to lodge at Saighton Grange in Cheshire, which was kept at her disposal by her brother. There she lived in total isolation with her youngest child, Richard. The other children totally ignored her. The girls, especially, despised her for the way she had behaved towards their father. In a letter to Dorothy on 21 April 1933, Lady Lettice attempted to explain herself. The girls, she implored, ought to realize that whatever she did, she had done it for 'Richard's future – to keep him clear of all the ill that

21   Quoted in Paula Byrne, *Mad World*, *op. cit.*, p. 168.
22   For particulars, see Jane Mulvagh, *Madresfield*, *op. cit.*, p. 390.
23   *Ibid.*, p. 390.
24   Quoted in *Ibid.*, p. 391.

otherwise would doubtless have befallen him. All I can do is to accept the inevitable and to trust Daddy to God's mercy, which never fails us when we turn to Him. The hardest part for me is not to be able to see Daddy.'[25] But how could she? It was she who had sent him into exile. There was little pricking of conscience, and yet she hoped and prayed that even if 'you have not felt able to keep yr love for me', they would understand 'some little part of what I have undergone and that the old love may yet be restored in its fullness, and even perhaps increased'. How could this love be 'restored', let alone 'increased', when no love ever existed between the girls and their mother? 'Mother,' observed Sibell (the fourth child), 'liked babies until they were two, and then she got terribly bored with them. When we were small we were each displaced by the next arrival. I had quite a long innings because I think she had a miscarriage in 1908. After that she never came into one's life, except as a vengeance; always in a bad temper.'[26]

Lady Lettice's hopes of reconciliation with her children were frustrated, her prayers left unanswered. She led an unhappy existence to which her own brother had largely contributed. Lonely, sad and sick, she died in the summer of 1936. Letters of condolence poured in, addressed not to Earl Beauchamp, who was in Venice, but to his eldest son, Viscount Elmley. Here we cite a few of them:[27]

1

J. F. Smith
Expert Valuers,
61 Elbury Street, London

30 July 1936

The Lord Elmley, M.P.
13 Belgrave Square, S.W.1

My Lord,

It is with profound regret that I have read in this morning's papers of the sudden passing of your Mother, the Countess Beauchamp, and I take this the earliest opportunity

25 The full text of the letter is printed in Jane Mulvagh, *Madresfield*, *op. cit.*, pp. 396–7.
26 Quoted by Jane Mulvagh, *Madresfield*, *op. cit.*, pp. 339–40.
27 Source: Beauchamp Papers, *op. cit.*

to tender on behalf of Messrs J. P. Smith, the Staff and myself our sincere sympathy with you, and the great Family to which you belong in your great loss. Her Ladyship whose kindly actions were extended to everyone she came in contact with has left a void, very difficult to fill, in this rapidly changing world.

Secretary

[Signature illegible]

2

Malvern Urban District Council

30 July 1936

The Right Hon. The Lord Viscount Elmley,
13 Belgrave Square,
London

My Lord,

In the absence of your Lordship's father abroad, may I, on behalf of the Chairman and Members of the Malvern Urban District Council, tender to your Lordship and your Lordship's sisters and brothers their sincere sympathy on the death of your Lordship's mother, Countess Beauchamp. The Members of the Council have very happy recollections of Countess Beauchamp at Madresfield and her great interest in Malvern and its people.

Clerk of the Council

[Signature illegible]

3

Halifax Rd., Bradford

30 July 1936

My dear William,

We were distressed to read of the death of your mother at such an early age. We want to join with so many others in assuring you of our sympathy. I am particularly sorry for your brother Richard who was so near & dear to his mother. You have still more responsibilities thrust upon you – you *can* stand up to them. ...

Ever yours,

George

Earl Beauchamp advised his lawyer, Richard Elwes to determine whether he could attend his wife's funeral. Elwes contacted the Home Secretary, Sir John Simon, who had once been Beauchamp's cabinet colleague. When the 2nd Duke of Westminster heard of Beauchamp's intention, he objected to it. He is alleged to have said that he could not allow Beauchamp to 'desecrate by his odious presence the interment of his beloved sister'.[28] The Duke exerted his influence upon Simon to refuse Beauchamp entry into Britain. Meanwhile, however, Earl Beauchamp had arrived in Folkestone, on the Kent shore, together with his daughter Dorothy, who had been with him in Venice. Elwes went aboard the cross-Channel steamer at the point of embarkation and informed Beauchamp that, if he landed on British soil, he would be arrested. Simon confessed to Sibell later that 'Bendor' (the 2nd Duke of Westminster) had been 'too strong for him – unstoppable!'[29] Beauchamp and Dorothy sailed back to France, and then caught a train back to Venice. It was a sad moment. But the saddest was yet to follow.

Hugh Patrick

Hugh Patrick, the second of Beauchamp's children, his darling son, went on a motoring holiday in Germany with his friend Henry Wynn in August 1936. On a hot Sunday, 19 August, they took a drive through the Bavarian countryside, reaching Rothenburg at dusk. Here they stopped for some rest. While stepping out of the car, Hugh fell and fractured his skull on the kerb-stone. He lost consciousness and never regained it,[30] dying in the early hours of the morning. Together with Dorothy and Sibell, Beauchamp managed to be at Hugh's bedside. The death of his son completely broke him up. Nothing would stop him from attending Hugh's funeral, not even

28 Quoted in Paula Byrne, *Mad World, op. cit.*, p. 253.
29 Quoted by Jane Mulvagh, *Madresfield, op. cit.*, p. 401.
30 A telegram to Viscountess Elmley: 'Hugh sinking fast. Love Mary.' Another telegram followed: 'Hugh passed away 7/30 this morning.' Source: Beauchamp Papers, *op. cit.*

the risk of arrest. It is alleged that Sibell induced her former lover, Lord Beaverbrook, to prevail upon John Simon, getting him to lift the warrant. This time the Home Secretary relented. When Beauchamp, Dorothy and Sibell arrived at Ostend, with the hearse containing Hugh's body, a telegram from Beaverbrook was waiting for Sibell on which was written: 'Safe for your father to land.'[31] Hugh was buried in Madresfield churchyard on 24 August.

Friends and relatives of the family were not aware that Beauchamp would be able to attend Hugh's funeral, so all letters of condolence were addressed to the eldest son, Viscount Elmley. We quote a few of these letters:[32]

1

Royal Lane Place,

16 August 1936

Dear Lord Elmley,

Thanks for your letter. This letter is *not* to be answered but I want you to know how sorry George & I are to hear of your sad loss. Please accept all our sympathy,

Yours ever,

Peggy Gripenberg

2

Boodle Hatfield & Co.

19 August 1936

Dear Lord Elmley,

I have just heard with the most profound regret of Mr Hugh Lygon's death. I venture to send you and the members of your family the expression of deep sympathy in your grievous loss.

[Signature illegible]

---

31   For details see Paula Byrne, *Mad World, op. cit.*, pp. 253–5; Jane Mulvagh, *Madresfield, op. cit.*, pp. 401–3.
32   Source: Beauchamp Papers, *op. cit.*

3

23 August/36

My dear Elmley,

I was grieved & distressed to read of Hughie's sudden death in Germany. ...

[signature illegible]

4

20 August, 1936

3 Wellington House, Great Malvern

Dear Elmley

My father joins me in sending you our very deep sympathy in your second [his mother Lady Lettice had died a month earlier] and most tragic loss ... My own words are most inadequate to express one's feelings, but I am indeed sorry and feel for your grief.

[Signature illegible]

5

City of Norwich Central Conservative & Unionist Association

21/8/36

Dear Lord Elmley,

It seems a dreadful thing to write two letters of condolence to you within so short a time. ...

[Signature illegible]

6

Malvern Cricket Club, Malvern

My Lord Elmley,

I present my apologies for being unable to be present at the funeral of the late H. P. Lygon. Also to offer the club's deepest sympathy to you in your family's great bereavement.

[Signature illegible]

7

Hull Place Sholden, Deal

Dear Elmley,

It seems too sad that I should again have to write to you to tell you how deeply I feel for you – another loss in your family in such a short time is really a calamity. ...

Yours ever,

R. Elliot

Thus with Hugh's burial ended Beauchamp's five-year exile. But it was not quite yet over. The warrant still stood. And Beauchamp could still be arrested.

CHAPTER 22

Last Will and Testament

Immediately after Hugh's funeral Earl Beauchamp returned to his rented *pallazo* on the Grand Canal in Venice. His companion at that time was David Smyth, his secretary. On 30 August 1936, Beauchamp sent a moving letter from Venice to his 'Darling Dorothy'. 'I want,' he said, 'to write a special line of thanks for all your loving sympathy these last dreadful days. You had more courage than I and I can never forget your help. How bad it has been I now begin to realise and have collapsed – not ill but just unhappy... your loving Daddy.'[1] A year later, in mid July 1937, Beauchamp was told that the charges against him had been dropped and the warrant revoked. How this happened we do not know. But we could conjecture that it may have occurred through Sibell's constant pestering of her former lover, Lord Beaverbrook. This so called 'baron of Fleet Street' was one of the most powerful men in Britain in the Thirties. He had been, even if for a short period, a cabinet member in Lloyd George's Coalition Government in 1918. Beaverbrook's *Daily Express*, with a circulation of over 2 million copies a day, could 'make or break almost anyone'. It is thus highly probable that Beaverbrook prevailed on the Home Secretary, Sir John Simon, to declare the warrant invalid. When this was done, Beauchamp returned to Madresfield as a free man. This was on 19 July 1937. One of the first things he did on returning to his home was to demolish all signs of the existence of the person who had caused him and his family so much agony. He had the image of Lady Lettice painted out of the Madresfield Chapel fresco with whitewash and her marble bust was thrown into the nearby moat.[2] That done, a period of relative peace returned to him. He spent most

---

1   Quoted in Paula Byrne, *Mad World*, op. cit., p. 256.
2   See Jane Mulvagh, *Madresfield*, op. cit., p. 404.

of his time at home with his children, especially with his youngest son, Richard, whom he had not seen for five years. He even took up knitting and some embroidery,[3] presumably to kill boredom. But he was restless, for his memories haunted him.

In October 1937, he again went to Venice with David Smyth, but returned in December to celebrate Richard's coming-of-age at Halkyn House, their London residence. Beauchamp hosted a lavish dinner-dance party. In January 1938, together with David, Beauchamp boarded the *Europa* and headed for Cuba, then sailed on to the Fiji Islands on the *Stella Polaris*. From Cuba he wrote to Dorothy, that he and David 'are both much better since we got here.'[4] They enjoyed drinking 'mint juleps made with Spanish Brandy'. In the summer of 1938 both seemed pleased to be back in the gardens of Madresfield, having tea surrounded by liveried footmen.[5] This was just an outward show. At heart Beauchamp was very sad. He had been diagnosed with cancer. He refrained from revealing this to his daughters. Instead he made a will on 19 August 1938, the full text of which we enclose below:[6]

I THE RIGHT HONOURABLE WILLIAM EARL BEAUCHAMP K .G. of Madresfield Court Malvern in the County of Worcester HEREBY REVOKE all Wills and Testamentary Dispositions heretofore made by me and DECLARE this to be my last Will and Testament I APPOINT my son WILLIAM VISCOUNT ELMLEY and my Daughter LADY MARY LYGON and my Secretary DAVID SMYTH of 5 Park Place in the County of London (who and the survivors or survivor of whom and the executors or administrators of such survivor or other the Trustees or trustee for the time being of this my Will are hereinafter called 'my Trustees') to be EXECUTORS EXECUTRIX and TRUSTEES of this my Will I GIVE to each of my three daughters the said Lady Mary Lygon and Lady Dorothy Lygon and Lady Sibel Lygon absolutely and for their use and benefit respectively such a sum free of

3   For details see Paula Byrne, *Mad World, op. cit.*, p. 262; Jane Mulvagh, *Madresfield, op. cit.*, p. 404.
4   Quoted in Paula Byrne, *Mad World, op. cit.*, p. 262.
5   For details see Paula Byrne, *Mad World, op. cit.*, pp. 262–3; Jane Mulvagh, *Madresfield, op. cit.*, p. 404.
6   Source: The State Records of the New South Wales Government, Australia under Deceased estate file: A2435, 20/2458, probate packet: Series 4–2379280.

death duties as will produce an annual income of £1000 I GIVE and BEQUEATH all my Australian property of whatsoever nature to the said David Smyth for his own use and benefit absolutely I GIVE DEVISE BEQUEATH and APPOINT all the residue of my real and personal estate and effects unto my Trustees Upon trust to sell call in and convert the same into money and after payment thereout of my just debts and funeral and testamentary expenses to stand possessed of the balance for my said son Viscount Elmley for his own use and benefit absolutely I WISH the said David Smyth to go through all my letters and personal effects I DECLARE that my Trustees may postpone the sale calling-in and conversion of any part of my real or personal estate for such period as they may in their absolute discretion deem fit without being liable to account notwithstanding that it may be of a wasting speculative or reversionary nature and that pending such sale calling-in and conversion the income (including the net rents and profits of real estate and chattels real after payment of rates taxes rent costs of insurance repairs and other outgoings property attributable in the opinion of my Trustees to income) of property actually producing income shall be applied as from my death as income and on the other hand on such sale calling in and conversion or on the falling in of any reversionary property no part of the proceeds of such sale calling-in or conversion or of such property shall be paid or applied as past income.

IN WITNESS whereof I have hereto set my hand this 19th day of August 1938.

SIGNED by the Testator THE RIGHT HONOURABLE WILLIAM EARL BEAUCHAMP K.G.

BEAUCHAMP

as and for his last Will and Testament in the presence of us both being present at the same time who in his presence at his request and in the presence of each other have hereunto subscribed our names as witnesses:

G. Haywood

7 Sansome Place

Worcester

Solicitors Clerk

W. Humphreys

Madresfield

Agent

(Will of The Right Honourable William Earl Beauchamp K.G, dated 19th August 1938. Hasties 65, Lincoln's Inn Fields, W. C.2)

Soon afterwards, in the autumn of 1938, Beauchamp sailed for New York, accompanied by his daughters Mary and Dorothy and his son Richard. They intended to attend a reunion dinner for the 'Ligon Kinsmen Association' in America at which the Earl was to deliver a biannual speech. This association consisted of people living in America, who bore the 'Ligon' surname, using its fifteenth-century spelling, originating from Madresfield, the ancestral estate of the Lygons.

After the reunion dinner, Beauchamp intended to travel further to Australia, to spend the winter months over there, and then return to Madresfield the next spring. His plans were never realized. In New York he fell seriously ill.

CHAPTER 23

The Earl's Death

On 15 November 1938, Earl Beauchamp died of cancer in a suite at the Waldorf Astoria Hotel in New York. His two daughters and his youngest son were at the deathbed, and the eldest son, Elmley, just managed to arrive in time. Beauchamp's last words were: 'Must we dine with the Elmleys tonight?'[1]

Again it was poor Elmley who had the misfortune to receive the letters of condolence:[2]

I

From the Chairman of the Malvern Urban District Council

To the right Hon. Viscount Elmley
Madresfield, Malvern

16 November 1938

My Lord,

On behalf of the Malvern Urban District Council, may I render to you and the other members of the family our sincere condolence on the death of your father, Earl Beauchamp. I, personally, knew your father for many years and remember what a great loss he was to public life when he gave up his public appointments a few years ago. I am aware of the great interest he took in matters affecting Malvern and district, as well as in public affairs generally, and can well understand the great loss that you have sustained. I beg, therefore, to tender the sincere sympathy of the Urban District Council and myself.

Yours faithfully,

---

1 Quoted in Jane Mulvagh, *Madresfield, op. cit.*, p. 405.
2 Source: Beauchamp Papers, *op. cit.*

Chairman

[Signature illegible]

2

42 Brynston Square
London, W.1

29 December 1938

Dear Lord Beauchamp,

Please accept my sincere condolences. I was so sorry that your father died. It is always sad to be left behind – for those that go it seems to me a relief as the world does seem mixed up. Don't answer this letter. It is merely to let you know I have thought of you & your Sweet Mona.

Love from

Pegg

Earl Beauchamp's funeral was described in detail by the local Worcester newspaper:[3]

Funeral of Earl Beauchamp
Buried within Shadow of His Ancestral Home

In the presence of mourners from a wide area, representing every sphere of public life, the funeral of Earl Beauchamp took place on Friday at Madresfield. The internment was in a grave by the side of that of his second son, the Hon. Hugh Patrick Lygon, in St Mary's Churchyard, a short distance from Madresfield Court.

On arrival at Southampton from New York, on the *Queen Mary*, in the early hours of Thursday, after a few hours' delay through the gale which swept all coasts of the British Isles, the coffin of American Oak, was conveyed to Madresfield by road. It rested in the Church for the greater part of the day draped with the family's house flag.

---

3   See *Berrow's Worcester Journal*, 3 December 1938. The microfilm copies of this are located in Worcestershire Archive & Archaeology Service, The Hive, Worcester. Printouts were made available to the present author by the Archives Assistant, Faye Sturgess, and this help is gratefully acknowledged.

A memorial service had been held at the Anglican Church of Old Trinity, Wall-Street, New York, conducted by the Rector, the Rev. Dr Fleming.

Accommodation at Madresfield Church was severely taxed, and from an early hour in the afternoon crowds lined the churchyard approaches and the graveside. Many county families were present, in addition to Madresfield Estate tenants, organisations with which Earl Beauchamp was associated by his gifts and support, and representatives of Liberal Party organisations.

The flag over Madresfield Court, and in the school-yard opposite the church flew at half-mast. There is no family vault at Madresfield. The grave was delicately lined with evergreen, cypress, yellow, red and white chrysanthemums, and pink, white and red carnations.

The high mass service at the Church and the graveside was conducted by the Rev. J. W. Greaves (Rector of Madresfield), and assisted by Revs F. J. Newson (Rector of Guarlford) and Hubert Jones (Rector of Hanley Castle). Other robed clergy present were the Revs F. C. Champion (Vicar of Powick) and R. W. Hatherly (Warden of St Leonard's Church, Newland).

Mr F. W. Reed played 'O, Rest in the Lord' (Mendelssohn) and Chopin's Funeral March, and accompanied the singing of the hymns 'Jesus, Son of Mary' and 'He who would valiant be', and the Psalm, 'Lord, Thou hast been our Refuge', which were led by the choir.

Family Mourning

The family mourners were Lord and Lady Elmley (son and daughter-in-law), Sir Richard and Lady Lettice Cotterell (son-in-law and daughter), Ladies Sibell, Mary and Dorothy Lygon (daughters), the Hon. Richard E. Lygon (son), the Dowager Lady Ampthill (sister), Sir Robert and Lady Susan Gilmour (brother-in-law and sister), Lady Agnes Peel (sister), Lady Dugdale (cousin), Mr Reginal Lygon (cousin) and Mr David Smith (Private Secretary of Earl Beauchamp). Others present included: ... Lord and Lady Coventry, Lady Deerhurst, Mayor of Worcester, High Sheriff of Worcester, Town Clerk of Worcester. ...

Local Associations

included: ... Gloucestershire Root, Fruit and Grain Society; Western Malvern Playing Field Association; Worcester City Football Club; Malvern Town Football Club; Callow End Men's Club; Worcester Diocesan Conference and the Church Music Committee. ...

[Widespread mourning and tributes from far and near: over 1000 persons were present.]

Floral Tributes

[Over a hundred wreaths from various persons and associations were placed beside the grave. Some of these included:]

'With all our Love, Elmley and Mona; with all love from Sibell; with love from Dickie; for Daddy, with love from Mary; with love, from Richard and Lettice; for Grandfather, from Rose, Anne and John; Uncle Willie, in affectionate remembrance from Mary and Reggie Lygon; with deepest sympathy, from the tenants of Madresfield; with deepest sympathy, from the staff of 13, Belgrave Square; with deepest sympathy from Bernards Green Cricket Club; with sympathy from the East Norfolk Liberal Association; in profound regret, from the officers and members of the Bewdley Liberal Association; from the officers of and members of the Worcester City Liberal Association with sincere sympathy, deepest regret and happy memories of our honoured leader; Worcestershire Women's Liberal Association unite in deepest and sincere regret, with memories of happy gatherings at Madresfield; ... Lord Bearverbrook: with kindest sympathy; ... deepest regret, and grateful memory of the most loving and honoured of friends, Richard R. and Mrs Fairbairn. ...

Memorial Service in London

A memorial service was held yesterday [2 December 1938] at St Paul's, Knightsbridge. The Rev. Bertram Chambers officiated, and among those present were:

Lieutenant-Colonel the Hon. Robert Lygon (half-brother), Mrs Reginald Lygon (also representing the Hon. Mrs Robert Lygon), the Hon. George Peel, Miss Juliet Peel, Captain the Hon. Guy Russell, the Hon. Leopold Russell, the Hon. Phyllis Russell, the Hon. Odo Russell, Lady Dorothea Head, Lady Lettice Ashley-Cooper. Sir Geoffrey Fry (representing Earl Baldwin of Bewdley), Mr A. J. Sylwester (representing Mr D. Lloyd George, MP), Mr G. D. Roseway (representing Mr L. Hore-Belisha, MP), Mr W. R. Davies (secretary, representing the Liberal Party Organisation), the Marquess of Crewe, Sir George Miller-Cunningham, Mrs B. A. Knowles Davies, Mrs Hastle, Mr W. T. Groom (representing the East Norfolk Liberal Association), Mr John Villiers, the Rev. A. and Mrs Linzee Giles, Captain W. H. Maybury, Mr S. L. Loney (representing the University of London), the Hon. Mrs Arthur Hope, Mr and Mrs W. West, Miss H. Sloane, the Hon. Sir Reginald Coventry, Mrs E. de Lancy, Mrs J. Lawrie. Geraldine Countess of Mayo, Mr C. Percy Park (representing the Worcestershire Association), Mr John W. Benson (secretary, the Eighty Club), ... Prince Vsevelode of Russia, ... Lady Bridget Parsons, ... the Duke and Duchess of Oylka, Viscount Mersey, Captain Oliver Fraser.

Lady Bertha Dawkins, ... the Earl and Countess of Granard, Lord and Lady Lamington, Lord Stanmore, Lord Denman, ... the Dowager Viscountess Gough, Lady Knatchbull-Hugessen. ... The Earl of Scarborough, the Dowager Lady Leconfield, the Hon. Lady Maxse, ... Mr Christopher Sykes (also representing the Earl of Antrim), ... the Hon. Patrick Balfour, ... Captain G. F. Gracey, general secretary, The Save the Children Fund.

Sir Samuel and Lady Maud Hoare and Kathleen Countess of Drogheda were unavoidably prevented from attending.

Callow End Memorial Service

A memorial service was held on Sunday evening at St James' Chapel, Callow End, for the late Earl Beauchamp. The service was taken by the Rev. F. J. Newson (Rector of Guarlford). In spite of inclement weather there was a large congregation, including Mrs Winsmore Hooper, Madresfield Estate tenants, and former servants.

Mrs C. L. Glenn was organist, and played 'What are These' (Stainer) and Handel's 'Largo' and accompanied the Hymns 'Let Saints on Earth', 'The King of Love', 'Ten Thousand times Ten Thousand' and the Psalm, 'Lord Thou hast been our Refuge', which were led by the choir.

Perhaps Rev. Newson's words got the measure of it when he spoke of 'the devotion and majesty of the late Earl and his many acts of kindness to the surrounding villages, which would never be forgotten'. The Earl, he said, had displayed 'loyalty to anything he undertook, which should be an example to all'.[4] This loyalty Earl Beauchamp had attempted to continue even after he had been forced into exile and was thrust into great agony of mind. The life of a remarkable man had come to an end. It was a life that had blossomed in security and luxury and had been blessed with a taste for beauty. But it had also been a life of well-earned merit. By the time of his fall, the Earl had done a great deal of practical good, working tirelessly for his party, for the House of Lords, and for numerous people and causes up and down the country – not to mention his earlier stint as Governor of New South Wales.

4   *Ibid.*

Each in their own way, the 2nd Duke of Westminster and the novelist Evelyn Waugh subjected Earl Beauchamp to such malicious treatment that anything good about him was erased from memory. Was his untimely death enough to satisfy them? Perhaps. But, even if this was the case, the damage had already been done. Now, for the first time since the Earl's fall, the evidence can be accessed and this book has laid it out for the reader's consideration. We see a very different figure from the one relegated to infamy. Is history ready to reinstate the 7th Earl Beauchamp?

Appendix: Execution of the Will

On Lord Beauchamp's death in 1938, his firstborn son, Viscount Elmley, succeeded to the title. The 8th Earl Beauchamp married but had no issue. He died in 1979. Thus ended the Beauchamp earldom. The 7th Earl's daughters followed their own careers. It is outside the scope of the present work to follow all this up, but it has been very well recorded elsewhere.[1] However, documentation relating to the execution of the 7th Earl Beauchamp's will in Australia does deserve a place in the present book.[2]

The Earl's will was reproduced in Chapter 22. In it, property on Australian soil was left to the Earl's secretary, David Smyth.

1

This [the will] is the document referred to in the annexed Affidavit of David Smyth sworn at Sydney this second day of March and shown to him at the time of swearing the said affidavit and marked by him in the margin hereof. Before me:

A Justice of the Peace

[Signature illegible]

Affidavit.

In the Supreme Court of New South Wales

---

1   See Jane Mulvagh, *Madresfield. The Real Brideshead: One home, one family, one thousand years* (London: Doubleday, 2008); Paula Byrne, *Mad World: Evelyn Waugh and the Secrets of Brideshead* (Hammersmith, London: Harper Press, 2009). Evelyn Waugh's fictional history, *Brideshead Revisited*, is fascinating. And Waugh's autobiography, letters and diaries make useful reading, as Waugh maintained a close friendship with the Beauchamp girls.

2   The documents printed in this chapter are located in the State Records of New South Wales Government, Australia under Deceased estate file: A2435, 20/2458, probate packet: Series 4–2379280. The present author is grateful to the Archivist, Bridget Reilly for making them available to him.

Probate Jurisdiction

In the Will of the Right Honourable William Earl Beauchamp Knight of the Garter late of Madresfield Court in the county of Worcester England and Bellevue Hill Sydney in the State of New South Wales Gentleman Deceased.

Affidavit.
Deponent – David Smyth
Sworn 22nd March 1939

2

In the Supreme Court of New South Wales

Probate Jurisdiction

In the Will of the Right Honourable William Earl Beauchamp Knight of the Garter late of Madresfield Court in the County of Worcester England and of Bellevue Hill Sydney in the State of New South Wales Gentleman Deceased.

On the twenty second day of March in the year One Thousand nine hundred and thirty nine David Smyth of Sydney in the State aforesaid Secretary being duly sworn makes oath and says as follows:

1. I am one of the Executors of the Will of the above named deceased and Applicant for grant of Probate to me reserving to William Viscount Elmley (now Earl Beauchamp) Lady Mary Lygon with the right to come in and prove.

2. Annexed hereto and marked with the letter 'A' is a certified copy of Probate with Certified copy of the Will.

3. The said William Viscount Elmley (now Earl Beauchamp) and the said Lady Lygon are resident without the jurisdiction of this Honourable Court being resident in England.

4. Annexed hereto and marked with the letter 'B' is an undertaking to furnish details to the Registrar of Probate of all assets liable to duty in New South Wales not included in the Stamp Affidavit and to pay any additional fees in consequence thereof.

David Smyth

Sworn by the deponent on the day and year first before-mentioned at Sydney Before me.

A Justice of the Peace.

[Signature illegible]

3

In the Supreme Court of New South Wales

Probate Jurisdiction

In the Will of the Right Honourable William Earl Beauchamp Knight of the Garter late of Madresfield Court in the County of Worcester England and Bellevue Hill Sydney in the State of New South Wales Deceased.

On the second day of March in the year One thousand nine hundred and thirty nine David Smyth of Sydney in the State aforesaid being duly sworn makes oath and says as follows:

1. The above named deceased departed this life at New York, America, on or about the fourteenth day of November One thousand nine hundred and thirty eight having first duly made and published his last Will and testament in writing dated the nineteenth day of August One thousand nine hundred and thirty eight whereby he appointed William Viscount Elmley (now Earl Beauchamp), Lady Mary Lygon and David Smyth this deponent executors thereof and I this deponent am also the sole beneficiary under the said Will in respect of the Australian Estate of the above named deceased.

2. Probate of the said Will was granted by the High Court of Justice England.

3. The document produced and shown to me at the time of swearing this my affidavit and marked by me by signing my name in the margin thereof and by the person before whom this Affidavit is sworn is I believe a copy of the last will and testament of the above named deceased and attesting witnesses thereof are G. Haywood and W. Humphreys.

4. The said deceased had whilst living and at the time of his death real and/or personal estate and effects within the State of New South Wales.

5. The testator did not marry subsequently to the execution of the said Will.

6. I will pay all the just debts and legacies of the said deceased so far as the estate of the said deceased will extend and the law bind me and I will render a just and true account of my administration thereof unto the Registry of the Supreme Court within twelve months from the date of grant of Probate herein.

7. The said Estate is under the value of Ten thousand five hundred and fifty pounds (£10,555).

8. I am over the age of twenty-one years.

David Smyth

Sworn by the deponent on the day and year first before-mentioned at Sydney Before me:

A Justice of the Peace.

[Signature illegible]

4

In the Supreme Court of New South Wales

Probate Jurisdiction

In the Will of the Right Honourable William Earl Beauchamp Knight of the Garter late of Madresfield Court in the County of Worcester England and of Bellevue Hill Sydney in the State of New South Wales Deceased Testate.

Take Notice that Application is being made herein that Probate of an Exemplified Copy of the last Will of the above named deceased dated 19th August 1938 may be granted to David Smyth one of the Executors therein named (leave being reserved to William Viscount Elmley, now William Earl Beauchamp and Lady Mary Lygon) to come in and prove.

Dated this Second day of March 1939.

Proctors for the Executor David Smyth
26 O'Connell Street,
Sydney

[Signatures illegible]

5

To

The Registrar of Probate
Supreme Court
King Street
Sydney

re. Earl Beauchamp Deceased

I David Smyth of Sydney in the State of New South Wales Secretary HEREBY UNDERTAKE to furnish to you details of all Assets liable to duty in New South Wales which are not included in the Stamp Affidavit and to pay any additional fees to you in consequence thereof.

Dated this twenty second day of March One thousand nine hundred and thirty nine.

David Smyth

This is the annexure marked 'B' referred to in the annexed affidavit of David Smyth sworn the twenty second day of March One thousand nine hundred and thirty nine sworn at Sydney Before me.

A Justice of the Peace

[Signature illegible]

In the Supreme Court of New South Wales, Probate Jurisdiction: In the Will of the Right Honourable William Earl Beauchamp Knight of the Garter, Malvern in the County of Worcester England and of Bellevue Hill, Sydney in the State of New South Wales Gentleman Deceased. AFFIDAVIT: Deponent – David Smyth. Sworn, 22nd March 1939.

McFadden & McFadden, Solicitors, 26 O'Connell Street, Sydney.

6

In the Estate of the Right Honourable William Earl Beauchamp Knight of the Garter late of Madresfield Court in the County of Worcester England and of Bellevue Hill Sydney in the State of New South Wales deceased Testate.

Schedule No. 1.

Real Estate

All That property situate in the District of Woollhara County of Cumberland Parish of Alexandria upon which is erected cottage known as No. 8 March Street Bellevue Hill having a frontage of 150 feet by a depth of 278 feet – 282 feet 1 inch being the whole of the land contained in Certificate of Title Volume 2727 Folio 229 Also in Conveyance No. 536 Book 1742

£9,000

Reserving the right to reduce and subject to Appeal.

Schedule No.2

2700 shares to Better Lighting Pty. Ltd. At 10/- d per share: £1,350

With reservation to reduce value.

Above are the Schedules numbered '1' and '2' referred to in the annexed Affidavit of David Smyth sworn at Sydney this day of March One thousand nine hundred and thirty nine. Before me.

A Justice of the Peace

[Signature illegible]

7

In the Supreme Court of New South Wales

Probate Jurisdiction

In the Will of the Right Honourable William Earl Beauchamp Knight of the Garter late of Madresfield Court in the County of Worcester England and of Bellevue Hill Sydney in the State of New South Wales Deceased.

Take Notice that the address for service of all Papers in this matter is at the under-mentioned address:

(Name) McFadden & McFadden

Solicitors

(Address) 26 O'Connel Street, Sydney

8

McFadden & McFadden

Sydney, 3rd April 1939

The Registrar of Probates,
Supreme Court,
King Street,
Sydney

Dear Sir,

re. Lord Beauchamp

Probate No. 237928

In connection with the above Estate, Probate whereof was granted on the 22nd of March last, we have to request the issue of a Certificate of Grant.

The same is required for the purpose of receiving certain deeds and documents from the Bank of Australasia Head Office, Sydney.

Yours faithfully

McFadden &McFadden

I Consent to the issue of a Certificate of the Grant of Administration in the above Estate only for the purpose Stated.

Commissioner of Stamp Duties

3/4/1939

[Signature illegible]

I CERTIFY that this is true copy of the Original Will deposited and proved in this Registry.

DATED this 8th day of March 1939.

Registrar

9

[Extracted from the Principal Registry of the Probate Divorce and Admiralty Division of the High Court of Justice]

In His Majesty's High Court of Justice
The Principal Probate Registry

BE IT KNOWN that The Right Honourable William 7th Earl Beauchamp K. G., of Madresfield Court Malvern in the county of Worcester died on the 15th day of November 1938 at Waldorf Astoria Hotel, New York, United States of America.

AND BE IT FURTHER KNOWN that at the date hereunder written the last Will and Testament (a copy whereof is hereunto annexed) of the said deceased was proved and registered in the Principal Probate Registry of His Majesty's High Court of Justice and Administration of all the Estate which by law devolves to and vests in the personal representative of the said deceased was granted by the aforesaid Court to The Right Honourable William 8th Earl of Beauchamp (formerly Viscount Elmley) of Madresfield Court aforesaid and Lady Mary Lygon of 13 Belgrave Square in the County of London spinster children of deceased two of the Executors named in the said Will.

Power reserved to the other Executor.

And it is hereby certified that an Affidavit for Inland Revenue has been delivered wherein it is shown that the gross value of the said Estate in Great Britain (exclusive of what the said deceased may have been possessed of or entitled to as a Trustee and not beneficiary) amounts to £ 140993–4–7 and that the net value of the personal estate amounts to £ 60530–19–5.

And it is further certified that it appears by a Receipt signed by an Inland Revenue Officer on the said Affidavit that £ 5891–11–9 on account of Estate Duty and interest on such duty has been paid.

Dated the 27th day of January 1939

Registrar

[Official stamp]: The deceased died domiciled in England.

Registrar

Noted pursuant to order dated: 18th of February 1939

Extracted by Hasties, 65 Lincoln's Inn Fields, London WC2.

I Certify that this is a true copy of the Original Record deposited in the Registry.

Dated this 9th day of March 1939.

Registrar

10

In the Supreme Court of New South Wales

Probate Jurisdiction

In the Will of the Right Honourable William Earl Beauchamp Knight of the Garter late of Madresfield Court Malvern in the County of Worcester England and of Bellevue Hill Sydney in the State of New South Wales. Deceased.

On the second day of March in the year One thousand nine hundred and thirty-nine David Smyth of Sydney in the State aforesaid being duly sworn makes oath and says as follows:

1. The above named deceased departed this life at New York, America, on or about the fourteenth day of November One thousand nine hundred and thirty-eight having first duly made and published his last Will and testament in writing dated the nineteenth day of August One thousand nine hundred and thirty-eight whereby he appointed William Viscount Elmley (now Earl Beauchamp), LADY MARY LYGON and DAVID SMYTH this deponent executors thereof and I this deponent am also the sole beneficiary under the said Will in respect of the Australian Estate of the above named deceased.

2. Probate of the said Will was granted by the High Court of Justice England.

3. The document produced and shown to me at the time of swearing this my affidavit and marked by me by signing my name in the margin thereof and by the person before whom this Affidavit is sworn is I believe a copy of the last will and testament of the above named deceased and attesting witnesses thereof are G. Haywood and W. Humphreys.

4. The said deceased had whilst living and at the time of his death real and/or personal estate and effects within the State of New South Wales.

5. The testator did not marry subsequently to the execution of this said Will.

6. I will pay all the just debts and legacies of the said deceased so far as the estate of the said deceased will extend and the law bind me and I will render a just and true account of my administration thereof unto the Registry of the Supreme Court within twelve months from the date of grant of Probate herein.

7. The said Estate is under the value of Ten thousand five hundred and fifty pounds (£ 10,555).

8. I am over the age of twenty-one years.

David Smyth

SWORN by the deponent on the day and year first before mentioned at Sydney Before me.

A Justice of the Peace

II

In the Supreme Court of New South Wales: Probate Jurisdiction

Inventory referred to in the preceding affidavit

Assets

Real Estate

Real estate possessed by the deceased at the issue of the time of his death, and Real Estate liable to duty under section 102 of the Stamp Duties Act, 1920–1933, as per Schedule No 1: £ 9000.-

Personal Estate

...

Dividends declared but unpaid, as per Schedule No: £1350. -

...

Money standing to credit Trust A/c D. R. Hall & Co.: £204 s.4 d.11

...

Durable Estate: £10554 s.4 d.11

Total debts that may be deducted under the Act, 1920–1933, section 107: £69, s.6, d.3

Final balance upon which duty is payable: £10484, s.18, d.8

To be signed here by executors or administrators making the affidavit:

David Smyth

Date 2nd March 1939

Nov. 1938

Bank of Australasia, Sydney, overdraft: £22, s.8, d.7 (Secured)

Metropolitan Water Sewerage & Drainage Board, Sydney, Rates £36, s.7, d.8 (Unsecured)

R. Hall & Co., Sydney, Legal costs (assessed): £10, s.10 (unsecured) Total

Total Debts: (Secured) £22, s.8, d.7; (Unsecured) £46, s. 7, d.8

Stamp Duties Department

Schedule of Freehold Lands in the Estate of

The Right Honourable William Earl Beauchamp Knight of the Garter late of Madresfield Court Malvern in the County of Worcester England and of Bellevue Hill Sydney in the State of New South Wales, deceased.

Date of Grant or Certificate of Title: 9/1/1917

Parish: Alexandria

County: Cumberland

Area: r. 2, p. 23 ¼

Reference: vol. 2727; Folio 229

Value as per Valuation: £9000. -

12

Form of affidavit to be lodged with application for administration

In the Estate of The Right Honourable William Earl Beauchamp Knight of the Garter late of Madresfield Court Malvern in the County of Worcester England and of Bellevue Hill Sydney in the State of New South Wales, deceased. Intestate.

On the Second day of March one thousand and nine hundred and thirty nine

David Smyth of Sydney in the State of New South Wales Secretary

being duly sworn, making oath, and saith as follows:

I am making application for the purpose of obtaining administration of the above named deceased and the party/parties liable for the payment of the duty, if any, on the estate herein included.

The above named deceased who died on the 14th day of November 1938, aged 67 years, was at the time of death Widower and was domiciled in New South Wales.

...

The final balance of the estate of the above named deceased is Ten thousand four hundred and eighty-four pounds eighteen shillings and eight pence.

In the event of any additional assets discovered, I will advise the Commissioner of Stamp Duties, and will pay any further duty found to be payable.

...

The deceased was not possessed of or entitled to any property in New South Wales at the date of his death other than the property set out in the annexed inventory.

David Smyth

Sworn by the deponent on the day first above mentioned at Sydney

before me

[Signature illegible]

A Commissioner for Affidavits

(or) Justice of the Peace

Bibliography

I. Archival Sources

Bodleian (Weston) Library, Oxford
Asquith MSS. Microfilm Asquith 27 (fol.188).
Carrington (The Marquess of Lincolnshire) Papers, MSS Film 1135 (2).

The British Library, London
MSS Eur F118/3/3–22: 1928–1931 [Title: Beauchamp, William Lygon, 7th Earl].
Personal and semi-official papers of 1st Marquess of Reading.

Cambridge University Library, Cambridge
Crewe Papers, C/2.

Gloucestershire Archives, Gloucester
Files: D 551/ 1–16.

Kent History and Library Centre, Maidstone
Fo/CPw10; Cpw/S7; Cpw/RPS8.

The Madresfield Archives, The Estate Office, Madresfield, Malvern
Boxes: 2–6.

The National Archives, Kew, London
Ref.: J 77/2899/9727 (C 632718).

Nuffield College Library Archive, Oxford
Emmott MSS, box no. 3, 5–7, 9.

The Parliamentary Archives, London
Lloyd George MSS, LG/ G/3/5/1–13.

Royal Archives
PS/PSO/GV/C/O/480/45, 46, 56.
GV/PRIV/GVD1894: 2 Apr.
PS/PSO/GV/PS/COR/56098/3.
PS/PSO/GV/PS/MAIN/2476/71.
PS/PSO/GV/PS/COR/56078/952.
PS/PSO/GV/PS/COR/56078/958.
PS/PSO/GV/PS/MAN/3742/5.
PS/PSO/GV/PS/MAIN/779/17.
PS/PSO/GV/PS/MAIN/2238/4.
PS/PSO/GV/PS/MAIN/2238/7.
PS/PSO/GV/C/O/396/2.
PS/PSO/GV/C/O/480/62, 65,66.
VIC/MAIN/P/2/223.
GV/ADD/COPY/2/3/67, 69,76,79.
VIC. Add. C/22.
VIC/Add/U/27/99–101, 162.
GV/ADD/COPY/2/3/67,69,76,79.
VIC/Add/U/27/99–101, 162.
VIC/ADD/B/11.613.
PS/PSO/GV/PS/SV/56079/7.
PS/PSO/GV/C/K/731/1.

Senate House Library Archives, University of London, London
File-05591: 1120 (AL 366); 1121 (UoL/VP 1/4); 1123 (UoL/CF 1/30/1502); 1124 (Uol/
CF 1/31/1502); 1125 (UoL/CN/4/8/1).

State Library of New South Wales, The Mitchell Library, Sydney
Manuscripts: Call No. ML A3295, Frame No. 259–301; Call No. ML A 3012; Call No.
ML DOC 2561; Call No. ML DOC 465b; Call No. ML A 1829 or C Y 3233;
Call No. ML D 233 or C Y 1164; Call No. ML A 3295, Frame No. 259–301; Call
No. ML A 3295, Frame No. 259–301; Call No. ML A 3012; Call No. ML DOC
465; Call No. ML DOC 339; Call No. ML D 233; Call No. A b 150/3; Call No.
ML A 3012; Call No. ML A 1829.

State Records of New South Wales Government, Australia
Deceased estate file: A2435, 20/2458, probate packet: Series 4–2379280.

Worcestershire Archives & Archaeology Service, Worcester
Deeds, 705:99/3375/67(v).

Other Archives
Christ Church Library Archives, Oxford.
Eton College Library Archives, Windsor.
Oxford Union Library Archives, Oxford.

II. Published Works

Amory, Mark (ed.), *The Letters of Evelyn Waugh* (London: Weidenfeld and Nicolson, 1981).
Asquith, Margot, *The Autobiography of Margot Asquith*, vol. II (London: Thornton Butterworth Ltd., 1922).
Beaverbrook, Lord, *The Decline and Fall of Lloyd George: And Great was the Fall Thereof* (London: Collins, 1963).
Berrow's Worcester Journal, 3 December 1938.
Birkenhead, the Earl of, 'Fiery Particles', in David Pryce-Jones (ed.), *Evelyn Waugh and His World* (London: Weidenfeld and Nicolson, 1973).
Blunt, Wilfrid Scawen, *My Diaries Being a Personal Narrative of Events, 1888–1914*. Part Two, 1900 to 1914 (London: Martin Secker, 1919).
Bruce, Alastair, Julian Calder, Mark Cator, *Keepers of the Kingdom: The Ancient Offices of Britain* (London: Weidenfeld & Nicolson, 1919).
Byrne, L. S. R. and E. L. Churchill, *Changing Eton: A Survey of Conditions based on the History of Eton since the Royal Commission of 1862–64* (London: Jonathan Cape, 1937).
Byrne, Paula, *Mad World: Evelyn Waugh and the Secrets of Brideshead* (London: Harper Collins, 2010 paperback edition).
Cannadine, David, *Aspects of Aristocracy: Grandeur and Decline in Modern Britain* (London: Penguin Books, 1995).
Cook, Chris, *A Short History of the Liberal Party, 1900–2001* (Hampshire: Palgrave, 2002, sixth edition).
Davenport-Hines, Richard, 'Lygon, William, seventh Earl Beauchamp (1872–1938)', in H. C. G. Mathew and Brian Harrison (eds), *Oxford Dictionary of National Biography*, vol. 34 (Oxford: Oxford University Press, 2004).

—— *Sex, Death and Punishment: Attitudes to Sex and Sexuality in Britain since the Renaissance* (London: William Collins, 1990).

—— *Universal Man: The Lives of John Maynad Keynes* (New York: Basic Books, 2015).

Davenport-Hines, Richard, and Adam Sisman (eds), *One Hundred Letters from Hugh Trevor-Roper* (Oxford: Oxford University Press, 2014).

Davie, Michael (ed.), *The Diaries of Evelyn Waugh* (London: Weidenfeld and Nicolson, 1976).

Card, Tim, *Eton Renewed: A History from 1860 to the Present Day* (London: John Murray, 1994).

Christabel, Lady Aberconway, *A Wiser Woman? A Book of Memories* (London: Hutchinson, 1966).

Clark, Alan (ed.), *A Good Innings: The Private Papers of Viscount Lee of Fareham* (London: John Murray, 1974).

Curthoys, Judith, *The Cardinal's College: Christ Church, Chapter and Verse* (London: Profile Books, 2012).

Curzon of Kedleston, the Marquess, *The Personal History of Walmer Castle and its Lords Warden*, (ed.) Stephen Gwynn (London: Macmillan, 1927).

David, Edward (ed.), *Inside Asquith's Cabinet: From the Diaries of Charles Hobhouse* (London: John Murray, 1977).

The Dover Standard, 25 July 1914.

Dutton, David, 'William Lygon, 7th Earl Beauchamp (1872–1938)', *Journal of Liberal Democrat History*, 23 (Summer 1999).

Ensor, Robert, *England, 1870–1914* (Oxford: Clarendon Press, 1968 edition).

Eton College Chronicle, 26 September, 1889.

The Evening News, Sydney, 27 September 1899.

Field, Leslie, *Bendor: The Golden Duke of Westminster* (London: Weidenfeld & Nicolson, 1983).

Fitzroy, Almeric, *Memoirs* (London: Hutchinson, 1925). Two Volumes.

Gilbert, Martin, *Churchill: A Life* (London: Minerva, 1992).

Gollan, R. A., 'Nationalism, the Labour Movement and the Commonwealth, 1880–1900', in Gordon Greenwood (ed.), *Australia: A Social and Political History* (London: Angus and Robertson, 1955).

Greenwood, Gordon (ed.), *Australia: A Social and Political History* (London: Angus and Robertson, 1955).

Grigg, John, *Lloyd George: From Peace to War, 1912–1916* (London: Penguin Books, 2002).

Heywood, Valentine, *British Titles: The Use and Misuse of the Titles of Peers and Commoners, with Some Historical Notes* (London: Adam and Charles Black, 1951).

Hinings, Edward, *History, People and Places of the Cinque Ports* (Buckinghamshire: Spur Books Ltd., 1975).

Jennings, Ivor, *Cabinet Government* (Cambridge: Cambridge University Press, 1951, second edition).

Knocker, Edward, *An Account of the Grand Court of Shepway: At Dover for the Installation of the Right Honourable Henry John, Viscount Palmerston* (London: John Russell Smith, 1862).

Lawson, Henry, *While the Billy Boils* (1896).

Lee, Sidney, *King Edward VII: A Biography* (London: Macmillan, 1927).

The London Gazette, Supplement, 4 August 1914.

Lygon, Dorothy, 'Madresfield and Brideshead', in David Pryce-Jones (ed.), *Evelyn Waugh and His World* (London: Weidenfeld and Nicolson, 1973).

McNaughtan, I. D., 'Colonial Liberalism, 1851–92', in Gordon Greenwood (ed.), *Australia: A Social and Political History* (London: Angus and Robertson, 1955).

Magnus, Philip, *Gladstone: A Biography* (London: John Murray, 1954).

Moore, Jerrold Northrop, *Edward Elgar: A Creative Life* (Oxford: Oxford University Press, 1987).

Mulvagh, Jane, *Madresfield: The Real Brideshead* (London: Doubleday, 2008).

Murray, K. M. E., *The Constitutional History of the Cinque Ports* (Manchester: Manchester University Press, 1935).

Nicolson, Harold, *King George the Fifth: His Life and Reign* (London: Constable, 1953).

Nicolson, Nigel (ed.), *Vita and Harold: The Letters of Vita Sackville-West and Harold Nicolson* (London: Weidenfeld & Nicolson, 1992).

Parliamentary Debates, House of Lords, vol. X, 14 March 1893 and whole relevant series.

Pimlott, Ben (ed.), *The Political Diary of Hugh Dalton, 1918–40, 1945–60* (London: Jonathan Cape Ltd., 1986).

Proceedings of the Oxford Union Society (1823–1924), v. 3 (M. T. 1890 to E. T. 1904) (Oxford: printed by W. R. Bowden).

Pryce-Jones, David (ed.), *Evelyn Waugh and His World* (London: Weidenfeld and Nicolson, 1973).

Raina, Peter, *House of Lords Reform: A History. The Origins to 1937: Proposals Deferred*, Book Two: 1911–1937 (Bern: Peter Lang AG, 2011).

Robb, Graham, *Strangers: Homosexual Love in the Nineteenth Century* (London: Picador, 2004 edition).

Rowse, A. L., *Homosexuals in History* (New York: Dorset Press, 1983).

Sackville-West, Vita, *The Edwardians* (London: Virago Press, 1983).

Schreuder, Deryck M., 'Empire: Australia and Greater Britain, 1788–1901', in Alison Bashford and Stuart Macintyre (eds), *The Cambridge History of Australia*, vol. I (Cambridge: Cambridge University Press, 2013).

Spate, O. H. K., *Australia* (London: Ernest Benn Ltd., third revised impression, 1971).

Spender, J. A., *The Life of Sir Henry Campbell-Bannerman* (Boston & New York: Houghton Mifflin Company, 1924). Two Volumes.

Stevenson, R. L., *The Works of R. L. Stevenson*, vol. II (London: Heinemann, 1922, Vailima edition).

Swift, Jonathan, 'A Treatise on Good Manners and Good Breeding', in John Gross (ed.), *The Oxford Book of Essays* (Oxford: Oxford University Press, 1991).

The Sydney Morning Herald, Sydney, 28 September 1899.

Taylor, A. J. P., *English History, 1914–1915* (Oxford: Clarendon Press, 1965).

Waugh, Evelyn, *Brideshead Revisited: The Sacred and Profane Memoirs of Captain Charles Ryder* (London: Chapman & Hall, 1960 edition).

Williams, Dorothy E., *The Lygons of Madresfield Court* (Logaston, Herefordshire: Logaston Press, 2001).

Wilson, Trevor (ed.), *The Political Diaries of C. P. Scott, 1911–1928* (London: Collins, 1970).

Index

By the same author:

House of Lords Reform: A History

Volume 1. The Origins to 1937: Proposals Deferred
Book One: The Origins to 1911
Book Two: 1911–1937
ISBN 978-3-0343-0749-9 | Book One: 632 pp., Book Two: 633 pp. | 2011

Volume 2. 1943–1958: Hopes Rekindled
ISBN 978-3-0343-0954-7 | 886 pp. | 2013

Volume 3. 1960-1969: Reforms Attempted
ISBN 978-3-0343-1764-1 | 956 pp. | 2014

Volume 4. 1971–2014: The Exclusion of Hereditary Peers
Book 1: 1971–2001
Book 2: 2002–2014
ISBN 978-3-0343-1856-3 | Book 1: 632 pp., Book 2: 654 pp. | 2015

A.V. Dicey: General Characteristics of English Constitutionalism: Six
Unpublished Lectures. With a Foreword by Lord Plant of Highfield
ISBN 978-3-03911-955-4 | 180 pp. | 2009

Bishop George Bell: House of Lords Speeches and Correspondence
with Rudolf Hess.
ISBN 978-3-03911-895-3 | 241 pp. | 2009

A Daring Venture: Rudolf Hess and the Ill-Fated Peace Mission of 1941
ISBN 978-3-0343-1776-4 | 278 pp. | 2014

To order, please visit www.peterlang.com